Systems Approaches to Managing Change:
A Practical Guide

Martin Reynolds · Sue Holwell
Editors

Systems Approaches to Managing Change: A Practical Guide

 Springer

Editors

Martin Reynolds
Department of Communication & Systems
The Open University
Walton Hall, Milton Keynes
United Kingdom MK7 6AA

Sue Holwell
Department of Communication & Systems
The Open University
Walton Hall, Milton Keynes
United Kingdom MK7 6AA

First Published in 2010 by
Springer London

In association with
The Open University
Walton Hall, Milton Keynes
MK7 6AA
United Kingdom

This book forms part of the Open University course TU811 *Thinking Strategically: systems tools for managing change*. Details of this and other Open University courses can be obtained from the Student Registration and Enquiry Service, The Open University, PO Box 197, Milton Keynes MK7 6BJ, United Kingdom: Tel. +44 (0)845 300 60 90, email general-enquiries@open.ac.uk

www.open.ac.uk

Whilst we have made every effort to obtain permission from copyright holders to use the material contained in this book, there have been occasions where we have been unable to locate those concerned. Should holders wish to contact the Publisher, we will be happy to come to an arrangement at the first opportunity.

ISBN 978-1-84882-808-7   e-ISBN 978-1-84882-809-4
DOI 10.1007/978-1-84882-809-4
Springer London Dordrecht Heidelberg New York

Library of Congress Control Number: 2010920841

Springer is part of Springer Science + Business Media (www.springer.com)

Preface

We live and work in a highly complex and interconnected world. Small decisions made by individuals may have large effects in a wider context. Actions taken within one organization can have an impact upon many different organizations, on government, on society and on the natural environment. This book has been motivated by a recognition that complex questions are increasingly asked of institutions and individuals in situations of change and uncertainty. The book addresses such questions not by offering 'new' tools, but rather by providing five approaches – systems tools – each embodying at least 25 years of experiential use. They not only provide robust methods, but moreover with the benefit of time and experience, the evolution of these approaches in different contexts has exposed new offerings; new enlightenment on how to use these approaches better in the light of experience. The five systems approaches presented in this compilation are presented not as 'new' tools to replace 'old' tools, but rather as evolving radical ways of thinking that have been nurtured in different contexts to complement and give added value to existing practices. They are specially updated for this publication, with each approach authored by the originators and/or experienced practitioners. This book is about intervention, or more precisely how to improve human intervention to help change situations for the better, to navigate the interrelated dimensions of making more effective strategic decisions in the twenty-first century.

Acknowledgements

The book was produced with the help of the Open University course team for TU811 *Thinking Strategically: systems tools for managing change* a core course for the postgraduate programme Systems Thinking in Practice. Special thanks go to three colleagues at the Open University: Robin Asby, John Martin, and Marilyn Ridsdale for their tireless efforts in supporting the editing process. Thanks also to Karen Shipp and Penny Marrington for their insightful contributions and to Pearl Cox for the production of the manuscript. Grateful acknowledgement is made to all sources for permission to reproduce material in this book, and particular thanks go to all contributing authors of the readings.

Contents

Contributors

Fran Ackermann is Professor of Management Science at Strathclyde University, Scotland. Her research interests focus upon the role that group decision support systems and causal mapping (a qualitative modelling technique sometimes referred to as causal mapping) can play in supporting the development and implementation of strategy and in risk assessment and forensic modelling. She is also keenly interested in how decisions are made and how managers operate within a complex and changing business world. She has wide experience with both public and private organizations through consultancy and action research. She has written widely in the areas of strategy, operational research and information systems, and is the author of three books. She is on the editorial board of three journals and has been invited to speak at MIT, Georgia State University, Curtin University, Perth, Western Australia, Tilburg University, the Netherlands as well as being an affiliate Professor at Bordeaux Business School.

Peter Checkland is currently Professor Emeritus of Systems at Lancaster University. After 15 years as a Manager in the synthetic fibre industry Peter Checkland joined the postgraduate Department of Systems Engineering at Lancaster University. There he worked with colleagues, including Dr Brian Wilson, in what became a 30-year programme of action research in organizations. Initially this work explored the use of Systems Engineering in dealing with management issues, rather than the traditional technically defined problems. The 'failure' of the early work highlighted a different direction that ultimately yielded Soft Systems Methodology (SSM) as an approach to tackling the multi-faceted problems which managers face. In doing this, it also established the now well-recognized distinction between 'hard' and 'soft' systems thinking. SSM is now taught and used around the world. Its development is described in many papers and five books: Systems Thinking, Systems Practice, in 1981; Soft Systems Methodology in Action (with Jim Scholes) in 1990; Systems Information and Information Systems (with Sue Holwell) in 1998; SSM: A 30-Year Retrospective in 1999; and Learning for Action (with John Poulter) in 2006.

His work has been recognised in a number of awards: honorary doctorates from City University, the Open University, Erasmus University (The Netherlands), and Prague University of Economics, a Most Distinguished and Outstanding Contributor Award from the British Computer Society, the Gold Medal of the UK Systems

Society, The Beale Medal of the OR Society, the I+M (Information and Management) award of Amsterdam University, the Pioneer Award of the International Council on Systems Engineering, and election to the Omega Alpha Association of the Systems Engineering Honor Society.

Colin Eden worked as an Operational Researcher in the engineering industry following his Ph.D., subsequently becoming Operational Research Manager. This was followed by a period as a Management Consultant specialising in small business problems and then he worked at the University of Bath until becoming Professor of Management Science at Strathclyde Business School in 1987. Until 2006 he was Director of the University of Strathclyde Graduate School of Business. Currently Colin is Director of SBS' International Division responsible for its ten overseas centres.

Colin is internationally known within the field of Management Science, Management, and Research Method through his research and publications. He has published over 150 articles in general management, management science, and project management journals, and published eight books. He has received research grants from the Leverhulme Trust, British Telecom, ICL, the Northern Ireland Office, SSRC, EPSRC, Bombardier, Inc., and ESRC.

His major research interests are into the processes of making strategy; the relationship between operational decision making practices and their strategic consequences; the use of group decision support in the analysis and making of strategy; managerial and organisational cognition; 'soft OR' modelling approaches and methodologies, including particular emphasis on the role of cognitive mapping; the process and practice of 'action research'; and the modelling of the behaviour of large projects disruptions and delays, including issues of the dynamics of productivity changes, and learning curves.

Sue Holwell has qualifications in accountancy, computing and information systems (IS). Before embarking on an academic career she worked for the Australian Public Service in Finance, Personnel and IS. The last few years were as the IS Manager, responsible for all aspects of IS in a mixed mainframe, PC technical environment with both commercial and design applications. A mid-career break brought her to the UK and a new career. Since 1988 she has worked on research and consultancy using Soft Systems Methodology in the NHS and multi-national companies in Europe, completed her Ph.D. in Soft Systems Methodology and IS and co-authored a book of 'conceptual cleansing' of the fundamentals of the field of IS. She joined Cranfield University as Senior Lecturer in 1998, teaching on the MSc in the Design of Information Systems and MBA. In April 2002 she joined the Systems Department at The Open University. She has published on soft systems methodology and action research.

Patrick Hoverstadt has worked as a Consultant since 1995 with organisations in both the private and public sector, mainly on issues to do with organisational structure and change. He specialises in using systems approaches for analysing and designing organisations and work processes. Patrick is a specialist in working with very large complex organisations including whole sectors. He has developed methodologies for several difficult business problems: large-scale organisational change, strategic risk, measuring management performance and collaborative governance. He has worked on many restructuring projects, analysing structural weaknesses, designing appropriate solutions and practical change plans.

Patrick ran an engineering business for 13 years before becoming a consultant. He has written numerous research papers, is a regular keynote speaker at conferences, has contributed to several books on organisation and management and is the author of a book on organisation published by Wiley in 2008. He chairs the largest group of systems practitioners in the UK, and is a Visiting Research Fellow at Cranfield School of Management.

John Morecroft is Senior Fellow in Management Science and Operations at London Business School where he teaches system dynamics, problem structuring and strategy in MBA, PhD and Executive Education programmes. He has served as Associate Dean of the School's Executive MBA and co-designed EMBA-Global, a dual degree programme with New York's Columbia Business School. He is also an Associate Fellow at Warwick Business School. He is a leading expert in strategic modelling and system dynamics and has written numerous papers and journal articles. He has co-edited three books and written a system dynamics textbook *Strategic Modelling and Business Dynamics* (Wiley 2007). He is a recipient of the Jay Wright Forrester Award of the System Dynamics Society and a Past President of the Society. His research interests include the dynamics of firm performance and the use of models and simulation in strategy development. He has led applied research projects for international organisations including Royal Dutch/Shell, AT&T, BBC World Service, Cummins Engine Company, Harley-Davidson, Ericsson, McKinsey & Co and Mars. Before joining London Business School he was on the faculty of MIT's Sloan School of Management where he received his Ph.D. He also holds degrees from Imperial College London and from Bristol University.

John Poulter is a Practitioner of SSM. He first used SSM formally when working with Peter Checkland in the UK's National Health Service in 1993. A founder member of the Soft Systems Research Group, he has presented papers and other publications on the use of SSM.

Martin Reynolds is an Academic at The Open University, UK with interests in systems practice, environmental decision making, and development studies. His previous work at the Institute for Development Policy and Management at Manchester University involved applying critical systems approaches to evaluating participatory approaches in natural resource management. He has since been involved with numerous collaborations including work with the Centre for Systems Studies at the University of Hull, the University of Guyana, the University of KwaZulu-Natal, and with internationally based colleagues associated with the American Evaluation Association and the European Evaluation Society. He has produced distance learning course material for postgraduate courses on Global Development, Environmental Decision Making, Environmental Responsibility, and

Systems Thinking in Practice. Martin is one of the founding members of the Open
Systems Research Group based at The Open University, UK. He provides workshop support for professional development in systems practice, applying critical
systems thinking for supporting public sector capacity in less developed countries,
and environmental responsibility in climate change initiatives. He has published
widely in the fields of systems studies, professional evaluation, international development, and environmental decision making. In 2009 he was lead editor of, and
contributing author to, *The Environmental Responsibility Reader* copublished by
The Open University and Zed Books.

Werner Ulrich is Honorary Visiting Professor in the Faculty of Technology of The
Open University, Milton Keynes, UK, and *Ancien professeur titulaire* in the Faculty
of Arts of the University of Fribourg, Switzerland. He is Founding Director of the
Lugano Summer School at the University of Italian Switzerland, which offers continuing education in systems thinking and reflective practice for professionals of
different fields. He has held appointments at a number of other universities and also
has extensive experience as a chief evaluator and policy analyst in the public sector.
He has some 175 academic publications thus far.

Werner's main interest is in the philosophical and methodological issues of
applied science and expertise, with special regard for reflective practice. A specific
contribution consists in his work on 'critical systems heuristics' and its methodological core principle of 'boundary critique'. Werner is now working to bring
together the methodological core principles of science, discourse ethics, pragma-
tist thought, and critical heuristics within a 'philosophy for professionals'. His
current research on 'critical pragmatism' explores the ways these sources of critical thought can contribute to competent and responsible professional practice in a
living civil society.

Chapter 1
Introducing Systems Approaches

Martin Reynolds and Sue Holwell

1.1 Introduction

Systems Approaches to Managing Change brings together five systems approaches to managing complex issues, each having a proven track record of over 25 years. The five approaches are:

1. System Dynamics (SD) developed originally in the late 1950s by Jay Forrester
2. Viable Systems Model (VSM) developed originally in the late 1960s by Stafford Beer
3. Strategic Options Development and Analysis (SODA: with cognitive mapping) developed originally in the 1970s by Colin Eden
4. Soft Systems Methodology (SSM) developed originally in the 1970s by Peter Checkland
5. Critical Systems Heuristics (CSH) developed originally in the late 1970s by Werner Ulrich

The accounts of the approaches that follow draw heavily on the extensive experience of the contributing authors. They are more than experienced practitioners, they bring the added quality of academic rigour to the reflection on practice that characterises their work. Drawing on the extensive experience of these contributing authors, some of whom are primary originators, this volume is an accessible exposition of the fundamentals of five compatible but different approaches and in addition is an opportunity to update guidance on the use of each approach.

We begin by examining, first, the nature of the complex situations to which systems approaches generally make a claim towards improving. Second, we examine how systems thinking might help manage complex situations more effectively. Third, some perspectives on the nature and development of systems thinking underpinning

M. Reynolds (✉) and S. Holwell
The Open University Communication & Systems Dept., Walton Hall, Milton Keynes,
United Kingdom MK7 6AA
e-mails: m.d.reynolds@open.ac.uk; s.e.holwell@open.ac.uk

M. Reynolds and S. Holwell (eds.), *Systems Approaches to Managing Change:*
A Practical Guide, DOI 10.1007/978-1-84882-809-4_1, © The Open University 2010.
Published in Association with Springer-Verlag London Limited

contemporary systems approaches are explored. Fourth, and finally, we provide our own perspective and rationale for the selection of the five approaches chosen and a brief description of each approach.

1.2   The Way of the World

It is Easter week 2009. A quick glance at the news media reveals several stories arising from complex situations calling for better human intervention. Here are just three such stories:

2009 is the twentieth anniversary of the Hillsborough football stadium disaster. Many people in the UK are joining with the families of the ninety six football supporters who were crushed to death shortly after the start of a FA Cup semi-final match between Liverpool and Nottingham Forest at the Hillsborough football ground in 1989. Although in reaction to the tragedy many improvements in the safety of football grounds have been generated, there remains a considerable sense of injustice amongst the families and friends of the deceased that no one has been held to account. In 1990 an official inquiry, which many considered flawed because it failed to give due voice to junior police officers and eyewitnesses, handed down the verdict of accidental death. Harrowing stories about victims who might have been saved continue 20 years on amidst growing evidence of confusion, non-communication, and general lack of leadership amongst emergency services, of police mismanagement and a subsequent police cover-up (senior police officers vetting statements presented to the inquiry), as well as some misguided tabloid news provocation. Aside from the bereaved families, for many groups of people associated with the football industry including the police, the circumstances of that afternoon, remain highly problematic.

The second story relates to a continuing saga of sea piracy – apparently the biggest industry for the troubled African country of Somalia. Individual pirates are among Somalia's wealthiest men. Using sophisticated equipment and modern weaponry, the pirates hijack sailing boats and large cargo ships, treating the ship, its cargo and its crew as hostages for ransom. Given the open seas in which they operate, there appears to be little hope of such attacks being curtailed: there is little chance of an effective military reaction, and little chance of the sea bandits ever facing justice. Although the Easter headline news focused on the deaths and rescue attempts of European and American victims of piracy, the effects of Somalia's sea bandits are far reaching. For the Seychelles it involves the loss of fishing grounds. For Kenya, there have been significant effects on tourism. Cruise ships have begun avoiding East Africa because of the piracy risk, thereby rendering thousands of Kenyan tourism workers jobless. Longer sea routes around Africa to avoid using the Suez Canal have increased costs for shippers and consumers. And Somalia itself is affected because ship owners are reluctant to take on UN contracts transporting the food aid that feeds half of Somalia's eight million people. Only with an expensively deployed European Union naval force were ships' crews willing to make the dangerous aid run into Mogadishu.

The third story is at first sight, and in fresh contrast, more agreeable and hopeful. In the mountainous forests of Indonesia environmentalists have discovered a population of Orangutans – one of the world's most endangered species of apes. Since the 1990s the rainforests in Indonesia have been systematically destroyed by burning at an alarming rate as plantation owners want more land for the production of Palm oil. Palm oil has become very lucrative because it is classed as a clean burning fuel. This fuel is at a premium as an ever demanding global population wants a source of fuel energy not dependent on the politics of crude oil supply and/or having the 'label' of being environmentally benign. The discovery of the Orangutans brings in to sharp relief the politics of food production, energy production, local livelihood strategies (including the widespread very poor working conditions of plantation workers), and of course conservation. Some experts estimate that the animals could be wiped out within two decades given the current rate of habitat destruction.

1.2.1 Big, Big Issues

So what might we learn from these three contrasting stories about the situations in which systems approaches might be helpful? Firstly, they illustrate how localised issues have causes and consequences that have a much wider impact. The Hillsborough disaster represents not just 'a problem' or 'difficulty' of infrastructure design and safety, but invites concerns ranging from basic community relations and policing methods, emergency service training, right through to the responsibilities of the media, politicians, and those financially benefiting from the football industry, even including football sponsors. The Hillsborough story continues to unfold and its consequences on the culture of football are not bounded by national frontiers. Similarly, the localised 'problem' of piracy in a country torn by war and conflict over the past 20 years is not one confined to the offshore waters of Somalia or one that can be easily 'fixed' by military or policing actions. There are many interrelated and interdependent factors involved, with contrasting perspectives on the situation that range from the rights of law-abiding Somali citizens wishing to develop livelihoods, to traders and tourists wanting to travel freely and safely, to sections of a community brutalised and attracted by greed into criminal activity. For the threatened communities of Orangutans, and conservationists concerned with their survival, the 'difficulty' is not just located in the mountainous forests of Indonesia but extends nationally and globally; to national logging concessions and the displacement of villagers from their forest dependent livelihoods, to global trade agreements on fuel. The ongoing, and growing, international concern and high level conversations over climate change suggest that matters of nature and conservation can no longer be regarded as localised issues, but rather are matters that should concern all of us.

In short, our three stories taken from a single day's news coverage over an Easter week-end in 2009 illustrate how localised issues can be translated into many big, big issues. They also illustrate how big issues are characterised by multiple and often conflicting perspectives. There are of course other big issues confronting us on a daily basis. As a backdrop to Easter 2009 we are continually reminded of the world crises of banking collapses, alongside increased abject poverty, and ecological dilemmas alongside increasing demand on natural resources. The G20 group of world leaders from the world's most powerful 20 economies attended an economic summit in London in March 2009. This was a meeting to tackle the worst economic situation since the 1930s Depression, a situation that is affecting both developed and less-developed countries. Also in the news are the increasingly familiar stories on the melting of huge swathes of the Antarctic ice shelf and predictions of growing shortages of fresh water supply that will have consequences more far reaching than the shortage of oil.

These are big, global issues and could be categorised as issues of sustainability and development, but that doing that does not give any indication about how they may be resolved. At the same time on a national level we face issues in our societies: children living in poor and violent neighbourhoods, an aging population with growing demands for care, how to manage policing in times of terrorist threat and still maintain civil liberties that have been hard won. In our organisations we are constantly trying to adapt to changing circumstances, whether it is for the public sector organisation new government legislation and/or targets forcing re-thinking of process, staff and structure or for the private sector organisation engaged in fierce competition beset by consumer demands and expectations. And for all, rapidly developing technologies can and do significantly change the environment for many organisations and their members.

And as individuals we face our own challenges, whether they be confronting our family concerns of 'what to do about grandpa' or overcoming substance abuse or, on a more fortunate footing, deciding where to go on holiday given some of the big issues above.

Human life is not often simple and straightforward, either professionally or personally. So what is the relevance of this to a book about systems approaches? To answer this, look at the kind of issues above; there are no obvious answers about what to do, different people will see different priorities, and when we begin to make changes unintended (and sometimes unwelcome) consequences emerge.

1.2.2   Messes and Difficulties

1.2.2.1   Is It a Mess or Is It Just Difficult?

Issues of concern to us vary enormously in terms of their complexity and seriousness, from minor hiccups to near-catastrophe, and we can think of all issues falling somewhere on a continuum between minor and straightforward to very complex and crucial. We can label one end of the continuum as being a 'difficulty' and the other a 'mess' (the term coined by Ackoff 1974). We can distinguish between the concept of a mess, and a difficulty, in several ways.

Messes usually have more serious implications; more people are likely to be involved; they include *many interlocking aspects* and may appear in different guises. As our three stories illustrate, messes usually have a longer time-scale; and they are often more complicated in terms of having many interdependent factors, than a difficulty. In addition to these broad characteristics there is a crucial difference between a difficulty and a mess and that is the extent of *uncertainty*.

If a situation is a mess there is much about it that is uncertain. The uncertainty starts with the situation itself: a mess is hard to pin down; it's difficult even to say what the situation of concern actually is, or what the source of the unease is, and yet things feel not right. With a difficulty we know roughly what an answer will look like: with a mess, we are not at all sure, not least because there are likely to be multiple possible trajectories. Indeed, with a mess it usually doesn't make much sense to talk about 'an answer'. It's more a matter of coping with the circumstances as best one can. With a difficulty we can take for granted the overall context and purpose of the activity; it's simply a matter of how it can best be done. But a mess calls into question priorities and assumptions; and raises questions about how much weight to give to different elements and viewpoints. Moreover, with a mess more aspects are beyond direct control. In short, a mess includes many different and changing perspectives and consequential actions, which contribute towards the overall level of uncertainty.

Some authors characterise a mess in terms of two dimensions, rather than a single continuum. Firstly, there is the multitude of factors that contribute to the scale of the situation. All three stories above have considerable histories attached to them as well as invoking multiple dimensions in terms of interrelated and interdependent human and natural variables, ideas and events. Secondly, a mess is characterised by significant levels of uncertainty, and this in turn is associated with there being multiple and, as evident in the three stories, often conflicting, perspectives on the situation. The first dimension alone signals the continuum from a simple difficulty, where few variables are involved, to a complicated difficulty. When the second dimension comes into play – dealing with uncertainty and multiple perspectives – this signals an engagement with a complex mess. Whereas difficulties, no matter how complicated, can be conceptualized in a straight-forward way and then worked upon, messes are experienced as being much more difficult to get to grips with conceptually.

Systems approaches aim to simplify the process of our thinking about, and managing, complex realities that have been variously described by systems thinkers as messes (Russell Ackoff), the swamp (Donald Schön), wicked problems (Horst Rittel), or in relation to environmental issues, resource dilemmas (Niels Röling). Systems thinking provides ways of selectively handling the detail that may complicate our thinking in a transparent manner, in order to reveal the underlying features of a situation from a set of explicit perspectives.

1.2.3 Traps in Conventional Thinking

Before examining how systems thinking might help our engagement with messes, let us look at how more conventional thinking can be counterproductive in resolving complex issues. Many aspects of our traditional thinking stem from confusing what is a mess with a simple or even complicated difficulty. For example, it is not unusual to approach the situations described in the three stories by adopting one or more of the following positions.

- Interconnections can be ignored – imagining that the survival of Orangutans has nothing to do with our own lifestyles – rather than looking at the bigger picture.
- A single cause may be assumed – tragic deaths of football supporters from inadequate physical football stadium physical infrastructure – rather than there being multiple interrelated causation.
- It may be assumed that an individual is to blame – a villainous pirate – rather than attempting to understand the ways in which a situation arose that led to a problematic outcome.
- There may be a focus on outcomes (and thus only on what can be measured) – numbers of Orangutans, all-seated football grounds, prosecution of pirates - rather than the processes by which beneficial change might best occur.

This last feature of traditional thinking has widespread relevance in Western societies blighted by the culture of targets, performance indicators and 'best' practice. Simon Caulkin, commenting on targets in the British National Health Service in a piece titled 'This isn't an abstract problem. Targets can kill' in the Observer newspaper on March 22, 2009 wrote:

> The Health Commission's finding last week that pursuing targets to the detriment of patient care may have caused the deaths of 400 people at Stafford between 2005 and 2008 simply confirms what we already know. … [T]argets distort judgment, disenfranchise professionals and wreck morale. Put concretely, in services where lives are at stake – as in the NHS or child protection – targets kill. Targets make organisations stupid. Because they are a simplistic response to a complex issue, they have unintended and unwelcome consequences – often, as with MRSA [infectious disease picked up in hospitals] or Stafford [hospital], that something essential but unspecified doesn't get done. So every target generates others to counter the perverse results of the first one. But then the system becomes unmanageable.

In summary, the traps of non-systems thinking lie in two simple dimensions; firstly avoiding the inevitable interconnectivity between variables – the trap of *reductionism*, and secondly, working on the basis of a single unquestioning perspective – the trap of *dogmatism*.

1.2.4 Systems Thinking Can Help

1.2.4.1 Systems Are Social Constructs

There are two major standpoints on the nature of *systems* that shape and distinguish different systems approaches. Cabrera et al. (2008) describe them in terms of the distinction made between 'thinking about systems' (e.g., accounting systems, personnel systems, ecosystems, health systems, legal systems, etc.) and 'systems thinking'. Elsewhere these traditions have been similarly referred to in terms of

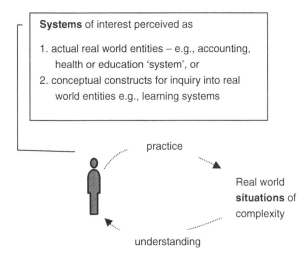

Fig. 1.1 Systems thinking and thinking about systems in a constructivist tradition

'hard' and 'soft' systems thinking (Checkland 1978 ; Jackson 1982). Both traditions have relevance and significance. More formally, the distinction is expressed in terms of the relative emphases of ontological traditions (systems as representing real world entities) and epistemological traditions (systems as learning devices to inquire into real world entities).

There is now agreement amongst systems practitioners that systems are *ultimately* conceptual constructs, and as such contemporary systems approaches can be regarded as belonging to a constructivist tradition. In short, 'systems' are constructs used for engaging with and improving situations of real world complexity (see Fig. 1.1).

Keeping this constructivist idea in mind, we can then examine two key aspects of systems thinking.

1.2.5   Two Aspects of Systems Thinking

> The core aspects of systems thinking are gaining a bigger picture (going up a level of abstraction) and appreciating other people's perspectives (Chapman 2004, p. 14)

The perspective on systems thinking that we use builds on this simple distinction made by Jake Chapman, which in turn builds upon the distinction made by Richard Bawden in identifying two transitions implicit in the history of systems thinking: one, towards holism, and another towards pluralism (Bawden 1998). The two transitions counter reductionism and dogmatism respectively. These two aspects are referred to in many guises by systems practitioners and writers. One of the most influential of these is C. West Churchman (1913–2004). Churchman described systems both as a process of unfolding, by which he meant heroically 'sweeping-in' as many factors as possible to our systems of concern, and as a process of looking at things from different viewpoints or, as he first coined the term, 'worldviews'. In this latter aspect, his description of a systems approach – *"A systems approach begins when first you see the world through the eyes of another"* (Churchman 1968, p. 231) – remains one of the most frequently quoted descriptions of systems thinking.

So how might we characterize these two aspects of systems thinking? Firstly, systems thinking is about gaining understanding by looking at the relationships between things. Most formalised thinking, including most scientific thinking and indeed most academic endeavour, tries to understand something by pulling it apart. By focusing on relationships you discover how something works by its effects on what surrounds it. Most people recognize they have been in situations where they 'can't see the wood for the trees'. Systems thinking is precisely about changing the focus of attention to the forest, so that you can see the trees in their context. Understanding the forest gives new and powerful insights about the trees. Such insights are completely inaccessible if one concentrates on the individual trees. So, systems thinking is a way of looking at (and making sense of) the world. It is based on an understanding that if one considers a situation as a whole, rather than focusing on its component parts, then there are properties which can be observed which cannot be found simply from the properties of the component parts.

Secondly, systems approaches start with the situation, with its complexity and uncertainty, where an acknowledged part of the problem is to establish and agree what the problem is, and where there will rarely be a single 'right' resolution. So the language of systems is about problem-situation rather than problem, and of resolution (improving the situation) rather than solution (solving the problem). Within complex situations involving multiple interrelated factors including multiple human interests, progress can be made as part of a process of inquiry in searching for, or thinking of relevant wholes, what in systems terminology are sometimes referred to as *systems of interest*. These are *sets of activity which could be described as being organised around a single/particular purpose.*

Such wholes are not pre-determined or existing. Rather they are selected, or identified by someone for a purpose – generally to learn about the complex situation in order to do something about it (change it, improve it). Given that when dealing with a 'mess' what counts as resolution is not clear at the outset then progress in a systems inquiry comes partly from learning what will count as resolution as the inquiry progresses.

1.2.6   Perspectives on Systems Thinking

Systems approaches have a rich historical tradition. Systems thinking in terms of promoting holistic views – particularly emphasising the integral relationship between human and non-human nature – can be traced back to the ancient spiritual traditions of Hinduism (e.g., through ancient texts like the Upanishads and Bhagavad Gita),

Buddhism (oral traditions of the Dhama), Taoism (basis of acupuncture and holistic medicine), sufi-Islam (in translations of the *Kashf al-Mahjûb* of Hujwiri, and the *Risâla* of Qushayri), ancient Greek philosophy (particularly Heraclitus and Aristotle), as well as being prevalent through the oral traditions of many indigenous tribal spiritual traditions which have existed for tens of thousands of years. The term 'systems' as recognised in contemporary usage, predominantly in Western cultures, was explicitly used first in eighteenth century European philosophy rooted in the works of Immanuel Kant (Ulrich 1983).

Bawden's two aspects of systems thinking – being holistic and being more pluralist – can be used to review systems approaches themselves. There are many different strands of systems thinking, and different perspectives on how to group them. So much so that whilst professing to deal with the complexities of real world situations in a manageable manner, we may well have inadvertently created a complex clutter of systems approaches. There have been many publications about systems thinking and practice in the 60 years since Bertalanffy published his first papers on systems theory. The four volume publication *Systems Thinking* by Midgley (2003) has nearly 100 chapters each dealing with a particular method and in 2001 Eric Schwartz identified 1,000 "streams of systems thought" (http://www.iigss.net/gPICT.jpg). The 1997 International Encyclopaedia of Systems and Cybernetics (François 1997) had 3,000 entries. So in the systems field there is no shortage of approaches; it is diverse with many concepts, methodologies, methods and techniques.

With the large number of 'systems approaches' it is not surprising that there are several ways of thinking about how systems approaches relate to each other and doing this produces different typologies. Typologies can themselves be regarded as system models; particular perspectives on organizing the interrelationships between different entities, each associated with a particular purpose. Here we briefly look at four 'typologies' or perspectives. As with any model, viewpoints are inevitably partial in the sense of being both incomplete and of being viewed from a particular or partisan perspective necessarily based on its own particular purpose. The following short overviews of these four perspectives represent a gradual shift in focus from the systems approach itself, to the situations in which they are used, and finally to the user.

1.2.6.1 Perspective 1: Three Traditions of Systems Thinking (West Churchman, Peter Checkland, Werner Ulrich, Mike Jackson and Others)

That traditions of systems thinking categorized as three sets – 'hard', 'soft' and 'critical', is perhaps the most widely used way of classifying systems approaches. It is intended to recognise prevailing systems approaches whilst also legitimizing new ways of thinking. The distinction is one that builds on Peter Checkland's earlier distinction between hard and soft systems. Checkland (1978) suggested that systems thinking prevailing at the time had rested on an unspoken assumption that systems exist in the real world. Checkland's questioning, and subsequent abandonment, of this 'hard' systems assumption paved the way for an extensive and influential

Table 1.1 Three traditions of systems thinking

Systems 'type'	Selected systems approaches
Hard systems	General systems theory (Bertalanfy 1956)
	Classical (first order) cybernetics, 'mechanistic' cybernetics (Ashby 1956)
	Operations research (Churchman et al. 1957)
	Systems engineering (Hall 1962)
	Socio-technical systems (Trist et al. 1963)
	RAND-systems analysis (Optner 1965)
	System dynamics (Forrester 1971; Meadows et al. 1972)
Soft systems	Inquiring systems design (Churchman 1971)
	Second order cybernetics (Bateson 1972)
	Soft systems methodology (Checkland 1972)
	Strategic assumption surface testing (Mason and Mitroff 1981)
	Interactive management (Ackoff 1981)
	Cognitive mapping for strategic options development and analysis (Eden 1988)
Critical systems	Critical systems heuristics (Ulrich 1983)
	System of systems methodologies (Jackson 1990)
	Liberating systems theory (Flood 1990)
	Interpretive systemology (Fuenmayor 1991)
	Total systems intervention (Flood and Jackson 1991a)
	Systemic intervention (Midgley 2000)

program of 'soft' systems action research based on the position that systems are epistemological constructs rather than real world entities. Meanwhile Churchman's student, Werner Ulrich, and others including Mike Jackson and colleagues at Hull University, identified the need for a distinct third systems thinking strand. Critical systems thinking (CST) shares the same epistemological shift as the soft systems tradition but addresses some of the perceived inadequacies in both hard and soft systems thinking, most notably the inadequate consideration of power relations. Table 1.1 is an example of grouping systems approaches using this schema.

Gerald Midgley uses the three distinctions in Table 1.1 to describe the historical evolution of current ideas of systems thinking and practice as evolving through a series of three "waves", or phases of inquiry (Midgley 2000). Each wave relates to a particular focus of the systems field which brought with it a new set of methods. Wave 1 focused on concrete issues of 'problems' and problem solutions for issues where there was perceived unity of purpose. Wave 2 began with the wider soft systems perspective on people and their perspectives on issues. And Wave 3 introduced added emphasis to power relations and how they affect what problems are addressed, and how they are perceived.

Whilst the three-part model remains very influential, not least because it addresses similar discourses in other disciplines, particularly those sharing ideas from critical social theory and Habermas' three knowledge constitutive interests (Habermas 1972, 1984), some difficulties are associated with the terminology of 'hard' and 'soft' as these have particular gendered connotations which can be difficult to discard. Other terms from critical social theory like functionalist, interpretivist, and emancipatory are sometimes substituted (cf. Jackson 2000). Another perceived difficulty is the limitation of defining systems thinking only in terms of these three categories. Does it not close up space for other potential synergies?

A question arising from this characterisation of systems approaches is what guidance would a practitioner find useful for using the different approaches in different situations. The focus here shifts towards the situation.

1.2.6.2 Perspective 2: Systems Thinking for Situations (Mike Jackson and Bob Flood)

The perspective here addresses the question of how might practitioners in different situations be guided in making use of the range of systems approaches available. System of systems methodologies (SOSM) builds on the triadic model associated with Perspective 1 with the primary aim to create a classification of systems methodologies that would allow for their complementary use in specified problem situations (Jackson 1990). The important shift in focus here is towards the situations in which systems approaches are applied. SOSM provides a matrix for classifying systems methods on two dimensions: one, the level of complexity of the problem situation (simple or complex), and the other, the degree of shared purpose amongst participant stakeholders (unitary, pluralist, or coercive relationships). It is this latter dimension that draws on the hard, soft, critical typology using metaphors as guiding principles – machine for the 'hard', living organism for the 'soft' and the metaphor of prison for the 'critical' situations. The classification yields a six celled matrix as illustrated in Table 1.2. Each cell defines a problem situation which then invites particular suitable systems methods.

The two dimensions of situations are helpful in delineating the two aspects of systems thinking described above. The simple/complex dimension relates to levels of interrelatedness and interdependencies, and the unitary/pluralist/coercive

Table 1.2 System of systems methodologies (Adapted from Jackson 2000, p. 359)

		Participants		
		Unitary 'hard' systems based on machine metaphor	Pluralist 'soft' systems based on organismic metaphor	Coercive 'critical' systems based on prison metaphor
'Systems' i.e., problem situations	Simple	Simple unitary: e.g. systems engineering	Simple pluralist: e.g. Strategic assumption surfacing and testing	Simple coercive: e.g., critical systems heuristics
	Complex	Complex unitary: e.g., systems dynamics, viable systems model	Complex pluralist: e.g. soft systems methodology	Complex coercive: (non available)

dimension relates to levels of engagement with multiple perspectives. Again such a model has been helpful in prompting systems practitioners to think more clearly about the nature of the problem situation – the 'mess' – in a simplified manner. It has helped with the appreciation that different systems methods might complement each other and indeed complement other approaches used for similar problem situations. Later, SOSM was adapted and became embedded in total systems intervention (TSI) by (Flood and Jackson 1991a, b) – a methodology for drawing different methods together through a three-fold process of (a) creatively exploring problematic situations, (b) choosing an appropriate systems approach, and (c) implementing it.

There are two significant difficulties in using this model. One is in assuming from the outset that a problem situation can somehow be easily identified as constituting one of the six 'problem situation' types depicted in the cells of the matrix. Another difficulty is in the 'fixing' or pigeon-holing of particular systems approaches as being only suitable for specific types of situation. First, there may be different opinions on where different systems approaches 'fit' based upon actual experiences of using the approach. Many approaches though understood as having roots in particular traditions can be used for different purposes. So for example, whilst some may classify VSM as a 'hard' approach – in the tradition of classic first order Cybernetics – others would describe the VSM as an interpretivist or even an emancipatory approach. Similar arguments may be expressed in relation to other approaches, particularly socio-technical systems and systems dynamics, both of which have many 'softer' and more 'critical' dimensions depending on the context of use and the user. Second, such pigeon-holing detracts attention from the potential for systems approaches to evolve and develop through use in different contexts by different users.

The perspective here and in the previous model prompt questions about other related traditions and approaches that might influence systems thinking, along with the influence of their domains or situations of interest. How might systems approaches draw upon and develop synergies with complementary traditions of practice and theory?

1.2.6.3 Perspective 3: Influences Around Systems Approaches (Ray Ison and Paul Maiteny)

This perspective illustrates some key relationships between different systems approaches and other closely related traditions. The authors were particularly concerned about the tendency of systems practitioners to be self-referential and insular. They wanted to recapture some of the wider influences and cross-fertilisation that continues to generate innovative development of systems approaches. The aim was to broaden the understanding and practice of spheres of influence both with respect to other *approaches* outside the traditional systems toolbox, and to other *situations* of interest in which such approaches were evident (Fig.1.2).

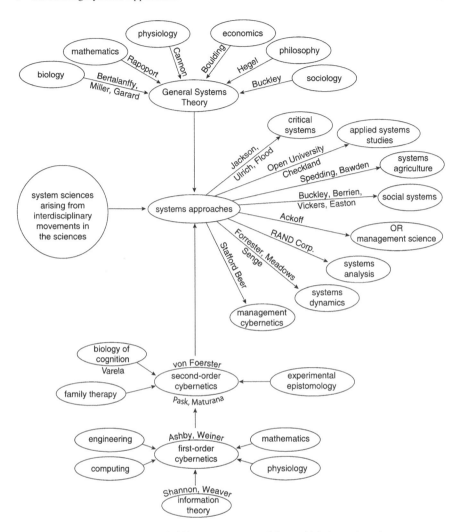

Fig. 1.2 An influence diagram of different systems traditions which have shaped contemporary systems practice (Maiteny and Ison 2000). Reprinted from Ison, R.L., Maiteny, P.T. and Carr, S., 'Systems Methodologies for Sustainable Natural Resources Research and Development', *Agricultural Systems*, p259, Copyright (1997), with permission from Elsevier

Some difficulties arising from such a perspective can be mentioned. Firstly, there are only one-way influences, whereas of course influences tend to be more dynamic (for example, family therapy has arguably been significantly influenced by systems approaches). Secondly, whilst arguably casting a wider net than prevailing perspectives (Tables 1.1 and 1.2), some significant contributors such as C. West Churchman appear not to be present. The difficulties raise some important questions though. A key question is how might systems practice develop synergies with other practices in different domains in order to keep alive its essential dynamism, and to maintain or raise its profile as being relevant to a range of complex situations in contemporary society. How might we ensure that systems thinking is not just sectioned off as just another academic discipline amongst the number of candidates vying for attention in ever-more challenging circumstances? Another question relates to the role of individual users of systems approaches and the influences that they can bring to bear on contributing towards developing systems approaches.

1.2.6.4   Perspective 4: Groupings of Systems Thinkers (Magnus Ramage and Karen Shipp)

The question regarding the contextual influence of individual systems practitioners is one addressed in the fourth perspective presented here. In *Systems Thinkers* (Ramage and Shipp 2009) the authors uniquely focus on the life and work of individuals behind the systems approaches rather than the systems approaches themselves. It is perhaps for this reason that their demarcation of systems approaches using the diagram below might be even more controversial. The prime intent behind this typology as acknowledged by the authors is to provide a foothold for the readers' engagement with the 30 systems thinkers covered:

> We had arguments with colleagues about the idea of providing any sort of 'map' of the territory. Of course there is no 'true' map – an individual might lay out the connections between these authors in any number of ways, to reveal a different pattern. By providing a model we emphasise certain connections, but underplay others. Yet to offer no map at all – no structure – is to deny the explorer a vital aid to their journey. Without some sort of map, the learner cannot even start to lay down the interconnections in memory. This map, which over time they will refine, extend, amend, embellish, and colour with their own experiences, preferences and insights, can only ever be an approximation, a starting point from which the individual can set out. (ibid, Afterward, p. 309)

Figure 1.3 illustrates the seven groupings: early cybernetics, general systems theory, system dynamics, soft and critical systems, later cybernetics, complexity theory, and learning systems.

As the authors suggest, the perspective here is unconventional and provocative, but was made with the intention of privileging the individuals rather than some abstract notion of either *systems* approaches (schools of thought) or perceived *situations* of interest: "The groupings were created from the starting point of our chosen authors rather than schools of thought, and thus they do not represent a comprehensive guide to a particular school of thought (for example, there are many more thinkers who have contributed to general systems theory than the four we cover)" (ibid).

A few other difficulties might be mentioned. For example, the grouping of soft and critical systems thinking together may cause some discomfort amongst traditional advocates of critical systems thinking who may prefer to hold on to a clear boundary of demarcation. Similarly the grouping of early (first order) and later (second order) cybernetics may appear to mask a very distinctive traditional divide. However, the refreshing and appealing aspect is that the authors are very explicit

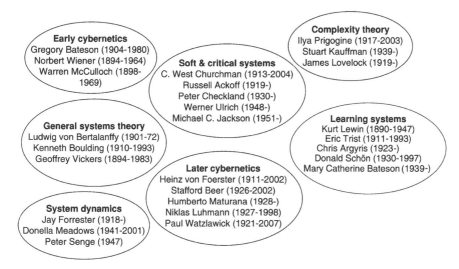

Fig. 1.3 The authors and groupings in Systems Thinkers (Ramage and Shipp 2009, p. 5)

about this being their own particular take on systems approaches. It is derived from a thorough reading around the personal circumstances and interrelationships of the systems authors in their context of practice. It raises questions regarding the role and circumstances of *people* in the development of practice.

There is a paradox here in any attempt at typography. Attempts to categorize tend to deemphasise links and ultimately break links, which arguably is the very problem that gave rise to contemporary systems thinking in the first place. So what perspective on systems approaches have we taken as editors of this reader? Moreover, what is the rationale behind selecting just five systems approaches?

1.2.7 Our Own Perspective

These four perspectives are all helpful in generating an understanding about how different systems approaches may be related to each other and to other schools of thought and practice, and also how they may be related to the situations in which they could be used. The five systems approaches presented in this reader have been chosen because they each demonstrate a rich interplay between the situation, the practitioner community, and the methodology itself. This interplay has generated a convincing and real sense of robustness and vigour for each approach. A second reason for selecting these particular five approaches relates to the different ways in which they take account of three motivations for the use of a systems approach in any systems intervention, namely: understanding interrelationships, dealing with different perspectives, and addressing power relations. All five approaches address each purpose in different ways and to a greater or lesser extent.

1.2.7.1 Systems Approaches in Practice

Peter Checkland identified three recurring attributes or entities relating to any intervention (Checkland 2000): the methodology being used, the context of use, and the user. The four perspectives outlined above provide different emphases on these three recurring themes:

1. The methodology or *systems* approach itself (particularly Perspectives 1 and 3)
2. The perceived problem *situation* (particularly Perspectives 2 and 3)
3. The *users* of the systems approach (including local people participating in the intervention and the practitioner community who lead such interventions) in the context of use (particularly Perspectives 2 and 4)

It is the interplay between these three attributes that determine the effectiveness of any approach to intervention. Figure 1.4 illustrates the dynamics of these attributes.

The approaches described in this book have each been internationally applied, in a wide and diverse range of contexts by diverse sets of practitioners. They are used in several languages and in countries with very different traditions of thinking. They can be applied over different time-scales – some studies are done in 10–15 minutes whilst others may take several years. They are also used in different domains of activity including organisational change, information systems strategy and development, environmental planning, international development, business strategy, etc. In short, they each embody a rich inheritance from practice.

The practices also have strong theoretical underpinnings which contribute both to their robustness and credibility amongst practitioners from different traditions. But perhaps the strongest attribute shared by these five approaches is their adaptability to change and modification. They have each proved resilient and adaptable given the challenges of different problem situations, involving different sets of users, bringing along different traditions of practice involving other conceptual approaches conventionally used for improving situations. Their value resides in their capacity to connect to a variety of professional traditions and schools of thought of different origins ranging from village-based participatory development initiatives in less-developed countries to multinational corporate enterprises and government.

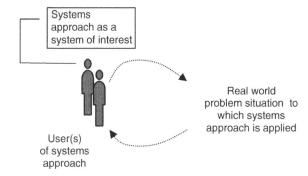

Fig. 1.4 Three aspects of using a systems approach: situation, user and system

1.2.8 Purposeful Practice

All five approaches in this book treat systems as social constructs. There is variation amongst them as to how much emphasis is put on the imperatives of *thinking about systems* as real world ontological entities, and *systems thinking* using systems more explicitly as epistemological constructs (see Fig. 1.1). Crudely, we might associate SD and VSM with the tradition of *thinking about systems* and SSM, SODA and CSH with the tradition of *systems thinking*, though in practice there is considerable variability amongst individual practitioners

But whether we consider systems as real world entities or not, we are reminded that *any* systems approach involving the conceptualization of systems might be characterized as serving some purpose (cf. Churchman 1968). We are also reminded by Churchman that purposeful intervention (where purposes can change and develop in the course of intervention) is preferable to purposive intervention (where purposes remain fixed). Drawing on Perspective 1 above, and a particular view of the *interrelatedness* between Habermas' three constitutive interests – technical, practical, and emancipatory – (Reynolds 2002) we suggest that any systems approach to intervention fulfils three generalised interrelated *purposes*. In serving these three purposes in an interrelated way, the input to intervention becomes purposeful (subject to change and modification). The outcome of purposeful intervention is systemic change. The three generalized purposeful orientations can be listed.

1. *Purposeful orientation 1*: Making sense of, or simplifying (in *understanding*), relationships between different entities associated with a complex situation. Notwithstanding the roots of some systems approaches in traditions of systems science, all systems approaches explored in this collection arguably present systems more as an 'art' form rather than as a 'science'. The prime intention is not to get some thorough comprehensive knowledge of situations, but rather to acquire a better understanding in order to improve the situation.
2. *Purposeful orientation 2*: Surfacing and engaging (through *practice*) contrasting perspectives associated with complex situations. The success of any systems approach discussed in these pages is ultimately dependent on the user, applying the ideas in a particular context rather than something inherent in a description of the approach. Whilst we may discuss different approaches in an abstract sense, any claims towards their value in creating beneficial change in a situation is dependent on the context of use, the purpose for which it is employed, and the skill and imagination of the practitioner.
3. *Purposeful orientation 3*: Exploring and reconciling (with *responsibility*) power relations, boundary issues and potential conflict amongst different entities and/ or perspectives. The aim here is not to provide yet another ready-to-hand matrix to offer clients through a consultancy, but rather to gently disrupt, unsettle and thereby provoke new systems thinking.

The five systems approaches are chosen for their particular strengths in serving one purpose to a greater extent over the other two purposes. So SD and VSM might be considered as having a primary strength and focus on making sense of interrelatedness and interdependencies between entities in a situation. For SSM and cognitive mapping associated with SODA, the primary strength and focus is on surfacing and engaging with different perspectives. CSH prompts particular attention to reflective practice and the need to address issues of power implied though our boundary judgements.

These particular strengths are an attribute of the historic roots of each approach. They do not necessarily signal a prescribed way of using the approach. Individual users of SD and VSM may for example experience a value in using the approaches as primary means of engaging with different perspectives and/or power relations. Likewise, users of SSM and SODA may in particular circumstances value its use in understanding interrelationships and interdependencies, or with engaging different boundary judgements. Users of CSH can sometimes attach more importance to understanding interrelationships and interdependencies, and/or engaging with multiple perspectives, again depending on the situation or context of use by individual users. Our rationale for choosing these five approaches is based not upon a prescriptive idea of 'best' *practice*, but rather upon an *understanding* of their particular pedigree – including (a) the experiences of interplay between the approaches themselves, communities of practitioners, and the situations in which they are used, and (b) the original dominant purpose to which they were serve. It is up to you, the reader (and user), to determine the further value of each approach in the context of your own traditions of practice, amongst your own communities of practitioners, and with respect to improving whatever situations of interest you are engaged with.

1.2.9 Five Approaches Described

1.2.9.1 System Dynamics (SD) Authored by John Morecroft

System dynamics was founded in the late 1950s by Jay W. Forrester of the MIT Sloan School of Management with the establishment of the MIT System Dynamics Group (Forrester 1961). At that time, he began applying what he had learned about systems during his work in electrical engineering to everyday kinds of systems. It is an approach to understanding the behaviour of complex systems over time. It deals with internal feedback loops and time delays that affect the behaviour of the entire system. What makes using system dynamics different from other approaches to studying complex systems is the use of feedback loops and stocks and flows in displaying nonlinearity. Forrester started work on servo-mechanism devices to control radar in the late 1950s, and then significantly moved into the field of, first, industrial relations, and later modelling global resource depletion, both of which involved Forrester himself (Forrester 1971). Sustainable development involved modelling of 'world systems'; work complemented significantly through sponsorship by the influential Club of Rome (Meadows et al. 1972, 1992). System dynamics later provided the crux of the systems approach advocated as the *Fifth Discipline* in the celebrated book of the same title authored by Senge (1990).

1.2.9.2 Viable Systems Model (VSM) Authored by Patrick Hoverstadt

The VSM is a model of the necessary and sufficient conditions for the viability of systems. A viable system is a system able to keep an independent existence. To do so it needs to be organised in such a way as to meet the demands of surviving in a changing environment. One of the prime features of systems that survive is that they are adaptable. The model itself was developed by the cybernetician Stafford in several publications, mainly *Brain of the Firm* (Beer 1972) and *Heart of Enterprise* (Beer 1979) for the theory, and *Diagnosing the System* (Beer 1985) for the methodology required for application. Beer's ideas arose out of a synthesis of Eastern and Western thought. His time in India as a very young man and subsequently his interest in Eastern thought, particularly Indian cultural traditions, was a very important factor in the emergence of the VSM. Beer's own engagement with practicing VSM was most notably carried out under invitation to Allende's Chile in the early 1970s before the military coup. Beer effectively founded management cybernetics – now known as Organisational Cybernetics – which is being developed and used extensively by cyberneticians worldwide. VSM , like SD and each of the other approaches in this compilation, has been and is continually being moulded for a variety of different levels of contexts including contexts with disparate purposes. Aside from different organisational fields, it has been used in contexts ranging from promoting efficiency in small organizations and communities to guiding major environmental policy at national and regional levels (cf. Espejo 1990; Espinosa et al. 2008).

1.2.9.3 Strategic Options Development and Analysis (SODA, with Cognitive Mapping) Authored by Fran Ackermann and Colin Eden

Cognitive mapping is a technique for revealing and actively shaping the mental models, or belief systems (mind maps, cognitive models) that people use to perceive, contextualize, simplify, and make sense of otherwise complex problems. SODA was built on Colin Eden's interest during the 1970s in Kelly's psychological work on 'personal construct theory' (Kelly 1955). The notion of cognitive mapping is based upon a process of meaning construction to facilitate negotiation and arrival at some agreed plans of action. Whilst being appropriate at the individual level in clarifying thoughts around a particular issue, work on SODA encompasses much wider contexts of *strategic* thinking; neatly encapsulated through the software acronym JOURNEY making (JOintly Understanding Reflecting and NEgotiating strategY). SODA is the methodology used for cultivating organisational change through attention to and valuing of individual perspectives in a concerted manner. The importance of facilitation (process) skills in consultancy practice is thereby emphasised in tandem with conventional knowledge management (content) skills. The techniques are used in developing strategies for improvement based on three hierarchical systems levels: (a) goals (cf. ideal planning); (b) strategic directions (cf. objective planning); and (c) potential options (cf. operational planning). The two key source publications for SODA are *Making Strategy: Journey of Strategic*

Management by (Eden and Ackermann 1988) and *The Practice of Making Strategy: A Step by Step Guide* (Ackermann et al. 2005). As noted in these publications, the context of their application has varied from dealing with individual decision making to small and large enterprises. It has also been recommended for dealing with wider international inter-organisational relationships (Hewitt and Robinson 2000).

1.2.9.4 Soft Systems Methodology (SSM) Authored by Peter Checkland and John Poulter

SSM is an approach to organisational process modelling. It was developed by Peter Checkland and colleagues at the University of Lancaster Systems Department through a 20 year program of action research. The primary use of SSM is in the analysis of complex situations where there are divergent views about the definition of the problem — 'soft problems' (e.g. How to improve health services delivery; How to manage disaster planning; When should mentally disordered offenders be diverted from custody? What to do about homelessness amongst young people?). In such situations even the actual problem to be addressed may not be easy to agree. To intervene in such situations the soft systems approach uses the notion of a 'system' as an interrogative device that will enable debate amongst concerned parties. The major texts on SSM are: *Systems Thinking, Systems Practice* (Checkland 1981) *Soft Systems Methodology in Action* (Checkland and Scholes 1990); *and Information, Systems and Information Systems* (Checkland and Holwell 1997). The most recent book, *Learning for Action* (Checkland and Poulter 2006) is a 'a short definitive account of SSM and its use' provides the source material for this compilation. SSM has been used to examine organisational change in large multinational corporations, with several hundred participants in the study; it can be used by an individual to manage, for example, personal recovery from substance abuse; it has been used to research Inuit fishing in Labrador; by an NGO volunteer to engage local people in mine clearance after war in the Middle East; by members of a women's forum in Japan to make sense of the impacts of societal changes on their lives; by consultants working on information systems planning in the NHS – these are just some of areas in which SSM has been applied.

1.2.9.5 Critical Systems Heuristics (CSH) Authored by Werner Ulrich and Martin Reynolds

Critical systems heuristics represents the first systematic attempt at providing both a philosophical foundation and a practical framework for critical systems thinking. CSH is a framework for reflective practice based on practical philosophy and systems thinking, developed originally by Werner Ulrich. The basic idea of CSH is to support boundary critique – a systematic effort of handling boundary judgments critically. Boundary judgments determine which empirical observations and value considerations count as relevant and which others are left out or are considered less important. Because they condition both 'facts' and 'values', boundary judgments play an essential role when it comes to assessing the meaning and merits of a claim. *Critical heuristics of social planning : a new approach to practical philosophy* (Ulrich 1983) is the principle text on this approach. CSH like SSM emerged from an ethical systems tradition promoted through the works of the American systems philosopher C. West Churchman. Werner Ulrich's own work in developing CSH as a means of supporting social planning was rooted in traditions of Churchman's systems philosophy (particularly Churchman 1971, 1979) along with American philosophical pragmatism and European critical social theory. Whilst the CSH case studies described in this compilation are rooted in environmental management, CSH has been deployed in a wide range of significant contexts ranging from health care planning, city and regional planning, and energy and transportation planning (Ulrich 1987, p. 276), enhancing prison service support (Flood and Jackson 1991b), towards promoting an alternative lens for corporate responsibility (Reynolds 2008a) and informing international development initiatives (McIntyre-Mills 2004; Reynolds 2008b).

1.2.10 Chapter Framework

The chapters in this compilation are summarized contemporary versions of the five approaches. For ease of comparison, each chapter is based on a template comprising three substantive sections:

(i) *Description of whole approach in broad terms*: what it is (nature/ essence of method); what it looks like (basic characteristics/ attributes); and what is its significance (why use it)?
(ii) *Detailed descriptor of the parts*: how it works (tools, concepts) together with the basic techniques, procedures and traps.
(iii) *Descriptor of whole approach in context of use*: why it is significant; a retrospective review of the rules of skilled practice in the application of the approach. What are the minimum claims that might be made on the use of the approach by a skilled practitioner?

Whilst the restricted space does not allow detailed expositions of the theoretical underpinnings of each approach, we trust that the reader will gain an appreciation of both theoretical foundations and practice. The experiences provided in these pages cannot possibly encompass the whole user experience, let alone all users' experiences over at least the last 25 years. Additional experiences of the use of each of these methodologies might be sought from the many readings associated with each approach. But no experiences are more valuable than your own. The approaches described here are not suggested replacements for your own skills, but rather sources for enhancing your skills for managing complex situations.

References

Ackermann, F., Eden, C. and Brown, I. (2005). *The Practice of Making Strategy*, London: Sage.

Ackoff, R. (1974). Redesigning the Future: a systems approach to societal problems. New York: John Wiley.

Ackoff, R. (1981). *Creating the Corporate Future: Plan or be Planned for*. New York: John Wiley.

Ashby, W. R. (1956). *An Introduction to Cybernetics*. London: Chapman & Hall.

Bateson, G. (1972). *Steps to an Ecology of Mind*. Toronto: Ballantine.

Bawden, R. J. (1998). "The Community Challenge: The Learning Response" *New Horizons (Journal of the World Education Foundation Australia)* 99 (October): 40–59.

Beer, S. (1972), *Brain of the Firm,* London and New York: John Wiley.

Beer, S. (1979), *The Heart of Enterprise*, London and New York: John Wiley.

Beer, S. (1985), *Diagnosing the System for Organizations*, London and New York: John Wiley.

Bertalanfy, L. V. (1956). General Systems Theory. *General Systems Yearbook* 1: 1–10.

Cabrera, D., Colosi, L., Lobdell, C. (2008). "Systems Thinking." *Journal of Evaluation and Program Planning*. 31 (3) pp. 317–21.

Chapman, J. (2004). *System Failure: Why Governments Must Learn to Think Differently*. London: Demos.

Checkland, P. B. (1972) Towards a systems-based methodology for real world problem solving, *Journal of Systems Engineering*, 3(2), 87–116.

Checkland, P. (1978). "The Origins and Nature of 'Hard' Systems Thinking." *Journal of Applied Systems Analysis* 5: 99–110.

Checkland, P. (1981). *Systems Thinking Systems Practice*. Chichester: John Wiley.

Checkland, P. (2000). "Peter Checkland at 70: A Review of Soft Systems Thinking." *Systems Research and Behavioural Science* 17(1): 11–58.

Checkland, P. and S. Holwell (1998). *Information, Systems and Information Systems* Chichester: John Wiley.

Checkland, P. and J. Poulter (2006). *Learning For Action: A Short Definitive Account of Soft Systems Methodology, and its use Practitioners, Teachers and Students*. Chichester: John Wiley.

Checkland, P. and J. Scholes (1990). *Soft Systems Methodology in Action*. Chichester: John Wiley.

Churchman, C. W. (1968). *The Systems Approach*. New York: Dell.

Churchman, C. W. (1971). *The Design of Inquiring Systems: Basic Concepts of Systems and Organizations*. New York: Basic Books.

Churchman, C. W. (1979). *The Systems Approach and its Enemies*. New York: Basic Books.

Churchman, C. W., and R. Ackoff, et al. (1957). *Introduction to Operations Research*. New York: John Wiley.

Eden, C. (1988). Cognitive Mapping: A Review. *European Journal of Operational Research*, 36 1–13.

Eden, C. and Ackermann, F. (1988). *Making Strategy: The Journey of Strategic Management*. London: Sage.

Espejo, R. (1990 guest editor). "The Viable Systems Model." *Systems Practice (special edition on VSM)* 3(3).

Espinosa, A., Harden, R. et al. (2008). "A complexity approach to sustainability – Stafford Beer revisited." *European Journal of Operational Research* 187: 636–651.

Flood, R. L. (1990). Liberating Systems Theory: Towards Critical Systems Thinking. *Human Relations* 43.

Flood, R. L. and Jackson, M. C. (1991a). Total Systems Intervention: A Practical Face to Critical Systems Thinking. *Critical Systems Thinking*. R. L. Flood and M. C. Jackson. Chichester: John Wiley.

Flood, R. L. and Jackson, M. C. (1991b). "Critical Systems Heuristics: Application of an Emancipatory Approach for Police Strategy Towards Carrying Offensive Weapons." *Systems Practice* 4(4): 283–302.

Forrester, J. W. (1961). *Industrial Dynamics*. Cambridge MA: Wright-Allen Press.

Forrester, J. W. (1971). *World Dynamics*. Cambridge Mass: Wright & Allen.

François, C., Ed. (1997). *International Encyclopaedia of Systems and Cybernetics*. München: K. G. Saur Publishing.

Fuenmayor, R. (1991). Between Systems Thinking and Systems Practice. *Critical Systems Thinking: Directed Readings*. R. L. Flood and M. C. Jackson. Chichester: John Wiley.

Habermas, J. (1972). *Knowledge and Human Interests*. London: Heinemann.

Habermas, J. (1984). *The Theory of Communicative Action Volumes 1 and 2*. Cambridge: Polity Press.

Hall, A. D. (1962). *A Methodology for Systems Engineering*. New York: Van Nostrand.

Jackson, M. (1982). "The Nature of Soft Systems Thinking: The Work of Churchman, Ackoff and Checkland." *Journal of Applied Systems Analysis* 9: 17–28.

Jackson, M. (1990). "Beyond a system of systems methodologies." *Journal of the Operational Research Society* 41(8): 657–668.

Jackson, M. (2000). *Systems Approaches to Management*, New York: Kluwer Academic/Plenum Publishers.

Kelly, G. A. (1955) *The Psychology of personal constructs. Volume One: A Theory of Personality* New York: W.W. Norton.

Maiteny, P. and Ison, R. (2000). "Appreciating Systems: Critical Reflections on the Changing Nature of Systems as a Discipline in a Systems-Learning Society." *Systemic Practice and Action Research* 13(4): 559–586.

Mason, R. O. and Mitroff, I. I. (1981). *Challenging Strategic Planning Assumptions: Theory, Cases and Techniques*. New York: John Wiley.

McIntyre-Mills, J. (2004). *Critical Systemic Praxis for Social and Environmental Justice: Participatory policy design and governance for a global age*. New York: Kluwer Academic/Plenum Publishers.

Meadows, D. H. et al. (1972). *The Limits to Growth: a Report for the Club of Rome's Project on the Predicament of Mankind*. London: Earthscan.

Meadows, D. H. et al. (1992). *Beyond the Limits of Growth*. Post Mills: Chelsea Green.

Midgley, G. (2000). *Systemic Intervention: Philosophy, Methodology and Practice*. New York: Kluwer/Plenum.

Midgley, G. (Ed.) (2003), *Systems Thinking (4 vols.)*. London: Sage.

Optner, S. L. (1965). *Systems Analysis for Business & Industrial Problem Solving*. New York: Prentice-Hall.

Ramage, M. and Shipp, K. (2009). *Systems Thinkers*. London: Springer.

Reynolds, M. (2002). "In defence of knowledge constitutive interests. A comment on 'What is this thing called CST?' (Midgley, 1996)." *Journal of the Operational Research Society* 53(10): 1162–1164.

Reynolds, M. (2008a). "Getting a grip: A Critical Systems Framework for Corporate Responsibility." *Systems Research and Behavioural Science* 25(3): 383–395.

Reynolds, M. (2008b). "Reframing expert support for development management." *Journal of International Development* 20: 768–782.

Hewitt and Robinson (2000) "Putting inter-organizational ideas into practice" in D. Robinson, T. Hewitt, and J. Harris, Eds. (2000). *Managing Development: Understanding Inter-Organizational Relationships*. pp.301–328. London: Sage.

Senge, P. (1990). *The Fifth Discipline*. New York: Currency Doubleday.

Trist, E.L., Higgin, G.W., Murray, H., and Pollock, A.B. (1963) *Organisational Choice*, London: Tavistock.

Ulrich, W. (1983). *Critical Heuristics of Social Planning: A New Approach to Practical Philosophy*. Bern: Haupt; paperback reprint edition, Chichester: Wiley (same pagination).

Ulrich, W. (1987). "Critical heuristics of social systems design". *European Journal of Operational Research* 31(3): 276–283.

Chapter 2
System Dynamics[1]

John Morecroft

Abstract System dynamics is an approach for thinking about and simulating situations and organisations of all kinds and sizes by visualising how the elements fit together, interact and change over time. This chapter, written by John Morecroft, describes modern system dynamics which retains the fundamentals developed in the 1950s by Jay W. Forrester of the MIT Sloan School of Management. It looks at feedback loops and time delays that affect system behaviour in a non-linear way, and illustrates how dynamic behaviour depends upon feedback loop structures. It also recognises improvements as part of the ongoing process of managing a situation in order to achieve goals. Significantly it recognises the importance of context, and practitioner skills. Feedback systems thinking views problems and solutions as being intertwined. The main concepts and tools: feedback structure and behaviour, causal loop diagrams, dynamics, are practically illustrated in a wide variety of contexts from a hot water shower through to a symphony orchestra and the practical application of the approach is described through several real examples of its use for strategic planning and evaluation.

2.1 Introduction

In this chapter the basic concepts of system dynamics are introduced. The approach helps you to develop a strategic overview of organisations and to visualise how the parts of a business, industry or society fit together and interact to create dynamics and change through time. You will first learn how to draw and interpret causal loop diagrams that show the main interdependencies in real-world problem situations. Examples based on transportation policy, hotel showers, drug-related crime and

---

[1] The chapter uses edited excerpts and selected figures from my book *Strategic Modelling and Business Dynamics* (1997), copyright John Wiley & Sons Limited. Reproduced with permission.

J. Morecroft (✉)
Management Science and Operations, London Business School,
e-mail: jmorecroft@london.edu

M. Reynolds and S. Holwell (eds.), *Systems Approaches to Managing Change: A Practical Guide*, DOI 10.1007/978-1-84882-809-4_2, © The Open University 2010.
Published in Association with Springer-Verlag London Limited

orchestra management illustrate how such diagrams reveal the big picture from underlying operating detail. Next you will see the steps required to create a full-blown system dynamics simulation model. Simulation is used to investigate the performance over time that arises from interlocking feedback loops. An example from the airline industry examines the dynamics of growth strategy and illustrates a fundamental tenet of the field that 'feedback structure gives rise to dynamical behaviour'.

2.1.1   Ways of Interpreting Situations in Business and Society

The idea there is an enduring structure to business and social systems, that some-how predetermines achievable futures, is not necessarily obvious. Some people argue that personalities, ambition, chance, circumstance, fate, and unforeseen events hold the keys to the future in an uncertain world. But an interpretation of what is happening around you depends on your perspective. What appears to be chance may, from a different perspective, have a systemic cause. For example, when driving on a busy highway you may experience sporadic stops and starts. Does that mean you are at the mercy of random events like breakdowns or accidents? Not necessarily. Trapped in a car at ground level you don't see the waves of traffic that arise from the collective actions of individual drivers as they try to maintain a steady speed while keeping a safe distance from the car in front. There is an invisible structure to the 'system' of driving on a crowded motorway that *causes* sporadic stops and starts, without the need for accidents (though, of course, they do happen too). You can sense such structure, or at least something systemic, in the pattern of traffic density (alternating bands of congestion and free flow) observable from a nearby hillside overlooking the motorway, where you have the benefit of an overview. The same benefit of perspective applies to all kinds of business and social problems. In particular there are two contrasting perspectives that people bring to bear on policy and strategy development: an event-oriented approach and a feedback (or joined-up) approach. In many ways they are polar extremes.

2.1.2   Event-Oriented Thinking

An event-oriented perspective is pragmatic, action oriented, alluringly simple and often myopic. Figure 2.1 depicts this mindset in the abstract. It reflects a belief that problems are sporadic, stemming from uncontrollable events in the outside world. Life is capricious. Events come out of the blue or at least there is no time to worry about their causes. What's important is to fix the problem as soon as possible.

The typical thinking style here is linear – from problem-as-event to solution-as-fix. The problem presents itself as a discrepancy between an important shared goal

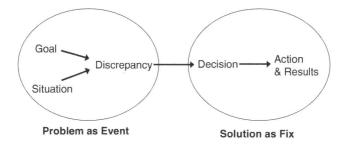

Fig. 2.1 Event-oriented world view

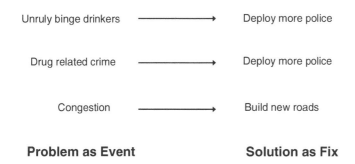

Problem as Event   **Solution as Fix**

Fig. 2.2 Examples of event-oriented thinking

and a capricious current situation. Through decision and action those responsible for the shared goal arrive at a solution and then move on to the next problem. Event oriented thinking is widespread and often compelling. It can lead to swift and decisive action. But there are limitations to this open-loop, fire-fighting mode of intervention.

Consider a few practical examples depicted in Fig. 2.2. Binge drinking is often in the news. Among other things it leads to unruly behaviour in towns and cities late at night. A local solution is to deploy more police to arrest the main troublemakers. Such an approach may reduce violence and accidents on a given night, but it does not get to grips with why people are binge drinking in the first place. Similarly a quick fix solution to drug related crime is to deploy more police in order to seize drugs and arrest drug dealers, but that does not deter addicts. In a totally different area of public policy, traffic congestion is a chronic problem for motorists and transportation planners alike. One practical solution is to build new roads, an approach that does work, at least in the short run. However experience suggests that in the long run congestion returns – as in the case of the M25 orbital motorway around Greater London, originally a six lane highway with a circumference of 160 miles, completed in the mid-1980s. More than 20 years later there are sections with 12 lanes and still it is overcrowded.

2.1.3   Feedback Systems Thinking

A feedback approach is different from event-oriented thinking because it strives for solutions that are 'sympathetic' with their organisational and social environment. Problems do not stem from events, and solutions are not implemented in a vacuum. Instead problems and solutions coexist and are interdependent. There is a long history to these ideas. They were lucidly brought to the attention of policy makers and business leaders in Senge's influential book *The Fifth Discipline* published in 1990. He presents four core 'disciplines' of successful organisational change that include team learning, shared vision, personal mastery and mental models. The fifth discipline is systems thinking which, by uniting the other disciplines, provides concepts and tools to visualise complexity and better understand sources of resistance to organisational change.[2] Although there are no formal simulation models or equations in the *Fifth Discipline* its approach to systems was inspired by the field of system dynamics, beginning with Forrester's seminal book *Industrial Dynamics* published in 1961 and further developed in the many ways described in the 50th anniversary review of the field (Sterman 2007). Moreover, system dynamics itself can be meaningfully placed among intellectual traditions that contributed to the evolution of feedback concepts in the social sciences, as described by Richardson (1991).

2.1.4   An Illustration of Feedback Systems Thinking

Consider Fig. 2.3, which is a causal loop diagram of factors contributing to road use and traffic congestion (Sterman 2000). The rules for constructing such a diagram are introduced later, but for now just focus on the cause and effect links that depict far-reaching interdependencies between highway capacity and traffic volume. Four feedback loops are shown. The top loop depicts road construction by the government agency responsible for transportation. As motorists experience an increase in travel time relative to desired travel time (the amount of time they are willing to spend on travel) there is growing pressure on planners to reduce congestion. This pressure leads to road construction which, after a time delay of several years, results in more highway capacity. More highway capacity reduces travel time as motorists are able to reach their destinations more quickly on less crowded roads. The four links described so far make a closed feedback loop labelled capacity expansion. Interestingly this loop includes an event-oriented link from 'pressure to reduce congestion' to road construction which is similar to the connection in Fig. 2.2 from congestion to 'build new roads'. But this isolated connection is now placed in context of many other factors, or side-effects, deemed relevant to the big picture.

---

[2] Here I use the term 'feedback systems thinking' to avoid confusion with 'systems thinking' often used in connection with Soft Systems Methodology (SSM), as described elsewhere in this book.

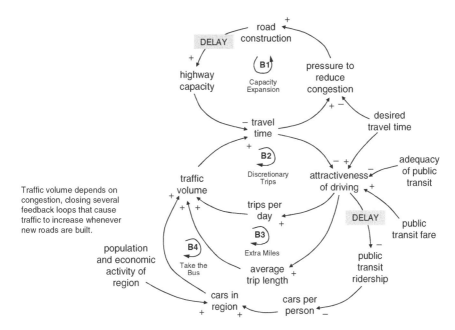

Fig. 2.3 A causal loop diagram about road congestion (Sterman 2000). *Business Dynamics: Systems Thinking and Modeling for a Complex World*, McGraw Hill, with permission from The McGraw-Hill Companies

One important side effect is shown in the middle loop labelled 'discretionary trips'. Here a reduction in travel time leads to an increase in the attractiveness of driving. Attractiveness itself depends on a variety of factors including desired travel time, adequacy of public transit and public transit fare. The greater the attractiveness of driving then (eventually) the more trips per day taken by motorists, the more traffic volume and the higher the travel time, thereby closing the loop. Here already is a vital side effect that can, in the medium to long term, defeat the objective of new road building programmes aimed at reducing congestion. Bigger and better roads make it more attractive to drive. So people make extra journeys. This particular side effect is largely responsible for the failure of London's M25 orbital motorway to relieve traffic congestion in and around the Greater London area, as drivers took to commuting regularly between places they would otherwise seldom visit.

The lower middle loop shows a related side effect labelled 'extra miles'. For the same attractiveness reasons drivers not only make extra journeys, they also take much longer journeys. The aggregate traffic effect is similar. Traffic volume increases leading to longer journey times.

The bottom loop labelled 'take the bus' shows another side effect, a potential long-term impact from public transit. Here, as the attractiveness of driving increases, public transit ridership decreases, causing cars per person to increase. (The direction of these causal effects can be read accurately from the diagram, but first you have to be familiar with the meaning of the '+' and '−'signs near the arrow heads which is explained later in the chapter.) With more cars per person there are more cars in the region and traffic volume increases, thereby closing the bottom loop.

If you reflect for a moment on the picture as a whole you realise it is a sophisticated view of the congestion problem. There are 15 concepts connected by 19 links. A lot of complexity is condensed into a small space. Compare the picture with the single stark arrow in Fig. 2.2 from an event oriented perspective. Obviously there is much more to think about and discuss in the causal loop diagram. Such richness is typical of good feedback systems thinking. The approach gives pause for thought by showing that often there is more going on (in public policy or in business strategy) than people first recognise. Where exactly to draw the boundary on the factors to include is a matter of judgement and experience. Usually there is no one right answer and therefore the process of constructing diagrams, and tying them to a dynamic phenomenon, is important too.

2.1.5   A Shift of Mind

People responsible for strategy development and facing problem situations often have in mind partial and conflicting views of these situations. It is therefore well worth spending time to capture their individual perspectives, develop an overview, share the big picture and thereby try to anticipate the ramifications, knock-on consequences, and side-effects of strategic change. These are the advantages of feedback systems thinking. In *The Fifth Discipline*, Peter Senge (1990) makes the point that feedback systems thinking is a 'shift of mind', a new way of interpreting the business and social world, and a kind of antidote to silo mentalities and narrow functional perspectives often fostered (inadvertently) by organisations and by our tendency to carve-up problems for analysis. Figure 2.4 summarises this shift of mind. Essentially problems and solutions are viewed as intertwined. The typical thinking style here is circular – starting from a problem, moving to a solution and then back to the problem. The important point, as shown on the right of the figure, is that problems do not just spring from nowhere, demanding a fix. They are a consequence of the cumulative effect of previous decisions and actions, sometimes intentional, but often with hidden side-effects.

As before, a problem presents itself as a discrepancy between an important goal and the current situation. Those responsible for achieving the goal arrive at a solution in the form of a decision leading to action and results that change the current situation. If all goes to plan then the current situation moves closer to the goal, the size of the discrepancy is reduced and the problem is alleviated. But this feedback response is not viewed as a once-and-for-all fix. It is part of a continual process of 'managing' the situation in order to achieve an agreed goal (or goals). Moreover, there is a recognition that other influences come to bear on the current situation. There are other stakeholders, with other goals, facing other

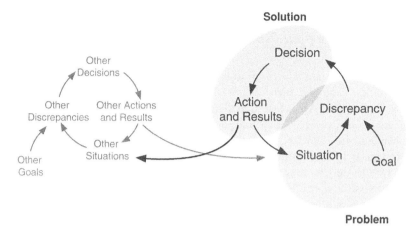

Fig. 2.4 A feedback perspective

situations and taking their own corrective action as shown on the left of Fig. 2.4. The performance of the enterprise as a whole arises from the interplay of these interlocking feedback processes, just as we saw in the transport example where the stakeholders included motorists, transportation planners, bus companies and bus passengers.

2.2   Concepts and Tools of System Dynamics

In this section we review the main concepts and tools used in system dynamics modelling. The material is divided into six parts labelled 2.2.1 through 2.2.6. Part 2.2.1 introduces the rules for constructing causal loop diagrams and for interpreting their likely problematic behaviour through time. A familiar example of a slow-to-respond hot water shower illustrates the central idea that feedback structure determines dynamic behaviour. Part 2.2.2 says more about causal loops and dynamic behaviour with an example in drug-related crime. Basic tips are then presented for constructing causal loop diagrams that are both conceptually and visually clear. Part 2.2.3 introduces additional modelling symbols necessary to build full-blown simulation models. Part 2.2.4 presents the equations for a simple drug-related crime model and uses them to illustrate principles of equation formulation. Part 2.2.5 shows system dynamics in action with an application to growth strategy for a low cost airline. The example includes causal loop diagrams, equation formulations, simulations and a gaming simulator that readers can operate themselves. Finally, in a very different organisational setting, Part 2.2.6 presents causal loops from a study of symphony orchestras and their success.

2.2.1   Causal Loop Diagrams, Feedback Structure and Behaviour Through Time

A causal loop diagram is a visual tool for the feedback systems thinker. As in the transportation example, such diagrams show cause and effect relationships and feedback processes. All causal loop diagrams are constructed from the same basic elements: words, phrases, links and loops – with special conventions for naming variables and for depicting the polarity of links and loops. Figure 2.5 is a very simple causal loop diagram, just a single loop, connecting hunger and amount eaten. Deliberately there is very little detail. Imagine the situation for yourself. You are hungry, so you eat. How would you describe the process that regulates food intake? Common sense and experience says there is a relationship between hunger and amount eaten and this is shown by *two* causal links. In the top link hunger influences amount eaten, while in the bottom link amount eaten has a reverse influence on hunger. Each link is assigned a polarity, either positive or negative. A positive '+' link means that if the cause increases then the effect increases too. So an increase in hunger causes an increase in the amount eaten. A negative '–' link means that if the cause increases then the effect decreases. So an increase in the amount eaten causes a decrease in hunger. In fact the assignment of link polarity is just a bit more sophisticated. In general it is better to imagine the effect (whether an increase or decrease) *relative to what it would otherwise have been*, in the absence of an increase in the cause. This turns out to be a more robust test.[3] In any case the two concepts, hunger and amount eaten, are mutually dependent,

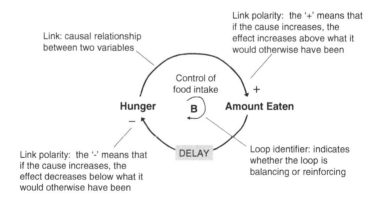

Fig. 2.5   Simple causal loop diagram of food intake

---

[3] This more sophisticated assignment of link polarity works equally well for normal straightforward causal links and for links that correspond to stock accumulation processes. The distinction will become clear when stock accumulation is introduced as a vital concept for modelling and simulating dynamical systems.

and this two-way dependence is shown as a closed feedback loop. The feedback loop represents, in outline, the control of food intake.

There are a few more details to explain in the diagram. The bottom link contains a box labelled 'DELAY'. This symbol shows a time delay in a causal link where a given cause leads to an effect, but not immediately. There is a lag. So here the more you eat the less hungry you feel, but it takes a while for hunger pangs to diminish. Such time delays add dynamic complexity because cause and effect is less obvious. Where eating is concerned a time delay of 20 min or so can make it much more difficult to regulate food intake. Overeating is a common result. In the centre of the diagram there is another special symbol, a 'B' inside a small curved arrow, a loop identifier to indicate a balancing feedback loop. Generally speaking a feedback loop can be either balancing or reinforcing. The names give a clue about the way the feedback process operates. In a balancing loop a change in the condition of a given variable leads to a counteracting or balancing change when the effects are traced around the loop.

A simple thought experiment illustrates the idea. Imagine you take a long walk and return home feeling hungry. Hunger rises and the feedback loop swings into action. Amount eaten rises and eventually hunger declines. The feedback effect of the loop is to counteract the original rise in hunger, which is a balancing process. By comparison a reinforcing loop amplifies or reinforces change. In a realistic multi-loop system, such as the transport example mentioned earlier, behaviour through time arises from the interplay of balancing and reinforcing loops. So it is useful when interpreting a web of causal connections to identify the main loops as a way of telling a story of what might unfold. At the same time it is a good discipline to name each loop with a mnemonic for the underlying feedback process. In Fig. 2.5 the balancing loop is called 'control of food intake'. Similarly in Fig. 2.3 a feedback view of road congestion is depicted vividly as the interplay of balancing loops for capacity expansion, discretionary trips, extra miles and 'take the bus?'.

2.2.1.1 Feedback Structure and the Dynamics of a Slow-to-Respond Shower

Causal loop diagrams are a stepping-stone to interpreting and communicating dynamics or performance through time. The best way to appreciate this point is to see a worked example. Here I present a hot water shower like the one at home or in a hotel room. In this example we start from dynamics of interest and then construct a causal loop diagram that is capable of explaining the dynamics. Our analysis begins with a time chart as shown in Fig. 2.6. On the vertical axis is the water temperature at the shower head and on the horizontal axis is time in seconds. Imagine it is a hot summer's day and you want to take a nice cool shower at 25°C. When you step into the cubicle the shower is already running but the water temperature is much too cold. The time chart shows three alternative time paths or trajectories for the water temperature labelled 'ideal, 'common sense', and 'most likely'. The ideal outcome is that you quickly adjust the tap setting by just the right amount and the water temperature immediately rises to the desired 25° after which it remains rock steady.

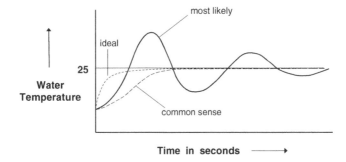

Fig. 2.6 Puzzling dynamics of a slow-to-respond shower

You are comfortably cool. Common sense says this ideal can't happen because, like most showers, this one is slow to respond. There is a time delay of a few seconds between adjusting the tap and a change in the water temperature. To begin with the common sense trajectory is flat and the water temperature remains too cold. Then after a while the temperature begins to rise and quite soon settles at the desired 25°. Unfortunately experience contradicts this common sense outcome. The most likely trajectory is much different. Again the temperature starts too cold. You adjust the tap and gradually the temperature rises. After a few seconds the temperature is just right. But annoyingly it continues to rise. Before long you are much too hot, so you reverse the tap. It makes no immediate difference. So you reverse the tap even more. At last the temperature begins to fall and after a few more seconds you are again comfortably cool at 25°. However, your comfort is short-lived as the water temperature continues to fall and you are right back where you started – too cold. The cycle continues from cold to hot and back again.

The most likely trajectory is a classic example of puzzling dynamics, performance over time that is both unintended and surprising. Who would deliberately set-out to repeatedly freeze and scald themselves? The feedback systems thinker looks for the structure, the web of relationships and constraints involved in operating a shower, that causes normal people to self-inflict such discomfort. It is clear from Fig. 2.6 that the dynamic behaviour is essentially goal seeking. The shower taker *wants* the water temperature to be 25°C, but the actual water temperature varies around this target. The feedback structure that belongs with such fluctuating behaviour is a balancing loop with delay, and that's exactly what we are looking for in modelling or representing the shower 'system'. This notion of having in mind a structure that fits (or might fit) observed dynamics is common in system dynamics modelling. It is known formally as a 'dynamic hypothesis', a kind of preliminary guess at the sort of relationships likely to explain a given pattern of behaviour through time.

Figure 2.7 shows a causal loop diagram for a slow-to-respond shower. First consider just the words. Five phrases are enough to capture the essence of the troublesome shower: desired water temperature, actual water temperature, temperature gap, the flow of hot water and the flow of cold water. Next consider the causal links. The temperature gap depends on the difference between desired and actual water temperature.

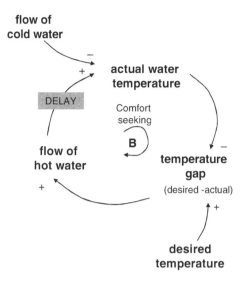

Fig. 2.7 Causal loop diagram of a slow-to-respond shower

The existence of a temperature gap influences the flow of hot water. This link represents the decision making and subsequent action of the shower taker. You can imagine a person turning a tap in order to change the flow of hot water and to get comfortable. The flow of hot water then influences the actual water temperature, but with a time delay because the shower is slow-to-respond. Also shown is a separate inflow of cold water, represented as a link on the left. The water temperature obviously depends on both water flows, hot and cold.

The end result is a balancing feedback loop, labelled 'comfort seeking', which is just what we are looking for to explain cyclical behaviour. The loop-type can be confirmed by adding signs (positive or negative) to each link and telling a 'story' about the process of temperature adjustment around the loop. For convenience imagine the desired water temperature is greater than actual at time zero – in other words the shower taker feels too cold and the temperature gap is greater than zero. Now consider the polarity of the first link. If the temperature gap increases then the flow of hot water becomes greater than it would otherwise have been. This is a positive link according to the polarity conventions. In the second link, if the flow of hot water increases, then the actual water temperature increases, albeit with a delay. This too is a positive link. (Note that in making the polarity assignment the flow of cold water, which also affects water temperature, is assumed to be held constant.) In the third and final link, if the water temperature increases then the temperature gap becomes smaller than it would otherwise have been. This is a negative link according to the polarity conventions. The overall effect around the loop is for an increase in the temperature gap to result in a counteracting decrease in the temperature gap, which is the signature of a balancing loop.

Incidentally, there is another way to work out loop polarity besides telling a story around the loop. It is also possible to simply count the number of negative links around the loop. An odd number of negative links (1, 3, 5, …) signifies a balancing loop while an even number of links (0, 2, 4, …) signifies a reinforcing loop. The reason this rule-of-thumb works is that any story about propagation of change around a loop will result in a counteracting effect for an odd number of negative links and a reinforcing effect for an even number. In this case there is one negative link around the loop (between actual water temperature and the temperature gap) and so it is a balancing loop. The other negative link in the diagram (between flow of cold water and actual water temperature) does not count since it is not part of the closed loop.

2.2.1.2 Processes in a Shower 'System'

A typical causal loop diagram shows a lot about connectivity in a small space. It is a purely qualitative model, a sketch of cause and effect, particularly good for high-lighting feedback loops that contribute to dynamics and to dynamic complexity. Usually there are many practical operating details that lie behind the scenes of causality. Although not shown in the diagram it is important to be aware of this detail, particularly when building an algebraic simulator of the same feedback structure. Then it is vital to be clear and precise about how such links actually work in terms of underlying behavioural responses, economic and social conventions, and physical laws. It is also important to know the numerical strength of the effects. This skill of seeing the big picture while not losing sight of operating detail is a hallmark of good system dynamics practice, known as 'seeing the forest and the trees' (Senge 1990; Sherwood 2002). It is a skill well-worth cultivating.

One way to forge the connection from feedback loops to operations is to ask yourself about the real-world processes that lie behind the links. In the case of the shower there is an interesting mixture of physical, behavioural and psychological processes. Take for example the link from the flow of hot water to actual water temperature. What is really going on here? The diagram says the obvious mini-mum: if the flow of hot water increases then sooner or later, and all else remaining the same, the actual water temperature at the shower head increases too. The sooner-or-later depends on the time delay in the hot water pipe that supplies the shower, which is a factor that can be estimated or measured. But how much does the temperature rise for a given increase in water flow? The answer to that question depends on physics and thermodynamics – the process of blending hot and cold water. In a simulation model you have to specify the relationship with reasonable accuracy. You do not necessarily need to be an expert yourself, but if not then you should talk with someone who knows (from practice or theory) how to estimate the water temperature that results from given flows of hot and cold water – a plumber, an engineer or maybe even a physicist. Consider next the link from actual water temperature to the temperature gap. Algebraically the gap is defined as the differ-ence between the desired and actual water temperature (temperature gap = desired water temperature – actual water temperature). But a meaningful temperature gap in a shower also requires a process for *sensing* the gap. The existence of a temperature gap alone does not guarantee goal-seeking behaviour. For example, if someone entered a shower in a winter wetsuit, complete with rubber hood and boots, they would not notice a temperature gap, and the entire feedback loop would be rendered inactive. Although this case is extreme and fanciful, it illustrates the importance of credibly grounding causal links.

The final link in the balancing loop is from temperature gap to the flow of hot water. Arguably this is the single most important link in the loop because it embodies the decisionmaking process for adjusting the flow of hot water. There is a huge leap of causality in this part of the diagram. The commonsense interpretation of the link is that when any normal person feels too hot or too cold in a shower, he or she will take corrective action by adjusting the flow of hot water. But how do they judge the right amount of corrective action? How quickly do they react to a temperature gap and how fast do they turn the tap? All these factors require consideration. Moreover, the key to over-reaction in showers arguably lies in this single step of causality. Why do people get trapped into a repetitive hot-cold cycle when all they normally want to achieve is a steady comfortable temperature? The answer must lie in how they *choose* to adjust the tap setting, in other words in their own decision-making process.

2.2.1.3   Simulation of a Shower and the Dynamics of Balancing Loops

Figure 2.8 shows the simulated dynamics of a slow-to-respond shower over a period of 120s generated by a simulation model containing all the processes mentioned above. As before the desired water temperature is a cool 25°C. However in this scenario the water temperature starts too high at 40°. Corrective action lowers the temperature at the shower-head to the desired 25° in about 10 s, but the temperature continues to fall, reaching a minimum just below 24° after 12s. Further corrective action then increases the temperature, leading to an overshoot

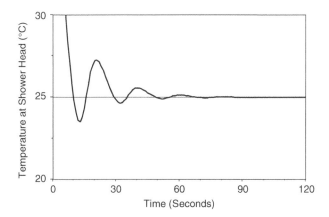

Fig. 2.8 Simulated dynamics of a slow-to-respond shower

that peaks at 27° after 21s. The cycle repeats itself twice in the interval up to 60 s, but each time the size of the temperature overshoot and undershoot is reduced as the showertaker gradually finds exactly the right tap setting for comfort. In the remainder of the simulation, from 60 to 120s, the temperature at the shower-head remains steady at 25°. The overall trajectory is a typical example of goal-seeking dynamics arising from a balancing loop with delay.

It is worthwhile to remember this particular combination of feedback structure and dynamic behaviour because balancing loops crop up all over the place in business, social, environmental and biological systems. Wherever people, organisations or even organisms direct their efforts and energy to achieving and maintaining specific goals in the face of an uncertain and changing environment there are balancing loops at work. Companies set themselves sales objectives, quality standards, financial targets and goals for on-time delivery. Governments set targets for economic growth, inflation, hospital waiting times, literacy, exam pass rates, road congestion, and public transport usage. The human body maintains weight, balance, temperature, and blood sugar. The ecosystem sustains an atmosphere suitable for the animals and plants within it. The vast global oil industry maintains a supply of oil sufficient to reliably fill our petrol tanks. The electricity industry supplies just enough electricity to keep the lights on. Economies generate enough jobs to keep most people employed. The list goes on and on. In some cases, like people's body temperature or domestic electricity supply, the balancing process works so well that it is rare to find deviations from the 'goal' – a degree or two from normal body temperature is a sign of illness and, in the electricity industry, it is unusual (at least in the developed world) for the lights to dim. In many cases, like sales objectives or hospital waiting times, the goals are known, but performance falls chronically short or else gently overshoots and undershoots. But in other cases, like employment in the economy or inventory levels in supply chains, the balancing process is far from perfect. Performance deviates a long way from the goal, too much or too little. Corrective action leads to over and under compensation and the goal is never really achieved, at least not for long.

2.2.2   From Events to Dynamics and Feedback Structure: Drug Related Crime

A shift of mind (from event oriented thinking to feedback systems thinking) is not easy to achieve. The best way to make progress is through examples of feedback systems thinking applied to real-world situations. So, instead of hot water showers we now consider something entirely different – drug related crime. A typical description of the problem, by the victims of crime, might be as follows.

> Drugs are a big worry for me, not least because of the crimes that addicts commit to fund their dependency. We want the police to bust these rings and destroy the drugs. They say they're doing it and they keep showing us sacks of cocaine that they've seized, but the crime problem seems to be getting worse.

Expressed this way drug related crime appears as a series of disturbing events. There is a concern about crime among the members of the community affected by it. They want action backed-up with evidence of police attempts to fix the problem by busting rings and seizing drugs. But, despite these efforts, more crimes are happening. The feedback systems thinker re-interprets the description and draws out those aspects concerned with performance through time (dynamics) that suggest an underlying feedback structure, one or more interacting feedback loops, capable of generating the dynamics of interest. Of particular significance are *puzzling* dynamics, performance through time that people experience but do not want or intend. Some of the most interesting and intractable problems in society and business appear this way.

Figure 2.9 shows the unintended dynamics of drug related crime that might be inferred from the brief verbal description above. This is just a rough sketch to provide a focus for structuring the problem. On the horizontal axis is time in years. On the vertical axis is drug related crime defined in terms of 'incidents per month'. There are two trajectories. The upper line is a sketch of crime reported by the community. We assume a growth trajectory because 'the crime problem seems to be getting worse'. The lower line is a sketch of tolerable crime, a kind of benchmark against which to compare the actual level of crime. We assume a downward sloping trajectory because the community wants less crime and fewer drugs, and the police are taking action to achieve this end by seizing drugs and arresting dealers.[4]

The divergence between reported and tolerable crime is of particular interest to the feedback systems thinker. What feedback structure could explain this phenomenon? Reported crime is growing and we know that growth arises from reinforcing feedback.

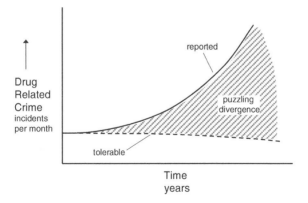

Fig. 2.9 Unintended dynamics of drug related crime – a rough sketch

---

[4] You may be thinking this method of creating time charts is rather loose and in a sense you are right because we have very little data about the problem. But even in practice, with real clients, the information sources for modelling are always a pragmatic blend of informed opinion, anecdote, objective facts and clear reasoning. For a good example of this balanced approach in the area of drug policy, see Homer (1993) and Levin et al. (1975).

So where could such a malignant feedback process come from and why would it exist at all if those involved want less crime, not more? The persistence of unwanted growth in crime suggests a feedback loop that weaves its way around society (crossing the boundaries between police, the community and drug users) and by doing so it goes unnoticed.

2.2.2.1 Feedback Loops in Drug Related Crime

Figure 2.10 is a causal loop diagram for drug related crime. First consider the words and phrases alone. They provide the basic vocabulary of the causal model, the factors that drive-up crime, or at least are hypothesised to do so. They also give clues to the boundary of the model, which parts of society are included. Of course there is drug related crime itself, the variable of central interest and concern to the community. There is a 'call for police action' and drug seizures that take us inside the police department. Then there is supply, demand and price that belong in the world of drug users who commit crime.[5]

These factors join-up to make a closed loop of cause and effect. The loop brings together disparate parts of society to reveal a surprise. Hidden in the connections is a reinforcing feedback process responsible for (or at least contributing to) escalating crime. To confirm let's trace the effect around the loop of an imagined increase in drug related crime. In this kind of analysis the reason for the initial increase does not matter, it is the feedback effect that is of central interest. The story begins at the

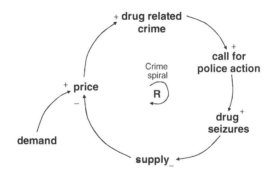

Fig. 2.10 Causal loop diagram for drug related crime

---

[5] Notice that all the terms in the diagram are nouns or so-called 'noun-phrases'. This is an important diagramming convention because you want concepts to denote things, attributes or qualities that can, in imagination, be unambiguously increased or decreased. Then, and only then, is it possible to cleanly assign polarity to causal links and thereby deduce the loop types – balancing or reinforcing. Take for example price and drug related crime. It is easy to imagine the price of drugs going up or down and separately to imagine drug related crime increasing or decreasing. Therefore, when a causal link is drawn between these two concepts, it is meaningful to ask whether an increase in one leads to an increase or decrease in the other. This thought experiment would make no sense if one or other concept were labelled as an activity, say pricing instead of price.

top of the diagram. An increase of drug related crime leads to a call for more police action. More police action (raids and arrests) leads to more drug seizures. So far so good. But the paradox lies in what happens next as available drugs are traded on the streets. An increase in drug seizures causes the supply of drugs to decrease. This supply cut then causes the price of drugs to increase, just like any traded goods subject to market forces, assuming of course that higher price does not depress demand. And crucially for illegal drugs, price has little effect on demand because most users are addicts, dependent on their daily fix. So an increase in price merely boosts crime as desperate drug users steal even more to fund their addiction. The reinforcing loop is plain to see. There is a 'crime spiral' in which any increase of drug related crime tends to amplify itself through the inadvertent actions of police, drug dealers and addicts.

2.2.2.2 Scope and Boundary of Factors in Drug Related Crime

There could be more, much more, to the problem situation than the six concepts shown. So I am not saying these six factors and this single reinforcing loop is a perfect representation of escalating crime in a community plagued with drug addicts. Rather it is a useful way of thinking about the problem that raises the perspective above the narrow confines of a single stakeholder. In fact three stakeholders are united in this particular view. And, just as we noted in the shower case, there is a lot going on behind the scenes of the stark causal links; detail that would need to be fleshed out in thinking more carefully about the problem and in building a simulation model to test alternative intervention policies. There is the community suffering from crime and calling for police action. There is the police department, concerned with all sorts of law enforcement, allocating police officers to priority tasks, among which is drug busting. And then there is the shady world of drug dealers sourcing drugs and covertly selling them to addicts who *must* consume, no matter what the cost. Later in the chapter we see how this qualitative feedback diagram is transformed into a full-blown simulator. But for now I want to end the discussion of drug related crime by inviting you to think about what else *might* be included in a conceptual model of the problem.

One place to expand the diagram is with demand and supply. (Another good idea in practice is to gather more time series data to help refine the dynamic hypothesis, but we will by-pass that step in this small illustrative example.) What if there is growth in demand because addicts and dealers themselves recruit new users? This possibility adds a whole new dimension to escalating crime not dealt with in our current picture, a new theory if you like. What if, as is surely the case, the available supply of drugs increases as the price rises? Does that mean drug seizures perversely expand the whole illegal drug industry (in the long run) by artificially boosting prices? Such industry growth could exacerbate the crime problem, particularly if the relevant time frame is a decade or more rather than just a few years. These questions, and others like them, are worth probing and may usefully expand the scope and boundary of our thinking. The point however, in any such conceptualisation task, is to avoid unnecessary complexity and focus on finding plausible loops, often unnoticed in the pressure of day-to-day operations, that not only challenge conventional event-oriented thinking but also produce dynamics consistent with the observed problem.

2.2.2.3   An Aside: More Practice with Link Polarity and Loop Types

I have explained the origin of the reinforcing loop in Fig. 2.10 by tracing an imagined change in crime all the way around the loop and showing it leads to even more crime. As mentioned earlier, another way to find the loop type is to use the counting rule. Count the negative links around the loop. If the number of links is odd then the loop is balancing and if the number is even the loop is reinforcing. Let's do this exercise now. First we need to assign link polarities using the standard test. Any individual link connects two concepts A and B where A is the cause and B is the effect. For each link imagine an increase in the cause A and then work out the effect on B. In this thought experiment all other influences on B are assumed to remain unchanged, the *ceteris paribus* assumption. The link is positive if, when A increases, B increases above what it would otherwise have been. The link is negative if, when A increases, B decreases below what it would have been. Note that the mirror image test works too. So when A decreases and B also decreases the link is positive, but when A decreases and B increases the link is negative. What matters for polarity is whether or not there is a reversal.

We start at the top. All else equal, if drug related crime increases then the call for police action (complaints from the community) increases above what it would otherwise have been, a positive link. When the call for police action increases then drug seizures increase, another positive link. Note there is a large leap of causality here that relies on all else remaining equal, *ceteris paribus*. We implicitly assume that a call for action really leads to action (in this case more police allocated to drug busting), rather than being ignored. Moreover, we assume that more police leads to more seizures. In the next link an increase in seizures leads to a decrease in supply, below what it would otherwise have been, a negative link. Then a decrease in supply leads to an increase in price, another negative link coming this time from a mirror image test. Here there is a particularly clear instance of *ceteris paribus* reasoning because price depends both on supply and demand. The assumption behind the polarity test is that demand remains constant. An equivalent test on the demand-to-price link shows it is positive: an increase in demand leads to an increase in price, assuming supply is held constant. Finally an increase in price leads to an increase in drug related crime, a positive link that completes the loop. Counting-up there are *two* negative links around the loop, an even number, so the loop type is reinforcing.

2.2.2.4   Purpose and Use of Causal Loop Diagrams: A Summary

As we have seen, causal loop diagrams offer a special overview of business and society, showing what is connected to what and how changes in one part of the system might propagate to others and return. People often say we live in an interconnected world. But we have no way, other than words, to express this complexity. Causal loop diagrams, concise and visual, reveal the interconnections, both obvious and hidden. Moreover, they can be used to elicit and capture the mental models of individuals or teams and to expand the boundary of people's thinking beyond the parochial.

Causal loop diagrams also capture hypotheses about dynamic behaviour. Here is the beginning of the shift of mind so vital to feedback systems thinking. The future time path of any organisation is partly and significantly pre-determined by its structure, the network of balancing and reinforcing feedback loops that drive performance through time. Causal loop diagrams embody this important philosophical view by making plain the important feedback loops believed to be responsible for observed performance.

2.2.2.5   Basic Tips: Picking and Naming Variables

The choice of words is vital. Each variable must be a noun. Avoid the use of verbs or directional adjectives. For example a causal diagram can use the word 'sales' but not 'sales planning' or 'increased sales'. Simple nouns like 'accounts' or 'staff' can be augmented with adjectives to give phrases like 'large accounts' or 'experienced staff'. Sticking to these simple naming rules helps when assigning polarity to causal links and explaining how changes propagate around loops.

Words are versatile, but they should also be grounded in facts. The range of concepts that can be included in causal loop diagrams extends from the hard and easily measureable, such as 'new products' and 'recruits', to the soft and intangible such as 'morale' or 'customer perceived quality'. A powerful feature of feedback systems thinking and system dynamics is its ability to incorporate both tangible and intangible factors. However, for any variable no matter how soft, you should always have in mind a specific unit of measure, a way in which the variable might be quantified, even if formal recorded data do not exist. So you might imagine morale on a scale from 0 (low) to 1 (high) or product quality on a scale from 1 (low) to 5 (high). And be sure to pick words that *imply* measureability, such as 'delivery lead time' thought of in weeks or months, rather than a vague concept like 'delivery performance'.

2.2.2.6   Basic Tips: Meaning of Arrows and Link Polarity

Arrows show the influence of one variable on another – a change in the cause leads to a change in the effect. The assignment of link polarity (+) or (−) makes the direction of change clear. So in Fig. 2.11 an increase in marketing budget leads to an increase in sales, which is a positive link.

Polarity assignment works equally well for intangible variables such as industry reputation in the lower half of Fig. 2.11. Industry reputation here is an intangible concept measured on a scale from 0 to 1. An increase in industry reputation leads to an increase in customers interested.

a change in *marketing budget* leads to a change in *sales*

marketing   + sales
budget   {units per month}
{£ per month}

a change in *industry reputation* leads to a change in
customers interested

industry   customers
reputation   Interested
{index on   {customers}
scale 0-1}

Fig. 2.11 Arrows and link polarity

A useful refinement in polarity assignment is to note whether the effect of a given change is an increase (or decrease) more than it would otherwise have been. The use of this extra phrase avoids ambiguity in situations where the effect is cumulative. For example customers are likely to be accumulating over time and therefore the effect of rising industry reputation is to attract more customers than there would otherwise have been.

2.2.2.7 Basic Tips: Drawing, Identifying and Naming Feedback Loops

For the systems thinker, feedback loops are the equivalent of the sketches created by political cartoonists. They capture something important about the situation or object of interest. Just as a few bold pen lines on a canvas can characterise George Bush, Osama bin Laden, or Margaret Thatcher, so a few feedback loops on a whiteboard can characterise an organisation. Like celebrity sketches feedback loops should be drawn clearly to identify the dominant features, in this case important loops. Sterman (2000) identifies five tips for visual layout:

1. Use curved lines to help the reader visualise the feedback loops
2. Make important loops follow circular or oval paths
3. Organise diagrams to minimise crossed lines
4. Don't put circles, hexagons, or other symbols around the variables in causal diagrams. Symbols without meaning are 'chart junk' and serve only to clutter and distract.
5. Iterate. Since you often won't know what all the variables and loops will be when you start, you will have to redraw your diagrams, often many times, to find the best layout.

As we have already seen, for the hot water shower and drug related crime, there are two main loop types, balancing and reinforcing. A loop type is identified by imagining the effect of a change as it propagates link-by-link around the loop.

A reinforcing loop is one where an increase in a variable, when traced around the loop, leads to a further increase in itself. Such an outcome requires an even number (or zero) of negative links. A balancing loop is one where an increase in a variable, when traced around the loop, leads to a counterbalancing decrease in itself. Such an outcome requires an odd number of negative links. Once you have identified loop types it is good practice to label them *R* for reinforcing and *B* for balancing, the letter encircled by a small curved arrow drawn clockwise for clockwise loops (and vice versa).

By following these tips and by studying the examples in the chapter you should be able to create, label and interpret your own causal loop diagrams. Often you will end-up with multiple interlocking loops that reach across conventional organisational boundaries. Then it is particularly important to follow the five tips for visual layout mentioned above. A good example can be found later, in Part 2.2.6, based on a study of orchestra management. Selected feedback loops show that factors affecting the success of an orchestra reach well beyond the boundaries of the concert hall.

2.2.3 *Modelling to Simulate Dynamic Systems*

Causal loops diagrams are very effective for expanding the boundary of your thinking and for communicating important interdependencies. But they are not especially good as the basis for a full-blown model and simulator that computes dynamics and performance through time. For a working model we need better resolution of the causal network. It turns out there is more to causality and dynamics than words and arrows alone. The main new concepts required to make simulators are introduced in this section. They transform a simple sketch of causality into a portrait (or better still an animation) that brings feedback loops to life, by specifying the realistic processes that lie behind causal links as the basis for an algebraic model and simulator.

2.2.3.1 Asset Stock Accumulation

Asset stock accumulation is a very important idea in system dynamics, every bit as fundamental as feedback and in fact complementary to it. You can't have one without the other. Asset stocks accumulate change. They are a kind of memory, storing the results of past actions. When, in a feedback process, past decisions and actions come back to influence present decisions and actions they do so through asset stocks. Past investment accumulates in capital stock – the number of planes owned by an airline, the number of stores in a supermarket chain, the number of ships in a fishing fleet. Past hiring accumulates as employees – nurses in a hospital, operators in a call centre, players in a football squad, faculty in a university. Past production accumulates in inventory and past sales accumulate in an installed base. All business and social systems contain a host of different asset stocks or resources that, when harnessed in an organisation, deliver its products and services. And, crucially, the performance over time of an enterprise depends on the balance of these assets and resources (Warren 2008). An airline with lots of planes and few passengers is out of balance and unprofitable. Empty seats bring no revenue. A factory bulging with inventory while machines lie idle is out of balance and underperforming. Inventory is expensive.

To appreciate how such imbalances occur we first need to understand the nature of asset stock accumulation – how assets build and decay through time. A process of accumulation is not the same as a causal link. Accumulations change according to their inflows and outflows in just the same way that water accumulates in a bathtub. If the inflow is greater than the outflow then the level gradually rises. If the outflow is greater than the inflow then the level gradually falls. If the inflow and outflow are identical then the level remains constant. This bathtub feature of assets in organisations is depicted using the symbols in Fig. 2.12. Here an asset stock or resource is shown as a rectangle, partially filled. On the left is an inflow comprising a valve or tap superimposed on an arrow. The arrow enters the stock and originates from a source, shown as a cloud or pool. A similar combination of symbols on the right represents an outflow. In this case the flow originates in the stock and ends up in a sink (another cloud or pool). The complete picture is called a stock and flow network.

Consider for example a simple network for university faculty as shown in Fig. 2.13. Let's forget about the distinction between professors, senior lecturers and junior lecturers and call them all instructors. Instructors teach, write and do research. The stock in this case is the total number of instructors. The inflow is the rate of recruitment of new faculty – measured say in instructors per month, and the outflow is turnover – also measured in instructors per month. The source and sink represent the university labour market, the national or international pool of academics from which faculty are hired and to which they return when they leave. The total number of instructors in a university ultimately depends on all

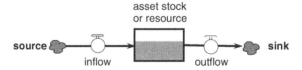

Fig. 2.12 Asset stock accumulation in a stock and flow network

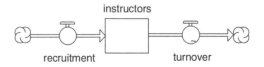

Fig. 2.13 A simple stock and flow network for university faculty

sorts of factors such as location, reputation, funding, demand for higher education and so on. But the way these factors exert their influence is through flow rates. Asset stocks cannot be adjusted *instantaneously* no matter how great the organisational pressures. Change takes place only gradually through flow rates. This vital *inertial* characteristic of stock and flow networks distinguishes them from simple causal links.

2.2.3.2   Accumulating a 'Stock' of Faculty at Greenfield University

The best way to appreciate the functioning of stocks and flows is through simulation. Luckily it is only a small step from a diagram like Fig. 2.13 to a simulator. Use this URL http://www.iseesystems.com/community/downloads/OpenUniversity.aspx to find the model called Stock Accumulation – Faculty and open it. A stock and flow network just like Fig. 2.13 will appear on the screen. To make this little network run each variable must be plausibly quantified. Imagine a new university called Greenfield. There is a small campus with some pleasant buildings and grounds, but as yet no faculty. The model is parameterised to fit this situation. Move the cursor over the stock of instructors. The number zero appears meaning there are no instructors at the start of the simulation. They will come from the academic labour market. Next move the cursor over the valve symbol for recruitment. The number five appears. This is the number of new instructors the Vice Chancellor and Governors plan to hire each month. Finally move the cursor over the symbol for turnover. The number is zero. Faculty are expected to like the university and to stay once they join. So now there is all the numerical data to make a simulation: the starting size of the faculty (zero), intended recruitment (five per month) and expected turnover (zero per month).

Press the Run button. What you see *is* stock accumulation as the 'bathtub' of instructors gradually fills-up. This steady increase is exactly what you expect if, each month, new instructors are hired and nobody leaves. Now double click on the graph icon. A chart appears, just like Fig. 2.14, that plots the numerical values through time of instructors (line 1), recruitment (line 2) and turnover (line 3). The horizontal time axis spans 12 months. The number of instructors begins at 0 and builds steadily to 60 after 12 simulated months. Meanwhile recruitment remains steady at five instructors per month and turnover is zero throughout. Numerically the simulation is correct and internally consistent. Recruitment at a rate of 5 instructors per month for 12 months will, if no-one leaves, result in a faculty of 60 people.

That's all very obvious, and in a sense, stock accumulation is no mystery. It is simply the result of taking the numerical difference, period by period, between the inflow and the outflow and adding it to the stock size. An equation shows the simple arithmetic involved:

instructors (t) = instructors (t – dt) + (recruitment – turnover) * dt
INIT instructors = 0

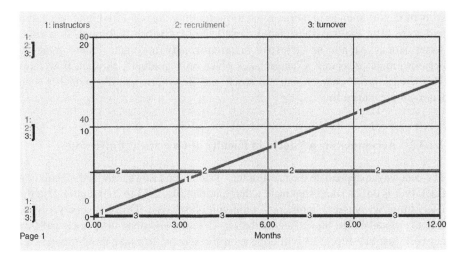

Fig. 2.14 Faculty size at Greenfield University – a 12 month simulation

Here the number of instructors at time t (this month) is equal to the number of instructors at time t-dt (last month) plus the difference between recruitment and turnover over an interval of time dt. The interval is a slice of time convenient for the calculation, the so-called delta-time dt. So if dt is equal to 1 month then the calculation is a monthly tally of faculty. The initial value of instructors is set at zero.

All stock accumulations have the same mathematical form, no matter whether they represent tangible assets (machines, people, planes) or intangible assets (reputation, morale, perceived quality). The relationship between a stock and its flows is cumulative and naturally involves time. It is *not* the same as a causal link. The stock of instructors accumulates the net amount of recruitment and turnover *through time.* Mathematically speaking the stock *integrates* its inflow and outflow. The process is simple to express, but the consequences are often surprising.

To illustrate let's investigate a 36 month scenario for Greenfield University. Recruitment holds steady at five instructors per month throughout, but after 12 months some faculty are disillusioned and begin to leave. To see just how many leave double click on the turnover icon. A chart and table appear. The chart on the left shows the pattern of turnover across 36 months and the table on the right shows the corresponding numerical values at intervals of 3 months. For a period of 12 months turnover is zero and faculty are content. Then people start to leave, at an increasing rate. By month 15 turnover is two instructors per month, by month 18 it is four instructors per month, and by month 21 it is six instructors per month. The upward trend continues to month 27 by which time faculty are leaving at a rate of ten per month. Thereafter turnover settles and remains steady at ten instructors per month until month 36. (As an aside it is worth noting this chart is a just an assumption about future turnover regardless of the underlying cause. In reality instructors may leave Greenfield University due to low pay, excess workload, lazy students, etc. Such endogenous factors would be included in a complete feedback model.)

To investigate this new situation it is first necessary to extend the simulation to 36 months. Close the turnover chart by clicking the OK button. Then find Run Specs in the pull-down menu called Run at the top of the screen. A window appears containing all kinds of technical information about the simulation. In the top left there are two boxes to specify the length of simulation. Currently the simulator is set to run from 0 to 12 months. Change the final month from 12 to 36 and click OK. You are ready to simulate. However, before proceeding, first sketch on a blank sheet of paper the faculty trajectory you *expect* to see. A rough sketch is fine – it is simply a benchmark against which to compare model simulations. Now click the run button. You will see the 'bathtub' of faculty fill right to the top and then begin to empty, ending about one quarter full. If you watch the animation very carefully you will also see movement in the dial for turnover. The dial is like a speedometer, it signifies the speed or rate of outflow. Now move the cursor over the turnover icon. A miniature time chart appears showing the *assumed* pattern of turnover. Move the cursor over recruitment and another miniature time chart appears showing the *assumed* steady inflow of new faculty from hiring. Finally move the cursor over the stock of instructors. The time chart shows the *calculated* trajectory of faculty resulting from the accumulation of recruitment (the inflow) net of turnover (the outflow).

All three trajectories can be seen in more detail by clicking the graph icon. The chart in Fig. 2.15 appears. Study the time path of instructors (line 1). How does the shape compare with your sketch? For 12 months the number of instructors grows in a straight line, a simple summation of steady recruitment (line 2). Then turnover begins to rise (line 3). The faculty therefore grows less quickly.

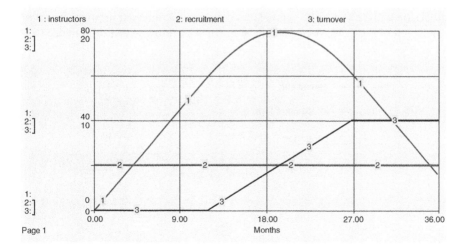

Fig. 2.15 Faculty size at Greenfield University – a 36 month simulation

By month 20 turnover reaches five instructors per month, exactly equal to recruitment, and line 3 crosses line 2. The process of accumulation is perfectly balanced. New faculty are arriving at the same rate existing faculty are leaving. The number of instructors therefore reaches a peak. Beyond month 20 turnover exceeds recruitment and continues to rise until month 27 when it reaches a rate of ten instructors per month, twice the recruitment rate. The faculty shrinks even though turnover itself stabilises.

Notice that although the number of instructors gently rises and falls, neither the inflow nor the outflow follow a similar pattern. The lack of obvious visual correlation between a stock and its flows is characteristic of stock accumulation and a clear sign that the process is conceptually different from a causal link. You can experience more such mysteries of accumulation by redrawing the turnover graph and re-simulating. Double click on the turnover icon and then hold down the mouse button as you drag the pointer across the surface of the graph. A new line appears and accordingly the numbers change in the table on the right. With some fine-tuning you can create a whole array of smooth and plausible turnover trajectories to help develop your understanding of the dynamics of accumulation. One interesting example is a pattern identical to the original but scaled down, so the maximum turnover is no more than five instructors per month.

2.2.3.3   The Coordinating Network

Feedback loops are formed when stock and flow networks interact through causal links, in other words when the inflows and outflows of one asset stock depend, directly or indirectly, on the state or size of other asset stocks. In principle *all* the stocks and flows in an organisation are mutually dependent because conditions in one area or function may cause or require changes elsewhere. Coordination is achieved through a network that relays the effect, direct or indirect, of particular stocks on a given flow. The symbols used for the coordinating network are shown on the left of Fig. 2.16. A causal link is drawn as an arrow with a solid line, exactly

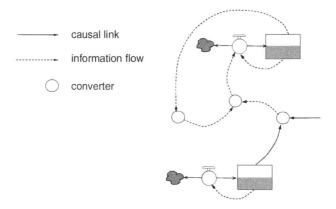

Fig. 2.16 Symbols in the coordinating network

the same as in a causal loop diagram. An information flow is drawn as an arrow with a dotted line. It too depicts an influence of one variable on another though in a subtly different way.

A converter represents a process that converts inputs into an output and is depicted as a circle. Converters receive causal links or information flows and transform them according to whatever rules, physical laws or operating policies apply. In a simulator there is an equation behind each converter that specifies the rules, as we will see shortly.

The diagram on the right of Fig. 2.16 shows how all the symbols fit together. There are two stock and flow networks joined by a coordinating network containing three converters. This is a feedback representation because the two flow rates not only accumulate into the two stocks but are themselves regulated by the magnitude of the stocks. The picture can readily be extended from 2 to 20 stocks or more depending on the complexity of the situation at hand. No matter how large the picture, it captures an elaborate process of bootstrapping that arises from nothing more than cause, effect, influence and accumulation found in all organisations.

2.2.3.4   Modelling Symbols in Use: A Closer Look at Drug Related Crime

To see all the modelling symbols in use we revisit the problem of drug related crime. Recall the original intention was to identify systemic factors that explain growth in drug related crime despite the drug busting efforts of police. Figure 2.17 shows the sectors of society involved and one important feedback loop, a reinforcing crime spiral. There are four sectors: the community itself (suffering from crime), the police department (trying to control crime), the street

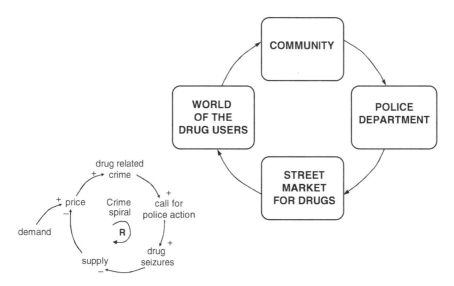

Fig. 2.17   Drug related crime – sectors and causal loop

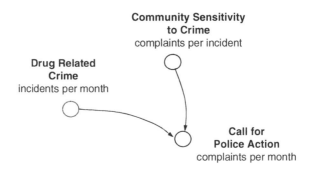

Fig. 2.18 Community reaction to crime

market for drugs and the world of the drug user. A simulatable model of this situation represents the stock accumulations, causal links, information flows and operating policies that lie behind the reinforcing crime spiral. The model is presented sector by sector.

Figure 2.18 shows the causal links in the community. The community is concerned about drug related crime and raises its collective concern through a call for police action. Notice that each concept is accompanied by units of measure that help ground the model and subsequently aid quantification. The search for practical and consistent units of measure is an important modelling and thinking discipline. Drug related crime is expressed as incidents per month. A practical measure of the community's 'call for police action' is complaints per month. The link here is the same as in the causal loop diagram. But the difference in units between the cause and effect shows the need for another concept, community sensitivity to crime, to operationalise the original link. Community sensitivity can be thought of in terms of complaints per incident. A community that is very sensitive to crime will generate more complaints per incident than a community resigned or indifferent to crime, thereby bringing to bear more pressure for police action.

Figure 2.19 takes us inside the police department. Notice that the police department converts the call for police action (in complaints per month) into drug seizures (in kg per month). In the causal loop diagram this conversion of complaints into seizures is achieved in a single causal link. The stock-and-flow diagram reveals the operating detail behind the link. In the middle of the diagram there is a stock accumulation representing the number of police allocated to drug busting.

The policy controlling the allocation of police is in the top half of the diagram and is a typical goal-seeking adjustment process. Call for police action leads to an indicated allocation of police – the number of police officers deemed necessary to deal with the drug problem. This goal is implemented by reallocating police between duties. The change in allocation of police (measured in police officers per month) depends on the difference between the indicated allocation, the current number of police allocated to drug busting and the time it takes to move staff.

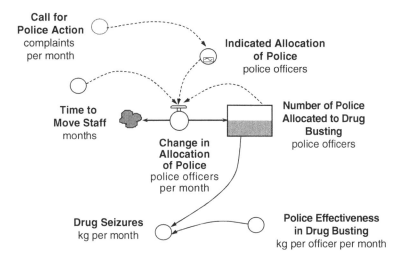

Fig. 2.19 Inside the police department

In reality the process of reallocating police takes time and organisational effort, all of which is captured by the stock and flow network for number of police.

Incidentally, the 'cloud' on the left of this network represents the total pool of police in the department, currently working on other duties, who might be called into drug busting.[6] The amount of drug seizures is proportional to the number of police allocated. To operationalise this link it is necessary to introduce a new concept 'police effectiveness in drug busting' measured in kilograms per officer per month – a kind of drug busting productivity.

The street market for drugs adjusts the street price of drugs according to the supply and demand of drugs, as shown in Fig. 2.20. The supply of drugs on the street is equal to the total supply of drugs less drug seizures. The drug supply gap is the difference between demand for drugs and supply on the street (all measured in kilograms per month). The existence of a supply gap generates pressure for price change which in turn drives the change in street price that accumulates in the street price (measured in £ per kilogram). The pricing 'policy' here is informal – an invisible hand. Note there is no target price. The price level continues to change as long as there is a difference between supply and demand.

In Fig. 2.21 we enter the world of drug-dependent users with an addiction and craving that must be satisfied at all costs, even if it involves crime. Addicts need funds (in £ per month) to satisfy their addiction. In a given geographical region the

---

[6] By using a cloud symbol we assume that the pool of police officers assigned to duties other than drug busting is outside the boundary of the model. If for some reason we wanted to track the number of officers in this pool, then the cloud symbol would be replaced by a stock accumulation with its own initial number of officers. It would then be apparent from the diagram that shifting more officers to drug-busting reduces the number available to work on other duties.

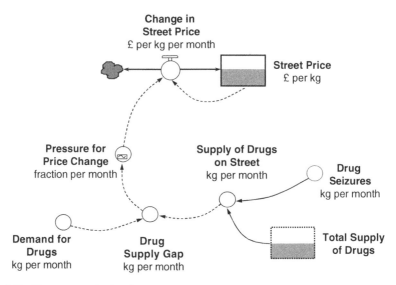

Fig. 2.20 The street market for drugs

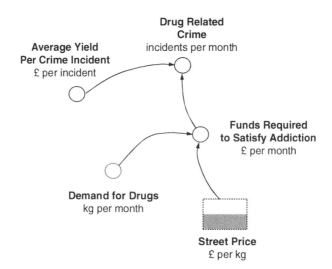

Fig. 2.21 World of the drug users

funds required by addicts are proportional to their collective demand for drugs (in kilograms per month) and the prevailing street price (in £ per kilogram). Drug related crime is the amount of crime (in incidents per month) necessary to raise the funds required. This conversion of funds into crime depends also on the average yield per crime incident (measured in £ per incident), which is a measure of criminal productivity and reflects the wealth of the burgled community.

2.2.4   Equation Formulations

The final step in developing a simulator is to write algebraic equations. Full structural diagrams are a good starting point because they show all the variables that must appear in the equations. Nevertheless there is skill in writing good algebra in a way that properly captures the meaning of the relationships depicted.

2.2.4.1   Drug Related Crime

Consider the formulation of drug related crime. We know from the diagram that drug related crime depends on the funds required (by addicts) to satisfy their addiction and on the average yield per crime incident. These two influences are reproduced in Fig. 2.22. But how are they combined in an equation? Should they be added, subtracted, multiplied or divided? The top half of Fig. 2.22 is a plausible formulation where drug related crime is equal to funds required *divided by* average yield. This ratio makes sense. We would expect that if addicts require more funds they will either commit more crimes or else operate in a neighbourhood where the yield from each crime is greater. So funds required appears in the numerator and average yield in the denominator. The ratio expresses precisely and mathematically what we have in mind.

An alternative formulation, such as the product of 'funds required' and 'average yield', contradicts commonsense and logic. A simple numerical example shows just how ludicrous such a multiplicative formulation would be. Let's suppose there are ten addicts in a neighbourhood and *collectively* they require £1,000 per month to

Drug Related   **Funds Required** / **Average Yield**
Crime   =   **to Satisfy Addiction** / **Per Crime Incident**
[incidents/month]   [£/month]   [£/incident]

Dimensional Analysis

Left hand side: [incidents/month]

Right hand side: [£/month]/[£/incident] = [£/month]*[incident/£] = [incidents/month]

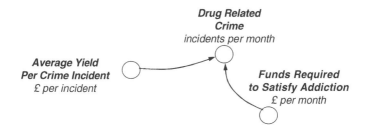

Fig. 2.22   Equation formulation for drug related crime

satisfy their addiction. On average each crime incident yields £100. A multiplicative formulation would imply that drug related crime in the neighbourhood takes a value of (1,000 * 100), in other words *one hundred thousand – which is numerically implausible and wrong.* The correct formulation results in (1,000/100), or ten incidents per month.

There are numerous guidelines for equation formulation to help modellers write good algebra that means what they intend. One of the most useful is to ensure *dimensional consistency* among the units of measure in an equation. This guideline is always useful in situations like the one above where the main formulation challenge is to pick the right arithmetical operation. Dimensional consistency requires that the units of measure on left and right of an equation match. In this case 'drug related crime' on the left is measured in incidents per month. So the operation on the right must combine 'funds required' and 'average yield' in such a way as to create incidents per month. Taking the ratio of funds required [£/month] to average yield [£/incident] achieves this outcome, as shown in the dimensional analysis box of Fig. 2.22. No other simple arithmetic operator such as +, –, or * leads to this result. For example the units of measure for a multiplicative formulation would be £^{2} per month per incident, a bizarre and meaningless metric that reveals a fatal formulation error.

2.2.4.2 Funds Required to Satisfy Addiction

The formulation for funds required is shown in Fig. 2.23. We know from the diagram that 'funds required' depends on demand for drugs and the street price. The greater is demand, or the higher the street price, the more funds required. Moreover, a combination of greater demand and higher street price calls for even more funds and therefore suggests a multiplicative formulation. So the equation for 'funds required' is expressed as the product of demand for drugs and the street price. A dimensional analysis shows the units of measure are consistent in this formulation.

2.2.4.3 Street Price and Price Change

The street price of drugs is a stock that accumulates price changes. The change in street price is a function of street price itself and 'pressure for price change'. This pressure depends on the drug supply gap, in other words whether there is an adequate supply of drugs on the street. The diagram and corresponding equations are shown in Fig. 2.24. The first equation is a standard formulation for a stock accumulation. The street price this month is equal to the price last month plus the change in price during the month.

The change in street price arises from informal, covert trading of illegal drugs on street corners. It is an important formulation that depends both on street price itself and the pressure for price change. This pressure is itself a function of the drug supply

Funds Required   =   **Demand for**   *   **Established Street Price**
to Satisfy Addiction   **Drugs**   [£/kg]
[£/month]   [kg/month]

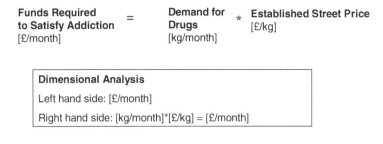

Dimensional Analysis

Left hand side: [£/month]

Right hand side: [kg/month]*[£/kg] = [£/month]

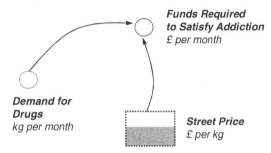

Fig. 2.23 Formulation of funds required

Street Price{this month} = **Street Price**{last month} + **dt * Change in Street Price**{during month}
£/kg   £/kg   month £/kg/month

Change in   =   **Pressure for**   *   **Street Price**
Street Price   **Price Change**   £/kg
£/kg/month   fraction/month

Pressure for   *Graphical*   **Drug**
Price Change   =   *function of*   **Supply Gap**
fraction/month   kg/month

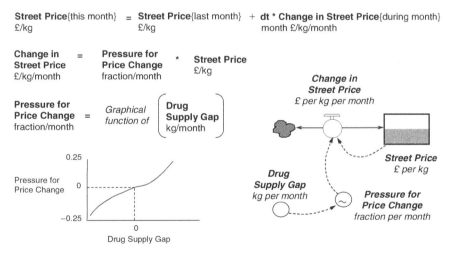

Fig. 2.24 Formulation of street price and price change

gap, a graphical function whose shape is sketched in the lower left of Fig. 2.24. To
understand the price change formulation, first imagine the drug supply gap is zero –
so there is just enough volume of drugs being supplied by dealers to satisfy demand.
Under this special condition the pressure for price change is logically zero and
so too is the change in street price itself. The multiplicative formulation ensures

no price change when the pressure for price change is zero. Now suppose there is a shortage of drugs on the street. The drug supply gap is positive and, through the graph, the pressure for price change is also positive. Moreover, as the gap grows the pressure rises more quickly than a simple linear proportion. The relationship is non-linear, with increasing gradient. A mirror image applies when there is a surplus of drugs and the drug supply gap is negative. Pressure for price change is expressed as a fraction per month, so the resulting change in price is the street price itself multiplied by this fraction per month. The units of price change are £/kilogram/month and an inspection of the price change equation shows the required dimensional balance.

Notice that the price itself feeds back to influence price change. This is quite a subtle dynamic formulation and has the curious, though realistic, implication that there is no pre-determined market price or cost-plus anchor toward which price adjusts. The only meaningful anchor is the current price. So if there is a chronic undersupply the price will relentlessly escalate, and conversely if there is a chronic oversupply the price will steadily fall. Price settles at whatever level it attains when supply and demand are balanced, no matter how high or low.

2.2.4.4 Allocation of Police

The formulation for the allocation of police is shown in Fig. 2.25. It is a classic example of an asset stock adjustment process. At the heart of the formulation is a stock accumulation of police officers guided by an operating policy for adjusting the allocation of police. The first equation is a standard stock accumulation in

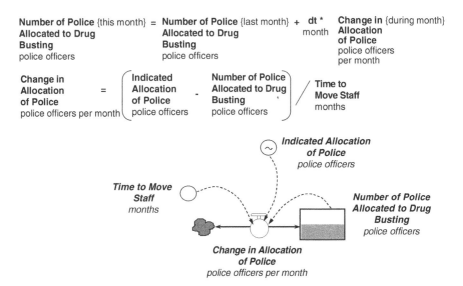

Fig. 2.25 Formulation for the allocation of police

which the number of police allocated to drug busting this month is equal to the number allocated last month plus the change in allocation during the month. The second equation represents the policy for redeploying police to drug busting. The change in allocation of police depends on the gap between the indicated allocation of police and the current number of police allocated to drug busting. If there is pressure from the community on the police department to deal with crime then this gap will be positive and measures how many more police officers are really needed. However officers are redeployed gradually with a sense of urgency captured in the concept 'time to move staff'. The greater this time constant, the slower the rate of redeployment for any given shortfall of police officers. The formulation divides the shortfall by the time to move staff, resulting in a dimensionally balanced equation with appropriate units of police officers per month.

2.2.5   System Dynamics in Action: The Rise of Low-Cost Air Travel in Europe

A modelling project is iterative. It begins with a concern about dynamics (performance over time) in the real world and preliminary ideas about feedback structure. Then gradually, in stages, a model takes shape that clarifies the concern and sharpens ideas about structure. But the purpose is not to create a perfect model that replicates the real world situation in every detail. Rather it is to use modelling as a learning process to investigate, discover and clarify feedback structure and the dynamic behaviour it implies.

To illustrate we examine a model about the early growth strategy of easyJet, one of the UK's most successful no-frills airlines, at the dawn of low-cost flights in Europe. To appreciate the model's boundary and scope it is important to imagine the European airline industry not as it is today but as it was back in the mid-1990s when full-service air travel was the norm and low cost flights were a new and unproven business concept.

2.2.5.1   easyJet: A Bright Idea, But Will It Work?

The historical situation is described in an article called 'easyJet's $500 Million Gamble' (Sull 1999). The opening paragraph sets the scene.

This case study details the rapid growth of easyJet which started operations in November 1995 from London's Luton airport. In 2 years, it was widely regarded as the model low-cost European airline and a strong competitor to flag carriers. The company has clearly identifiable operational and marketing characteristics, e.g. one type of aircraft, point-to-point short-haul travel, no in-flight meals, rapid turnaround time, very high aircraft utilisation, direct sales, cost-conscious customer segments and extensive sub-contracting. easyJet's managers identified three of its nearest low-cost competitors and the strategy of each of these airlines is detailed in the case study. But easyJet also experienced direct retaliation from large flag carriers like KLM and British Airways (Go). These challenges faced easyJet's owner, Stelios Haji-ioannou, as he signed a $500 m contract with Boeing in July 1997 to purchase 12 brand new 737s.

Imagine yourself now in Mr. Haji-ioannou's role. Is it really going to be feasible to fill those expensive new planes? In his mind is a bright new business idea, a creative new segmentation of the air travel market to be achieved through cost leadership and aimed at customers who are interested in "jeans not business routines". Feasibility checks of strategy are natural territory for business simulators, especially dynamic, time-dependent, strategy problems such as rapid growth in a competitive industry. At the time there were differences of opinion within the industry and even among easyJet's management team. Some industry experts had a dismal view of easyJet's prospects (in stark contrast to the founder's optimism), dismissing the fledgling airline with statements such as "Europe is not ready for the peanut flight".

To bring modelling and simulation into this debate we have to visualise the dynamic tasks that face Mr. Haji-ioannou and his team in creating customer awareness (How do you attract enough fliers to fill 12 planes?), and dealing with retaliation by rivals (What if British Airways or KLM engage in a price war, could they sustain such a war, what would provoke such as response?). The starting point is a map of the business, a picture created with the management team, to think with some precision about the task of attracting and retaining passengers and the factors that might drive competitor retaliation.

2.2.5.2   Winning Customers in a New Segment: A Process that Involves Stock Accumulation and a Reinforcing Feedback Loop

Recall that the building blocks of system dynamics models are stock accumulations, causal links and feedback loops. Causal links show simple cause and effect relationships. Feedback loops depict closed paths of cause and effect and are of special importance because they generate dynamics. Feedback loops can be either reinforcing or balancing. Reinforcing loops are responsible for growth dynamics whereas balancing loops are responsible for goal-seeking dynamics and oscillations. By combining stock accumulations, causal links and feedback loops it is possible to create visual models of a wide variety of dynamic strategic business situations, including easyJet's $500 million gamble.

Figure 2.26 uses one stock accumulation, one reinforcing feedback loop and several causal links to show how a start-up airline attracts new passengers and communicates its new low-cost, no-frills service to the flying public. The marketing task is far-from-trivial, because when you think about it (and modelling really forces you to think hard about the practical details that underpin strategy) the company has to spread the word to millions of people if it is to fill 12 brand new 737s day after day.

Potential passengers are shown as an asset stock representing the cumulative number of fliers who have formed a favourable impression of the start-up airline.

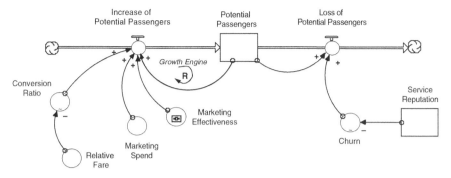

Potential Passengers(t) = Potential Passengers(t-dt) + (Increase of Potential Passengers –Loss
of Potential Passengers) * dt
INIT Potential Passengers = 5000
Increase of Potential Passengers = Potential Passengers *Conversion Ratio + Marketing
Spend*1000*Marketing Effectiveness
Conversion Ratio = GRAPH(Relative Fare)
Marketing Spend = 2500{£thousands per year}
Marketing Effectiveness = 0.05 {Passengers wooed per £spent}

Fig. 2.26 Creating awareness of low-cost flights among potential passengers: word-of-mouth and
marketing

Note that these passengers have not necessarily flown with easyJet, but would if
they could.[7] This rather abstract way of thinking about passengers is a convenient
simplifying assumption that enables us to focus on *growth of interest* in low-cost
flights without the need to model the detailed operations of the company. Bear in
mind however that the scope of a model always depends on its purpose. For example
a model to study the growth of the whole airline (rather than simply growth of
potential passengers) would include the company's internal operations such as hiring
and training of staff and investment in planes, as in Sterman's (1988) well-known
People Express Management Flight Simulator.

The number of potential passengers starts very small (just 5,000 in the model)
and grows over time. But how does growth take place? The remaining parts of the
figure show the factors that determine both the increase and loss of passengers.
In practice this information comes from the management team, coaxed-out by a facilitator
who is helping the team to visualise the business.

The driver of growth is a reinforcing feedback loop shown at the centre of
Fig. 2.26 and labelled 'Growth Engine'. In this loop potential passengers attract
new converts through positive word-of-mouth. The more potential passengers, the

---

[7] We are drawing a distinction between *wanting* a product or service and actually buying it.
The distinction is important in practice because customers often go through stages of adoption.
First they become aware and interested. Then, with more time and further persuasion, they buy.
The most basic feasibility check is whether the firm can generate enough interested customers to
fill 12 planes.

greater the rate of increase of potential passengers. The increase of potential passengers then accumulates in the stock of potential passengers leading to even more potential passengers and a greater rate of increase in potential passengers, thereby completing the reinforcing loop. The strength of word-of-mouth is captured in a concept called the conversion ratio, which itself depends on relative fare. As relative fare increases the conversion rate decreases, a causal link with a '−' sign on the arrow head to indicate negative polarity.

These effects are captured algebraically in the equation for increase of potential passengers. The first part of the equation states that the increase of potential passengers depends on the product of potential passengers and the conversion ratio. Intuitively the lower easyJet's fare relative to established rivals the higher the conversion ratio and the more potent is word-of mouth. An exceptionally low fare is a talking point among the travelling public, just as happened in real life.[8] Such a relationship would normally be sketched as a graph, based on expert opinion from the management team. The shape of the graph can be seen by browsing the Fliers Mini-Sim on the website at http://www.iseesystems.com/community/downloads/OpenUniversity.aspx. The graph shows that when easyJet's fare is just 30% of rivals' fare the conversion ratio is 2.5, meaning that each potential passenger converts 2.5 new potential passengers per year. However at 50% of rivals' fare the conversion ratio is reduced to 1.5 and at 70% it is only 0.3. Eventually, if easyJet's fare were to equal rivals' then the conversion ratio would be zero because a standard fare cannot sustain word-of-mouth.

The increase of potential passengers is also influenced by marketing spend, another causal link. This link is formulated as the product of marketing spend and marketing effectiveness (shown in the second part of the equation for increase of potential passengers). Marketing spend is set at a default value of £2.5 million per year. Marketing effectiveness represents the number of new potential passengers per marketing £ spent. It is set at 0.05 passengers per £, so marketing brings 125,000 potential passengers per year (2.5 million per year * 0.05).

The loss of potential passengers depends on service reputation. The lower service reputation, the greater the churn. The greater the churn the more the loss of passengers. Industry specialists say that service reputation depends on ease-of-booking, punctuality, safety, on-board service, and quality of meals. For short-haul flights punctuality is often the dominant factor. The model does not represent all these factors explicitly but simply represents service reputation as a stock accumulation that can be initialised anywhere on a scale between 0.5 (very poor) and 1.5 (very good). If reputation is very good then fliers retain a favourable impression of the airline, so the annual loss of potential passengers is small, just 2.5% per year – an assumption made in the graph function for the churn. If reputation is poor then the loss of potential passengers per year is damagingly high, up to 100% per year. Notice there is no inflow or outflow to reputation even though it is a stock variable. The reason is that the factors driving change in reputation are outside the boundary of the model.

---

[8] In some cases very low fares may deter passengers due to concerns about safety. But in this particular case easyJet was flying a fleet of brand new 737s which instilled confidence.

2.2.5.3   Retaliation by High-Cost Rivals: A Process That Involves Stock Accumulation and a Balancing Feedback Loop

Figure 2.27 shows one possible way to visualise the retaliatory response of powerful European flag carriers to low cost airlines in the early years. It is important to emphasise here the phrase one possible way, because there are many ways that a management team such as easyJet's might think about competitors. Part of the team model-building task is to achieve the simplest possible shared representation, drawing on the sophisticated (and sometimes conflicting) knowledge of the team members. A fundamental question is whether it is necessary to model competing firms in-depth. Do you really need a detailed portrayal of British Airways or KLM to understand the threat such rivals might pose to the feasibility of easyJet's growth strategy?

The leader of a team-modelling project should not impose a rigid answer on this question of how much detail to include. The modeller should be sensitive to the opinions of the management team while always striving for parsimony. After all to achieve buy-in the model must capture managers' understanding of their world in their own vocabulary. In these situations it is useful to bear in mind that experienced business leaders themselves simplify their complex world. If they did not then it would be impossible to communicate their plans. Good business modelling, like good business communication, is the art of leaving things out – focussing only on those features of reality most pertinent to the problem at hand.

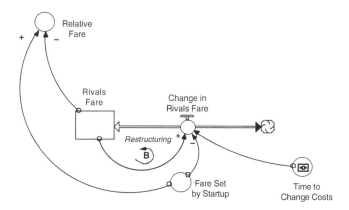

Rivals Fare(t) = Rivals Fare(t - dt) + (Change in Rivals Fare) * dt
INIT Rivals Fare = .25 {£/passenger mile}
Change in Rivals Fare = (Fare Set by Startup – Rivals Fare)/Time to Change Costs
Fare Set by Startup = .09 {£/passenger mile}
Time to Change Costs = 4 {years}
Relative Fare = Fare Set by Startup / Rivals Fare {dimensionless}

Fig. 2.27 Rivals and relative fare

Figure 2.27 shows just enough about competitors to indicate how, collectively, they could stall easyJet's growth ambitions.[9] Recall that word-of-mouth feedback relies for its contagion on the start-up's fare being much lower than rivals. But what if competing firms try to match the start-up's low price? The figure shows how such price equalisation might take place. At the heart of the formulation is a balancing loop labelled 'Restructuring'. Rivals' fare is shown as a stock that accumulates the change in rivals' fare which in turn depends on three factors: the fare set by the startup, rivals' fare and the time to change costs, all depicted as causal links. The use of a stock accumulation implies that it takes time and effort for the established airlines to lower their fares. They cannot reduce fares until they cut costs, and a flag carrier like BA may take years to achieve cost parity with a low-cost start-up. The process of achieving cost parity is essentially a goal-seeking process represented by the balancing loop.

To understand the operation of the balancing loop let us suppose, for the sake of argument, that rivals begin with an average fare of 25 pence (£0.25) per passenger mile and set themselves a goal for average fare of only nine pence (£0.09) per passenger mile – equal to the average fare set by the start-up. (Of course nowadays all airlines use revenue management systems with variable fares. But our focus is on the huge discounts originally offered by low-cost airlines that were available on most seats and enabled easyJet to grow. So a very low fixed fare for the start-up is a reasonable simplifying assumption.[10]) The magnitude of the underlying cost equalisation task is now clear – it is the 64% difference between rivals' initial fare of 25 pence (£0.25) and easyJet's fare of nine pence. Such an enormous change can only be achieved through major restructuring of the business. The change in rivals' fare is controlled by the 'restructuring' balancing loop that gradually reduces the fare to equal the fare set by the start-up. The pace of restructuring depends on the time to change costs. Normally one would expect this adjustment time to be several years, and in the model it is set at 4 years.[11] The equations show a typical asset stock adjustment formulation. The change in fare is equal to the difference between the start-up's fare and rivals' fare divided by the time to change costs. This expression takes a negative value as long as rivals' fare exceeds the start-up's fare, thereby leading to a fare reduction. So, at the start of the simulation, the change in fare is

---

[9] Rivals are portrayed at a high level of aggregation. The purpose is to capture in broad (but dynamically accurate) terms how rival airlines respond to price competition.

[10] Large carriers will match low seat prices regardless of cost by providing some seats at a discount. Price cuts can be implemented very quickly through on-line yield management systems that allow dynamic pricing according to load factors. But narrowly targeted discounts are an ineffective weapon for companies like BA and KLM in the competitive fight with low-cost airlines. For example, out of 150 seats there may be only 15 cheap ones. For very popular flights there are no cheap seats at all. Only cost parity can deliver competitive prices and profitability in the long-term for large carriers catering to a growing population of price-conscious fliers.

[11] An empirical study of cost and productivity convergence among US airlines, conducted by Peter Belobaba from MIT's International Centre for Air Transportation, confirms significant cost convergence between Network Legacy Carriers and Low Cost Carriers spread over several years.

(0.09–0.25)/4 which is a brisk reduction rate of £0.04 per passenger mile per year. This rate prevails over the first computation interval to arrive at a new and lower fare for the next computation interval, and so on as the simulation proceeds.

2.2.5.4   Feedback Loops in the easyJet Model

Figure 2.28 summarises the main feedback loops in the model, including the two loops described above and two more loops that capture route saturation and churn. In the centre of the figure is the reinforcing growth engine from Fig. 2.26. More potential passengers lead to more conversion from word of mouth, a greater increase of potential passengers, more potential passengers, and so on.

In the bottom right of the figure is the important balancing loop from Fig. 2.27, involving restructuring of costs, which determines rivals' fare. There are just two concepts in the loop: rivals' fare and cost cutting rate. The dynamic significance of the balancing loop is that it tends to equalise rivals' fare with the start-up's fare. As a result relative fare (defined as the ratio of start-up's fare to rivals' fare) converges gradually to parity thereby reducing the strength of word-of-mouth in the reinforcing loop.

These two loops form the core of the model and are central to the evaluation of easyJet's start-up strategy. Qualitatively, if the reinforcing loop is strong (and stimulates rapid growth) while the balancing loop is weak (and leads to very slow price equalisation) then easyJet's $500 million gamble is likely to succeed and the company will fill its planes. However, if the balancing loop is strong (and price

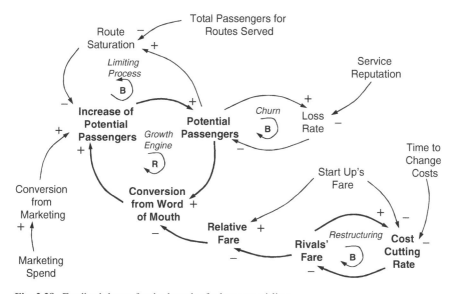

Fig. 2.28 Feedback loops for the launch of a low-cost airline

equalisation happens quickly) then the window of opportunity for rapid growth is much reduced and easyJet's gamble may fail.

In addition to the two loops depicted in bold there are two further loops in Fig. 2.28 that capture the effects of route saturation and churn on passenger interest. These extra loops are peripheral to the immediate question of whether or not easy-Jet can fill 12 planes, but are important in the long run to ensure realistic limits to the growth of potential passengers in the region served by the fledgling airline. At the top of the figure is a balancing loop (labelled 'Limiting Process') in which route saturation eventually restricts the increase of potential passengers. Finally in the centre-right is a balancing loop (labelled 'Churn') showing the effect of the start-up's service reputation on the loss rate of potential passengers.

Of course this brief model of passengers and fares is a sketch of a more complex reality. Nevertheless, it contains sufficient detail for an informative team discussion about passenger growth and price retaliation. And when simulated the model contains sufficient dynamic complexity to yield thought-provoking growth scenarios that help management to rehearse strategy.

2.2.5.5 Strategy and Simulation of Growth Scenarios

The purpose of the model is to investigate easyJet's $500 million gamble to purchase twelve brand new Boeing 737s. Is it wise to order so many planes? Will it be possible to fill them? And assuming a large potential market for low-cost air travel, will easyJet be able to capture a big enough slice? A rough calculation suggests the airline needs one million fliers if it is to operate 12 fully-loaded aircraft[12] – which is a lot of people. What combination of word-of-mouth and marketing will attract this number of potential passengers? How long will it take? What are the risks of price retaliation by rivals? These are good questions to explore using the what-if capability of simulation.

Figure 2.29 shows simulations of the growth of potential passengers over the period 1996–2000 under two different approaches to marketing spend (bold and cautious) *and* under the assumption of slow retaliation by rivals. Bold marketing spend is assumed to be five times greater than cautious spend (at £2.5 million per year versus £0.5 million per year). In both cases the horizontal straight line shows the 'required' number of passengers to fill 12 planes. This line is a useful reference

---

[12] Let's assume each aircraft carries 150 passengers and makes three round-trip flights a day. So a fully loaded plane needs 900 passengers each day (150*3*2). A fully loaded fleet of 12 planes needs 10,800 passengers a day, or 3,888,000 passengers each year, which is very nearly four million. If we make the further assumption that each potential passenger is likely to fly the available routes twice a year on round-trip flights, then the start-up airline needs to attract a pool of almost one million fliers to ensure commercially viable load factors. This rough calculation is typical of the sort of judgmental numerical data required to populate an algebraic model. Perfect accuracy is not essential and often not possible. The best estimates of informed people, specified to order-of-magnitude accuracy (or better), are adequate, drawing on the informal but powerful knowledge base derived from experience.

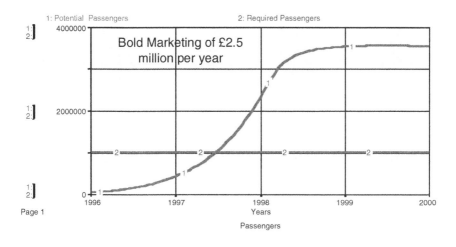

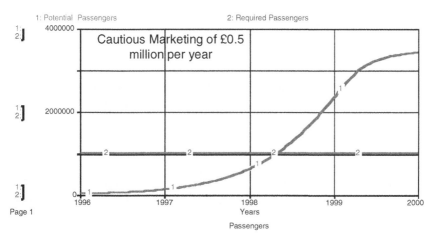

Fig. 2.29 Simulations comparing bold marketing (*top chart*) with cautious marketing (*bottom chart*). Assuming slow retaliation

against which to compare the number of potential passengers. If and when potential passengers exceed required passengers, the strategy is deemed feasible.

Consider first the timeline for bold marketing in the top half of the figure. The simulation begins in 1996 with a very small number of potential passengers – just 5,000. The fledgling airline is virtually unknown to the flying public, despite its ambitions. In the first year of operation, bold marketing brings the airline to the attention of a growing number of fliers. By the end of 1996 there is a band of several hundred thousand enthusiastic supporters. Moreover, this band of supporters is beginning to recruit more followers through positive word-of-mouth. In the interval 1997–1998 the number of potential passengers rises sharply as word-of-mouth continues to stoke exponential growth. By mid-1997 the number of potential passengers has reached the target of one million required to fill the fleet. In the remainder of the year, reinforcing growth continues. There is a huge leap of more than one million potential passengers in the last 6 months of 1997 as the powerful engine of growth continues to gather momentum. Then, in the second quarter of 1998, growth ceases abruptly as the airline's message reaches all 3.5 million fliers in the imagined catchment region it serves.

The strategically important part of the timeline is the growth phase between the start of 1996 and early 1998. Bold marketing coupled with strong word-of-mouth unleashes a powerful engine of growth which, in classic exponential fashion, begins small (and therefore invisible) and snowballs rapidly after 18 months.

Now consider the timeline in the bottom half of Fig. 2.29, which traces the build-up of potential passengers from cautious marketing. Spend is cut by four-fifths from £2.5 million a year to only £0.5 million a year. As before, the simulation starts in 1996 with only 5,000 potential passengers. In the first year the airline wins few passengers – not surprising because marketing spend is much reduced. In the second year there is healthy growth in passengers, despite the low marketing spend. Word-of-mouth is now beginning to draw-in lots of new passengers. Once the growth engine is primed it gets rolling and in the second quarter of 1998 carries the airline's passenger base beyond the target required to fill the fleet. Growth continues into 1999 until nearly all 3.5 million fliers are aware of the new low-cost service. Cautious marketing simply defers growth (by comparison with bold marketing) but doesn't seem to radically alter the ultimate size of the passenger base. One can begin to appreciate a persuasive rationale for caution. By the year 2000 the simulated airline has saved £8 million in marketing spend (4 years at an annual saving of £2 million) yet has still got its message out to 3.5 million fliers!

Figure 2.30 shows the same two marketing approaches (bold and cautious) under the assumption that rivals retaliate quickly. Price equalisation happens in half the time previously assumed and as a result both timelines are noticeably changed by comparison with the base case. But from the viewpoint of strategic feasibility the bold marketing timeline tells much the same story as before. At the start of 1996 the airline is almost unknown among the flying public, and by the third quarter of 1997 it has attracted enough potential passengers to fill 12 planes. Fast-acting rivals seem unable to prevent this rise of a new entrant from obscurity to commercial viability, though price equalisation measures do curtail the ultimate dissemination of the start-up airline's low-price message.

A strategically significant change is observable in the timeline for cautious marketing. The startup airline is no longer able to fill its planes because it is unable to attract passengers. The rise from obscurity to prominence never happens. Cautious marketing attracts few converts and fails to ignite word-of-mouth. By the time the low-price message has reached a few hundred thousand fliers (at the end of 1997) it is no longer distinctive. Rivals are low price too. If this future were easyJet's its planes would be flying half-empty and it would be losing money. Fast retaliation can prove fatal in a word-of-mouth market.

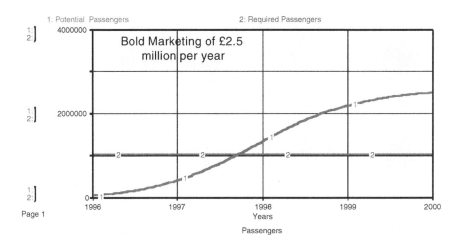

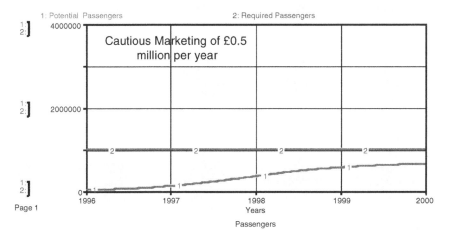

Fig. 2.30 Simulations comparing bold marketing (*top chart*) with cautious marketing (*bottom chart*). Assuming fast retaliation

2.2.5.6 Using the Fliers Simulator to Create Your Own Scenarios

The Fliers simulator enables you to explore a variety of scenarios for a start-up low cost airline. You can replay the simulations shown above, create new scenarios, and investigate the behaviour of many more variables. Open the model called Fliers Mini-Sim on the website at http://www.iseesystems.com/community/downloads/OpenUniversity.aspx to see the opening screen as shown in Fig. 2.31. There is a time chart for potential passengers and required passengers, numeric displays for potential passengers and relative fare, and slide bars for marketing spend and time to change costs. Marketing spend is 2,500 (in £ thousands per year) and the time to

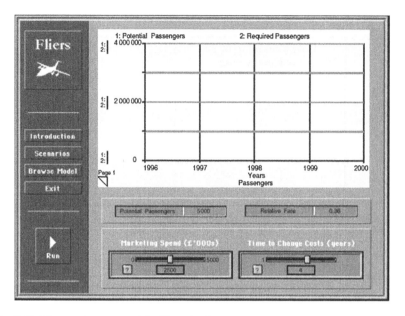

Fig. 2.31 The opening screen of the fliers simulator

change costs is 4 years. These are the conditions for the base case scenario of bold marketing and slow retaliation already seen in Fig. 2.29.

To get started press the 'Run' button *without altering either of the slide bars*. The first year of the simulation plays out. Scroll through the time charts to view the behaviour of the conversion ratio, the effect of route saturation, churn and the increase/loss of potential passengers. Press the Run button again to see the next simulated year and so on to the end of the simulation in the year 2000. For a guided tour of the simulation press the scenarios button on the left. A new screen appears containing a menu of pre-prepared scenarios. Press the large green button for a year-by-year analysis of the base case. At the end of the analysis press 'scenario explorer' to return to the opening screen. Then conduct your own experiments with other combinations of marketing spend and time to change costs. At any time you can learn more about the simulator by pressing the navigation buttons on the left of the screen. The introduction is a review of the easyJet case and the feedback structure of the model. The scenarios button offers a guided tour of the four pre-prepared scenarios already covered in Figs. 2.29 and 2.30. 'Browse model' allows you to see the detailed model structure and documented equation formulations.

2.2.6 Excerpts from 'Orchestras in a Complex World'

Sometimes casual loop diagrams are used in a purely qualitative way, without algebraic modelling and simulation. Although the emphasis of this chapter has been on mapping that leads to simulation, it is also useful for readers to see that conceptual maps are helpful in their own right: for expanding the boundary of people's thinking about organisations; and for providing an overview from which novel insights may arise.

To illustrate I present an application to orchestra management carried out by Bernhard Kerres while he was an associate with Booz-Allen Hamilton in Munich. Over a period of 3 years he worked with various orchestras in Europe to assist in the development of their strategic agendas. In the course of the study he spoke with orchestra managers, concert promoters, musicians, agents and others close to the industry. Together they explored the questions of what is success for an orchestra and how can an orchestra become successful. Drawing on his experience as a professional musician and knowledge of system dynamics from an MBA at London Business School he was in a good position to help orchestra managers and other stakeholders to address these questions.[13] Collectively the interviewees identified five major indicators for successful orchestras:

– High quality orchestral concert performances with the ability to attract and retain excellent orchestra musicians, as well as guest artists and conductors
– Challenging and interesting programming which attracts audiences and raises the interest of new audiences
– Attracting well-qualified managers and staff, and also enthusiastic volunteers and supportive sponsors
– Maintaining a media profile, including recordings and broadcasts, as well as favourable reviews
– Successful outreach and education work through provision of musical services to their communities, with an outcome of raising the understanding and appreciation of music

Causal loop diagramming was used to show how these indicators are related to each other. Here I present an *edited subset* of the diagrams that appeared in Bernhard Kerres' published article. Note how he communicates complexity. He adds interlocking loops one-by-one and writes a vivid accompanying narrative that is well-grounded in the real-world situation.

2.2.6.1   Success of Performances and Quality of Orchestra

To build a conceptual map for orchestras in larger cities, the success of metropolitan performances seems to be a good starting point. What is a successful performance? What makes it successful? Successful performances can be seen mainly in two ways: artistic success and financial success.

---

[13] I am grateful to Bernhard Kerres (1999) for this example which is based on excerpts from an article entitled 'Orchestras in a complex world' first published in *Harmony*, 8, pp. 45–58 (Forum of the Symphony Orchestra Institute). Bernhard is now Intendant and CEO of the Vienna Konzerthaus, one of the most active concert houses in the world.

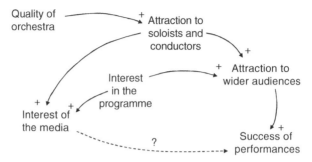

Fig. 2.32 Success of performances

Artistic success includes the quality of the performance and the challenge of the programme. Financial success includes the ability to sell tickets for the performance and to attract sponsorship. The comparable dimension of intermediate or longer-term artistic and financial success would be the ability to sell season subscriptions and to increase the audience base.

When considering what makes the actual success, audience attraction is a major point as shown in Fig. 2.32. Financial and artistic success can only be achieved if audiences are attracted. Audiences are often attracted by their interest in the programme and/or the attraction artists hold, including the fundamental quality of the orchestra. Programmes and artists are often cited as the main reasons why audiences attend concerts. Sometimes the venue itself plays a role. The state-of-the-art Benaroya Hall in Seattle, Symphony Center in Chicago, or the Konzerthaus in Vienna are attractive and unique places in themselves, and attract audiences who want to say "I've been there".

And one should remember that audiences are not the only people who come to listen to a concert, broadcast, or recording. Audiences also include supporters, volunteers, and others who endorse the work of an orchestra. This wider definition of audience is critical for the success of orchestral institutions. Without the support from the wider audience, an orchestra would be limited to silent listeners. It would be hard for an orchestral institution to become a lively organisation which attracts great artists and musicians, or to be successful in the longer term.

And undoubtedly the media have a role in attracting audiences for performances. But what exactly is that role? Media includes print, as well as recordings, broadcasts and many other forms. Media is a very large industry in itself and often crosses paths with the music industry. Media attention includes not only reviews, but also any form of publicised information about the orchestral organisation's activities. This can range from advertising at the local bus station to dedicated slots on the local radio station.

Technical developments in the media industry over recent years have lowered barriers to the media world, but also raised the level of competition. Orchestral institutions face the challenge of how to use these developments to their advantage.

The options are immense, and might include selling recordings over the internet or entering into partnerships with various media companies. Just consider the Berlin Philharmonic which has recently started to make all their concerts available on the internet with great sound and video quality in a subscription model.

With these thoughts in mind we have now covered the first part of the conceptual map shown in Fig. 2.32. The map establishes connections between the quality of an orchestra and the success of performances. However it does not adequately explain the influence of the media on success (shown as a dotted line with an accompanying question mark). Neither does the figure yet show any reinforcing feedback loop. If one or more such loops can be established for an orchestra, that orchestra would have found a success engine to drive growth.

2.2.6.2 The Importance of Brand

So far we have not spoken about the "brand" of the orchestra. In today's world a brand for an orchestra is just as important as for any other good. Such examples as Virgin demonstrate how powerful brands can be. But there are also examples of powerful brand names in the orchestra world. Such orchestras as the Vienna Philharmonic or the Berlin Philharmonic are associated with world-class quality and other attributes. The names of these orchestras have developed into brand names, even if these orchestras do not actively promote their brands. And so have certain artists like Anna Netrebko, Lang Lang and many others.

But what lies behind a brand name? A brand relies on the image it generates in people's minds. A brand links the values of a product or organisation with the qualities people associate with the product or the organisation. We therefore should consider not only such well-known brands as Coca-Cola. The local shop in a small town actually has a brand because the local population links the image of the shop with the values the shopkeeper represents. The only differences are that fewer people know the brand, and it may not be as well managed as Coca-Cola.

One example of an orchestra developing its image into a brand is the Detroit Symphony. With its surprise encores and the friendliness it exhibits towards its audiences, the Detroit Symphony is creating a certain favourable image in the minds of its audiences. It is building a brand with this image to differentiate itself from other orchestras, and from other performing arts groups in Detroit. The correct conclusion is that orchestral institutions in any city have to think hard about the qualities and values they want people to think of when they hear or see the orchestra.

Take the example of the Florida Orchestra, which works hard on its image of being informal and creative. On one occasion the orchestra performed an all-Frank Zappa concert as part of its frequent testing of the boundaries among classical music, jazz and pop music. The *Washington Post* reported that. "Roars of applause followed every piece.... Symphony patrons in tuxedos edged past colourful eccentrics decked out in Willie Nelson braids and Harley leathers".

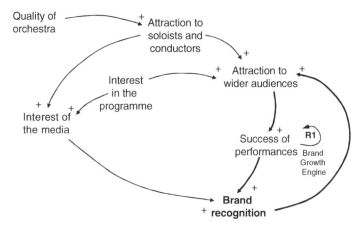

Fig. 2.33 The importance of the brand

We now add brand to the conceptual map as shown in Fig. 2.33. Because brand recognition can be measured, it is a good parameter for a conceptual map. Brand establishes the first feedback loop in our model: the stronger the brand recognition of an orchestra, the higher the attraction to audiences and the better the success of performances. This feedback loop is represented by the symbol R1 on our map and is labelled 'Brand Growth Engine' to indicate its potential to generate growth. However it is important to note that the same loop could change from a virtuous circle to a vicious circle under adverse circumstances. For example if the success of performances is low, then brand recognition could decline and even become negative. Negative brand recognition can lead to lower audience attraction, which in turn can lead to less successful performance. Keep in mind this possible switch in behaviour as we extend the map by adding more reinforcing loops.

Figure 2.33 also helps to better understand the media's role in the success of performances. Media – in its full variety – directly influences brand recognition and indirectly affects success through loop R1. The more an orchestral institution appears in articles, broadcasts, shows and reviews, the higher the brand recognition and the greater the knock-on consequences to success.

2.2.6.3 Attracting Musicians

So far the map is missing one element vital for an orchestra's success. An orchestra could not exist without its musicians. Figure 2.34 shows how musicians can be attracted. Musicians consider important the orchestra for which they play. They take into consideration the brand of the orchestra as well as the soloists and conductors with whom they work.

If an orchestra is attractive to well-known conductors, it will also be attractive to musicians. Attracting good and enthusiastic musicians is critical for the success of

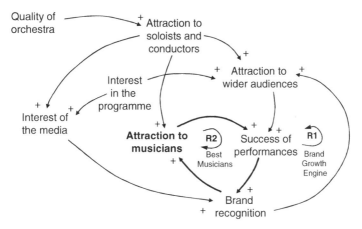

Fig. 2.34 Attracting musicians

an orchestra and its performances and establishes a second reinforcing feedback loop R2, labelled 'Best Musicians'.

2.2.6.4 Success with Fundraising

Our map so far has not touched upon a very important issue for any arts organisation: fundraising. In general, few orchestras in the United States ever really experienced the system of public funding which was well known until recently in Europe and Canada. In Europe, funding for the arts was historically reserved for the sovereign. The shortfalls in state households and the focus on other issues have led to a steady decrease in public funding in most European countries. Private fundraising has now become as important in Europe and Canada as it has been historically in the United States. A conceptual map for orchestra organisations needs to take this development into account.

Fundraising success – from individual, corporate and public sources – depends heavily on the brand recognition of the arts organisation. An organisation with a good brand recognition will also be able to attract the right supporters and volunteers to make fundraising a success. The success of the orchestral institution itself depends on the ability to raise sufficient funds. Fundraising success must therefore be included in the conceptual map.

As Fig. 2.35 shows, fundraising success depends heavily on brand recognition. It is easier to raise funds for an organisation which is well known and well thought of than for an unknown organisation. Well-known orchestras can attract higher levels of funding and can also attract prominent individuals to leadership of their fundraising campaigns.

Survival for lesser-known organisations is a real issue, especially in Europe. Lesser-known organisations in countries which traditionally had high public funding face not only drastic reductions in public funding, but also see corporate sponsors attracted to the top institutions (which, ironically, still receive a certain level of

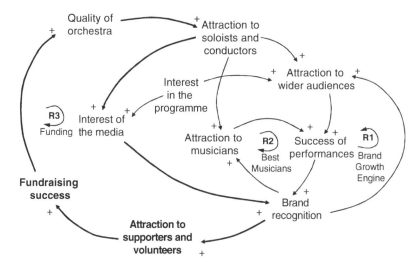

Fig. 2.35 Success in fundraising

public funding). Public and private funding become focussed on a few well-known organisations, leaving fewer funds available for lesser-known institutions.

Success in fundraising starts another reinforcing feedback loop R3. Only if enough funds are available will well-known soloists, conductors and musicians be attracted to perform with the orchestra. High-level artistry is necessary to develop audiences and to generate sufficient media interest. This process again leads to better brand recognition.

Similar to brand recognition, fundraising seems to be a key success factor for orchestras in today's environment. Many orchestral organisations in the United States have professional fundraising staffs, either in-house or outsourced. Orchestra organisation board members in the United States take active roles in fundraising, often giving significant donations to their organisations.

Private donors are the strongest supporters of US arts organisations. They may not necessarily be interested in a well-marketed brand, but they are interested in the image behind the brand. If they see their own interests and values represented in the image behind the brand, they will be inclined to support a particular orchestral institution.

The climate in Europe is very different. Fundraising is rather new. Some organisations in the United Kingdom are taking the lead. Nevertheless, many boards, if they exist at all, see their roles primarily in governance and not in fundraising. A learning process will obviously be necessary.

2.2.6.5   Conclusions from Orchestra Study

A conceptual map represents ways in which the organisation's main features and activities interrelate with one another, and with the environment in which the organisation functions. Building a conceptual map is normally done in an iterative team effort. The map represents the group's consensus of the operating environment.

A successful conceptual map requires the support of the whole team. Therefore, it is valuable to work not only with the management and the board of an orchestral organisation, but also to include supporters, sponsors and representatives of audiences. The success of an orchestra is not based on a few people on the orchestra's payroll. In today's world, staff, musicians, volunteers, audiences, supporters, and many others take an active interest in the future of their orchestral institutions. Incorporating their views, with the help of a trained facilitator and map builder, increases the chances for a successful process.

2.3   Summary and Conclusion: An Overview of the Modelling Process

The previous examples have covered the main concepts and tools used in system dynamics. In summary, five steps of modelling can be identified as shown in Fig. 2.36. Usually there is lots of to-and-fro between the steps as understanding of the situation improves by sketching diagrams, quantifying concepts, writing friendly algebra, and making simulations. Step 1 is problem articulation. It is the most important step of all because it shapes the entire study. Here the modeller or modelling team identify the issue of concern, the time frame, the level of analysis (business unit, firm, industry, etc.), the boundary of the study and the likely scope of factors involved. Step 2 is a dynamic hypothesis, a preliminary sketch by the modeller of the main interactions and feedback loops that could explain observed or anticipated performance. Step 3 is formulation, the transformation of a dynamic hypothesis into a reasonably detailed diagram of feedback processes and corresponding algebraic equations. Step 4 is testing. The model is simulated to see whether or not its behaviour over time is plausible and consistent with available

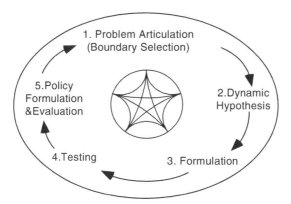

Fig. 2.36 Modelling is an iterative learning process (Sterman 2000). *Business Dynamics: Systems Thinking and Modeling for a Complex World*, McGraw Hill, with permission from The McGraw-Hill Companies

evidence from the real world. Step 4 fixes errors and begins to build confidence in the model's integrity. Step 5 is policy formulation and evaluation. By now there is confidence that the model's structure is sound and that it is capable of reproducing the dynamic symptoms of the original problem. So attention shifts to policy changes intended to improve performance and to alleviate the perceived problem. The new policies are then simulated to see how well they work.

Notice these steps are shown as a cycle and *not* as a linear sequence. The web-like symbol in the middle of the diagram and the circle of arrows around the edge mean that iteration is a natural and important part of the process. For example it is common for modellers to revise the problem and model boundary as they develop a dynamic hypothesis and causal loops. So step 2 influences step 1. Similarly formulation and testing can reveal the need for new equations or new structure because simulations contradict common sense or else reveal that the original dynamic hypothesis is incapable of generating observed or expected behaviour over time. So steps 3 and 4 can influence steps 1 and 2 or each other.

Consider such iterations as they arise in the drug-related crime model. According to the dynamic hypothesis, escalating crime is attributable to police drug busting that removes drugs (and drug dealers) from the streets. A side-effect is to push up the street price of drugs and this price inflation inadvertently forces addicts to commit *more* crime, leading to more drug busting and so on. The structure is a reinforcing loop and the resulting simulator (based on formulations outlined in Figs. 2.18–2.25) shows that crime escalation is possible given reasonable operating assumptions about the police department, street market, the community and addicts themselves. However, when the simulator is run for 5 or more years this logic is pushed beyond the limits of common sense and reveals a world in which the price of drugs is sky high, crime has increased sixfold and the supply of drugs on the street is *negative*![14]

A modeller faced with these contradictions returns to the model's assumptions to find the fallacy. A few possibilities come to mind. The simplest, and least disruptive to the integrity of the model, is that police effectiveness in drug busting is not constant (as assumed) but depends on the supply of drugs on the street. As supply is reduced through drug seizures it becomes more and more difficult for police to trace the few drugs that remain – an example of the 'law of diminishing returns'. This formulation requires a new causal link and a graphical converter that shows police effectiveness as a non-linear function of the supply of drugs on the street. Another more radical idea is to include the dynamics of supply. The current model assumes the total supply of drugs is fixed, so drug seizures create a permanent shortage on the street. But if the street price is high then, sooner or later, the supply of drugs will increase to compensate for drug busting, thereby re-establishing an equilibrium of supply and demand. In other words the dynamic hypothesis needs to be modified and the boundary of the model expanded in order to create plausible long-term dynamics.

---

[14] The simulations are not included in this chapter. Readers who wish to see them should refer to Chapter 3 of *Strategic Modelling and Business Dynamics*.

2.3.1 Dynamic Hypothesis and Fundamental Modes of Dynamic Behaviour

From a modeller's perspective a dynamic hypothesis is a particularly important step of 'complexity reduction' – making sense of a messy situation in the real world. A feedback systems thinker has in mind a number of structure-behaviour pairs that give valuable clues or patterns to look for when explaining puzzling dynamics. Figure 2.37 shows six fundamental modes of dynamic behaviour and the feedback structures that generate them.

The trajectories in the top half of the diagram arise from simple feedback processes. On the left is pure exponential growth caused by a single reinforcing feedback loop in isolation. In the centre is pure goal seeking behaviour caused by a balancing loop. On the right is s-shaped growth that occurs when exponential growth hits a limit. In this case a reinforcing loop dominates behaviour to begin with, and then later (due to changing conditions) a balancing loop becomes more and more influential.

The trajectories in the bottom half of the diagram arise from more complex feedback processes. On the left is classic oscillatory, goal-seeking behaviour with repeated overshoot and undershoot of a target, caused by a balancing loop with a time delay. In the centre is growth with overshoot, a pattern of behaviour where growth from a reinforcing loop hits a limit that is not immediately recognised. This lagged limiting effect is represented as a balancing loop with delay. On the right is overshoot and collapse, which is a variation on growth with overshoot. But here the limit itself is a floating goal that adds an extra reinforcing loop. This set of six structure-behaviour pairs is not exhaustive but illustrates the principle that any pattern of behaviour over time can be reduced to the interaction of balancing and reinforcing loops.

Some of the most intriguing and complex dynamics arise in situations where multiple feedback loops interact and each loop contains time delays and non-linearities. Even quite simple models with two or three interacting loops can prove to be very

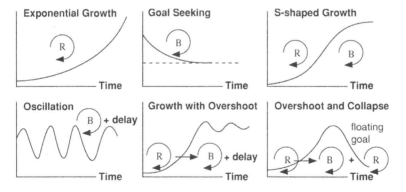

Fig. 2.37 Dynamic hypothesis and fundamental modes of dynamic behavior (Sterman 2000). *Business Dynamics: Systems Thinking and Modeling for a Complex World*, McGraw Hill, with permission from The McGraw-Hill Companies

interesting as we saw in the airline model presented earlier. The main point for now is to realise that all such models take shape in a structured yet creative process of discovering feedback processes in everyday affairs.

2.3.2   A Spectrum of Model Fidelity

Models range in size from large-and-detailed to elegantly small and metaphorical. The spectrum is illustrated in Fig. 2.38. On the left-hand side are realistic high-fidelity simulators epitomised by aircraft flight simulators used to train pilots. They are realistic enough for pilots to practice take-offs and landings and to prepare for emergencies such as engine failure. Often people expect business and public policy models to be similarly realistic; the more realistic the better. But very often small and simplified models are extremely useful as metaphors for more complex situations.

My favourite example of a metaphorical model is a simulator of Romeo and Juliet intended for high school students studying Shakespeare in English literature classes. Clearly a simulator cannot possibly replicate Shakespeare's play, but it can encourage students to study the play more closely than they otherwise would. By simulating the waxing and waning of love between Romeo and Juliet, students become curious about romantic relationships, both in the model and the play. A metaphorical model is small and can be explained quickly. The Romeo and Juliet simulator fits on a single page and involves just a handful of concepts,[15] a far cry from the large and detailed model that lies behind an aircraft flight simulator. It is important to realise that business and public policy models typically lie somewhere in the middle of this spectrum of model fidelity, as indicated by the oval in Fig. 2.38.

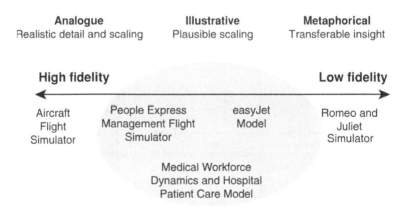

Fig. 2.38 Modelling and realism – a spectrum of model fidelity

---

[15]The Romeo and Juliet simulator is described in chapter 6 of an edited book entitled *Tracing Connections, Voices of Systems Thinkers* (Morecroft 2010). See the list of references for a full citation.

2.3.3   Growth Strategy in Low-Cost Airlines: A Small Model and a Much Larger One

The easyJet case gives us a taste of a small but nevertheless quite insightful model – 'a back of the envelope model' – to address a dynamic challenge in a rapidly evolving market where timing to market is very important. The easyJet model condenses this core timing issue in just a few variables and feedback loops allowing quick feasibility tests of the strategic initiative to complement managerial judgement and to challenge prevailing wisdom. This type of model rehearses the basic intuition of the manager in order to find out hidden pitfalls. It is also small enough to illustrate fundamental concepts in system dynamics such as stock accumulation and feedback loops and therefore serves a useful pedagogical purpose too.

In contrast Sterman's People Express Management Flight Simulator, about the growth strategy of a US low-cost airline in the 1980s, is a much larger model of several hundred equations. It examines the problem of coordinating investment and hiring in a fast-growth no-frills airline (a service business) while maintaining staff motivation and high-quality service. The scope of the problem situation is defined more broadly than for easyJet and the dynamic phenomenon to be explained – growth and unintended collapse of the firm – requires a more sophisticated dynamic hypothesis and model.

2.3.4   Public Policy: A Medium-Sized Hospital Model

In 2004, the European Working Time Directive EUWTD, a measure intended to limit the working week to 48 h for *all* workers within the European Union (EU), became mandatory for junior doctors working for the National Health Service (NHS) in Britain. The intuition behind this piece of health and safety legislation was to reduce the fatigue experienced by junior doctors by limiting doctor's working hours and so improve the quality of patient care. This rationale, though compelling, does not address the non-clinical effects of the EUWTD, in particular, the fundamental change that the directive has on doctors' working patterns, in-service training and work-life balance.

These concerns were of personal and professional interest to Dr. Mark Ratnarajah, a paediatric specialist registrar based in London who, at the time, was also enrolled on the Executive MBA programme at London Business School. He decided to conduct a project to consider the effects of the directive on junior doctors' career decisions and the consequences of these decisions on the medical workforce and quality of patient care. Based on his experience and knowledge of the UK National Health System NHS he developed a system dynamics model to consider the broad implications of the directive and to explore alternative courses of action.[16]

---

[16]For more information about the model see Chapter 9 of *Strategic Modelling and Business Dynamics*.

The project was conducted in two stages. In stage one a workforce planning model was built to explore how hospitals will cope with the expected loss of junior doctor cover and the transition to full-shift work patterns. This model focuses on the tangible effects of the directive on the total hours available from junior doctors. In stage two the model was extended to include intangible effects of the working time directive on the work-life balance and morale of junior doctors and potential knock-on consequences to doctors quitting the medical profession. The models' structure was derived from the modeller's own decade of personal experience as a physician trained in the NHS. Parameters were gleaned from government health-care policy documents and from journal articles about the medical profession.

2.3.5   Reflections on Model Fidelity and Size

These examples show that system dynamics models of varying fidelity can support the process of strategic development. There is no one perfect model of an organisa-tion that will reveal the future outcome of strategy and policy with certainty. Modelling is fundamentally the art and science of interpreting complexity, and there is always a choice about how much detail to include, depending on the pur-pose. On the one hand there are small scale models, mere sketches of a complex reality, whose purpose is to reflect managerial intuition and rehearse the implica-tions. On the other hand there are larger, more sophisticated models whose purpose is to facilitate strategic change by developing shared understanding of complex situations and by testing the effect of specific policies.

2.3.6   Required Skills of Practitioner

The skills needed to conduct projects depend on the problem situation, model size and whether or not a simulator is required. Someone who is familiar with the rules of causal loop diagramming (and who is confident with group facilitation) can conduct projects of similar scope to Bernhard Kerres' study of Orchestra Management. However the expertise necessary to create clear and insightful loops should not be underestimated.

Simulators, both large and small, require skills in formulation, equation writing and simulation analysis. As the drug related crime model shows, there is a significant step in going from a causal loop diagram to a full-fledged simulator of the same feedback structure. Normally such work is done with project teams that include both policymakers and expert modellers/facilitators. The relevant modelling expertise can be found among members of the system dynamics community, in niche consulting companies, and among graduate students who have specialised in system dynamics. Useful gateways to members of this community are the websites of the System Dynamics Society www.systemdynamics.org and the Society's UK Chapter www.systemdynamics.org.uk.

I should emphasize that is not easy to build full-blown simulators and there is always room to improve modelling skills. Even small metaphorical simulators present significant formulation challenges for the novice as the following story about the Romeo and Juliet model illustrates. The tiny model contains just two stocks: Romeo's love for Juliet and Juliet's love for Romeo. They are mutually dependent. Two strikingly simple connections are all that is needed to produce a cyclical pattern of love in the time chart. At least that is the dynamic hypothesis. If the change in Romeo's love for Juliet depends on Juliet's love for Romeo, and vice-versa then an endless cycle of waxing and waning love is possible. This hypothesis comes as a big surprise to many people.

From the stock and flow diagram it is a further step to a full-blown simulator. In my experience this step is not easy. In executive education programmes I sometimes ask participants to formulate equations themselves. First they write equations for the two stock and flow networks (copying the standard syntax that applies to all stock accumulations). Then they tackle the tricky task of formulating equations for causal links between the two lovers. I allow participants the freedom to introduce auxiliary concepts in order to operationalise the links. This exercise, conducted in pairs, provokes a lot of thinking and discussion. Participants try their best to capture the imagined sensitivity of lovers and argue whether Romeo and Juliet respond to being loved in exactly the same way or somehow mirror each other's affections. The model is small enough that everyone manages to formulate a full-set of equations and run simulations. The result is a wide variety of time charts. Some charts show escalating growth of love while others show a collapse of love to a permanent state of cold lovelessness (zero units of love).

In the limited time available it is very rare indeed for anyone's model to reproduce the intended cyclical pattern of love (although the exercise provokes much fruitful thought about the relationship between Romeo and Juliet, just as a metaphorical model should). Nevertheless participants learn a useful cautionary lesson. The exercise shows that it is difficult to write equations that mean what you intend (and of being absolutely clear about what you really mean). Herein lies an enduring challenge of good system dynamics modelling. The same challenge applies to business and public policy models, only more-so. It can take 2 or 3 days of the project team's time to come-up with a conceptual model worthy of the problem situation. It can take weeks or months more of the modellers' (or modelling team's) time, depending on model size, to formulate equations and then create a calibrated and fully-tested simulator suitable for evaluating new policies and strategies. In other words, don't expect a credible simulator to appear overnight. It is necessary to carefully work through all five iterative steps described earlier in order to build confidence in the model, its structure, equations and fitness for purpose.

2.3.7 *Enhancing Your Skills in Feedback Systems Thinking and System Dynamics*

This chapter on system dynamics is necessarily condensed. If you wish to learn more about the subject then there are several good sources to consult. My own book *Strategic Modelling and Business Dynamics* (Morecroft 2007) covers all stages of model building from problem articulation to mapping, equation formulation and simulation. It includes a range of in-depth practical examples that vividly illustrate important or puzzling dynamics in business, society and everyday life. The book also includes software and simulators that allow readers to run models described in the text and to role-play in dynamically complex systems.

Another good source is *Business Dynamics* (Sterman 2000). This comprehensive and definitive textbook thoroughly explains the philosophy, theory and practice of system dynamics modelling and simulation. It is exceptionally well written and provides a wealth of case model examples from business and society. Although the book is used in advanced courses on system dynamics, several chapters are well-suited to beginners. For example, causal loop diagramming is covered in Chapter 5, with many well-documented examples. Then, in Chapters 6 and 7, there is an excellent treatment of stocks and flows and the dynamics of stock accumulation.

For those who are interested in strategy and system dynamics there is *Strategic Management Dynamics* (Warren 2008). This textbook provides the basis for an entire strategic management course based on sound dynamic principles of asset stock accumulation. It includes explanations of how these principles connect with many of the most widely used frameworks in the strategy field. There are also extensive worksheets and exercises to develop skills in mapping a firm's strategic architecture in terms of interlocking tangible and intangible asset stocks. Simulations show how this architecture delivers performance through time.

A final suggestion is to sample a PhD dissertation with the intriguing title "How and Under What Conditions Clients Learn in System Dynamics Consulting Engagements" (Thompson 2009). The author tackles the important yet slippery topic of model-based learning drawing on his considerable experience as a businessman, keen observer of system dynamics, serious student in the field and system dynamics consultant. The work involves documented histories, from ten consulting engagements, of clients' learning experiences in modelling projects they themselves initiated. A combination of direct observation, survey, interview and personal reflection provides compelling stories of client insights, significant learning events, 'aha' moments, and some setbacks. Among the client organisations are a pharmaceutical company, a medical care provider, a development bank, a medical insurer, a memory device firm, a community hospital, a shipyard and a manufacturer of steel balls or "boules" (used in the bowling sport of petanque). With applications spanning service and manufacturing, private and public sector, system dynamics is indeed a versatile systems approach to managing change.

References

Forrester J.W. 1961. *Industrial Dynamics*, Waltham, MA: Pegasus Communications (reprinted 1990; originally published by MIT Press 1961).
Homer J. 1993. A System Dynamics Model of National Cocaine Prevalence, *System Dynamics Review*, 9 (1), 49–78.

Kerres B.H. 1999. Orchestras in a Complex World, *Harmony* (Forum of the Symphony Orchestra Institute), 8 (April), 44–58.

Levin G., Roberts E.B., Hirsch G. 1975. *The Persistent Poppy: A Computer-Aided Search for Heroin Policy,* Cambridge MA: Ballinger.

Morecroft J. 2010. Romeo and Juliet in Brazil: Use of Metaphorical Models for Feedback Systems Thinking, chapter 6 in *Tracing Connections, Voices of Systems Thinkers* (editors Joy Richmond, Kathy Richmond, Joanne Egner and Lees Stuntz, dedicated to the memory of Barry Richmond), Hanover, NH: isee systems Publications.

Morecroft J. 2007. *Strategic Modelling and Business Dynamics,* Chichester: John Wiley.

Richardson G.P. 1991. *Feedback Thought in Social Science and Systems Theory*, Philadelphia: University of Pennsylvania Press.

Senge P.M. 1990. *The Fifth Discipline: The Art and Practice of the Learning Organization*, New York: Doubleday.

Sherwood D. 2002. *Seeing the Forest for the Trees: A Manager's Guide to Applying Systems Thinking*, London: Nicholas Brealey Publishing.

Sterman J.D. (editor) 2007. Exploring the Next Great Frontier: System Dynamics at 50, *System Dynamics Review*, 23 (2–3), 89–370.

Sterman J.D. 2000. *Business Dynamics: Systems Thinking and Modeling for a Complex World*, Boston: Irwin McGraw Hill.

Sterman J.D. 1988. *People Express Management Flight Simulator: software and briefing materials*, Cambridge MA: MIT Sloan School of Management.

Sull D. 1999. easyJet's $500 Million Gamble *European Management Journal*, 17 (1) 20–38.

Thompson J.P. 2009. How and Under What Conditions Clients Learn in System Dynamics Consulting Engagements, PhD Thesis, Strathclyde Business School, Department of Management Science.

Warren K. 2008. *Strategic Management Dynamics*, Chichester: John Wiley.

Chapter 3
The Viable System Model[1]

Patrick Hoverstadt

Abstract The Viable System Model (VSM) is a conceptual model which is built from the axioms, principles, and laws of viable organisation. It is concerned with the dynamic structure that determines the adaptive connectivity of the parts of the organisation or organism; what it is that enables it to adapt and survive in a changing environment. It can be used as a comparison against an actual organisation in order to identify weaknesses, mismatches or missing elements in diagnosing a problem and then as a framework for organisation design to resolve a diagnosed problem. Also it can be used for purposes of design from a clean-sheet. At the foundation of the model is the concept of variety, the number of possible activities of the parts and the necessity to limit these to those required for survival. The breakthrough in developing the model was the understanding that this could only be achieved with a fractal (recursive) layered structure. Furthermore at each level the pattern of the regulation of the variety of possible activities must be fractal. The chapter takes the reader through the development of the model and shows how the VSM supports autonomy and adaptablility.

This chapter, written by a highly experienced practitioner, Patrick Hoverstadt, describes the model and its elements from a practitioner perspective supported by practical advice and helpful recommendations on its use.

---

[1]This chapter uses edited excerpts and selected figures from Hoverstadt (2008) *The Fractal Organization: Creating Sustainable Organizations with the Viable System Model*, copyright of John Wiley & Sons Limited.

P. Hoverstadt (✉)
Fractal Consulting
e-mail: patrick@fractal-consulting.com

M. Reynolds and S. Holwell (eds.), *Systems Approaches to Managing Change:*   87
A Practical Guide, DOI 10.1007/978-1-84882-809-4_3, © The Open University 2010.
Published in Association with Springer-Verlag London Limited

3.1   Introduction

3.1.1   What Is VSM and What's It for?

In the 1950s Stafford Beer was a senior manager in a steel company and began to develop new thinking in management by drawing on his understanding of control systems as described by the then new science of cybernetics and on systems theory, particularly from the fields of social research and biology. The complete VSM model was first published in 1972 in 'Brain of the Firm' where he first set out the development of the model through an application of cybernetic principles to the functioning of the human body. When he developed the Viable System Model (VSM), Stafford Beer was seeking to develop a "science of organisation", using systems and cybernetic principles that underpin all organisations (Beer 1959, 1966, 1974, 1978, 1979, 1981, 1985, 1994). His criterion was how organisations create viability, which is the capacity to exist and thrive in sometimes unpredictable and turbulent environments. This requires that organisations are or become ultra-stable, that is capable of adapting appropriately to their chosen environment, or adapting their environment to suit themselves, even if they find themselves in a situation that has not been foreseen. This doesn't just mean that we are looking at a system to fulfil some given or ascribed purpose, we are also looking at how systems create their own purposes and maintain or change those through time.

I'm going to concentrate on the use of VSM to model human activity systems, though as I mention in the "reflections" at the end, there are a number of other uses it can be put to and is put to. In using VSM with Human Activity System organisations as the term is commonly used, there are three principle uses: diagnosis, design and self knowledge. Diagnosis and design are fairly self explanatory. In diagnosis, the modeller uses VSM as a normative model to compare against the real world situation to look for weaknesses, mismatches or missing systemic elements that explain the problem being experienced or at least give a handle on it. Design can either be a clean sheet exercise (let's sit down and design this new organisation), or following on from diagnosis (let's redesign this part of the organisation to deal with the problem). The third common use comes from Conant–Ashby Theorem (Conant and Ashby 1970), one of the basic tenets of systems and part of the internal logic of the VSM. Conant–Ashby says that "every good regulator of a system must be a model of that system" – in other words, your ability to manage an organisation depends on how good your model of that organisation is. Overwhelmingly, the most common organisational model in use is the hierarchical model. Hierarchy is originally a religious concept and is about "nearness to god". The fundamental belief is that the higher up you are, the closer you are to infallibility. In practice, what a hierarchical model actually models is the overt power structure or more prosaically, the blame structure. It doesn't model a number of quite important things you need to know to understand an organisation, such as: what it does, how it does it, how and where performance is managed, how the parts are coordinated, how the organisation adapts, how or where it takes decisions, and on what information those decisions are taken. All of which the VSM does cover. The reason I came to use VSM was simply that it allowed me to understand how organisations work when they do and why they don't work when they don't – far better than anything else I had come across. And so far, I haven't found anything else that comes close to it in dealing with problems to do with organisation.

3.1.2 Overview of the Model

The VSM is presented as a graphical model – a picture with a number of critical components (five sub-systems and an environment) that are connected together in a particular way and are needed for viability (see Fig. 3.1). The subsystems are:

- System 1 – the set of activities that the organisation does which provide value to its external environment, the primary operations (System 1 is drawn in the standard diagram below as a set of circles)
- System 2 – the set of activities or protocols to coordinate operations that are needed to stop the different operations causing problems for one another (represented by the triangles on the right hand side of the diagram)
- System 3 – the management activities to do with allocating resources to operations and ensuring they deliver the performance the organisation needs, which we might call 'managing delivery'
- System 4 – the management activities to do with understanding the environment and the future, with planning and change, the outcome of which is to develop the organisation
- System 5 – the set of management activities to do with ensuring that the organisation works as a system, specifically that there is a balance in decision making between Systems 3 and 4, and also maintains the organisation's identity and ensures that activities undertaken are consistent with acceptable practice, what we would normally call governance.

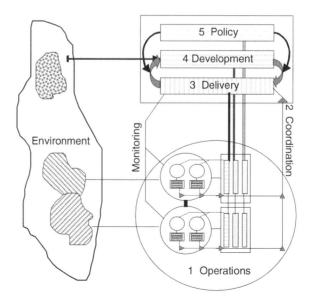

Fig. 3.1 Viable systems model

- The environment is modelled as outside the system in focus and conventionally is represented as an amorphous blob.

I've gone into these sub-systems in more depth in the following sections. The five subsystems are different types of activity that are connected together in a particular way. They aren't necessarily different people or teams or departments. Particularly in a small organisation one person can be performing several of the functions identified above and can be active in several areas of the model if they do different types of activity. Conversely, one circle on the diagram might represent the activity of a whole division of a multi-national organisation. So the model is fundamentally different to a conventional organisation chart in that it represents types of activity rather than "things".

3.1.3 Key Concepts

Beyond this basic graphical model which shows the static systemic structure of the organisation, broken down by type of activity and by the connections between those activities, there are a number of key concepts that we need to address. Mostly these have to do with complexity and the ways in which VSM handles complexity.

The basic VSM model with its five subsystems is fairly simple, how then to deal with a large complex organisation? VSM does this by being a recursive or fractal model. This means that within the "operations" circle of System 1, there will be a set of operational sub-activities, each of which will also be a viable system with exactly the same systemic needs and systemic structure as the whole. So, we have viable systems made up of viable systems which are made up of viable systems and all of which use the same systemic architecture (see Fig. 3.2).

So, a team needs to manage its resources and performance and change, just as the department it's part of does, just as the division the department sits in does, just as the corporation the division is part of does. In practical terms then, we can use a relatively simple model to deal with organisations of any degree of complexity.

The connections in the VSM diagram are just shown as lines, but they actually represent two way communication channels and "variety equations". The VSM is a working through of Ashby's Law of Requisite Variety (Ashby 1956) which says that "only variety can absorb variety", where variety is a measure of complexity – "the number of possible states of the system". What this means is that if we have an environment that demands six varieties of service or product from us and we can deliver all six, then we have "requisite variety", whereas if we can only deliver five we don't have "requisite variety". Which seems pretty obvious – about as obvious as Newton's observation that apples fall from trees – and in management terms about as significant as Newton's Law of gravity was to physics. Why? Because, the environment our system sits in and relates to has much higher variety than the organisation's operations and the operations have higher variety than management, so the question of how to balance these inherently unbalanced variety equations so that the organisation can be managed to carry on delivering what the environment needs is a non-trivial one and the fundamental problem that VSM sets out to address.

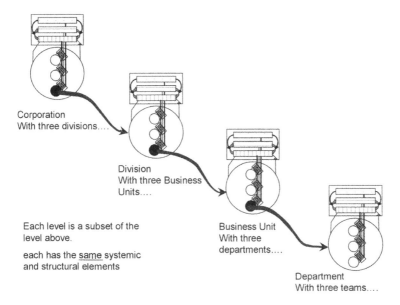

Corporation
With three divisions....

Division
With three Business
Units....

Each level is a subset of the
level above.

each has the <u>same</u> systemic
and structural elements

Business Unit
With three
departments....

Department
With three teams....

Fig. 3.2 A fractal structure

This problem of balancing variety equations which are intrinsically weighted against the management of the organisation drives the two most critical tensions in the VSM: the tensions between the autonomy of the parts versus the cohesion of the whole and the tension between current delivery and future need. Both of these have their own section in what follows.

They are also intensely relevant to two of the fundamental concepts in systems generally: wholeness and emergence. The original basic tenet of systems approaches is that there are attributes – emergent properties – that systems have as a whole that they do not have as components. So, they can only really be understood as cohesive wholes. The autonomy – cohesion tension within VSM is about this. Too much autonomy and all cohesion – the wholeness is lost. Too much cohesion, too little autonomy and emergence is reduced and "wholeness" is impoverished. VSM provides a language to debate how to set this critical balance.

3.2   The Model: Underpinning Concepts, Structure, and Use

3.2.1   Autonomy Versus Control

3.2.1.1   The Horns of the Dilemma

There are few issues in management that are quite as contentious, quite as likely to trigger strong emotional reactions as the question of authority and autonomy. Even within the same organisation, you can find managers who argue passionately that centralised control by a hierarchy is critical and next to them managers who are equally passionate that centralised control dooms organisations to fatal rigidity in a fast changing world. The two sides often caricature one another. The advocates of hierarchy complain about anarchists and the advocates of greater autonomy depict the supporters of hierarchy as slightly sinister control freaks.

The passion betrays the underlying fears on both sides of the debate. Both sides know that the other's arguments have some validity, but aren't completely right. Organisations that are too centralised are too rigid, do find it difficult to adapt to changes in their environment and do die as a result. Organisations that have no centralising decision making structures are incapable of acting as coherent wholes and do fall apart. The problems are real. The dilemma is real and part of the reason for the emotions is that many managers recognise that they are caught in a dilemma – which is not a comfortable position to be in.

3.2.1.2   The Complexity Equation

When Henry Ford started production of the Model T Ford, the world's first mass produced car, he was famously reported as saying that his customers could have it "any colour – so long as it's black". His manufacturing philosophy was in line with Frederick Taylor (Taylor 1911) the great advocate of management control. Taylor reasoned that one of the principal roles of management was to control work practices to reduce proliferating variety. Following the Taylorist line, several generations of managers sought to set down and control how staff did their job, sometimes in great detail.

For many years now, Taylorism has been seen as outdated, as an approach that inhibits change and innovation. For me, the interesting question, and one that is frequently ignored is "what has changed?" For make no mistake, if Taylorism is rightly seen nowadays as generally being an unhelpful approach in today's environment, it wasn't always so. Time was when it worked and worked well. The stunning success of Henry Ford's Model T – 15 million were made between 1908 and the late 1920s at a time when most other makers' models were produced in hundreds or fewer – proves just how successful the Taylor approach was. So if it did work once and doesn't now, why is that? What has changed? The answer is two things, one external to organisations and one internal.

Internally what changed to make the Taylorist formula redundant was increased complexity of technology and skills. At the beginning of the twentieth century, it has been estimated that 95% of workers couldn't do their job as well as their immediate boss. At the beginning of the twenty-first century, it is estimated that this statistic has pretty much reversed, so that 95% of workers can do their job better than their boss. A century ago, when a factory needed to appoint a new supervisor for a machine shop, they would simply promote the best machine operator working in the shop and they would become the new supervisor. Because the most skilled were promoted, of course they could do the job better than their staff. In that context, the Taylorist approach of managers dictating not just what was to be done, but how it was to be done made sense.

Nowadays, it is normally the case that staff understand how to do their job better than their bosses and management is seen as a separate skill-set in its own right, not just something that the best operators will acquire through osmosis. In this context, the idea that managers can centrally control all aspects of operations is simply nonsensical and the level of autonomy of staff has to be radically different from the Taylorist model.

Externally what has changed is the complexity of the environment we operate in. No car company these days could realistically survive, never mind prosper to become the biggest car manufacturer in the world if it was only prepared to offer cars in one single colour. A market that Henry Ford was able to treat as if it was largely homogenous has become progressively more and more segmented and fragmented – more complex. Henry Ford's dream was to bring car production to a position where it could create a new mass market. Whilst other producers were hand crafting individual commissions at luxury prices, the Model T was designed and built by semi-skilled workers and was sold at a price to compete with horse drawn buggies. The market accepted the Model T as a basic no frills product because customers were new to the car market and had low expectations. So out in the environment, the market was simple for the Model T and Ford was keen to keep it that way, hence "any colour – so long as it's black". The problem that Ford did face in his environment was sheer volume, how to build something as complicated as a car in millions, not tens or hundreds. The answer was in the simplification and standardisation of the production process – the Taylor solution.

What Ford created was a balanced equation: outside, a simple undifferentiated market demanding high volume and inside a standardised process capable of producing standard products in high volume. The internal organisation was able to match the complexity of needs of the market by treating customers as essentially the same and offering a simplified product in great numbers. Where there were differences in customer needs, these were not addressed by Ford. They were dealt with by a huge sub-industry that sprung up to service, maintain and customise the basic car. For Ford, business success came from getting the right balance of complexity either side of the equation between the company and its environment.

Of course this equation wasn't stable through time. Increasing customer diversity between customer groups increased the complexity of the market. With the Model T, Ford had effectively been able to ignore differences between customers (other than geographic ones), but as the market matured, customers increasingly wanted not just a basic machine, but one that was suited to their needs and their tastes. To address this emerging problem, Alfred Sloan (Sloan 1962) developed the divisional organisation model used by General Motors. This brought in an organisational structural for GM that had specific units within GM each with its own branding and tasked with servicing a specific market segment. The increased complexity of the market environment was matched by a corresponding increase in the complexity of the organisation and so the equation between operations and environment was balanced once again. To do it, Sloan had to develop new managerial practices. These were designed specifically to cope with the autonomy divisions needed to cope with their different markets. The divisional management structure allowed a degree of autonomy for divisions whilst still retaining overall cohesion. So as well as the complexity equation between environment and operations being in balance, the complexity equation between management and operations was also re-balanced. The formula was successful and propelled GM to become the biggest car manufacturer in the world (Fig. 3.3).

The next revolution came with the creation of the Toyota Production System (Monden 1983; Liker 2003) and here again there was an increase in autonomy to deal with an increase in complexity and now Toyota has taken over from GM to become the biggest car manufacturer in the world.

In the development of the car industry from 1908 we can see three huge shifts in organisational model. In each case, the change was designed to balance the fundamental problem of matching environmental complexity with an adequate operational response that could cope with the complexity of market demands. At the same time, increasing operational complexity demanded an increase in management response and this response was in the form of increased autonomy. The problem the industry faced was a simple problem of balancing complexity using Ashby's Law of Requisite Variety, which simply states that "only variety can absorb variety" which means that complex environments need organisations that are sufficiently complex to match those environments, and organisational complexity needs to be matched by management. Failing to match environmental complexity means that organisations fail to meet what the world demands of them and fail. Failing to match organisational complexity means that management cannot manage effectively, takes arbitrary decisions and fails. The problem is that simple. The same fundamental dynamic that has driven the development of the car industry affects every organisation of every size and in every sector. Every organisation faces the challenge of matching environmental complexity.

The trouble is that the complexity of the environment is theoretically infinite, so we have to be selective as to which aspects of the environment we are bothered about. Similarly, the organisation is more complex than management.

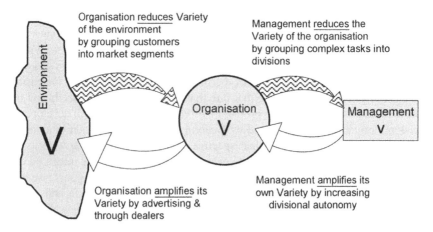

Fig. 3.3 Balancing the complexity equation

Reconciling what is a fundamental set of imbalances is what the VSM is all about. The balance can only be achieved by amplifying management's variety and attenuating that of the organisation and by amplifying the response of the organisation to the environment whilst attenuating environmental variety. Typical attenuators are to standardise and group. So we group individual customers into market segments and the organisation treats them as if they were the same. Similarly management groups complex tasks into divisions and departments and treats them as production systems with common reporting standards, not as individual tasks. Typical amplifiers include advertising to the market, but the most important is probably increasing the autonomy of operational units to address differences in demand. Understanding the level of environmental complexity that needs to be absorbed gives us a practical metric – admittedly a fairly crude one – for understanding the degree of autonomy we need for any organisation. The tension between sub-system autonomy and system cohesion is one of the most important tensions in the VSM.

3.2.1.3   Recognising Autonomy

One of the problems with hierarchy is that it is often an illusion. Even if you take an extremely coercive system such as a prison, where it would appear that the prison staff have huge power over prisoners, the reality is that the system can only function on a consensual basis. If the prisoners really decide they aren't going to play the game, then the system breaks down very quickly. This is even more true in more ordinary organisations where the apparent power of the hierarchy is very often more illusion – or at least consensual, than real.

In a large service organisation, the senior executive team operated a tight control regime. All decision making was centralised including detailed operational and resourcing decisions. There was absolute control of processes in the best Taylorist fashion, with detailed descriptions of how every aspect of operations was supposed to be carried out. Some of the executive team and senior and middle management argued they needed to get away from this "command and control culture". But, you didn't have to look very far before you came across lots of examples of staff ignoring the rules to ensure that the job got done. Overwhelmingly, when staff could see that the prescribed process was dysfunctional and where they could, they exercised the autonomy which was officially denied to them and went outside the official process. Procedures were regularly ignored and processes changed, steps omitted and others introduced. All this was done despite management decree. This wasn't a culture of "command and control", it was a culture of "command and ignore". The senior managers responsible for laying down the processes were blissfully unaware that middle managers were routinely taking control of their own processes. It was all done with the best of intentions and for the benefit of customers.

Leave aside any moral questions about the rights or wrongs of managers wresting control of their processes from senior managers, these managers were exercising their autonomy. They weren't gifted this autonomy. They weren't "empowered" to do it. It wasn't sanctioned. They just did it because they thought it was the right thing to do.

They had the power to do it and their bosses didn't actually have the power to stop them – because they didn't know it was happening.

This was Ashby's law at work again – as inexorable as the law of gravity. There was a mismatch between the complexity of the operational situations these managers were confronting and the responses provided by the officially endorsed processes. So given spare management decision-making capacity in the form of a bunch of smart well educated middle managers, they filled the vacuum and exercised their autonomy. People have autonomy to act whether we like it or not. As managers, we can choose to utilise that capacity, or to try to stifle it, but it exists and when we try to restrict it too much, it will find other outlets.

3.2.1.4   The Resolution of the Dilemma

So what's the difference between a hierarchy and VSM as far as autonomy and control are concerned? The fundamental difference is that in the VSM, it is clear that different levels of the organisation deal with different aspects – different types of complexity. This means that as the organisation is built up from its basic operations, there is a clear focus for management decision making at each level, and generally it isn't about the same things as at the level above or below. This gives a clear marker as to what management at each level should be focused on and what they are equipped to take decisions about and just as importantly, what they aren't competent to take decisions about. This is quite different from a hierarchy where the assumption is that senior managers know more than juniors about everything – down to knowing more about how to shovel coal into a boiler than the guy doing the shovelling. Using VSM, managers at different levels see different issues in the complex world they manage (both organisation and environment) from those at other levels. This means there is a need to have conversations between levels about how to proceed, if decisions at one level are not to destabilise decisions at another level. This doesn't imply that one level is subservient to another, since each is, or needs to be the expert in their particular environment.

The hierarchical model is about power. About who has the power to take decisions and it carries with it the assumption that higher in the hierarchy means better equipped to decide. The VSM is about managing complexity and difference and it carries the assumption that different managers in different parts of the organisation will be best placed to take decisions about their part of the organisation. Neither hierarchy nor anarchy, VSM provides a solution to the perennial debate about autonomy and hierarchy.

Many people have come to the study of VSM with one of two preconceptions. The first is that it is a hierarchical model and it has been severely criticised for this – quite unjustifiably. The second preconception is the exact opposite; that this is a model for organisation without control – almost an anarchist's charter. Both views are wrong. Viability demands that organisations have the capacity to balance the demands of their environment – which in complex environments rules out centralised hierarchies but it also demands systems that can act coherently so as to be effective – which rules out anarchy.

So our attack on the variety problem, requires that management at a particular recursive level agree with its operational subsystems a set of frameworks within which the operational subsystems should operate. The frameworks can only be obtained and maintained by agreement since the knowledge and expertise necessary to manage the whole system lies both in the management and in the operational subsystems. To set up and maintain this set of frameworks is the purpose of system two.

3.2.2   The Structure of Value Creation: System 1

3.2.2.1   Primary and Support Activities

Organisations are difficult things to build and run so there has to be a good reason for having one. The main reason for having an organisation is to do things that an individual cannot do on their own because the task is too complex. Either it is too big, requires more diverse skills than that individual has, or it needs to be carried out in several different places or at different times. In other words organisations are simply a way of coping with different types of complexity.

One of the critical steps in modelling an organisation either for design or analysis is to understand the structure of how the organisation deals with the complexity of the tasks it carries out. When I say tasks here, I'm referring specifically to "primary activities". These are the tasks that the organisation does that deliver value to the external "customers" of the system and I'm specifically not referring to all the tasks the organisation has to do to keep itself in being. In VSM, this is a vital distinction and however we choose to define identity, the distinction between primary and support activities is at the heart of understanding identity – of understanding "what business are we in" (Hoverstadt 2008; Beer 1985). There are different ways of distinguishing between primary and support functions, but the definition I use is based on the concept that there is some sort of value exchange between an organisation and its environment that keeps the organisation in being and that the activities that deliver this value are primary.

As an example, if we take the task of doing accounts in a building contractor, this is not a primary activity. It isn't the accounts that deliver value to the builder's customers. What they value is the building work the company does. By contrast, if we take the task of doing building maintenance in a firm of accountants, the building work isn't a primary activity, whilst doing accounts for customers is primary, because that is the service that external customers value. This distinction between primary and support activities is roughly analogous to the distinction of profit and cost centres in management accounting.

The term primary is a statement of the purpose the organisation exists to fulfil and the expectations that customers have of the organisation. It isn't a comment on the importance of tasks. Doing the accounts in the building company may be vitally important to ensuring that the company stays in existence and is able to service its clients, just as maintaining the building may be equally vital to the firm of accountants.

3.2.2.2   Organisation Structure and Complexity Drivers

So, starting with the primary activities of the organisation, the next question is
"what is the best way of structuring these?" Each primary activity is made up of
other sub-activities which in turn are made up of sub-sub-activities and we can
decompose the tasks as far as we need to go to understand it. Building houses may
be a primary activity of our building contractor, and that might be split down by
building site, by individual building plot, by the different trades involved. If we
wanted, we can carry on the task decomposition to the point where we are focused
on the task of laying an individual brick, or knocking in a nail. Similarly with the
firm of accountants, we could split the task up by specialism: tax, audit, management accounting etc. We can split the task up by sector, by customer, by geographic
area: the London office or the New York office and just like the building company,
we can carry on breaking down the task to the point where we focus on an individual calculation or check carried out. Since the organisation exists to do tasks
more complex, more diverse in terms of skills, geography or time than an individual
can cope with, the way primary activities break down level by level reflects the sort
of complexity the organisation is trying to address. There are four principal drivers
of complexity in primary activities (Espejo & Harnden 1989):

- Technology
- Geography
- Customers
- Time

"Technology" is about doing different things, so plumbing is a different job to
bricklaying in the building firm and auditing is a different job to personal tax advice
in accountancy – these are "technology" differences.

"Geography" is about structuring the organisation according geographic differences: different teams working on different building sites, or in different offices in
the accountants.

"Customers" fairly obviously is about structuring activities according customers, so our accountancy firm might have a team specially set up to deal with big
accounts and keep that quite separate from the team dealing with small clients.
The builders might have a team dealing exclusively with "executive developments".
In both cases, the rationale might be the specialist skills required for those sorts
of customers.

"Time" is about continuing the job beyond the staying power of the individual
or single team. So the most common example is shift systems in manufacturing or
in 24 h services such as the emergency services, but it can take many forms such as
having a duty officer to deal with "out of hours" emergencies.

Whatever the drivers of complexity, in analyzing any primary activity, it is
important to realise that we are simply repeating the analysis process in unpacking
the complexity. The resulting layered structure of system, sub-systems, and sub-
sub-systems, etc. is called a recursive structure. The word 'recursive' indicates that
the structure has the same pattern and properties at each level.

3.2.2.3   The Impact of Complexity Drivers

Primary activities are broken down into sub-activities according to one of these four drivers at each level. The order in which this is done – in other words the order in which the organisation's structure unfolds the complexity that it faces, can have an absolutely massive impact on how the organisation performs.

Let's take as a hypothetical example a government's provision of roads. This might involve two activities – road construction, and roads maintenance, giving us two organisational units using the same technology and in the same geographical area and for the same customers. Most likely one road repair team and one construction team will not cover the whole country, it may only operate in a particular location, let us say Erehwon. So to cover the whole country, there may be many such units that are divided by geography, perhaps on a county basis, all contained within the "Roads" agency, and each in turn containing a road construction and a road maintenance unit.

The "Roads" agency will itself of course be a part of a larger public sector body, say "Transport Infrastructure". In this case, it will be just one of several units that may be differentiated on the basis of technology, so roads may be one agency, railways another, urban light railways another. In this scenario, the diagram shows how the provision of roads is structured from the level of central government to an individual road project, and most importantly, the way that the complexity of this provision has been handled (Fig. 3.4).

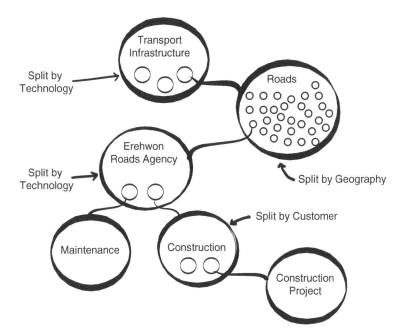

Fig. 3.4 Road Transport Organisation – Option 1

Although we have postulated this as a possible way of carrying out the structural division of transport infrastructure, it is by no means the only way of doing this. It could be done on a regional basis, with each county managing its own infrastructure: rail, roads, light rail, airports, etc. Or alternatively, it could be that regional division is done at the lowest level, and that all road infrastructure, both construction and repair is centrally controlled. A model for this might look like Fig. 3.5.

The critical issue is that the provision of roads to all areas of the country is a complex task, and the way that this complexity is dealt with has profound implications for the way that the organisation operates and the way that it is managed.

For example, in the first model in which we postulated an Erehwon Roads Agency that handled both maintenance and construction, we can easily imagine that it would be possible for the two to coordinate resource usage and swap both personnel and plant as needed. The implications of this may be a more efficient use of resources, but a drop in the speed of response of the road repairs service when maintenance resources were committed to construction.

In contrast, such a pooling of resources would be near impossible using the second model, since construction is controlled centrally, and only maintenance is managed at a local level. There are of course many other implications not only for the operations but also for the management. It is necessary to unfold the organisation's complexity in this way if we are to understand what these implications are for any organisation. In particular, this method allows us to start to look at where within an organisation decisions can be taken, and how resources may be allocated.

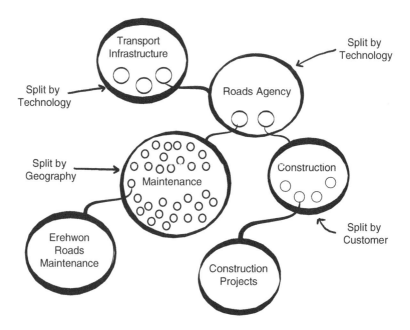

Fig. 3.5 Road Transport Organisation – Option 2

One common example of changing the order in which complexity is unfolded in an organisation's structure and the dramatic effects it can have is the switch in manufacturing organisations from functional departments to "cellular manufacturing". Back in the first half of the twentieth century, it was the norm that engineering factories were laid out in functional departments. So typically, there might be a turning department, full of lathes, a milling shop with milling machines, a drilling shop etc. Jobs would be passed back and forth between these shops having a series of separate operations done on them. This derived in part from the Tayloristic tradition of job specialisation and description which took task decomposition to extreme and assumed that restricting workers scope of work to a relatively few simple tasks would result in greater standardisation and improved productivity. Having worked on a production process with a cycle time of around 90 seconds I can vouch from personal experience that you do indeed get very good at doing it and you do get very fast, but it does get just a trifle boring.

The logic that this sort of task specialisation would be the most efficient seemed irrefutable, until firms started experimenting in the 1950s and 1960s with what was then variously called "group engineering" or as became more commonly know "cellular manufacturing". In this approach, groups of machines were put together in "cells". So rather than different types of machines being used in separate functional departments, there might be a mixture of lathes, millers, saws, drills etc. grouped together, with all the machines being used by a small team of multi-skilled operators. Each cell had the equipment necessary to carry out all the operations to make either a complete product or a complete sub-assembly that would go into a finished product. The results were dramatic. The accompanying table from a study of typical improvements with cellular manufacturing comes from a study done by London Business School of ten engineering companies (Table 3.1).

Don't forget, these improvements came simply from altering the structure of the organisation and therefore the way work was done. Some of the improvements are not too surprising. Reductions in work-in-progress, stocks and throughput time are easily accounted for; in functional departments, delays between operations in different departments are inevitable. A component would sit in one department while all the components in that batch were finished and would then wait (in some cases for days or weeks) till it was sent off to another department to have the next operation in the process done on it. By contrast, in a cell, as soon as each operation was carried out on a component it could be passed directly on to the next machine. In some cases,

Table 3.1 Improved performance from manufacturing cells

	Maximum %	Average %
Reduction of WIP	85	62
Reduction in stocks	44	42
Reduction in throughput time	97	70
Reduction overdue orders	85	82
Increase in sales	32	–
Increase in output per employee	50	33

process cycle times were slashed from weeks to minutes. This meant that at any time, there was drastically less WIP hanging round, fewer jobs in process (so less stock) but all of them moving very much faster.

Reduction in overdue orders is also easily explained, as production planning is very much easier and predictable. If a process that used to take several days because of all the delays built in now takes minutes, it becomes much easier both to accurately predict finish dates and also easier to push through a rush job.

Exactly the same design principles but applied to business process instead of manufacturing, formed the basis of the BPR revolution in the 1990s. Often the results were similarly dramatic, but often, the significance of the fact that what was now being streamlined were now often not primary, but support processes was lost. Very often, there were two ensuing problems: business processes that were hopelessly out of balance with the rest of the organisation and collateral damage to other processes as a result of not recognising the systemic role the process played. An Arthur D. Little survey of BPR initiatives found that of the successful ones, 68% threw up unforeseen harmful side effects.

3.2.2.4   Unpacking Complexity: Diagnosis and Design

Changing the order in which complexity drivers are addressed can change the organisation and its performance dramatically. Many corporate restructurings are about changing this order. Very often though, this is done without any clear rationale as to the relative benefits, or any method for working out why or indeed how one formulation will be better than another. The VSM provides a clear way of addressing this issue and a framework for working out the relative pros and cons of each structural option. There is never one single answer but in considering changes, we can be guided by the natural flow of the work. Each of the tasks we identify as a part of a primary activity is itself a primary activity. It will have its customers within the organisation.

Whenever we make decisions about how an organisation unpacks its complexity, this should be done by mapping this against the complexity of the environment and the complexity drivers operating there. But this isn't a static decision; each organisational response redraws the boundary between the organisation and its environment. When we do that, we can create or shut down opportunities. Each has its opportunities and dangers, but understanding what those are is critical to the decision. Changing the organisation to match unmet need in the environment – addressing a new or different complexity driver – has the effect of enlarging the organisation and changing the organisation's boundary with its environment. Changing the boundary means changing the organisation's exposure to its environment and so can lead to new opportunities or dangers. In health provision, research on new treatments which are intended to address unmet need often end up creating the possibility for yet more research into even more illnesses. Health provision is locked into a cycle of each new treatment creating the possibility for other new treatments, so the "market" for healthcare grows. This is not necessarily a bad thing, but it is certainly a factor that needs to be considered when deciding on the organisation's basic operational structure. Some choices will expose the organisation to areas of the environment with many opportunities and dangers, others will offer far fewer.

In analysing an existing organisation, when looking at how the basic structure deals with the complexity drivers in the environment, as well as looking for the stress each option would put on System 2, we need to check how well each option addresses the complexity of the environment. Are we ignoring important distinctions between customers? Beyond the complexity drivers the organisation needs to address in the here and now, there is also the issue of what direction this will take the organisation in for the future, will it open up or close down future options. We like to think that we direct our organisations, and in a sense we do, but it is also true that our organisations circumscribe the sorts of strategy we are able to envisage and pursue. Our current decisions about how we deliver what we need today will largely determine how we relate to the world and that in turn will determine the future we are able to create. Mostly these choices are unconscious; they need to be conscious if we are not to have organisations that are simply driven by their history.

3.2.3   Maintaining Balance Between Primary Activities: System 2

3.2.3.1   Identifying Needs

We like to think of our organisations working as well oiled machines, where all the parts fit together, working in harmony with one another. Of course, it doesn't always work quite like that. Whenever we have a set of primary operational activities operating with any degree of autonomy, there is the possibility that one operation will do something that will disrupt the activities of another. The function of System 2 is to reduce or prevent inter-operation disruption (Hoverstadt 2008; Beer 1985).

The need for coordination increases with three factors:

1. The number of operational activities
2. The degree to which these can affect one another, or are interdependent
3. The degree to which they affect the same parts of the environment

The more integrated and more numerous our operations are, the more likely this sort of disruption becomes. The integration may be within the organisation, so if operation "A" supplies operation "B" they need to be coordinated. Equally, the connection can be through the environment. If two departments of the same organisation compete for the same customer, or send contradictory messages to the same market, that's a coordination issue. To prevent this sort of internally generated disruption we need some form of coordination between the operational activities at each level of recursion.

An extreme example of coordination problems was a large teaching hospital. With 60 service delivery units, there were too many different disciplines for practitioners to understand what all the other departments were doing. This might not have mattered, if the care each offered was a discrete care pathway, but of course, because they were treating patients, they were related. Patients were no respecters of clinical boundaries. The patient who had come in with a broken hip was the same patient as suffered with Parkinson's disease and dementia, was malnourished and was in the process of getting bedsores. In this sort of situation, coordination problems go way beyond purely administrative issues such as having common standards for patient's notes. Different care needs can conflict and so need some way of sorting the prioritisation of clinical needs. Similarly, for a patient presenting at a hospital with a complaint that cannot be easily diagnosed, coordinating different disciplines to get the right specialist to correctly diagnose and prescribe the appropriate care pathway can be a very hit and miss affair.

Coordination problems have many symptoms that help in identifying them once they're happening:

- Oscillations in performance – the "shock wave" problem
- Low level ongoing chaos
- Cyclical recurring problems in operations – having to solve the same problem repeatedly
- Turf wars and inter-team or interdepartmental disputes

These are all classic indicators of missing or failing coordination. Of course it is always better to identify potential problems before they happen, so look for where there are connections between operational units, either where these are interdependent, or need to be but aren't.

Coordination problems rarely go away on their own. They tend to either occur periodically, simmer away constantly under the radar of management or are escalated to higher management for resolution. When this happens, they often trigger the "control dilemma" which can in turn jeopardise management including threatening strategy, so what appear to be low level and even insignificant operational issues can have a damaging effect on the organisation at a strategic level (Fig. 3.6).

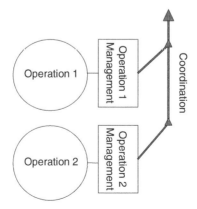

Fig. 3.6 System 2 coordination mechanisms to reduce disturbances between operations

Whenever organisations change, there will be a shift in coordination needs and addressing these will be a critical success factor for achieving change. Where they aren't addressed, they can prevent change happening and in a high proportion of change projects failure to plan new coordination is a key cause of failure. If department "A" is trying to change, but is also dependent on department "B", and there is no way of handling new aspects of their interdependence, managers are faced with changing and risking a breakdown of delivery or of staying with the status quo. Almost invariably given this choice managers opt for the status quo and change programmes stop. So anticipating coordination needs is important for both smoothing operations in the present and for enabling future change.

3.2.3.2   Coordination Mechanisms

Coordination failure, or rather the absence of coordination mechanisms, is one of the three most common systemic problems we see in analysing organisations. Generally, coordination is taken for granted when it is effective and is not correctly identified as the problem when things go wrong. It isn't as glamorous as heroic fire fighting for managers, but it is vastly more effective. We tend to praise and reward problem solving in organisations, but far more powerful than problem solving is problem anticipation and avoidance and this is what coordination does. The reason we take it for granted is because good coordination is so much a part of the infrastructure that we hardly notice it. Imagine a school without a timetable and the chaos that would follow trying by any other means to get 100 teachers synchronised with 1,200 pupils in each of 40 periods in the week to do the right one of 30 different subjects at three different levels in 45 different classrooms. Yet the miracle of organisation that is the school timetable does this and is taken totally for granted (apart of course from by the individuals who slave through the summer holidays to put them together). And it is the same for most coordination mechanisms. We don't notice them when they work and we don't always recognise the need for them even when they aren't present and we are frantically trying to solve the problems the lack of them has caused.

The school without a timetable may seem like a fanciful example, but perhaps no more fanciful than the bank that didn't coordinate training between branches. They sent all its customer service staff off on a 3-day customer care course at the same time so there was nobody actually left to do any customer care. Failed or missing schedules are very common. Production scheduling is one of the most common areas of failure, and particularly the need to keep different operations "balanced". When this fails, we get overproduction in some areas and underproduction in others and work-in-progress piling up in factories.

As well as scheduling, production or otherwise, typical coordination mechanisms include: protocols, mutual adjustment, boundary agreements, common standards, common language, and culture.

In a training department, individual trainers decided what courses they though were needed, and then designed, set up and ran courses. Trouble was that they actually needed the cooperation of their fellow members of the training team to deliver the courses and they needed access to shared training resources such as the training suite and facilities. Because they operated independently without coordination, facilities and people would be double booked. Each time was treated as a new occurrence, with arguments and appeals to the head of training to sort out the mess. In this case there was clearly a need for some sort of schedule for use of shared facilities but also for some protocols for negotiating and contracting colleagues to work on one another's projects.

Boundary issues are a frequent coordination issue. One of the areas where this is most prevalent is in sales territories. Where the boundaries are geographic, this is fairly easy to define, but where the boundaries are more nebulous, it is obviously harder.

An IT company increased the autonomy of its operational units but failed to put in adequate coordination. A salesman turning up at a client to sell a document manage- ment package could find that two competitive offerings from the same company had already been offered to the client. With no coordination, the company was competing against itself and wasting resources duplicating development, sales and support.

In a hospital, there was no coordination mechanism for handling the boundary between cardiac surgery and cardiac medicine. If a patient got referred to a cardiac surgeon, then they invariably got sent for surgery. Occasionally the cardiac medics would refer patients for surgery, but generally, they prescribed drugs. Patients pre- senting with heart problems could end up in either surgery or medicine. The basis on which this life critical decision was taken was the length of the waiting list for the surgeons. If there was a gap in a surgeon's waiting list, then the next patient would be sent in that direction. Coordination problems can have serious and sometimes bizarre repercussions.

In 1999, NASA had the embarrassing and expensive experience of crashing a probe into Mars. It emerged that the problem had been that two teams were using different measurement systems, one metric and one imperial. The thrust applied by rockets to control the probe's position for entering Mars atmosphere was calculated by one group in Newtons and by the other group in pounds force. Each assumed they were both using the same common measurement standard, but they weren't and because there are just over 4 lb force to the Newton, the probe wasn't where it should have been. The issue of coordination by common standards or rather a lack of them is very common and isn't limited to tangible things like measurement stan- dards. Within one single company of just 60 staff, the five operational departments each used different standards for management accounts. With no common basis for comparison, it was impossible to establish which operations were actually profitable. This generated a series of ill-judged investment decisions that destabilised opera- tions when some departments were under-funded whilst others were over-funded. Inevitably, it also created political turmoil.

Working on restructuring a bank in a post-communist eastern European country, a team of western consultants were disconcerted part way through the project to discover that whenever they'd talked with the bank's management about "cash", they had been talking about completely different things. To the westerners, cash was actual tangible money. To the eastern bankers, it was any money that wasn't part of the government's planned economy.

This sort of problem over common language isn't limited to national differences. Amongst a group of pharmacists operating within the same hospital, there wasn't common use of language – not even of their specialised technical language. Different individuals used a range of different terms for the same thing and used the same technical term to mean different things. This is a little disconcerting when we are talking about a group of people trained to be precise and scientific, all working in the same discipline in the same organisation, and especially when they are dealing with potentially life critical treatments. Problems over common language are even more common between departments and different technical disciplines and extend to the choices we make about using the same IT platforms and programmes and of course to the mental models we use. Wherever a message crosses a system boundary: between two individuals, two departments or two companies, it undergoes "transduction" a process of translation in which it inevitably gets changed to some extent. The distortion can be trivial or critical, but the purpose of creating common languages is to build effective transducers that reduce distortion as far as possible.

3.2.3.3   System 2 and the Design of Structure

Within many organisations there is a constant battle going on between support functions trying to get operations to adopt common languages and standards and operations seeking to go their own way. This is one facet of the autonomy – cohesion dilemma. Finance wants everyone to do their budgets and reporting in the same way. IT departments want everyone to use the same programs so support is easier, whilst operational departments often find reasons why they need a non-standard IT program. Both sides of this tension can be legitimate, although it's hard to see the validity of having 400 different knowledge management systems within the same organisation, as one high tech company did. Especially since the purpose of knowledge management is to allow knowledge sharing and this is prevented by system fragmentation.

Sometimes this tension which manifests as a sort of guerrilla warfare over System 2 coordination mechanisms is actually a sublimation of the autonomy – cohesion tension at the level of strategy. Operational departments denied autonomy in the direction of their operations, sometimes exercise autonomy in subverting the common standards that IT, finance, or other departments seek to impose. Whatever the politics, coordination is explicitly about restricting complexity and autonomy. The trick is to identify where there is unnecessary complexity that is destabilising operations and remove that whilst leaving differences that reflect genuine differences between operations. The payback for operational managers of accepting the reduction in their autonomy represented by coordination mechanisms is a reduction in disturbance to their operation by other departments, less conflict and much less fire fighting.

As well as being significant in their own right, System 2 mechanisms are also important in helping to work out the optimal solution to the question of how to organise the structure of value creation. Wherever possible, the basic structure of the organisation should be worked out to reduce System 2 issues. In my view the loading on System 2 is one of the most critical design features and is probably the single most important factor in deciding between structural options.

One of the reasons that cells are so much more productive than functional layouts in engineering is because the structure eases System 2 coordination issues between operations.

3.2.4 Managing Delivery: System 3

3.2.4.1 Line Management

The structure of value creation breaks the organisation down, operational level by operational level and provides the basic seed structure for the viable system (Hoverstadt 2008; Beer 1985). The essential function of line management is to build these component operations back up into a cohesive coherent organisation that can create synergy. I use the term line management in its traditional sense, management responsible for a set of operations – sometimes the term is used to describe someone who has a personnel management role over an individual. In essence, line management is a relationship between an individual, or a team, department or division and the organisation of which it is a part, in which an agreement is made that the organisation will provide X resources in return for the individual, team or department delivering Y performance. This basic equation of resources for performance is key.

The basic design concept is extremely simple, but conventional practice goes against it in several ways, some of them fairly obvious, some of them quite subtle and mistakes in designing a structure to deliver synergistic performance are more than common.

For each set of operational activities identified in the basic operational structure, there needs to be a corresponding set of management activities, starting with the line management role to build cohesion. The purpose of this is to take a set of operations and to create synergy from them. Each level of the organisation delivers some aspect of performance that its individual components can't provide on their own. To do this, management has to ensure that when the performance of the operational sub-systems it manages are combined, they will deliver the performance this level of the organisation itself is responsible for (Fig. 3.7).

The twin strands involved in managing this relationship are resources and performance. The combination of the two into a negotiated agreement between, say, a departmental management and its constituent sub-systems is critical.

For this to work, what is needed is agreement rather than imposition. Arbitrarily imposing performance targets or budgets risks loading impossible burdens onto operations and also risks management basing their decision making and strategy on levels of performance that are not achieved and which may have been totally unrealistic.

Fig. 3.7 System 3 delivery – managing delivery and Synergy, bargaining resources for performance

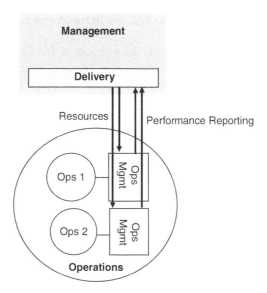

The traditional approach to managing resources is the annual budgeting cycle. So prevalent is this approach that it may come as a surprise to many that it is relatively new and grew to popularity in the post war drive for strategic planning. Relying on a plan meant that both performance and the resources that drive performance also had to be planned. This planning and budgeting system has become a monster that has taken over much of managers' lives – typically between 20% and 30% of senior manager's time. As well as consuming valuable management time, it encourages all sorts of dysfunctional behaviour, particularly gaming and "creative" accounting in resource negotiations. The alternative model being developed by the members of the Beyond Budgeting Round Table is one that will be familiar to many smaller entrepreneurial businesses (Hope and Fraser 2003). Typically, it uses a much more flexible approach to decide on and manage resource deployment –a combination of discretionary agreements that allow managers more autonomy within agreed limits and with the option to decide on new resourcing commitments whenever circumstances demand rather than being locked into a fixed planning cycle. This allows managers more autonomy to manage their resources flexibly whilst still leaving them accountable for results and also allows the organisation to respond quickly to any opportunities or threats that may emerge in their environment.

The key to understanding the autonomy within the recursive structure is the realisation that the management at any one level manages a set of subsystems which (a) operate within the agreed operational framework established and maintained (System 2), and (b) operate to the resource bargain agreed (System 3) beyond that the subsystems have autonomy in the way they achieve their purposes. By these means the operational variety is absorbed at each recursive level in a combination of management and self-management.

3.2.4.2   Common Failures in the Performance Management Structure

Organisations that do not measure performance do not and cannot know how well they are doing whatever it is that they do, so performance measurement has an absolutely key role to play in building an effective organisation. Which is easy to say, but is very often not done well.

The first structural element to getting it right is to not miss out performance measures. In a lot of organisations, performance measures are generalised and are not designed as specific links between elements of the organisation. For every operational element at every level of recursion, there needs to be adequate and appropriate performance measures. This means performance measures specific to each level. Performance measures follow and define the line management structure. They are one of the fundamental links between a set of operations and management at the next level. Missing out levels undermines the viability of the organisation. Missing performance measurement from one or more levels means that there are managers at that level who do not know how well the operations they are supposed to be managing are doing. This is pretty fundamental to doing the job of a line manager which is to take the resources provided by the organisation and use these to deliver performance.

The second common problem is to split resourcing decisions from performance measurement. Often operations find themselves negotiating the performance levels they are supposed to deliver, quite separately from the negotiation about the resources necessary to achieve that level of performance. Since resources come in many forms – people, skills, infrastructure, equipment, IT, money etc. all of which may be managed quite separately, combining all these resources together with an agreement about performance is not always a simple task. Where this fails, then one of two outcomes is likely, either over-resourcing – certain activities have more resource than they can use effectively, or under-resourcing – which leads to a failure to deliver performance, or at least considerable stress in trying.

Problems of misattribution are extremely common in organisations. Measures that are actually about the process carried out by department "A" are attributed to department "B". Although this may sound unlikely and the sort of thing that should be easy to spot, it is actually endemic. The reason is that predominantly, performance measurement systems are not built as feedback systems to inform decision making about specific processes and specific units. The traditional model increases the probability of sloppy attribution, because hierarchical structural models give little clue as to where processes sit and who is actually responsible for which aspects of performance.

In a small national supermarket chain, the performance of both stores and their managers were measured by sales. This is a common conflation between measuring an area of activity or process and measuring the management of that process. In this case, the measure was intended to inform the board about the performance of the store managers so that the board could take decisions about both them and their stores: which managers to promote, or fire, and which stores to expand, change or close. In reality, a store manager's area of discretion had very little impact on sales. Overwhelmingly, the decisions that did affect this measured output were taken by buyers and marketers at central office. What store managers could actually decide about were issues around managing their staff. They couldn't decide what was sold in their store, or for what price, or how it was presented, or where it would sit in the store or when to run promotions, or any of the things that have the biggest impact on sales. These key issues were all taken centrally. So, the performance measures attributed to store managers were actually measures of central staff functions As a result, there were critical control deficits at two levels: at the level of the store and at the level of the central marketing and purchasing functions. At both these levels, appropriate performance measures were not being used to inform management decision making. The store manager's actual performance wasn't being measured, but the board thought it was and made judgements accordingly. At the same time, the set of measures that actually measured the central staff functions weren't used in taking decisions about them. Using a systemic model allows us to look at the systemic consequences of this sort of failure, and in particular what decision processes and hence what decisions are undermined by a lack of information, or misinformation. In this case, that was a whole series of judgements and decisions about individual managers, their stores, and about the management and effectiveness of a set of central functions such as buying, marketing and product positioning. In addition to the diagnostic advantage, this modelling also provides a design template for the design of more appropriate performance measures that do actually provide information where it is needed about the activities that are supposed to be being measured.

The most common problem though is the "control dilemma" (Espejo et al. 1996). Usually regarded by those experiencing it as a personality issue, it is also a structural problem and the structural solution lies in getting the structure of performance management right and specifically in monitoring. The control dilemma occurs when management worries about its loss of control over operations and so burdens operational staff with more and more demands for performance reporting. The increase in demands for performance reports is usually driven by a lack of trust that the information being given is providing either a complete picture or indeed is giving managers the answer they want. The solution is not simply to ask for more reports and more detailed or frequent performance reports, but to monitor. There is a clear distinction between 'performance measuring' and 'monitoring'.

The word "monitoring" is fairly loosely used in management. Here, I am using it to describe a particular set of activities conducted in a particular way. It is an in depth, occasional check by management, not of what their immediate subordinates are doing, but of the reality of their operations. Where performance reporting is by its very nature largely quantitative, monitoring is largely qualitative. A performance report may tell you that late deliveries go up at the end of the month. What monitoring does is let the manager who gets those reports every month, experience the semi-chaos of the shopfloor on the last Friday of the month as production tries to juggle a deluge of increasingly fractious customers and managers demanding that their job be prioritised before the weekend. Armed with that experience, the reports take on a completely different meaning. What seemed perverse and frustrating behaviour by your operations team that prevented you from hitting your target and keeping your promise to your boss is now seen for what it is, a hopeless task in the face of impossible pressures (Fig. 3.8).

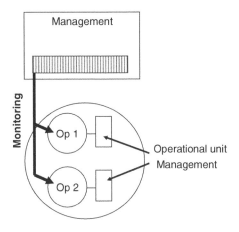

Fig. 3.8 Monitoring channel – supplements performance reporting with sporadic in-depth check of operations at next level down, bypassing one level of management

The requirements of good monitoring can be summed up in four simple rules:

1. It needs to be sporadic.
2. It needs to be unannounced.
3. It needs to skip a level of management.
4. It needs to be in depth.

Monitoring needs to be sporadic if it isn't to become too heavy handed and leave staff feeling as if they are being constantly watched. It needs to be unannounced if it is to show reality, if its predictable, then "window dressing" can hide what's really going on and the exercise becomes destructive. It needs to bypass a level of management if it is to reassure both staff and managers that management has a realistic view of what is going on in the organisation. Whole organisations have collapsed because this simple rule was ignored and managers thought that it was more comfortable just to rely on reports without checking out the reality. If monitoring doesn't jump a level of management, it provides a cover that allows unscrupulous managers to engage in all sorts of unsavoury practices from bullying, through financial irregularity to major undeclared changes in objectives, strategy or working practices.

3.2.5 System 4 – Outside and the Future – Managing Development

3.2.5.1 Systemic Function

The systemic role of System 4, the development sub-system is to ensure that the organisation maintains a healthy fit with its environment (Hoverstadt 2008; Beer 1985). In other words it has to ensure that the organisation is doing the right things

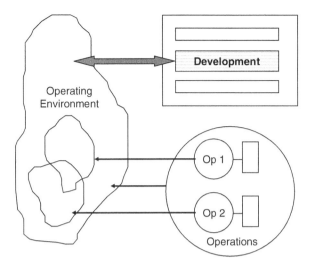

Fig. 3.9 System 4 development – surveys operating environment: Technical, competitive and market developments predicts, plans, creates the future

and able to maintain some sort of value exchange with its environment so that it can remain viable into the future. Essentially, this involves preparing the organisation to deal with changes in the environment and preparing the environment for changes in the organisation, so, predicting and creating the future (Fig. 3.9).

To do this, it has to fulfil several connected but subtly different roles, all of which relate to understanding: the future, the environment outside the organisation and the fit between organisation and environment. Typically these involve:

1. Scanning the external environment for changes or potential future changes and specifically scanning for strategic risks
2. External communications (other than those directly related to operations)
3. Innovation
4. Managing change
5. Building and holding the organisation's model of itself

Failure or weakness in System 4 is endemic in organisations and is one of the commonest pathologies encountered in looking at organisations. This is true for commercial organisations, public sector organisations and also for the third sector. To some extent, this bias against dealing with the future has been enshrined in conventional management doctrine with its emphasis on efficiency.

The failure rates of commercial organisations are evidence of just how common this systemic problem is. Of the original S&P 500 index (the Standard & Poor index of the top 500 US companies) 85% were no longer in business in 2007, so they had failed to survive 40 years. The median life expectancy of European companies used to be 60 years, it has fallen to 12.5 and is still going down. Commercial companies are failing to adapt to their environments at an increasing rate. In the public sector of course, organisational failure rarely leads to bankruptcy.

Where the System 4 sub-system is weak, disconnected or missing entirely, there are problems, both passive and active. Passively, organisations are unable to anticipate changes coming from their environment, are surprised when they happen, are unable to adapt to these changes and fail. In failing to be active, organisations don't innovate, fail to create changes in themselves or in their environment and their relationship with their environment atrophies. Where the capacity to adapt is missing or weak, systems tend to fail when their circumstances change. Of course the more complex the system the more there is that may need to adapt. So large complex systems can collapse spectacularly quickly, although it's usually easy to spot their blind spots, or lack of capacity for adaptation and consequent vulnerability, well in advance

Where System 4 fails, there are a set of mostly very common symptoms.

- Creating new products with no markets for them
- Creating markets without products to fit them
- Failing to adapt to changing markets
- Failing to adapt to changing technology
- Persisting with outdated products
- Overcome by Strategic Risks

Although, these are couched in commercial terms, exactly the same types of failure apply to the public and third sectors, so for example, an international development charity that created a type of intervention that could not be "sold" to intended users in the theatre of operations and simultaneously was failing to recognize or address new crisis areas that had opened up. International development agencies are often unable to match their response times to the pace of unfolding events – a simple lack of requisite variety.

Where development management fails, the organization fails. Often this can be seen long in advance of the actual failure and can be addressed, but many organisations with a lack of development capability are disasters waiting to happen.

3.2.5.2   Managing Change

The statistic generally quoted is that around 80% of change projects fail and when I ask groups of change agents about this, they generally agree that this figure is about right. Clearly, there is something fundamentally wrong with an approach that fails most of the time – if my car didn't get me to my destination 80% of the time, I'd think seriously about an alternative….

The traditional model for managing change not surprisingly is based on hierarchy: change is planned and implemented from the top across the whole of the organisation and cascaded down through successive tiers of management.

It is my experience that traditional change programmes ignore the essential differences between departments or teams and treat the whole organisation as if it was the same. But of course, organisations are not the same throughout. In any change programme, there are always parts of the organisation that can change more easily than others and parts where there is a greater impetus for change. These natural differences mean that change programmes always fragment and this causes two problems. First is the perception that there is resistance. Second is the problem of consistency across the boundaries between parts of the organisation that have changed and those that haven't. These boundary issues become the grit in the change process that creates friction and drives resistance. Gaps quickly develop between teams and departments that are engaging with change and those that are not. These gaps fragment change programmes. Invariably at this stage of programme failure, managers responsible for change switch their efforts away from those areas where they are failing into the areas where they are enjoying relative success. As well as being a pragmatic response to a difficult situation, and a sensible use of their inadequate resources, this is also a very human response. Faced with a task with a high failure rate and given the option between nurturing those parts of the programme that show some hope and those where change is proving difficult, it is entirely natural to support the successes rather than confront the failures. The effect of this focus on the easy targets is to amplify the differentials that emerge, thereby further fragmenting the homogeneous nature of the programme.

In effect, change programmes that are intended to be homogeneous and 'whole company' programmes break down into discrete patches of change. This concentrates the impetus and resources for change coming from management on to just a few individuals or teams. Homogeneous undifferentiated change becomes in practice, heterogeneous, highly differentiated and discrete change. This is an entirely natural process and seems almost inevitable given the circumstances.

This isn't primarily a problem of leadership and it isn't primarily or initially a problem of resistance. In practical terms, problems occur where processes cross organisational boundaries. Where a process crosses two departments, so department 'A' hands information or components over to 'B' and where 'A' is trying to change to the new way of working and 'B' isn't, then managers are faced with a dilemma. If they carry on with change, the process will fail and if they stick with the existing process, then the change will be reversed or stalled. Faced with the dilemma – carry on with change and break a critical work process or forget the change and carry on with business as usual – managers generally take the only possible decision – go back to business as usual.

In Viable Systems terms of course, this problem of resolving cross boundary conflicts is a failure to manage the co-ordination issues and since coordination is one of the three most common pathological archetypes, it isn't very surprising that this happens.

But of course for the plan to succeed, all parts of the organisation would have to move all together and at the same pace. This is clearly unrealistic. Each department is different. Its operational demands and constraints are different. Its people are different. Their ability to handle change is different and the number of changing processes they may be handling at any one time is also different. So of course it is absolutely inevitable that they will change at different rates. Once again, Ashby's law applies, any plan that assumes change will be uniform, lacks requisite variety.

A VSM based approach to organisational transformation approaches the problem in quite a different way. It involves breaking change down into discrete, "do-able" packets and introducing these in a sequence of planned initiatives. These allow managers to concentrate on changing elements of the organisation in a discrete way, whilst managing the interfaces between that element and the rest of the organisation so that change is not prevented by resistance through boundary issues. The sequence of change needs to be planned so that each stage helps prepare for subsequent changes either by creating structural redundancy (often in the form of management time released from fire-fighting) or by removing structural obstacles to subsequent changes.

The two key elements in this "mosaic" approach to system transformation are utilising structural redundancy and discrete packets of change. Change a component, and any other components it directly interfaces with, don't change everything at once.

Structural redundancy is about having spare capacity in the system and the amount and rate of systemic change is directly related to structural redundancy. Change requires requisite variety in the form of spare resources. The scale of change will depend on the availability of resources. Release more, and you can change more. Tackle too much and the resource will be spread too thin and nothing will work. This is of course pure Ashby's Law.

Planning mosaic change starts with a Viable Systems analysis of the organisation, both in its current state and its desired future state. Mapping these two organisational models against one another gives you a list of those bits of the organisation that will be directly affected – in other words all the parts that need to change. As well as giving you this list of potential change packages, it should also tell you about all boundary issues involved in carrying out change. There are direct transfers, such as department "A" being upstream in the same process as department "B", so if you change "A" you know "B" may well be affected. In addition, the VSM should give you all the known connections that department has with others. Existing or future co-ordination issues are particularly sensitive and important.

Following a systemic overview, the next stage is deciding where to start change. This can involve several factors. The general rule is that change must be practicable and worthwhile. Assessing practicability should include evaluating the relative capacity for change of the units concerned. The factors that affect this include:

• Group cohesion
• Experience of and attitude to change
• Skill at changing
• Quality of leadership
• Number and severity of probable boundary problems
• Management resources available to assist change

Assessment of which changes are most worthwhile at any point in the process must take into account both the intrinsic value of the change – i.e. how far it takes the organisation towards the intended destination – and critically, the capacity of the change to create structural redundancy or other factors to aid subsequent stages of mosaic transformation. The factors that aid further development will include removal of structural or process obstacles to subsequent change.

Weighing up these various factors presents quite a complex decision. In many cases, there will be an option between an initiative that is more easily achievable, but less desirable, and one that is more difficult, but will yield bigger dividends. Although, in many cases this will be a matter of judgement, there are some hard rules that will need to be obeyed. First, the proposed change must be matched by the resources available. Although this "mosaic" inherently reduces the probability of management overstretch, it doesn't eliminate it. In some organisations, management resources available to effect change are so stretched that only the smallest systemic changes are practical. Second, there is often in major systemic change a natural chain of progress. This is almost a critical path within the plan of change, such that 'A' has to be changed before 'B' becomes practicable. This interdependency of issues or problems is a systemic feature, and is one reason for the need for a systemic overview of the organisation. Once these two basic rules have been applied, the major consideration is the creation of structural redundancy, since this can be used to create the momentum for further change.

Once change is being undertaken, boundary problems can become as big an issue as the change itself. As well as a functional analysis to identify where these are likely to occur, consideration also needs to be given to non-functional relations, and in particular the political dimension of the context needs to be considered. By making change incremental and planned, a mosaic approach helps to concentrate change management resources, so these can be more tightly focused on the interfaces of the change area and manage boundary disputes.

3.2.6   Strategic Balance

3.2.6.1   The Traditional Strategy Model

The traditional model for strategy development has three principal features. It is linear, it is deterministic and it is based on a hierarchical model. In other words, a management team or board decide a fixed goal or vision and set down a straight path of things the organisation needs to do to move towards this fixed goal and hopefully arrive at the desired destination.

This linear deterministic approach to strategy has been the prevailing paradigm since the 1960s and is based on an assumption that management can reasonably decide on a set of goals about the future of the organisation and that performance can then be measured relative to these goals. This deterministic approach is usually encapsulated in some sort of methodology that follows a linear path that runs: vision, mission, strategy, targets, performance measures. Each step is determined by reference to the previous step (Fig. 3.10).

Fig. 3.10   Traditional model – strategy and performance management

The three basic elements, determinism, linearity and hierarchy are mutually supporting and consistent. If you can determine a goal – your vision – into the future then logically the rest of the strategic process should be a linear development that follows from that vision to get you there. So determinism requires linearity and of course, linearity requires determinism. You can't have a linear process unless you know the destination. Similarly, hierarchy supports them both. It's difficult to get a large group to agree on a single vision. For that, you need a small group of decision makers or even a single (preferably inspirational) leader. Once fixed, the rest of the organisation is targeted by the hierarchy to meet the vision. It is difficult (but not impossible) to do deterministic strategy without a hierarchy and its difficult for a hierarchy to do strategy in any other way.

Unfortunately though, this traditional model has several very major shortcomings. The most important of which is that it very rarely works. Figures vary, but most surveys conclude that over 90% of strategic plans are never implemented and one survey found that 98% of strategic plans were not carried out.

The roots of failure of the traditional model are found in its features, its linearity, its determinism and hierarchy. Firstly, the deterministic approach assumes a degree of environmental stability that is rarely found today. Following a goal that was set in a strategy formulated often years earlier is only sensible if the world still looks the same as it did when the strategy was decided. In many environments, in both the public and the private sector, this is rarely the case. If our operating environment changes faster than we can achieve our strategy, then that goal based strategy is likely to be irrelevant and can even deliver us prepared for a world that no longer exists.

Take for example a leading electronics firm specialising in defence systems. They followed a goal centred strategy to become a global player in the communications market and invested heavily in a market that was new to it – optical fibre technology. By the time the strategy was fulfilled, the market for optical fibre had already peaked and the company was poised for a world that no longer existed. Typically, the planning cycle is run on an annual basis, which means that there can be a very long time lag in the feedback process that tells you that the plan isn't working. In the case of the electronics company, the strategy proved fatal.

Secondly, because it is a linear model, it has performance measures as an output of strategy. You set measures that tell you whether your strategy is working. So this approach ignores the need for performance measures to inform the strategic process as an input. In the absence of suitable performance information, strategy is inevitably misinformed and the result is a proportion of strategic plans that the organisation does not have the capability to deliver. Performance measures need to be, not merely an input to strategy rather than an output of the strategic process, but also designed specifically to provide the information that strategic decision making will need. So a strategic process that reduces performance measures to being an output has problems.

The problems with the linear deterministic model are compounded because of its connection with the hierarchical model of organisation. This may seem paradoxical because the whole point of a hierarchy is to centralise decision making, precisely to make it easier to set strategy. Hierarchies are designed specifically to be unstable structures that allow a single individual or small team to move a whole organisation. So, it may seem odd that in practice, they aren't actually very good at formulating strategies that actually work. What hierarchies are really good at is taking decisions. What they aren't good at is taking decisions that actually get implemented. There is a strong inverse correlation between involvement in a decision process and rejection of the decision or resistance to it. The more hierarchical the decision process, the fewer people involved. The fewer people involved, the less the rest of the organisation will trust it. The less they trust it, the less likely they will be to carry it out and actually implement it.

3.2.6.2   Strategy as an Emergent Property of Structure

The connection between strategy and structure is both complex, and dynamic. Strategy often determines structure, and drives changes to the organisational structure. Less obviously, organisational structure also has an enormous effect on strategy. The two are linked together not just at any one point in time, but also through the passage of time, and this is the dynamic that drives the evolution of organisations.

It is easy to see how strategy drives organisational change. The outcome of strategy is often either a new direction for the organisation or a change of pace. To put these into effect requires some changes either to formal structures (departments, teams etc.) or at least to work patterns and communications.

What is often unseen is the way in which structure determines strategy. The strategic options open to an organisation are limited by the information that is fed into the strategic decision making process. These limitations are not arbitrary, they are structural. Messages come in to the organisation from its environment all the time, some good, some bad, but the organisation can only hear the sorts of messages it is structured to hear. If there isn't a part of the organisation that is tasked with hearing messages on a particular set of topics, then the organisation will not hear those messages. Individuals within the organisation may hear them, but the organisation cannot, unless it has structured itself to hear them. The information may come in to an individual in the organisation but then it just dissipates through the organisation because there is nowhere for it to go.

This may seem bizarre, but we experience it on a regular basis. Ever tried complaining to organisation that doesn't have a customer complaints department? Gradually it dawns on you that you are engaged in a totally futile exercise. As you try to explain to someone in the organisation what has gone wrong, they wait for you to get off the phone so they can get on with their job – which isn't dealing with your problem. The poor employee has heard your problem, but without a structure, it rarely gets any further because they have nowhere to send the information. Exactly the same principles apply to the classic strategic topics. Without some part of the organisation tasked with understanding the market, or changes in technology or economic trends or competitive pressures, decisions will be taken in absolute or relative ignorance of those key topics.

So, the classical assumption that the organisation is an outcome of the strategy because you change the organisation to suit the strategy is true, but it's only half-true. The reverse is also true, because the organisation's strategy is also an outcome of its structure. This may seem contradictory but of course, what it means is the structure and strategy are linked together in an evolutionary cycle in which the structure affects the strategy, which affects the structure. The obvious outcome is that the organisations follow evolutionary pathways that are largely determined by who they are now and they progressively evolve to become more "themselves". This is a natural evolutionary process of organisations structurally coupling to their environments and is quite different to trying to force change through goal setting. This approach does carry a risk of the organisation becoming increasingly culturally and informationally closed. The way to avoid this danger is by ensuring that the intelligence function is operating effectively. If it is pulling in diverse information about what is happening in the environment and specifically monitoring strategic risks then threats to the relationship that is emerging with its chosen environment can be avoided.

3.2.6.3 Strategic Conversations

Systemically, good strategic decision making relies on balancing the capabilities of the organisation as it is now, in its current operating environment, against the demands that it needs to address in its environment and in the future. As the environment changes, as demands change, those changes need to be detected, or better still anticipated, and brought into the strategic debate. Seeing a need for change creates a "strategic gap", a gap between what can currently do, and what we have identified that we are going to need to be able to do in the future. The process of strategic decision making is then to work out which of the identified strategic gaps the organisation should close, and how this should be done. And this is what strategic decision making does, it opens and closes the strategic gap to drive the organisation's continuous evolution and adaptation through time. Closing the gap is primarily the job of "delivery management" (System 3). Opening up the gap, in the sense of perceiving it, making it explicit to the organisation, and making practicable is the job of "development management" (System 4).

All management disciplines tend to have their own areas of interest and their own language. Consequently communication between them can be difficult. Marketing and operations don't talk the same language. They don't see the world in the same way and indeed aren't even looking at the same bits of the world. Both are different from the finance department who speak another language and view another landscape. And yet, despite these very real differences, we need all these different specialist interests and others to come together if we are to come up with strategies that are practicable and appropriate. Robust decision-making, coming up with a strategy that actually gets implemented, requires that all aspects of the strategy are examined (Fig. 3.11).

If our strategy involves introducing a new product currently in R&D for example, then R&D (System 4) need to check with operations (System 3) that they can produce it. Finance needs to be involved over both short term cashflow implications

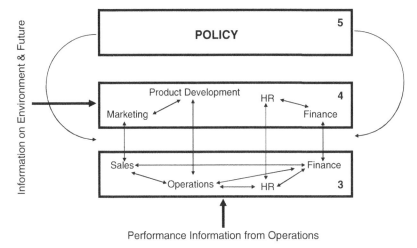

Fig. 3.11 Management decision structure. Typical set of strategy conversations, connecting different disciplines on a range of interdependent issues. With System 5 ensuring the decision structure's integrity by integrating internal and external issues

(System 3) and longer term investment planning (System 4). HR may well need to be involved on short term staffing arrangements for operations (System 3) and for either recruitment or training (System 4) if current capability doesn't already exist. Similarly marketing (System 4) needs consulting early on about market opportunities for the new product and sales (System 3) about how the new product might disrupt existing sales. This is a complex set of conversations and not one that can follow any pre-set process. In reality, these are interdependent not independent issues and the outcome of one conversation may require us to go back and revisit another. So operations may agree with HR that they need to recruit new staff and retrain others to make the new product, but a conversation with finance may force them both to think again.

3.2.6.4   Getting the Balance

Within this decision structure there are two very different types of management behaviour. On the one hand, there is that part of management engaged in running the organisation as it is now, and all the behaviours that go with that. Trying to optimise, measuring performance and resource usage and seeking greater efficiency. On the other hand, there is that part of management engaged in developing the organisation and creating the future. This involves scanning trends, analysing market needs, creating options, researching and developing products, technologies and markets and planning how to move forward into the future. These two sets of activity are both essential, but are pulling in opposite directions.

Good management of the organisation as it is now, so it operates efficiently is essential. Without it, the organisation will struggle to survive in the short term and as the saying goes "without a short term, there is no long term". Equally important however is the need to envisage and create a future for the organisation. Without development and adaptation, the organisation will lose its "fit" with its environment. It, will fail to provide goods or services that a changing world values and will die. So both types of management activity are essential to survival.

The problem is that whilst both are essential, they are also in tension, and in several different ways. They require different types of thinking, so individual managers are predisposed to one or the other. They require different types of information, so the organisation's management information system can provide biased support. Most obviously, they are in tension because creating the future inevitably involves reducing the efficiency of the present.

Any action to change the organisation to meet future needs, inevitably involves using resource. No adaptation – not even one aimed at improving efficiency is entirely cost free. There always has to be at least some "pump priming" and if we are talking about major strategic change in the direction or identity of the organisation, then this generally requires a significant call on resources and particularly management resource. All of this inevitably reduces the short term efficiency of the organisation and disrupts managers' attempts to run a "well oiled machine". As well as diverting resource, it also diverts attention away from the efficiency issue and so has a political effect of tending to undermine the importance of those managers focused on the here and now.

The result of this dynamic tension between stasis and change is that organisations are often unbalanced to either one side or the other. This strategic balance is acted out in the 3–4–5 balance. Where this favours System 3, strategic decisions tend to be of the "do more of the same" or "do less of the same" variety, so strategies are about growth or retrenchment, but not about doing something different. This can be fatal if the nature of the environment has changed and requires something different from the organisation. Where the imbalance is in favour of System 4, then organisations can develop strategies that involve changes of direction, the development of new markets, new innovations, or new technologies. This can be fatal if the new direction isn't within the capability of the organisation and the strategy is unrealistic or unachievable. Where it is in balance, organisations are able to develop strategies that do involve genuine changes of direction but ones that are within their capacity for change.

3.2.7   Identity and Governance: System 5

This is a tricky section both to write and to get to grips with, because we need to address two different issues in parallel. Firstly there is the issue of "how to analyse/design System 5 of the VSM" – the bit responsible for governance and identity. Secondly there is the issue of "how do we define the identity of the system we are analysing/designing using the VSM so we know what we are looking at". This a paradox, because in the

VSM we are not just talking about modelling a system to which we have ascribed an identity, we are looking at how an organisation modelled as a system creates, maintains and recreates its own identity for itself. Inevitably then, these two: the identity ascribed by the modeller and the identity the organisation creates for itself, connect at some point and need to connect. So in this section I'll be flipping between these two perspectives. In practice, this flipping is a necessary sense check – is the model of the system we are building actually aligned with the organisation's own self construction of identity. This does not mean, modelling the system as it has been described in some sort of "mission statement". Organisational identity isn't the prerogative of senior management, so the comparison is between the view of identity the modeller started with and what the analysis reveals of how the organisation builds its identity. A further complication is that there are different ways of defining identity depending on the purpose of modelling.

3.2.7.1   Defining Identity

When building a VSM I use two different approaches to defining the identity of an organisation as a system, depending on the purpose of the modelling exercise (Hoverstadt 2008). The first is a fairly conventional one which is to define the system by "purpose", by what the system does. The second is to define it by its "structural coupling".

The first uses a formula "a system to do x by means of y for purpose z". This type of definition is embedded in a set of stakeholder relationships which can be categorised using the mnemonic TASCOI (Espejo et al. 1999)

T = Transformation, what the system changes from what into what
A = Actors, those carrying out the transformation
S = Suppliers to the transformation process
C = Customers, those in receipt of the transformed product
O = Owners, those responsible for ensuring it happens
I = Interveners, those with an interest in the process

I use the approach of defining by purpose when designing a new system and when problem solving. In this latter case, because problems are not things in the real world, they are essentially a gap between how someone thinks the world should be and how they perceive it to be, defining perception is critically important. More specifically the perception of the person who wants their problem solved as to the purpose of the system is critically important.

I use definition by structural coupling in any other situation and specifically when analysing an existing organisational system. Rather than looking at purpose and from a specific viewpoint, this is definition by relationships. So the organisation is defined as a system that has a set of relationships with different parts of its environment in which some value exchange happens which affects the structure of activities (in other words causes you to do something different). The advantage of this approach is that it involves modelling the same organisation from multiple viewpoints at the same time. The organisation will have multiple relationships each of which may have radically different perspectives of purpose, value and significance. Since the interaction of these perspectives and value judgements may be significant, this approach gives a more rounded model than modelling from a single named perspective.

Defining identity by structural coupling is actually to define the system in a very literal sense – to define by its de-fined limits, by its boundaries. Whenever we put a boundary around something, and in our case around a part of an organisation, we are defining something. We are deliberately separating what is inside from what is outside the boundary. We are saying that inside the boundary is different in some way from everything else outside. This creates an identity for what is inside. This happens whether we like it or not, every time we build a boundary. Every time we set up a new team or department, or business unit, we create a new identity. So, identity is an aspect of structure and the boundaries we create or the ones that we or other people recognise.

The significance of boundaries and identity here is that confusion over boundaries and therefore identity is becoming an increasingly common source of mismanagement as organisations adopt new forms in an increasingly complex global environment. From a modelling point of view, when you have an organisation that has outsourced key systemic functions, there are sometimes difficult decisions to be taken as to where you define the boundary of the organisation.

3.2.7.2   Systemic Function of System 5

The systemic function of "System 5" is to do three distinct but related things. Firstly it has a governance role for the organisation, ensuring that the organisation is functioning as a system capable of managing itself and of steering a course that will keep a healthy fit between the organisation and its environment (occasionally, this will involve dissolving the organisation if that is the most appropriate thing to do). Secondly, it needs to create, maintain, or recreate the identity of the organisation. Thirdly it needs to maintain an understanding of the relationship between the system-in-focus and the meta-system, the system within which it is embedded.

Each of these roles is fairly nebulous and in practice, this is often the most difficult of the VSM sub-systems to identify, not least because when it's working well, it's nearly invisible.

Given the elusive nature of System 5, it is often difficult to spot where the capacity is that performs its roles and in practice, it's often easier to look for connections than actual tangible resources like a team. Once we get high up an organisation, we'd expect some sort of "board" which should be fulfilling some of these roles. If we look at the specific System 5 task of ensuring there is a balanced debate between System 3 and System 4, within a board (where we might expect such a debate to take place) this is the role fulfilled by a good chairman.

In formalised project management environments, "project boards" nominally at least play some of these roles, although often this is pretty nominal. Once we get down to the level of a department or team though it may be much less formalised.

If we think about the roles of System 5 in the context of a board (because that's where it's most obvious) and the connections needed, and how we might spot those, then there are three we need to look at:

1. The governance connection – specifically to maintain the balance between System 3 and System 4 in formulating strategy.
2. The governance connection into lower levels of recursion in the organisation to hear alarm calls that levels of management might filter out.
3. The connection to the wider system within which our system-in-focus is embedded.

In looking at the connection to ensure a balanced board debate to create a viable strategy, when you watch a well chaired meeting of this sort, the role of the chair is almost invisible, but everyone has had space to voice their views, and been listened to.

There has been much talk in the public sector about whistle-blowers. Much of this has been slightly schizophrenic, they are approved of by ministers when the whistle is being blown on public sector bodies behaving in a way ministers don't approve of, whilst they are pilloried when the whistle is being blown on ministers themselves. Part of the System 5 governance role is to be able to hear these messages from deep in the organisation that things are not as they should be. External whistle blowing – going public is a sure sign that this function isn't being discharged. There is no single right answer as to how this particular connection should operate, some CEO's and chairmen do it effectively by "walking the floor" by physically making themselves available to staff, but there is a limit on the size of organisation you can cover effectively in this way. Informal networks can work well and in organisations, there often are particular individuals or chains of individuals who fulfil this systemic role, conveying messages up the organisation that all is not as it seems or is reported and that there are problems being hidden.

The third connection to understand the system-in-focus's place within the wider system in which it's embedded – which of course impacts on its understanding of its own identity. Formally, this includes things like engagement in industry bodies, professional or trade associations and societies. Benchmarking exercises to compare your organisation to others in the same sector can also help. It explains the systemic role or potential systemic value of the time CEOs and chairmen spend on golf courses and other similar apparently trivial activities. This sort of networking with peers outside of the organisation's immediate stakeholder network is vital to the role.

For each of these types of connection, there are equivalents at any level of recursion. Some of these will be easier to assess (like being accessible to danger messages) others less so.

3.2.7.3 Symptoms of Failure and Pathologies

Where governance fails, we see the disintegration of the organisation. The most sensitive areas are the balance between delivery (maintaining the status quo) and development (change) and the measuring and monitoring of performance.

Where either of these are under-resourced, disconnected or simply missing, the organisation is likely to fail whenever circumstances become unfavourable. These are disasters waiting to happen. A common manifestation of this is the "Death Spiral". Systemically, the problem starts with a failure of governance to ensure that there is a balance of strategic decision making and specifically a failure to address external and future factors. When the complexity of the environment changes, this isn't noticed. Because of the failure to prepare adequately, operations respond to the environmental changes erratically. This triggers either inter-unit instability or inter-vention by higher management (control dilemma) or both. This reduces the ability of the organisation to respond at both the operational and the strategic level. As a result, operational responses to environmental change are inadequate and the organisation starts to fail. If management notices – and often they don't – they usually go into crisis mode – bunker mentality. This further reduces their ability to address the problems and reinforces the initial isolation from external intelligence. At this point, the organisation can usually only be saved by external intervention. Either an injection to the management team, or a further change in the environment is needed. In other words, organisations in this state only survive by luck. The process starts with a failure of governance (Fig. 3.12).

For me, the Death Spiral illustrates two things well – apart of course from showing this all too common mode of collapse for organisations. The first is just how critical Governance is for the sustainability of organisations and the second is the systemic nature of organisations and the problems they have.

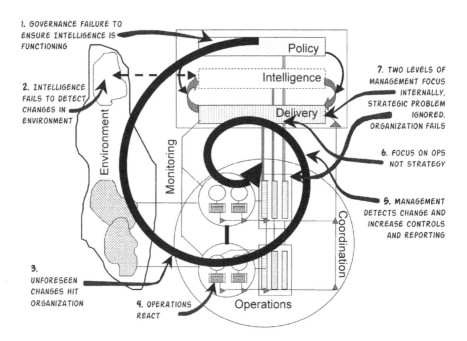

Fig. 3.12 The Death Spiral

Where governance is weak or focused on compliance or on internal control, in other words for most organisations, the death spiral is a disaster waiting to happen. As our organisations become increasingly complex internally and operate in increasingly uncertain and turbulent environments externally, failures in the critically important role of governance will continue to drive up the failure rate of organisations.

The Death Spiral is also a good example of how organisations operate and fail systemically. Failure of one part of the organisation can cause a chain reaction throughout the rest of the system. A possibly long standing failure of governance creates a flawed strategic decision structure, which goes unnoticed until the environment changes which then causes a sudden failure in operations which in turn triggers a collapse of strategic response. As the spiral winds its way inexorably inwards, so the time the organisation has to react shortens. Usually, the governance problem could have been addressed years in advance of the crisis, but by the time the crisis hits the senior management team cut off in their mental bunker, there may be only days or occasionally even hours to save the organisation.

This means that understanding these systemic linkages is critically important and also that doing so gives us the opportunity to deal with many organisational weaknesses well in advance of their manifesting as actual problems. This all relies on understanding how different aspects of decision making need to interact, understanding how these relate to operations and to the environment. In short it depends on understanding how the organisation operates as a system. In this way, the model of organisations outlined in this book is totally different to other models of organisation such as the hierarchical model which model organisations as static structures. The essence of this approach is that it models organisations as dynamic systems co-evolving with their changing environments.

3.3 Reflections

3.3.1 Model or Methodology

It's easy (particularly in this sort of context) to lose sight of the fact that the VSM itself is a conceptual model not a methodology – you do need some sort of methodology to apply it, but it is not itself a methodology, it's a model of organisation. As a model, it encapsulates some principles, laws and axioms of organisation, but it isn't itself a methodology – a way of addressing a situation, much less a method – a step by step process of investigation. The differences this makes are profound. A lot of systems knowledge is bound up in methodologies and some of the rest of this reader covers some popular methodologies, but VSM isn't really like that. It has often been criticised for not being a methodology on the grounds that this makes it harder to use. Well it does and it doesn't.

I think there are two reasons why VSM practitioners have often been reluctant to go down the methodology route. The first is that methodology tends to be focused around one type of application – say problem solving, whereas people use the VSM in a very wide range of fields and for a very wide range of purposes, so methodology can be perceived as restricting. The second is that the basic methodology for VSM is so simple that it hardly warrants the term. Essentially VSM methodology consists of pattern matching – you take a real world situation, compare it to the VSM as a normative model, see where there are differences between what you perceive in the world and the normative model, and then see whether those differences tell you anything useful or interesting about what you see as this real world situation. Which is pretty simple, but also pretty non-specific.

Beginners often struggle with the question "so where do I start then?" and of course the one sentence methodology above doesn't help you with that. The good news is that it doesn't necessarily matter where you start although some routes to building a model will take you much longer than others. Some practitioners have resorted to some quite linear methods to help and these take you through a series of modelling steps to build up a "complete" model. Some of them are even quite good.

But, if you talk to seasoned users, they don't usually do that. They very often don't even bother building a "complete" model. They just seem to go quite quickly to the core of the organisational issue, whether this is to do with analysis or design and they focus on that. Part of the reason is that they tend not to use linear methodologies and partly it's that they often start their analysis in a completely different way to beginners.

Beginners to the VSM will often see it as a sort of static model, maybe not much more than a rather complex organisational chart, and proceed by doing a "filling in the boxes" exercise. But of course this is only part of the picture. Systems models tend to be more about the connections than the things they connect – after all, it's the way things are connected that gives rise to emergent properties. In the VSM, although it's presented as a graphical model and the connections between the component subsystems of the model are shown as lines or arrows, what each of these represents is a feedback loop and a complexity equation. What we are actually looking at is how the organisation reconciles the fact that the environment is more complex than itself and that its operations are more complex than management. Each of these complexity equations has a dynamic or expresses a dynamic tension. If we can maintain requisite variety, we have some degree of order, if we don't have requisite variety then we have chaos. In the terms used by complexity theorists, Ashby's law defines the edge of chaos and what the VSM models is the organisation's ability to walk the edge of chaos. It's very far from being a static model. So, experienced modellers become acutely sensitive to spotting chaos or stasis, either actual or potential and analysing the systemic roots of these two weaknesses. At the same time as they are "filling in the boxes" they look for these imbalances and focus their attention around those. In problem solving of course this is particularly useful, most presenting problems in organisations have a requisite variety component – either as their root cause or as a symptom, so sniffing these out and chasing them down can often provide blisteringly fast diagnosis.

So the pattern of investigation is often much more of a "natural" hunting pattern than a linear methodology. Different areas of the model may be briefly explored – maybe an initial sketching in of the boxes, and if that shows up a missing connection or a lesser failure to maintain requisite variety, then that deserves deeper attention, otherwise move onto another area of the model and sketch that out.

The dynamics of complexity imbalances also provide a rich source of prediction. If for example you know the environment is changing faster than the organisation can plan its response, it isn't hard to work out the sorts of symptoms you are likely to find and to check out whether those are present. As well as being a reassuring sanity check on your analysis for the modeller, this loop from initial analysis, through checking symptoms and feeding back into the model can have dramatic impact with anyone in the organisation. Being able to explain the systemic causes of existing pain and predict future problems can have a very strong emotional impact and help "buy in" to the model and the modelling process.

So experienced modellers tend to flip between modelling the static elements of the model (people and teams fulfilling specific systemic roles at particular levels of recursion), to the dynamics and back again. To the untrained observer this process can appear rather arbitrary. The comforting thing is that while in any particular situation there are some routes though an analysis that may be very much faster than others, the slow routes should still work, they just take longer. This means that for the inexperienced practitioner, the question of "where do I start?" is much less important than with many systems approaches.

Following a "dynamic" approach is easiest when problem solving, as very often the presenting problem will be analysable as a variety imbalance issue. Once this is established, the next step is to model which variety balance it is, so where in the VSM it fits – for example, is it between two operations or between operations and the operating environment, and then to model the static elements around that imbalance.

When tackling an analysis from the other direction, starting with the static structure, most modellers may start by defining the identity and then unfold the recursive structure of primary activities that fulfil that identity. From there the other subsystems from 2 to 5 are added. One approach is to progress from static to dynamic across the subsystems. So once the identity and recursive structure are defined, first look at whether there is capacity to fulfil the systemic role of each of the five subsystems, then whether it has the connections it needs as set down in the graphical model, then whether there is requisite variety across each of these relationships. This progressive approach has two advantages, it's thorough and it can save time by leading you quickly into an analysis of requisite variety and therefore of dynamics. Obviously, if there is no capacity to maintain a systemic link, there can't be any connection and if there isn't a connection where there needs to be one, then the system cannot have requisite variety. So this approach can lead you fairly quickly from tangible aspects of analysis – "is there anyone fulfilling this systemic role?" through to "if not then we can't have requisite variety so are these sorts of issues being dealt with?" to "so does that explain the chaos/pain/uncertainty?"

3.3.2   VSM as a Source of Methodology

VSM has been described as a "master organising idea" and what was meant by that was that in providing a model of organisation, it offers a framework to understand how other management approaches fit together (or don't). This can be massively important.

For example in a recent (2009) project on Business Intelligence in commissioning in the NHS, the distinction which is very clear in the VSM, between Business Intelligence information (System 4 to the environment) and performance management information (System 3 to System 1), was critical in the diagnosis that some trusts were missing the intelligence information altogether because they'd confused the two. With no clear model of the difference between intelligence and performance measurement, all "data" was treated as if it was the same – irrespective of its source or true meaning. What this meant was that instead of taking decisions based on System 4 intelligence about the health needs of the population and commissioning services to address those, they were taking decisions based purely on how hospitals performed in discharging their contracts. The implications of this were that they would base their decision making purely on performance management data about the status quo, leading to a cycle of repeating old patterns. With no intelligence to tell them when provision was out of step with need in the environment, the status quo could not be successfully challenged and areas of health inequality could not be addressed. In practice, this diagnosis was confirmed, trusts that didn't incorporate intelligence, but only relied on performance data were unable to take "cycle breaking" decisions.

As well as acting as a framework that provides a context for other approaches, the VSM has also been a fruitful source to develop methodology for some common management issues. So there are "VSM" derived methodologies for: software development, change management, performance measurement, strategy development, strategic risk, innovation strategy, knowledge management, finance management, management accounting, and governance. Generally these are radically different to the traditional models and methodologies which tend to be linear and deterministic rather than systemic.

3.3.2.1 Different Applications

I've talked about VSM in terms of an organisational model to look at "human activity systems" and the emphasis has been on formalised, systems that the casual observer would recognise as entities in the real world – companies, hospitals, charities that sort of thing. But of course, VSM isn't just a model of organisations it's a model of **organisation** and it's relevant in many other domains.

Firstly it's widely used to model systems made up of a number of organisations, from the socio economic system that is a nation state downwards. So for example one project I was involved with was to model the system for decision making about nuclear waste in an EU country. This wasn't a single "organisational entity" it was a system composed of around 20 different organisations interacting to do decision making about what to do (or indeed not to do) with nuclear waste. Whereas other organisational models really struggle with this sort of situation, the power of the VSM to make sense of big complex systems really comes into its own.

The first book Stafford Beer wrote on the VSM was "Brain of the Firm". In it he mapped the VSM to a known viable system – a human being. The VSM is a model of the human nervous system. For many years, "Brain of the Firm" a book on management was a standard teaching text in medical schools as the best available text on the working of the human nervous system. In fact more copies were sold to medical schools than to business schools. Since then, it's been used to model a number of biological systems, from single celled organisms to bee colonies. The "mosaic" approach to change which is based in VSM is also the way species evolve – structurally redundant components get recycled and used for new and different functions to create new capabilities.

As well as being a biological model of the individual human, VSM can also be used to understand individuals as activity systems. A whole variety of personal issues such as identity – the maintenance of structural coupling, personal integrity, "work life balance", personal decision making, managing personal change and relationships can all be usefully modelled with VSM. I personally struggle to maintain a balance between System 3 and System 4 – I find it all too easy to create more new opportunities and developments than I can deliver on. In true Conant–Ashby style, modelling that dynamic does help me to manage it better.

The VSM has also been used to design software. There have been databases and operating systems designed using VSM as a structural model. Two of the holy grails of software development are adaptive self regulating software and reusable software. Operating systems designed using VSM made significant steps towards those goals. The database design approach that uses VSM allows for a much more evolutionary approach to handling big systems development and integration than conventional approaches. The adoption path here has been software designers and computer scientists looking for a model that would allow them to do what they needed and finding VSM rather than VSM enthusiasts running off to develop some software in a fit of enthusiasm – in other words, it has been adopted by necessity.

To my eyes the oddest application of VSM has been in the arts. Whatever you think of their music, once you know that both Brian Eno and David Bowie are VSM aficionados, its hard not see their musical careers in a completely different light. In the visual arts, there have been a number of artists who have incorporated some of the concepts underlying VSM into their work and more broadly, cybernetics have been widely taught in art colleges where it gave a handle on the issues of how identity , the mutability of identity and meaning is constructed. In popular culture, cybernetic concepts have been a major influence on science fiction, not merely at the very superficial level, but again in the issues of the construction and self construction of identity and meaning.

3.3.2.2 Ethics

It may seem odd that quite a lot has been talked about and written on the VSM and ethics. Indeed some of the early critiques of the VSM were based on an ethical criticism of what it was supposed (incorrectly) that the VSM represented – an improved model of hierarchy that would help those in power to control people more easily. Conversely, some have seen the VSM as negating all centralisation and taken the handle it gives on the significance of autonomy as an anarchist's charter. In fact of course the VSM is not a charter for either anarchists or dictators and in both these cases, it will show the limitations of each position, although the "anarchistic" faction have been less sensitive to the messages the VSM has about the limits of anarchy than the dictators have about what it has to say about the limitations of totalitarianism. But then I guess you only get to be a dictator by being intolerant of any limit to your power, real or implied, so they would be sensitive.

There's another aspect to the ethical debate which rarely gets mentioned and that's to do with ethics and recursion.

As you go up levels of recursion, you go up levels of logical concern. If you take a particular level of recursion as your system-in-focus and define its identity in terms of "what" it does, then the level below will be defined by "how" it does it and the level above by "why". These are different levels of logic and at each level the system engages with different issues and looks at a slightly different bit of the environment. What may seem appropriate at one level may seem very inappropriate when viewed from a different level even within the same system, because another level of recursion will see different consequences of the same action. A lot of common ethical problems fit into this architecture, something which is seen as a good at one level of the system which is seen as bad at another. This isn't just a phenomenon you can observe, it provides a basis for predicting and modelling ethical issues, both their appearance and their structural and systemic drivers. This in turn feeds into the design and running of governance.

References

Ashby, W. R. (1956), *An Introduction to Cybernetics*, London: Methuen.
Beer, S. (1959), *Cybernetics and Management*, London: English Universities Press.
Beer, S. (1966), *Decision and Control*, Chichester: John Wiley.
Beer, S. (1974), *Designing Freedom*, Chichester: John Wiley.
Beer, S. (1978), *Platform for Change*, Chichester: John Wiley.
Beer, S. (1979), *Heart of Enterprise*, Chichester: John Wiley.
Beer, S. (1981), *Brain of the Firm*, 2nd Ed, Chichester: John Wiley.
Beer, S. (1985), *Diagnosing the System for Organisations*, Chichester: John Wiley.
Beer, S. (1994), *Beyond Dispute*, Chichester: John Wiley.
Conant R. C. and Ashby W. R. (1970), *Every Good Regulator of a System Must be a Model of that System*, Int J. Systems Sci, vol. 1 No. 2 p. 89–97.
Espejo, R., Bowling, D., and Hoverstadt, P. (1999), *The Viable System Model and the Viplan Software*, in Kybernetes, Vol 28 Number 6/7, 661–678.
Espejo, R. and Harnden, R. (Eds) (1989), *The Viable System Model: Interpretations and applications of Stafford Beer's VSM*, Chichester: John Wiley.
Espejo, R., Schuhmann, W., Schwanger, M., and Bilello, U. (1996), *Organisational Transformation and Learning*, Chichester: John Wiley.
Hope, J. and Fraser, R. (2003), *Beyond Budgeting*, Boston, Mass: Harvard Business School.

Hoverstadt, P. (2008), *The Fractal Organization*, Chichester: John Wiley.

Liker, J. (2003), *The Toyota Way: 14 Management Principles from the World's Greatest Manufacturer*, New York: McGraw Hill.

Monden, Y. (1983), *The Toyota Production System*, Industrial Engineering and Management Press.

Sloan, A. P. (1962), *My Years with General Motors*, New York: Doubleday.

Taylor, F. W. (1911), *The Principles of Scientific Management*, New York: Harper and Brothers.

Chapter 4
Strategic Options Development and Analysis

Fran Ackermann and Colin Eden

Abstract Strategic Options Development and Analysis (SODA) enables a group or individual to construct a graphical representation of a problematic situation, and thus explore options and their ramifications with respect to a complex system of goals or objectives. In addition the method aims to help groups arrive at a negotiated agreement about how to act to resolve the situation. It is based upon the use of causal mapping – a formally constructed means-ends network – as representation form. Because the picture has been constructed using the natural language of the problem owners it becomes a model of the situation that is 'owned' by those who define the problem. The use of formalities for the construction of the model makes it amenable to a range of analyses as well as encouraging reflection and a deeper understanding. These analyses can be used in a 'rough and ready' manner by visual inspection or through the use of specialist causal mapping software (*Decision Explorer*). Each of the analyses helps a group or individual discover important features of the problem situation, and these features facilitate agreeing a good solution. The SODA process is aimed at helping a group learn about the situation they face before they reach agreements. Most significantly the exploration through the causal map leads to a higher probability of more creative solutions and promotes solutions that are more likely to be implemented because the problem construction process is wider and more likely to include richer social dimensions about the blockages to action and organizational change. The basic theories that inform SODA derive from cognitive psychology and social negotiation, where the model acts as a continuously changing representation of the problematic situation – changing as the views of a person or group shift through learning and exploration. This chapter, jointly written by two leading practitioner academics and the original developers of SODA, Colin Eden and Fran Ackermann, describes the SODA techniques as they are applied in practice.

F. Ackermann (✉) and C. Eden
University of Strathclyde Business School, 40 George Street, Glasgow, Scotland G1 1QE

M. Reynolds and S. Holwell (eds.), *Systems Approaches to Managing Change: A Practical Guide*, DOI 10.1007/978-1-84882-809-4_4, © The Open University 2010.
Published in Association with Springer-Verlag London Limited

4.1   Summary

The underlying essence of SODA (Strategic Options Development and Analysis) is that it is an approach that enables *problematic situations* to be explored more fully before making a decision. This process is carried out using a technique called cognitive or cause (or causal) mapping which is a fundamental part of the SODA approach. Mapping allows views to be captured and structured in a 'means-end' format (for example, this issue might lead to this outcome) thus generating chains of argument. Therefore a map can be seen as a representation of how somebody or a group construes a situation and therefore helps them makes sense of it before considering action. Thus it is synthetic. In the figure below some of the considerations surrounding the issue of writing a good second edition of a book can be seen. The central statement is the issue of concern, those statements linking out (consequences) reflect the objectives, and those linking in are options and constraints. Where there are minus signs at the head of the arrow, this represents a negative link namely managing teaching and admin demands may lead to NOT finding the time.

The unfolding map thus enables exploration of the situation. This can be done through a simple visual examination of the map, or when working with a large model, can be assisted through the use of specific analyses designed for mapping. By capturing the full extent (as much as is possible given time and resource constraints) the approach helps enable participants to take a more holistic view allowing the analyses to reveal the 'nub of the issue' – the one or more statements that are most central and which have a significant impact upon desired ends (individual values or organizational goals). The exploration will also highlight options, causes and constraints. The analyses can also uncover self-sustaining vicious or virtuous cycles suggesting dynamic behaviour. When working with large maps (comprising

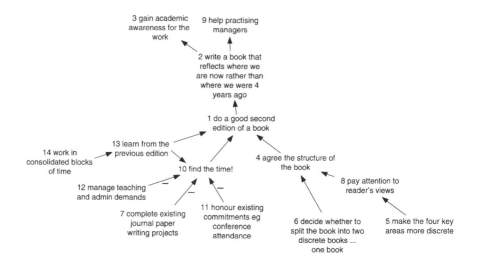

the views of many participants) specially designed mapping software – *Decision Explorer* – can be used.

Although SODA is most commonly used with groups, the approach has also been used at the individual level to explore how best to manage a particular situation (whether it be personal or managerial) (see Bryson et al. 2004b, for examples). However, as noted in Chapter 1, one of the key emphases of SODA is the capture and structuring of multiple perspectives, and to facilitate this emphasis, there are a number of different modes. These modes range from manual interventions to those that are extensively supported through technology.

In most of the modes of working, the capturing, and knitting together, of perspectives is carried out in a publicly viewable manner which ensures that participants feel that the process is procedurally just (Kim and Mauborgne 1995) through all being involved in contributing. Furthermore by opening up the apparent problem situation and exploring all of its facets, participants gain a wider and more sophisticated appreciation and feel that the resultant direction appears more robust and procedurally rational (Simon 1976). As such, participants feel both emotional and cognitive commitment to the outcomes, increasing their likelihood of implementation. Widening the scope and involving participants therefore helps avoid making poor decisions that are either unsustainable or not owned (Nutt 2002). It also helps to protect against the traps of reductionism and dogmatism.

Thus SODA is an approach which aims to encourage the facilitator/consultant to bring together two skills. Firstly, skills relating to the *processes* involved in helping a problem solving team to work together efficiently and effectively in reaching workable – politically feasible – agreements. Secondly, skills pertaining to the adoption of a framework which enables the construction of a model comprising the *content* – the interconnected issues, problems, strategies and options – which members of the team wish to address.

4.1.1   What Does It Look Like (Basic Characteristics/Attributes)?

The SODA framework constitutes four important and interacting theoretical perspectives. These perspectives include: the individual (cognitive psychology); the nature of organizations and groups (as negotiated enterprises); consulting practice (the interaction between a facilitator and client group); and the role of technology and techniques (to allow the construction of a visually interactive model). Each of these perspectives leads to the core notion that drives SODA: the application of a facilitative device – the construction of a publicly viewable model amenable to continuous change and analysis to support group working.

Recognition of the *individual* implies drawing on a theory of cognition particularly in relation to the psychology and social psychology of problem solving. This is evidenced in SODA through one of the main tenets underpinning the approach, that of a Theory of Personal Constructs' (Kelly 1955). Within SODA, construct theory has practical significance through cognitive mapping (Eden 1988).

As noted above, the 'cognitive map' is a model of the 'system of concepts (or statements) used by a person to communicate the nature of the situation – the way they make sense of their world'. The model represents the meaning of a concept by its relationship to other concepts – providing context – and through an action orientation. Thus, any statement about an aspect of the situation is given meaning either by suggesting consequences/purposes – why this 'fact, assertion, proposal' is important, or by providing explanations for the statement being made – how this circumstance or proposal has been derived or come about. In other words, statements are made as a way of representing a person's 'making sense' of the situation/ problem they believe is faced by the group.

Thus, in an organizational setting the manager is taken to be involved actively in the psychological construction of the world rather than the perception of an objective world (Thomas and Thomas 1928). So it is the interpretation of an event that is reality. Action arises out of the meaning of situations, and the meaning will vary from one person to another even if the summary descriptor of the event is agreed by both individuals to be similar. Thus individuality – expertise, wisdom and experience – is legitimate and allowed to blossom within a SODA intervention.

In *organizations*, teams are created in order that each member of the team may bring a different perspective to an issue. A different construction of a problematic situation comes from having a different role and from a different set of experiences and wisdom. Individuals, within an organizational setting, thus will use all methods of communication in order to negotiate with and persuade others to their viewpoints. However, exploiting individuality implies deliberately encouraging more richness in problem construction by accentuating complexity within problems – complexity of multiple perspectives and complexity from more data. Moreover, a view of organizations which focuses on the individual will inevitably also focus on the organization as a changing set of coalitions in which politics and power are significant explanations of decision making.

Consulting practice centres on the role of negotiation in effective problem solving. The consultant is the instrument for facilitating the negotiation, and for managing consensus and commitment. The consultant is taken to have a central professional role in both *designing and managing* this negotiation. Finally the *tools and techniques* employed by SODA comprise the use of cognitive or causal mapping and associated software – *Decision Explorer*. This software acts as a means of both visual interactive modelling (Ackermann and Eden 1994) and analysis.

4.1.2   What Is Its Significance (Why Use It)?

SODA's main contribution is that the approach helps groups manage complexity inherent in messy complex problems-balancing the management of content with the management of process. It pays explicit attention to all three of the purposes argued to be behind systems thinking in Chapter 1.

Underlying this notion of success is a view of problem solving that focuses on the point at which people feel confident to take action that they believe to be appropriate. The use of SODA recognizes that there is never a right answer to complex problems but rather a better or worse answer. Complex situations suggest dilemmas and paradoxes for a team, and consequently approaches such as SODA encourage informed judgment as opposed to a search for optimal solutions.

4.2   Strategic Options Development and Analysis (SODA): A Detailed Exploration

SODA has its foundation in working with 'multiple perspectives' in order to more fully understand a situation. Each member of a client group is held to have his or her own personal subjective view of what they regard as the 'real' problem(s). Thus tapping the wisdom and experience of participants is a key element in developing decisions with which participants feel confident. And, it is because of the complexity and richness that arises from attention to subjectivity that SODA provides a means for managing *process* as well as *content*. Thus SODA through attending to behaviour, judgement, and decision making in organizations sees experience-gathering as an act of 'scientific' endeavour, where managers experiment with their organizational world, learn about it, develop theories about how it works, and seek to intervene in it.

To facilitate an appreciation of both the approach and its practice, we begin with a short introduction to the method before examining each of its constituent parts. Commencing with an examination of the cognitive/cause mapping technique (its formalisms and benefits), we will then address the analysis of maps, before concluding with the processes and considerations of working with groups.

4.2.1   Introduction to the SODA Method

4.2.1.1   Where Has SODA Been Used?

The SODA method was initially developed in the 1980s (Eden et al. 1983) and has been used extensively with organizations public and private, large and small, at senior and middle management levels. Example organizations include: Shell International, Reed Elsevier, Grant Thorton (Australia), the Northern Ireland Prison Services, the National Health Service, Scottish Natural Heritage, Quantum Media, Scottish Water, AMEC Process and Engineering, Strathclyde Poverty Alliance, Cardonald College, IKAD (France), SES Global, Bombardier, Strathclyde Police. A SODA intervention may take as little as half a day where there is urgency or significant resource constraints or can encompass a number of days. SODA has also been used for individual problem structuring (see Bryson et al. 2004b).

4.2.1.2   Conceptual Background

Alongside taking cognisance of the four perspectives as noted in the summary, the overall approach is essentially based on the framework shown below (see Fig. 4.1). This draws on the theoretical frameworks mentioned earlier and also illustrates how the tools and techniques support the overall approach.

As can be seen from the framework, the bedrock of the methodology is based on theories relating to psychology (Personal Construct Theory) and organizational behaviour. These theories are augmented by further concepts attending to both the intervention impact (the role of the consultant/facilitator in an organization) and its implementation. In the centre is the method – which not only takes cognisance of the theories but also recognises the need to manage the environmental consider-ations, the desires of the client, and effective group working. The tools and tech-niques support the method. Below are further details for each of the five elements.

4.2.1.3   The Theoretical Framework

Personal construct theory: This theory was developed by a psychologist called George Kelly who argued that people continually and actively anticipate events

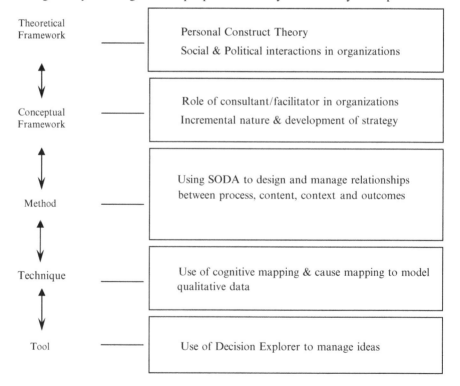

Fig. 4.1 A Framework illustrating the various theories, techniques and processes underpinning SODA

through a process of hypothesising what might occur in the future based on existing experience and subsequently testing out these hypotheses (Kelly 1955). From this experience new constructs are added to the existing set of constructs. Thus people make sense of their world by comparing and contrasting events, observations, facts, etc. to determine their meaning and to help navigate the future. The body of knowledge, what Kelly referred to as a "construct system", is finite, and is made up of bipolar constructs. A bipolar construct is one which contains the contrasting or opposite pole and can be expressed as "this rather than that". For example, I wish to study Management Science rather than Financial Accounting.

Kelly proposed 11 corollaries, five of which are particularly pertinent to SODA's focus on problem solving and therefore through that particular lens can be seen as:

Construction: constructs are used to model an individual's experiences and build up a worldview. This relates closely to Karl Weick's notion of sense making (Weick 1979) which was influenced by Kelly.

Organization: individuals organize constructs hierarchically; they have super ordinate, core and peripheral constructs. As such at the top of the SODA hierarchy are values/beliefs – driving forces for us as individuals – with those further down the hierarchy either representing issues (events that affect positively or negatively our values) or options/constraints (explanations and alternative courses of action). This structure helps us organize and make sense of the constructs and experiences.

Individuality: individuals construe events differently through differently perceiving and interpreting things from a situation. An example here might be that it is raining (something it does frequently in Glasgow). One person might construe this as being a good thing (maybe they are from a water board) as it ensures that the reservoirs and dams are filled. Another might perceive it as a bad thing – they have forgotten their umbrella. Finally a third, particularly if it is winter, might perceive it as a good thing – if it is raining in Glasgow then there is a good chance it is snowing in Glen Coe and they can go skiing this weekend. Each has an entirely different interpretation of the same event. Recall a meeting you have recently attended. Was your view of what occurred during the meeting the same as others? Did the minutes of the meeting bear any resemblance to your understanding of what was agreed?

Commonality: the success of a decision making team depends upon the ability of member's to understand how each interprets the situation as there will be similarities and differences between their experiences. Returning to the exercise suggested above (thinking about a meeting), by surfacing and understanding the different experiences gained, a shared or common language can be developed. A good article to read for further insights on this is Eden et al. (1994).

Sociality: which relates to the fact that decision makers need to find a common way of not only construing events (especially future events) but also in designing and working with options in order to be able to reach a consensus.

4.2.1.4 The Conceptual Framework

Social and political interactions in organizations: As noted in Section 4.1.2, rational analysis alone does not achieve change – organizations are made up of people who are persuaded to carry out some activity or change some operation. Thus organizations might be considered as "political cauldrons" where different and shifting coalitions emerge in order to get things done. Understanding who has power (in its different forms) is key to making changes – if any meaningful changes are to occur then there will be winners and losers and thus a change in the balance of power. Some will work to stop the changes going ahead and others will work towards ensuring their implementation. Understanding who these stakeholders are, and what their bases of power are, is an important aspect of change management. (For a good understanding of stakeholders and their management, see Ackermann and Eden 2010.)

Role of consultant/facilitator: There are two important aspects of facilitation worth considering when planning a SODA (or any) intervention. Firstly any intervention made by a consultant/facilitator (regardless of whether they are internal or external to the organization) raises expectations that something might change (for the better or worse). This has a number of consequences. One is that those involved will act to 'manage' this intervention in a way that is most beneficial to them. Another is that expectations will be established that need to be dealt with.

Secondly the act of talking to someone changes people's minds. As Huw Wheldon of the BBC put it: "How can I know what I think until I hear what I say?" (Huw Wheldon of the BBC quoted in Life on the Air, by David Attenborough BBC books, London, 2002, p. 216), and notably paraphrased by Weick as – 'how do I know what I think until I see how I act' (Weick 1979). For an example of this at work, think back to when you have had a problem and you have gone to talk it over with a colleague. Half way through your explanation, you see the way forward; thank your colleague and leave. The very act of having to frame/structure the problem in a way your colleague can understand and therefore help you, provides sufficient aid to help you move forward.

Incremental nature and development of strategy: As noted above, change is difficult and the greater the change, the more resistance will be exhibited. Therefore it is important to find ways of gaining the commitment of those involved through involvement and understanding. As Lindblom (1959) wrote "often constant nibbling is a better substitute for a large bite".

4.2.1.5 The Method

Process, content, context and outcomes: As noted above, SODA comprises paying attention to both Process (namely considering power, politics, personalities, and people – the skills traditionally encompassed by Organizational Development facilitators) and Content (traditionally Operational Research skills of capturing, structuring and analysing problem statements). The significant aspect being that one informs

Fig. 4.2 The relationship
between Process Management
and Content Management

or influences the other – P × C (see Fig. 4.2 from Eden (1990)). An example of this
might be that as a result of the analysis of the data one particular issue emerges as
central and therefore the most appropriate place to start the workshop – content is
therefore informing process design. However an alternative might be where one
particular issue is contentious and therefore should not be tackled first as the emotional state of the group is not ready – here process is informing content
management.

Understanding the context is also important. Attending to context along with
reflection on the outcomes agreed during the intervention requires decision makers
to consider (a) whether there are sufficient resources available – both in terms of
cash and staff time and (b) whether there is sufficient support for it – from both up
(senior management) and down (staff) the organization. Most of the contextual
implications arise as participants discuss the nature of the problem situation –
thus, options are contextualized through beliefs about the possibility of their implementation. In this way problem definition arises from issues of problem solution.
The 'outcomes' attend to what the 'client' (the person initiating the intervention)
hopes to achieve. It is important to spend time exploring the aims and objectives
of the intervention in order to ensure that SODA is best suited to help resolve the
situation. For further information see Eden and Ackermann (2004b).

4.2.1.6   The Technique

Cognitive mapping and cause mapping: This technique, the bedrock of SODA
encapsulates the strongest link to Kelly's work. Building on the Repertory Grid
technique developed by Kelly, cognitive mapping was designed to enable a representation of somebody's construal of an issue to be created. It is important to note
that both representation and construal are significant to the process. Returning to
the corollary of individuality – construal deals with how the person whose views
are being 'mapped' sees the world. It is a subjective picture (rather than an objective truth) and one that gives insights into how the particular individual might act
in the manner articulated by Thomas and Thomas, namely "if men define events to
be real, they are real in their consequences" (Thomas and Thomas 1928).

Maps in essence are networks (directed graphs) comprising nodes (constructs/
statements) and links (causal arrows). As such, chains of argumentation are built up
revealing both the richness of the area of concern and also particular characteristics

of it – for example, different aspects or themes, dilemmas, significant concerns and contradictions.

Cognitive maps are those maps that attempt to represent cognition – and therefore are focused on a single individual. Causal maps are those that are produced either from the amalgamation of cognitive maps, or from using the Oval Mapping Technique or mapping live using *Decision Explorer* (see later on in the chapter). The notion of group cognition is problematic as even if the constructs being captured appear to say the same thing, the map will not reflect a single cognition but rather fragments of a number of different cognitions.

Cognitive Mapping has been used extensively and not just in problem structuring (Ackermann and Eden 2004; Bryson et al. 2004b). The mapping technique, its use, attributes, and guidelines will be presented in the next section along with some exercises. For further information on the origins and theoretical underpinning of cognitive mapping see Eden (1988).

4.2.1.7   The Tool

Use of decision explorer to manage ideas: *Decision Explorer* (formerly *COPE*) is a software package that replicates the mapping process whilst also enabling rapid search and analysis, and providing the means to view as much or little of the captured material as desired. Working as a form of relational database, the software allows maps to be viewed and amended (either in groups or individually) and helps manage the complexity of the situation at hand (rather than simply reducing the complexity).

4.2.2   SODA and Cognitive/Cause Mapping

4.2.2.1   Mapping: What Is It? Where Can It Be Used?

It is first worth noting that there are many forms of cognitive or cause mapping each corresponding to a different theoretical basis. Whilst all forms of mapping aim to elicit causality they do so using a variety of coding procedures. Some examples include the work undertaken by Laukannen (1998), Langfield-Smith and Wirth (1992), Bougon, Weick and Brinkhorst (1977), Huff (1990), and Huff and Jenkins (2002). Understanding that the nature of cognitive and cause maps can vary will avoid later confusion when reading around the field.

Mapping has been used to great effect for a wide range of different purposes and applications. Below are a few of the main reasons mapping is used in the SODA method:

- *To structure thinking through capturing chains of argumentation, dilemmas, etc.* By being able to capture all of the statements (constructs) along with their relationships (causal relationships) maps present the means of being able to identify the key issues, consider the breadth of considerations, and identify inconsistencies in our arguments. This relates back to the corollary of construction and organization. Let's look at an example experienced by one of the authors:

> A while back a member of our department had a messy problem. She was a lecturer (on probation), who was working on her PhD, whilst looking after her 18 month year old son. In addition, her husband was working in the Middle East and her main home was in Cumbria (around two hours drive away from where she was working). Things were tough. Whenever she thought about her job she remembered that she needed to get the PhD completed in order to get off probation. However that meant working in the evenings and weekends. Having Raymond (her son) however meant that if she was working full time as a lecturer along with completing her PhD she needed to keep on the nanny. In fact a large percentage of the money she earned went to pay for the nanny! Her husband couldn't help – he was too far away. And then there was the issue of the house and all the things to do there. She found herself awake at night constantly worrying about the situation. Knowing I used mapping to help decision makers she asked me to do a map for her. Over the course of an evening we produced a map. There was nothing new on the map – she was aware of all of the statements captured. However the fact that the map did capture all of the concerns, assumptions, aspirations and issues in one place and showed how they impacted one another meant that she could stand back and see the 'wood for the trees'. Her immediate response was a sense of relief, now she could begin to make sense of it all and plan appropriately. She could see the implications of doing option A compared with option B, she could understand exactly what it was that she wanted (her goals) and identify the major issues. After some time deliberating upon the map, and another evening spent adding further material to it, she made her decision. She went and saw the Head of Department and stated that she was resigning. She explained why she was doing this, and showed him the map along with the concerns and options to demonstrate the rationality of the decision.

It is not untypical for the nodes/concepts on the map to be well known and understood – the advantage lies in taking what is often a mess and *reformulating it into a structure* that can then be worked with. Complex problems like these, with lots of interconnected issues or decision areas (Friend and Hickling 1987), are sometimes referred to as 'wicked' (Rittel and Webber 1973) or 'messy' (Ackoff 1981).

The map also provides insights and a sense of control that can sometimes result in there being enough clarity to move forward to action without doing any further analysis (see Eden 1987).

- *To present ideas in a graphical, rather than linear, form.* In many, if not all, situations there are links between the various pieces of information. Think back to when you take notes: often you find yourself drawing a link in from one point to another to show a relationship. The graphical format not only allows some rough analysis to be carried out (see next point) but also enables more material to be captured on a single sheet of paper facilitating further exploration. In this type of use there is some similarity with 'mind mapping' (Buzan and Buzan 1993), although mind maps are not constructed in a formal manner and so are not amenable to analysis.
- *To carry out 'rough' analyses.* For example by looking at a completed map it is possible to determine which are (a) the key issues (those with lots of statements linking to and from them), (b) potential goals/values (those that are at

the top of the map hierarchy with statements only linking in to them), as well as (c) properties such as self-sustaining or controlling feedback loops. This scan of the map to detect its emerging properties often can be a powerful way of summarizing what has been said as it provides added value and highlights areas not yet captured. When doing it for yourself it also provides the opportunity for further reflection.

- *To share more easily, through capturing more statements and links on one single A4 page.* Connecting with the idea of presenting statements in a graphical form, not only does the map help its constructor understand the situation better but also it will help others appreciate the construal. For example, when working with a group from Shell involved in the development of an Expert System, one of the comments from a member of the group involved in the project was that maps were a great way of (a) ensuring that the knowledge captured from the expert was valid and comprehensive as the map reflected what had been said in a natural and transparent manner, and (b) sharing the complexity of this knowledge with colleagues. This was because all the *statements were on one page together with how they related to one another.* Meaning could be deduced from concepts that were linked to, or from, one another.
- *To allow a more 'objective' stance to be taken.* Returning to the earlier example about the benefits of structuring thinking, one of the advantages of mapping is to be able to stand back, to reflect on the various explanations and consequences and therefore take a view that is more 'objective', in the sense of being *a fuller view*. Therefore it is possible to 'play' with the material, exploring how different options might achieve objectives and reflecting on which are the significant or busy statements.
- *To capture wisdom, 'tacit' knowledge and experience.* One of the difficulties experienced when trying to understand a situation is that the material provided, at least in the first instance, can be fairly superficial. People revert to well rehearsed scripts. Think about a particular event currently unfolding – it might be something global, like the credit crisis, or it might be something more local and relevant to your organization. In either case, you have probably had numerous conversations about this to the point that whenever anyone asks you about it, you are easily able to respond, without much cognitive effort. Essentially you have built up a repeatable script.

  Mapping however enables further exploration of the issue or problem through its focus on *teasing out* explanations (laddering down) for particular assertions/statements along with determining the reasons why (laddering up) particular issues matter. In this way a deeper level of insight is gained.
- *Improve interviewing capability.* It is often very difficult to do a good interview. If the interviewee speaks in a monotone, and it is a warm sunny afternoon, and you are tired, then the propensity to mentally 'drop off' or begin thinking about something else is very high. Moreover, taking linear notes is very passive – you don't have to understand what is being said – just note them down. Mapping however demands that more *active listening* takes place. As

such, there is an overhead in terms of effort because it forces you to not only capture the points but understand what they mean – otherwise it is not possible to be able to capture the relationships. As a result you are likely to understand far better what is being proposed rather than finding yourself in the position of either not understanding your linear notes (or the point being made) or realising that you missed a vital question, such as whether one aspect had an impact on another.

4.2.2.2 Building a Map: How a Map Is Constructed

There are a number of aspects to consider when mapping. If we go back to the point about mapping's origins being based on Kelly's Personal Construct Theory and that each construct can be seen as bipolar then we need to attend to the content of the statement. But we also need to consider its context.

A good way of illustrating this is to start with an *attribute map* (see Fig. 4.3). In the centre is the focus of the map – 'good rather than other teachers'. The three dots (an ellipsis) is used as a short hand for 'rather than'. Having the contrast to 'good' namely 'other' provides some additional meaning by providing *content*. For example, the contrast could have been 'poor', 'excellent', or 'innovative'. In each case the contrast adds depth to our understanding. If we then look at the attributes surrounding this statement (*the context*) we can see that they are also bi-polar giving the reader more of an understanding of what is meant by each of them, and an enhanced understanding of what is meant by a good teacher. Try thinking of a few more attributes that might denote a good teacher along with their opposite poles.

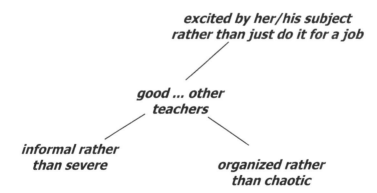

Fig. 4.3 An attribute map (From Eden et al. 1979, p. 45). Reprinted from Eden, C., Jones and Sims, D., '*Messing About in Problems: An Informal Structured Approach to Their Identification and Management*', p. 45, Copyright (1983), with permission from Elsevier

If we take seriously the premise that meaning can be derived from context lets look at Fig. 4.4. We can see that in both instances the same central focus (A) has been used. However, the context around it (B, C, & D or Q, R & P) is different suggesting quite different interpretations. Let's consider an example. Imagine we are all together at the end of a class and we agree that it would be nice to have a great evening together – this seems very straightforward until we try to implement it. What does a great evening constitute? Going to the Pub for lots of drinks? Having a meal in an expensive and high-class restaurant? Trying out the latest ethnic food café? Frequently we find ourselves in the situation where language itself is *very imprecise (in terms of meaning)* and can cause complications re action.

Keeping this in mind, now consider the alternative (see Fig. 4.5 below). Here we have differently worded central foci, X and Y, but the context surrounding them is identical (J, K & D). This too can cause problems. Reflect back, have you ever been in the middle of a good argument with someone only to find you are both arguing the same

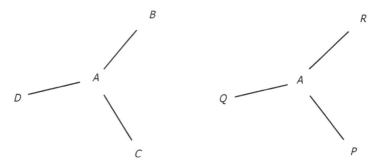

Fig. 4.4 Two attribute maps that appear to have *the same* central focus (A) (see Eden et al. 1979, p. 46). Reprinted from Eden, C., Jones and Sims, D., '*Messing About in Problems: An Informal Structured Approach to Their Identification and Management*', p. 45, Copyright (1983), with permission from Elsevier

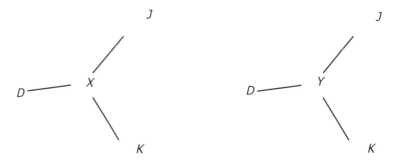

Fig. 4.5 Two attribute maps with what appear to be *different* central foci (see Eden et al. 1979, p. 46). Reprinted from Eden, C., Jones and Sims, D., '*Messing About in Problems: An Informal Structured Approach to Their Identification and Management*', Copyright (1983), with permission from Elsevier

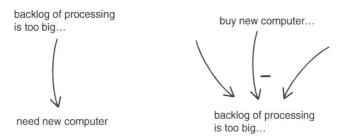

Fig. 4.6 Exploring causality (see Eden et al. 1979, p. 49). Reprinted from Eden, C., Jones and Sims, D., '*Messing About in Problems: An Informal Structured Approach to Their Identification and Management*', p 45, Copyright (1983), with permission from Elsevier

point! You are in violent agreement! What has happened is that through the argument, you have provided one another with the context and thus realised that *although the words are different the meaning is the same*. This situation is common particularly as we work with those from different backgrounds (national, industrial, communal, etc.).

Moving on from content and context lets begin to *consider the relationships*. In the previous examples, the links have simply been arbitrary attributes. However when undertaking cognitive and cause mapping the arrows have a particular meaning – that of causality – A may lead to B, or this 'Option' may lead to this 'Outcome' or this 'Means' may lead to this 'End'. However the direction of the arrow will depend on the value system of the individual (or group) being mapped. Lets consider Fig. 4.6 above.

The two concepts/statements on the left hand side might be from an interview with an IT manager. Here he is arguing that because the *backlog of processing is too big*, they should *buy a new computer* (he is interested in getting one of the latest machines with extremely fast processing time and various other features). However on the right are two statements from the Finance Manager. Her view is that *buying a new computer* is only one option for *reducing the backlog* and that there are others.

Thus we see two things here. The first is a *difference in values/aspirations* and the second is that you can *have negative links*. In reviewing the Finance Manager's map note that the arrow linking from '*buy a new computer*' to '*backlog of processing is too big*' has a minus sign at its head. This indicates a negative link and can be read as A leads to [not] B (in this case '*buy a new computer*' may lead to *NOT* '*backlog of processing is too big*'). As a consequence we can capture statements that have both positive and negative ramifications thus illustrating dilemmas.

4.2.2.3 Guidelines for Mapping

So let's have a look at a map in a little more detail. What does it look like? Fig. 4.7 below is part of a map produced when working with a group of staff interested in developing a new Information System for monitoring students. The map was created in the mapping software (Decision Explorer) and has used various styles of statement to denote constituencies. For example those statements which are in shaded rectangles emerged from the IT staff who would be responsible for managing the system and those that are in italics represent the views of academics. In addition there are numbers attached to each of the statements e.g. 10 reduce rates … drop out rates are too high. These numbers are simply tags or reference numbers to allow effective manipulation of the each of the statements. They do not have any weighting except to reflect when in a conversation the statement was made relative to others.

The arrows can be read as "may lead to" therefore the chain of argument shown by statements 62, 63, 68 and 37 reads 'being able to archive old data' may lead to 'avoid clogging up the system' which in turn may lead to 'able to get fast and easy access' and therefore lecturers being 'able to access student records while counselling'. Finally the dotted arrows with numbers show that there are other statements within the whole map which are linked to the material shown in the map but which are not at this point displayed on this extract of the whole map. Thus it is possible to show as little or as much detail to be revealed as demanded.

The map (Fig. 4.7) shows the hierarchy with goals/values at the top (boxed statements) and assertions at the bottom (dotted boxes).

Some of the mapping guidelines to watch for therefore are:

1. *Separate sentences into distinct phrases.* Frequently when we speak we encapsulate three or four causally linked phrases into a single utterance. For example "we need to *expand our business into new areas*, and therefore must focus on

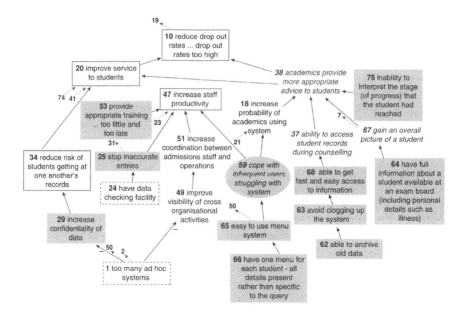

Fig. 4.7 An example of a cause map

building strategic alliances, and *tapping and developing our skills base*". Here there are four potential linked statements: expand our business into new areas, build strategic alliances, tap our skills base and develop our skills base. Note that the last part has been separated into two – tapping the skills base and developing it – this is because different activities are needed in order to do either of these and also they are likely to have different ramifications. A common pair that benefits from separation is "improve and increase" – what you do to increase something doesn't necessary lead to improvement. An example from the above map might be "if we can stop inaccurate entries through having a data checking facility then we will be able to increase staff productivity".

2. *Build up the hierarchy.* As noted above (section 4.2.1.3) when discussing the second of Kelly's corollaries, laddering up and down the chains of argument enables a more complete representation to be captured. Questions such as "how might that be done" or "what are some of the constraints preventing that from happening" help ladder down to options; whereas "why is that important" helps tease out ramifications. Therefore, returning to the above map, one question that might be asked is "why do you want to increase staff productivity"? (laddering up) and another might be "how could you have a data checking facility?" (laddering down).

3. *Identify the option and outcome (means and ends) within each pair of ideas.* Checking the direction of the link is important. For example, consider the two statements 'buy Microsoft Office' and 'standardise our software'. For most people *'buy Microsoft Office'* is one option/route to *'standardise our software'* – but there may be others. However it is unlikely that you would *'standardise our software'* in order to (may lead to) *'buy Microsoft Office'* (unless of course you were Bill Gates!). Another example from the above map – 49 and 51 – might be do you *'improve the visibility of cross organizational activities'* to *'increase coordination between admissions staff'* or the reverse.

4. *Watch out for values/beliefs/goals and strategic/key issues and mark them.* Values and goals are statements that can be seen as 'good in their own right'. An obvious private sector candidate might be 'build shareholder value' and a personal goal might be 'feel fulfilled at work'. Strategic or key issues are those that either have a lot of links around them or a lot of emotion behind them. In an interview setting watch out for the non verbals, namely the gestures made and tone of voice as they provide a lot of useful information. There is no prescribed way of marking them. One method might be to use an asterisk for key issues and circle goals but it is up to personal preference. In the above map, the software allows us to identify these using particular styles e.g. goals are black text in a rectangular box.

5. *Add meaning by wording the statements in an imperative form.* By making the statement action oriented, that is an imperative, it is usually much easier to correctly link the statement. Thus the verb is quite significant. Whereas a statement that simply contains the word 'marketing' could probably be linked throughout the map as it has multiple interpretations, identifying the action e.g. "improve marketing's resources" or "outsource the marketing department" or "develop a

marketing campaign" helps make sure that the appropriate links are captured. Look at the map in Fig. 4.7 to see how many of the statements commence with verbs. Where they don't e.g. *'too many ad hoc systems'* then these might be assertions or facts. Typically these appear at the bottom of the chain of argument as they are usually uttered as being an explanation for a particular action.

6. *Use the person's own language.* There is always the temptation to paraphrase, particularly if you know the issue/subject well. However it is important to capture exactly what is said (as much as possible given the above guideline) so as to ensure that the map is recognisable to the interviewee. Furthermore, paraphrasing might result in a different meaning being derived from that which the person being mapped had in mind.

7. *Capture contrasting poles.* Obviously not every single statement will have one, but where they are provided make sure you capture and reflect these on the map. Sometimes they are immediately obvious. For example 'we need to do this rather than that'. At other times however the first pole is noted and subsequently elaborated before the 'rather than' is mentioned. It is worth being alert to this possibility. Finally using this device as a means for better understanding what is being said can be helpful. Where a statement is not immediately clear, try asking the question "rather than...?" This can often provide the clue.

8. *Tidy up your map by looking for isolated statements and examining heads and tails.* Look for statements that have no arrows linking them to other statements. Where these do occur it is worth asking the person being mapped more about them. For example, "I notice that you mentioned '*X*', I wonder if you could explain to me how it relates to the other material we have already discussed". This usually leads to more information being surfaced along with gaining an understanding of the particular statement's position in the map. Checking whether the end points – the heads (those with no links leaving from them) – are goals/values will enable these to be determined, or further questioning to take place. Likewise exploring tails (those statements with no links going into them) and checking to see if they can be further developed in terms of options will help build the map.

9. *Consider the following tips* including: (a) use blank paper, (b) start two-thirds up the page, (c) write in rectangular blocks of text and (d) use a self propelling pencil. Blank paper is useful because it allows statements to be positioned in a more appropriate place rather than feeling constrained to writing on the line! We are so well trained from childhood that we can find it hard to stop writing on lines so as to allow a more graphical representation to unfold. Starting two-thirds up the page (and usually in a portrait orientation) works well as most interviewees' start with the main issues bothering them and thus there is more detail supporting them (explanations, options, constraints) than ramifications and consequences. Working in rectangular blocks of text enables links to be drawn in so that the flow is retained – it is easy to see the chain of argument – whereas if the statements are one long sentence then arrows will have to 'wiggle' around them giving no visible assistance. Finally a propelling or mechanical pencil is best as mistakes can be rubbed out whilst always being sharp enough to write clearly.

4.2.2.4   Have a Go!

Below is a piece of text. Have a go at mapping it. It is probably best to first read it through once to understand what is being said. Then underline what you see as the phrases. Finally write these on a blank piece of paper and capture the links that are contained in the text – map *just what is in the text*. Once you have done this, return to the above coding guidelines, and check whether you have taken them all into account.

The text is based on some work that the authors did with Scottish Natural Heritage.

> To influence the attitude and policy of others to care for the natural heritage, SNH could well be advised to use those protected areas owned by SNH as demonstrators for good care of the natural heritage. To meet this need and to secure practical management of the natural heritage (another of SNH's goals) SNH must develop and deliver a strategy for protected areas. Various ideas such as gaining a general awareness of global resource depletion, SNH addressing sustainability (they are currently the only organization doing so) and using their knowledge of how the natural heritage is changing with time may go some way towards achieving a strategy for protected areas. Management of the marine environment, and of those species which cause conflict, for example deer and seals may go some way towards balance maintaining natural heritage features with addressing increasing complex environmental problems which adds to the knowledge of the natural environment (Fig. 4.8).

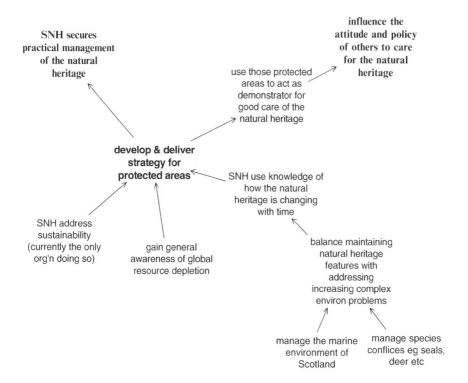

Fig. 4.8 A possible map from the SNH text

4.2.2.5   Comments on the Map

How did your map look? Did you get the values/goals (there were some hints). Did you manage to break down the text into statements? Did you find it easy? If you answer 'no' then that is pretty typical. Most of us actually find mapping text harder than mapping discussion. This is because we can ask questions in a discussion to ascertain the links. Furthermore, the temptation to add our own links (which appear to be obvious and natural) is considerable – particularly as we want to make sense of the argument. See Eden and Ackermann (2004) for further discussion on mapping text.

Hopefully the above map should also have prompted you to ask

- "Shouldn't *developing* and *delivering strategy for protected areas*' be separated?"
- "Shouldn't *influence the attitude and policy of others ...*' be split?"

In the first case you would be absolutely right – they should. The actions that might be necessary to achieve 'developing a strategy' are quite different from those of 'delivering it'. However, in the second case, interestingly enough the answer is no. The person whose views/perceptions it represents felt that they were not separable. In his mind they were two sides of the same coin and separating them would add complexity and be a false image. This highlights an important point that the interviewee (whose map it is) is the only one who can say what is right and what isn't.

Probably the hardest of the concepts to capture correctly is the one reflecting the 'balance'. Don't worry, this is usually the case.

4.2.2.6   Additional Coding Guidelines

The coding guidelines below extend those noted above. They are taken from a book on mapping called *Visible Thinking* by Bryson et al. (2004).

4.2.2.7   Getting the Wording Right

- Try to use around six to eight words for each statement – by including more words you will have a better sense of what was meant, BUT including too many words may mean that there are multiple statements.
- As part of the above guideline, think about incorporating who/what/when into the statement.
- As much as possible avoid words such as 'should', 'ought', 'must', etc. as these are both prescriptive and unnecessary. Instead of capturing *we must invest in a new information system*, simply note down *invest in a new information system* – it saves time!
- Check your statements to see if they include phrases such as "in order to", "due to", "through". These all imply a link and therefore comprise two statements rather than one.

Don't forget the earlier guidelines, that of using their language, and adopting an action orientation.

4.2.2.8   Direction of the Arrow

- Make sure links are causal, showing means to ends or options to outcomes. Frequently novice 'mappers' end up producing a more chronological or flow diagram type of representation.
- Check that you really have options leading to outcomes – when getting started it is not unusual to produce 'upside down' maps where the links flow from outcomes to options (as often this is the way people speak).
- As a rule of thumb, link specific instances into generic statements. For example you might have *'privatise prison services'* as the generic with *'privatise cleaning'*, *'privatise catering'* and *'privatise maintenance'* as specific options.
- Seek to have those statements that appear to be assertions or facts at the bottom of the map. These often are not action oriented but they matter to someone because they imply action is necessary, and so the action is higher up the map.
- Avoid double-headed arrows and check feedback loops. Double headed arrows imply feedback (i.e. dynamic behaviour). However as only two statements are involved it is difficult to (a) determine whether they are 'true' feedback loops and (b) if they are loops, how best to manage them. Try to explore how A might lead to B by adding an intervening statement and do the same for elaborating the link between B to A. This loop, now containing four statements, is more amenable to review. Once this is done, or where you have a feedback loop – check whether it makes sense. For example are you *developing a marketing plan* in order to *create more awareness* in the market so as to *get more products sold*, and thus *have more revenue*s, which in turn can be spent on *developing a marketing plan*. At first glance this might look like a feedback loop. However the second mention of marketing plan is a redevelopment of the first and therefore chronologically inconsistent.

Remember you are working to build an understanding of the particular issue facing the person being mapped (or yourself if the map is about your issue). By knowing what facts mean and why they fit together as they do – the mechanism and the structure – we are able to determine the basis for pulling a mess into a system of interacting issues.

4.2.2.9   Developing Practice

There are a number of ways you can gain more practice in mapping. Three are listed below – each providing different benefits.

The first method is to try to map another piece of text and see how you get on, and whether it gets any easier. A good source of text might be to use an article in a well written newspaper which is discussing a particular current concern with its attendant issues, values and options. However, don't worry if you find that many of your statements are unlinked – this is likely to say as much about the structure of the writing as the quality of your mapping!

The second method is to try the technique out on an issue that you are currently grappling with. Start by capturing the main issues (using an action orientation as this will stimulate a better understanding of the issue) and how they relate to one another. If, in linking them together, further concepts are needed to explain the relationship note these too. Next consider why they are issues – are the issues either attacking or supporting some desired outcomes – thus eliciting some of your personal values (laddering up). Finally think about what might be some of the options and constraints and capture these (laddering down). This material will give you some idea of the consequences of each option, helping arrive at one that is potentially more sustainable as it addresses more of the goals. Throughout the process use the guidelines to help you sharpen your thinking.

A third method is to try creating a map through an interview. Here the aim is to find a colleague, friend, or family member who currently is wrestling with a difficult issue and try interviewing him or her whilst building a map to record and guide the interview. Try to make sure that the issue is something that is 'live' rather than past as this will provide a more realistic event (post rationalising an issue can result in the interviewee talking very fast but also in a structured manner). Review your map together and find out if it helped their thinking about the issue. Alternatively, try mapping a television presentation or a work presentation. However, as with the text option, this option does not provide the benefits of being able to ask questions to elicit relationships and enhance understanding.

4.2.3   Reflections on Mapping: Some Hints and Tips

Don't worry about appearance. One of the most common concerns particularly regarding sharing the map is "but it looks so messy". It is worth bearing two things in mind here. The first is if the interviewee is struggling with the issue because it is difficult and messy, the chances of you being able to produce a perfect map are extremely small (and if you did manage it, would be very humbling! Why couldn't they unravel the problem themselves?). Secondly, as long as it captures their language (rather than yours!) then in our experience interviewees are happy to work with the messy handwritten image. Allowing them to see the map is also a great way to validate what you have captured and demonstrate that you have been actively listening. Often interviewees are curious about the different form of note taking being used, which gives you a perfect opportunity to start explaining the process – and get some confirmation of the captured material. A tip here is, where you can, sit at right angles to the person you are mapping – this way you can both read the map, but you don't encroach onto the interviewee's personal space.

Capture the constructs/statements first. By doing this, you can begin to gain an understanding of what is being said and as you begin to get an overall understanding of the material, you can begin the process of linking one statement to another. It is far easier to add links once the statements are captured than the other way around. Imagine the concepts/statements as landmarks. However, if statements are very obviously linked then by all means put in the arrows immediately.

Use natural breaks productively. When the interviewee pauses, having contributed a number of ideas, use these breaks to feedback material to him/her. This will provide a number of benefits. The first is that it will demonstrate you really have been listening and capturing their views thus gaining you more credibility and building the consultant client relationship. This is important if you want to come back and interview them a second time. Secondly it enables you to test your understanding of the material and get feedback if it isn't correct or there is more to add. You are therefore more likely to get a better understanding of how the issue is understood.

Finally, and sometimes the most important reason, as you are feeding back the material make sure you write down what you are saying which is in your brain but hasn't yet been translated onto paper – before you forget it! Often, particularly at the beginning of an interview, there isn't time to write down all the material and so the statements are 'half formed'. Use these opportunities to flesh them out more fully ensuring that they adhere to the guidelines.

Build in time for review. Before ending the interview try to ensure you have at least five minutes to review the map with the interviewee. Start by recounting what appear to be the key issues (those with lots of links in and out) to ensure that all have been captured. Next check whether there are any 'orphans' – statements that have no other statements linking to them – and enquire how they might be woven into the map. Finally review the apparent goals (statements that are "good in their own right" and typically have no statements linking out from them) and whether they are legitimate or need further laddering up. By taking the interviewee through the map you are not only able to further validate the representation, but also to provide him/her with an intuitive understanding of how mapping works. This can be useful if a workshop is to follow. It also provides value for the interviewee as they are able to see the particular situation structured and thus more amenable to management.

Consider the shape of the map. Is your map very broad but somewhat shallow (not having lengthy chains of argument)? This usually suggests that the perspective being mapped is one that encompasses a very wide range of the issues and concerns (perhaps a senior managerial perspective). This is in contrast to a map that is narrow and deep suggesting in-depth knowledge of a relatively small part of the business.

Make sure you capture the interviewee's (not your) key issues. Sometimes when you are doing a series of interviews and someone else has already mentioned a particular option or issue, it is tempting to skip capturing it again. However, the interviewee does not know this, so the omission may raise anxieties. Rather than follow *your* agenda, always ask the interviewee what he/she sees as the key issues – this way you will develop a far better understanding of what they see as important.

Consider how you manage the interview. Starting with a very broad question (one that does not result in a 'yes/no' answer) is best. For example, "how can the organization grow its business over the next 3 years" allows interviewees to surface all of their concerns and opportunities and therefore provides the agenda for subsequent questions (e.g. how might an issue be resolved, what are some of the constraints, what are the consequences, etc.). Don't feel the need to prepare lots of questions, question emerge as the map does as there are always uncertainties about meaning and structure.

Carefully introduce the process. Don't spend time at the beginning explaining that you are using cognitive mapping. This is partly because in saying you are going to do "*cognitive mapping*" individuals might feel concerned about what this actually involves, and partly because you will end up spending time explaining the technique which reduces the amount of time you have building the map. Wait until they comment on your unusual note-taking format and then explain the process – but don't necessarily say it is cognitive mapping, but rather a two-dimensional way of taking notes. The more you can jointly develop the map, the better the representation will be and the more shared.

Manage multiple 'opposite poles'. If you find yourself with a statement that seems to have more than one 'opposite pole' then this might mean you have a series of options. For example, you might start off with '*centralise marketing rather than have a profit centre*'. However, later on in the interview the interviewee notes that it might be beneficial to have marketing as a cost centre rather than a profit centre. There are now three different options – have a centralised marketing department, or set up marketing as a cost centre or as a profit centre.

A few final pointers: Try not to learn all of the guidelines at once. Start by just noting down statements and drawing in some rough links. Then move to thinking about causality i.e. which way the link should be positioned. Finally consider the action orientation. Always try to avoid writing down statements that simply comprise one or two words as the more complete the statement the better the understanding. As a final tip, try to write in lower case rather than capitals – not only is it quicker but some handwriting experts believe it to be more readable.

Sometimes an interviewee will take no interest in the map you produced; very often this is because you have produced a map that belongs to you rather than to the interviewee. There is always a great danger in translating the words used by the interviewee into something that is more meaningful to you. Often the maps that are of no interest to interviewees turn out to be summary maps. For example, we have often found that we might produce a map comprising 60 statements from a 45 min interview where a novice interviewer, in the same interview, might produce a map with only 15 statements. This is because many of the statements are summarised rather than captured with their richness and subtlety.

4.2.3.1 How Does Mapping Compare with Other Graphical Processes?

There are a number of different graphical representation modes ranging from the well known Mind Maps (Buzan and Buzan 1993) to influence diagrams (Richardson and Pugh 1981). Table 4.1 compares three common diagrammatic forms (word and arrow diagrams) against a few characteristics.

Table 4.1 Comparison of three diagramming forms

–	Cause mapping	Mind maps	Influence diagrams
Nodes	Formal guidelines for capturing material i.e. action orientation and six to eight words	No formality – anything goes	Formal guidelines for capturing material i.e. variables
Links	Formal guidelines for linking material i.e. hierarchical causality	No formality – anything goes	Formal guidelines for linking material – flows of a single unit of analysis
Size	Aims to build up rich and detailed pictures – individual maps may comprise 100 statements, group maps 1,000	Usually fairly small – around 30 or 40 statements	Focuses on only capturing the stocks, flows and intervening variables
Analysis	Open to analysis – including detecting feedback, identifying central statements	No analysis usually carried out	Analysis crucial
Format	Graphical format – so easier to remember and understand underlying structure	Graphical format – so easier to remember and understand underlying structure	Graphical format – so easier to remember and understand underlying structure

4.2.4 Where Has Causal Mapping Been Used?

4.2.4.1 To Elicit Representations of Individual Thinking

As noted above, mapping can provide a very powerful means of understanding your own thinking or helping someone else develop theirs. Remember the example earlier of the lecturer trying to manage the job, her PhD and her personal life. Being clear about your (or others) goals – and the various options and dilemmas that exist – can help provide a sense of relief as the map's structure helps make sense of the complexity. Some consultants use mapping as a way demonstrating their skills to clients. Through building a model of the client's thinking of the issue the consultant is seen to be able to provide added value. Another example is when commencing a project – spending time mapping out the objectives of the particular project, the issues and options can help clarify the situation. For further examples see Ackermann and Eden (2004) which provides examples of three different individual uses of mapping.

4.2.4.2 To Support Group Working

When working on developing strategy or resolving messy complex problems typically groups – rather than an individual – are involved. This is for two reasons.

The first relates to the fact that organizations are political and social constructions (as noted above when discussing the framework). Many researchers argue that in order to get things done in organizations, participants have to 'own' or 'buy into' the change – and therefore it is important to attend to ensuring the outcomes are 'politically feasible'(see Eden and Ackermann 1998). The importance of ensuring commitment was well expressed by Machiavelli who noted that "*It must be remembered that there is nothing more difficult to plan, more doubtful of success, nor more dangerous to manage than the creation of a new system. For the initiator has the enmity of all who would profit by the preservation of the old institutions and merely lukewarm defenders of those who would gain by the new ones*". Paying attention to gaining emotional commitment through building in the means to allow participants to 'have their say' and be listened to (procedural justice (Kim and Mauborgne 1995)) is thus important. The mapping process – using the group methods discussed below – provides this.

The second reason focuses on the added value gained from eliciting and structuring the contributions from a range of different perspectives and enabling the model to facilitate an action plan that is more robust. In the decision making literature this could be seen as ensuring that the process used is procedurally rational (Simon 1976). Moreover, and returning to earlier comments, surfacing and structuring the issues, goals, options and assertions of different participants can help the group as a whole begin to develop a shared sense of understanding and a common language. This facilitates negotiation and therefore increases the likelihood of a successful outcome.

4.2.4.3   To Analyse Models

Models can often became very large – group models in particular reaching up to 1,000 nodes. As such it becomes difficult, if not impossible to be able to effectively examine manually the structures to determine emergent properties and gain insights into ways forward. However, computer-based analyses can yield important insights into significant emergent properties that can either reveal counter intuitive and damaging outcomes or offer up new and creative opportunities. A sample of the analyses techniques available has therefore been provided below (in the next section).

4.2.4.4   To Support Other Forms of Modelling

Whilst SODA (and any form of modelling) can be used on their own and provide significant value, combining SODA with either more quantitative models or other qualitative processes can extend the use and power of the method. SODA – particularly causal mapping – has been used as a starting point for modelling complex projects that have experienced considerable disruption and delay (Ackermann et al. 1997), and multi-criteria decision making (Belton et al. 1997) amongst a range of other applications.

4.2.5   *Analysis for Strategic Options Development and Analysis (SODA)*

Regardless of the particular method for generating the initial map (see the next section on different options of using mapping/SODA with groups) the following analytical routines provide a powerful means of exploring a causal model's structure and properties and gaining insight into possible avenues of action. These analyses are typically carried out using the *Decision Explorer* software but could be undertaken manually – although for some analyses it would be a time consuming and potentially laborious job. The analyses range from simple routines for tidying and structuring the map to more complex ones assisting in examining the underlying structure.

The analyses are dependent on the coding formalisms being adhered to. One particular characteristic that often occurs when mapping is when duplication of links occurs through redundancy. For example, the chain of argument might be $A \rightarrow B \rightarrow C \rightarrow D$ however there might also be links from $A \rightarrow C$ and $B \rightarrow D$. In this case it is worth checking whether these two further links are unique in their own right, rather than duplications – a summary link where $A \rightarrow C$ summarizes $A \rightarrow B \rightarrow C$. It they are unique, could further material be added showing the variation? This process avoids the model having extraneous links and thus ensures clarity of thinking.

As the maps may represent a single interview or a series of interviews or workshops they may contain anywhere from a few dozen to several thousands concepts. As the number of concepts increases, the 'map' usually starts being referred to as a 'model' because it can no longer be represented as one single easy-to-read document. Rather than attempting to depict all of the concepts at once – an impossible task when using the software and working with over 60 concepts – *Decision Explorer* has the facility to create a number of 'views' – windows which can reveal a section of the overall model. These views allow aspects/themes/areas to be explored and amended as required. Changes made to the concepts and links are reflected throughout the model, though changes to the content of the views are local. Thus views can have material either made visible or hidden without copying or deleting concepts from the model.

Although the analyses have been used for a range of different purposes, the analytical processes covered in this section particularly relate to the resolution of messy complex and often strategic problems. Thus Fig. 4.9 depicts a three stage process. The first stage centres on the analysis of the model (although obviously some capture of the information, knowledge, wisdom and experience needs to have been already completed – maybe through individual interviews or a group modelling process). This stage is typically carried out in the 'back room' enabling the analyst/facilitator to both tidy the model and review its structure in preparation for a workshop. The analysis process is iterative (although below it is presented in a linear form) and often helps the facilitator/analyst to gain a good understanding of the whole in preparation for facilitating a group workshop.

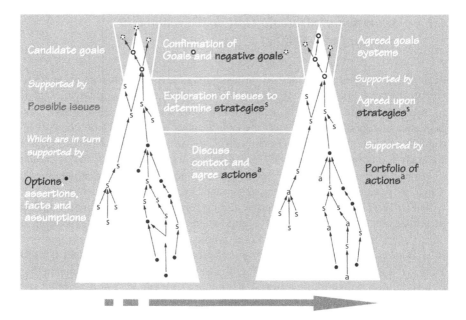

Fig. 4.9 Developing agreement for the direction

4.2.5.1 Identifying Goals

Identifying candidate goals is usually a good place to begin – remembering that a goal, according to SODA principles, is something that is "good in its own right". An example of a goal in a University setting might be '*be research excellent*'; for a private sector organization it might be '*become No 1 in the market*'. Each of these goals may also support other goals and/or be supported by other goals. Understanding the goals (or values) can provide assistance in understanding the objectives of the individual(s) and thus allow for exploration of their variety and coherence. To find the goals, an obvious starting point, therefore, is to examine the 'top' of the model (using the *List Heads* or *LH* command in the software – a 'head' is a statement that has no other statement linking from it). Reviewing the resultant list usually provides a mix of statements, some of which are candidate goals whilst others are issues, options, and assertions, etc. that have not yet been laddered up to goals. Those that are candidate goals ('candidate' until confirmed by the group) can be given a particular style (a typical goal style might be bold, black, Times Roman, 14 point) to easily distinguish them. Those that are 'heads' but not goals can then be examined to see where are missing links and dealt with accordingly. This is particularly the case when weaving together material from different individual interviews as it is possible to miss capturing some of the links.

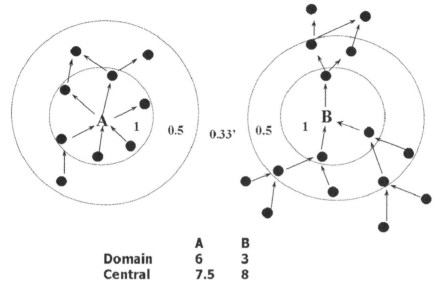

	A	B
Domain	**6**	**3**
Central	**7.5**	**8**

Fig. 4.10 A comparison between the central and domain analysis results

4.2.5.2   Identifying Issues

The next stage is to determine which of the statements are key issues. An issue can be seen as something that is broad, requires resources (time and money) and may take a while to put in place. An example might be '*keep good people*' or '*avoid being taken over by a competitor*'. Issues can be positive or negative but either way should be of some concern to those involved. There are two analyses that help here (see Fig. 4.10).

4.2.5.3   Carrying Out a Domain Analysis

The first analysis – *Domain* – examines each statement and calculates the number of links in and out (essentially determining how busy it is). Those that have a high score are considered as potential key issues. If the model is around 200 statements and the analysis depicts that there are three statements that have eight links around them, five that have seven links around them and then 19 that have five links around them, then a natural breakpoint is evident and the top eight are selected as being candidate key issues. This is obviously dependent on the size of the model and will also reflect the adherence to the coding rules. Those identified as issues can be attributed with a specific style (a typical issue style might be italic, purple, 12pt). Often this analysis can be conducted visually rather than having to use the software.

4.2.5.4   Carrying Out a Central analysis

A second way of considering issues (and one that both reinforces the domain analysis as well as suggesting new issues) is to review the overall model's structure to
see which statements are '*central*'. To understand this analysis, consider the structure of a molecule (see Fig. 4.10). Here elements are connected to one another with
bonds – with some of the elements being relatively peripheral with few bonds connecting them whilst others are more central. By identifying those statements that
are both busy and central a greater sense of confidence in revealing the key issues
is acquired. This analysis is usually impossible to do without the software.

It should be noted that the results of the central analysis provide a more 'accurate'
view of potential key issues than domain analysis. This is because the domain analysis results can be influenced through a participant spending a considerable amount
of time on a single topic that is currently of concern to them – a hot button – but
which is peripheral to the whole, and which later on becomes less significant.

To confirm the emergent set of key issues two further analyses are useful. The
first 'slices' the model into *clusters* (possible themes) through comparing how similar each pair of statements are. The second analysis uses a different approach to
'slice' the model – that of producing sets comprising all of the supporting material
for each of the potential key issues, or goals, and thus provides *hierarchical sets or
clusters*. Both provide useful ways of feeding back information to participants.

4.2.5.5   Carrying Out a Cluster Analysis

The clustering analysis works using an algorithm to check link similarity. Two statements are 'similar' if they have many linked statements in common. It is rather like
having shared friends. If I am friendly with A, B, C, and D, and you are friendly with
B, C, D, and E, then we both 'share' friendships with B, C, and D. The higher the
proportions of our friends we share, the more 'similar' we would be on this measure.
Figure 4.11 shows that when you have a number of statements with many links
amongst them, but rather few links with other statements, you can think of it as a
cluster. In Fig. 4.11 the dotted and lined selected pairs have little similarity and therefore are components of two separate clusters. Thus the material within the clusters is
closely related (due to the linking) enabling the clusters to reveal the emergent themes
in the model. Each theme potentially contains at least one key issue. If there isn't a key
issue within the cluster then examination might suggest further candidate key issues.

This analysis, more than any other, relies on good mapping coding – particularly
avoiding redundant links. It is also affected by any feedback loops (see below) as
these tend to result in large clusters as everything that is captured in the loop is
placed into a single cluster. It is difficult to undertake this analysis without the
software. However, the principle of causally related clusters (as opposed to topic
based clusters) is an important one, and it is possible to undertake rough cluster
analyses based on structure. Note that although the analysis is based on structure,
the structure was based on content, and so clusters are content analyses.

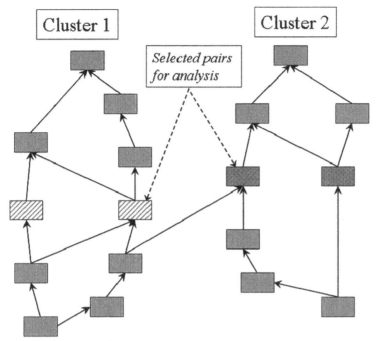

Tight intra-cluster links with few inter-cluster links (bridges)

Fig. 4.11 Cluster analysis: Tight intra-cluster links with few inter-cluster links (bridges)

4.2.5.6 Carrying Out a Hierarchical Set Analysis

Hierarchical sets – as their name suggests – take each member of the seed set (in this case the key issues) and drills down the chains of argument. Each of the statements linking into the seed (see Fig. 4.12), along with all of the material that links into them is captured, essentially producing a tear-drop shaped set.

As with clustering, where the resultant hierarchical set (called hieset in the software) is very large (over 40 statements) consideration should be given to whether a further key issue exists within the set. In both cases – 'cluster' or 'hieset' – it is possible to just examine the contents of one cluster or hieset at a time. For further help, reviewing the results of the central and domain analyses alongside the large set can give insights into which might be candidate key issues (i.e. those that are relatively busy or central). Likewise if the set is very small (less than 10) then examining whether the issue is a key issue – for example does it directly relate to another similar concept that is key – can be helpful.

As with the cluster analysis, these sets are also useful for providing feedback to those involved in the intervention as they reveal each key issue with all its attendant supporting material (they are therefore NOT mutually exclusive as are cluster sets).

Undertaking this analysis with the software is quick and easy. However, as with cluster analysis, the principle of hierarchical clusters/sets is an important one because it seeks to show all of the options that can influence a chosen outcome (key issue or goal).

4.2.5.7 Finding Options

Identifying Potent Concepts

Once a hierarchical set analysis has been carried out, it is possible to determine which options are '*potent*' (i.e. those that have consequences for a number of key issues or goals are more potent than those that support only one or two). This is a means of prioritising options. Figure 4.12 shows those statements in the light shaded area having an impact on three of the key issues.

Identifying Composite Tails

Another analysis that helps both with determining options and giving some insights into the key issues is the composite tail analysis. A composite tail ('cotail' in the software) is where a concept has multiple out-bound arrows – hence being labelled composite.

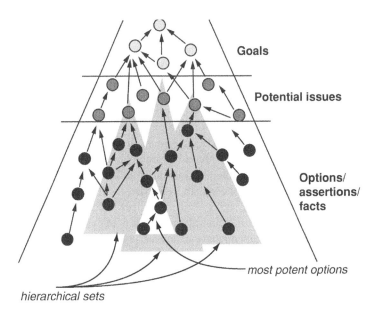

Fig. 4.12 Hierarchical sets drilling down from the potential issues and producing tear drops of supporting material

The analysis thus starts at the 'bottom' of the model examining tails and laddering up until a branch point is reached. This is then listed and the analysis starts with the next tail. The results provide a source of useful information as they refine the results of the potent analysis. This is achieved by detecting which of the potent concepts are also composite tails and therefore pinpointing those that have the greatest effect. Any options beneath them only hit the potent option identified and so can be chosen as implementation strategies for the cotail. For example, in Fig. 4.12 there are two concepts that are potent, however, it is the top one of the pair that is of significance as it represents the branching point – the lower is simply elaboration.

Detecting Feedback Loops

Identifying whether there are any feedback loops in the model can not only give valuable insights into the structure but can also help tidy up the structure of the model. As with both cluster and hieset, the software places the components of each loop into a set which is then amenable to listing or mapping (the latter tends to provide more useful insights). Once detected it is worth checking that the loops are legitimate – sometimes when weaving the different maps together errors can occur through incorrect causal links. Where they are valid, then the loops can be examined further to determine whether they are controlling loops or comprising a vicious or virtuous cycle. Loops can give those involved in the intervention some powerful insights as they depict a dynamically changing situation. Moreover, identifying loops and the events that are triggering them can provide a powerful way of providing the structure for a System Dynamics model (see Ackermann et al. 1997; Howick et al. 2008). Finding feedback loops visually is notoriously difficult – loops are often missed. However, their identification and exploration is usually very important.

Producing an Overview of the Model's Content

As noted above, developing the model and then working on the model with the group tends to take the form of a three stage process with the analysis aiming to ready the model for a group workshop. (Although it is important to note that all the analyses are fast enough to be undertaken by the software with the group.) As a last step before bringing the model to the group to review the material and negotiate a set of outcomes some further means of helping those participating navigate maps is helpful. Therefore constructing an overview 'road map' of the model is carried out. This is similar in concept to a road atlas, which on the front cover depicts the country along with the major cities/towns and their apparent associated road connections. However this picture typically suggests direct routes between the major cities (for example a direct route between Glasgow and Edinburgh) which when examined in further depth prove not to be the case (e.g. the Glasgow to Edinburgh route actually travels through Linlithgow, Falkirk, etc.). The same process is possible with the model, resulting in a 'collapsed' picture of the goals and key issues (Cities and towns) with the various chains of argument (routes) between them (both those that are direct as well as those that traverse additional argumentation).

4.2.5.8 Summary

To summarise, the software analyses provide a means of making sense of a large amount of qualitative data through being able to tidy the model along with gaining new insights from the emergent properties that unfold. As a result they might give clues regarding how best to act in the situation. Moreover, the analyses make it possible to test thinking and reveal uncertainties. However two things should be noted; firstly that all the analyses are based on the structure of the model and therefore vulnerable to the quality of the mapping coding, and secondly that analysis of models isn't easy – the first few times it is often overwhelming to keep in mind the mapping guidelines, software commands and underlying purposes of the analysis.

For additional reading on analysis see Bryson et al. (2004), Eden (2004), or Ackermann et al. (2005).

4.2.6   SODA for Group Problem Structuring and Resolution

4.2.6.1   Introduction

Although SODA has been used to support individual working, its predominant use is with groups. As such, consideration has to be given to assessing which of the different possible modes of working is best suited to the group in question. Issues worth reflecting upon include:

- The degree of *openness* within the participant group. In some organizations (or countries – see Hofstede (1980) for further insights) participants are more constrained by social conformity pressures. As such they are hesitant to raise contradictory views and the material generated therefore does not reflect the situation accurately.
- Related to the above concern, participants may believe that their *view is 'out on a limb'* from the rest of the group, and so feel they may be subject to ridicule for expressing an alternative view (it is possible that everyone in the group feels this way also) (Harvey 1988).
- Existing social and political relations. Participants may have *'trading agreements'* with others in the group which would be broken if they expressed a view which opposes that of their trading partners – to do so would have consequences for support on other issues.

- To dissent from the view of the group may risk damaging *team cohesiveness* … the camaraderie of being a team (Janis 1972).
- *Time available.* In some circumstances the situation demands a fast response. Sometimes the complexity of getting the appropriate people together results in a constrained duration for working.
- *Resources available.* There may also be limitations in other resources, such as consultant time, or facilities and equipment.
- *Objectives of the client.* Whilst there is usually a prime objective which centres around the situation of concern, there may be other objectives such as building teams, etc.
- *The skills and abilities of the facilitator.* Where the facilitator is a novice, starting with a mode of working that reduces the amount of load is likely to be helpful.
- *The context.* This goes beyond basic issues of time and resources, to consider the culture of the organization, the views of other stakeholders (particularly those more senior in an organization), other organisational concerns, etc.
- *The participants.* Paying attention to the personalities of those involved along with their ability to work together will also shape the intervention.

These issues influence which of the possible modes for working with groups should be adopted. However, combinations of the modes are possible. Also pertinent is recognising that whilst the above considerations might suggest a particular design for the intervention, this design might change sometime during the intervention as the process of working together suggests different options. Therefore paying attention to the pre-workshop phase is very important and is part of the facilitation process (Ackermann 1996).

The modes of working centre on the level of 'technology' used in each. One mode of group working is essentially manual. This might involve interviewing each of the participants (using cognitive mapping) before weaving together the views or it might involve manual group mapping using the Oval Mapping technique (see below). Another mode is where the facilitator, using *Decision Explorer* and a public screen (through a projector) works with the software and allows the group to interact with the model. Each has its own benefits and disadvantages and therefore careful consideration regarding their fit with the particular group and issue being considered is important (see Ackermann and Eden 2001).

Figure 4.13 provides one possible design; though it must be noted that there are many others (another is provided in Pidd (2003)). This figure shows a combination of manual and computer supported working taking place. Starting initially with interviews a *Decision Explorer* model is built combining all of the views. This is followed by an oval mapping workshop – maybe with the more junior members – to elicit further views. These views are added to the *Decision Explorer* model. Finally, a workshop with the decision making team is undertaken. Here the facilitator operates the software on behalf of the group allowing for changes as the group negotiates a way forward. The resultant model then allows easy assessment of progress.

One possible route...

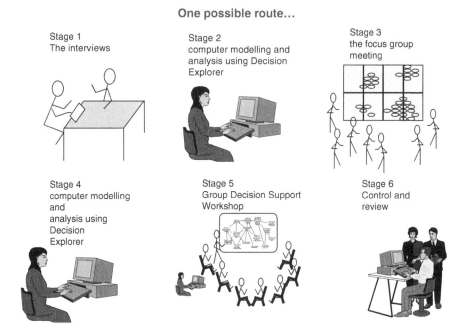

Stage 1
The interviews

Stage 2
computer modelling and
analysis using Decision
Explorer

Stage 3
the focus group
meeting

Stage 4
computer modelling
and
analysis using
Decision
Explorer

Stage 5
Group Decision Support
Workshop

Stage 6
Control and
review

Fig. 4.13 One possible route (Microsoft Clipart)

Particularly powerful is the ability to determine whether the actions agreed are done in relation to the objectives they have been set up to achieve – the relationship – the arrow – being significant.

4.2.6.2 Working Manually: Using the Oval Mapping Technique (OMT)

The Benefits of Oval Mapping

Oval mapping is initially much like brainstorming, except that very significantly it is not about lateral thinking but about surfacing current aspects of the problem. It depends on participants contributing their views directly through writing them on to an oval shaped adhesive, or sticky putty based, card and posting them publicly (see Fig. 4.14). There are a number of benefits including:

- Building teams – as the process is manual, interactive, and participatory participants begin to learn more about one another's roles and responsibilities and gain a wider appreciation of the organisation as a whole. From this they can develop a sense of being part of a team. This ties into the above comment about client's having more than one objective – sometimes more covert in nature.

Fig. 4.14   Getting started – writing, reading and placing ovals

- Providing a social context – which not only helps build teams but also provides participants with a means of learning more about the organisation, contributing to the outcomes as well as having fun.
- Relatively little role ambiguity – most groups have experienced some forms of brainstorming and so are less concerned about their relative performance.
- Flexibility in location and relatively easy to set up – particularly important in organizations where there are few resources (it is also a good way to limit the number of demands on the facilitator – as there is no need for the software).
- It provides the group with the ability to see the whole picture. Through being able to capture all of the concerns, issues, objectives, assertions and facts with their relationships in one single large map, participants can develop a better understanding and begin to work towards a sustainable and negotiated set of outcomes.
- It allows participants to contribute simultaneously and therefore avoids contributions being lost and increases productivity. It also engenders a sense of procedural justice (Kim and Mauborgne 1995) as everyone is able to contribute and listen.
- It is transparent – which enables participants to easily see where the process is going. As such this procedural rationality (Simon 1976) increases its credibility with participants. They are more likely to contribute and engage with the process.

Starting an Oval Mapping Session

As noted above, when starting any form of group workshop there are a number of important aspects to consider. With Oval Mapping, there are a couple of tasks that need to be covered before the workshop (falling into the 'pre-meeting' stage). The first is determining who is going to attend – both to ensure that a range of views and perspectives are covered and secondly to get buy in from those that have the power to make it happen (or not happen). OMT workshops work best when there are around seven to nine people (more than this is hard to manage) and therefore there is always the trade-off between getting buy-in and emotional commitment from participants versus ensuring all have airtime.

It is also worth considering where the workshop is to be held, when, what is to be told to the participants, etc. Whilst location might not sound significant, it can have a fundamental effect on the outcomes. Choose a room that has plenty of wall space which is amenable to flip chart sheets being posted onto the walls (Blu-tack or sticky putty is best for this). Typically OMT works best when there are at least 14–16 sheets of flip chart paper set up – see Fig. 4.14) and the surface is conducive to being able to write on the sheets easily (wood panelling or textured wall paper are to be avoided). OMT workshops are usually effective over about 3 h and running the workshop in the morning can ensure participants are mentally fresh. Whilst getting these details right won't guarantee success they will help to reduce problems that could derail a successful intervention (McFadzean and Nelson 1998).

For the workshop itself, it is important to provide clear directions to the group covering issues such as agenda, objectives and ground rules. The first 10 min of a meeting can be critical towards the overall meeting's success (Phillips and Phillips 1993). Below are a set of steps which have been found to be useful.

1. Encourage participation by going through guidelines for writing up statements (see 3 and 4 below) – helping participants in this way can settle their concerns.
2. Explain that this process is aimed to get at their expertise – note that they are the experts and therefore it is important for them to surface all of the considerations around the particular topic being discussed. This is their opportunity and anything not raised in this forum can't be considered.
3. Stress one statement per oval – this ensures that the writing on the ovals is sufficiently large to be able to be read by all and will also facilitate linking. When there is more than one statement on the oval they will need to be disaggregated.
4. Recommend six to ten words each contribution – that they follow the mapping formalisms in that they avoid single words and questions and so work to write up action oriented statements.
5. Warn that there is no removing of other's ovals! This is one that always gets a laugh when it is mentioned but nevertheless is important. Encourage participants to write up on a new oval why they agree/ disagree with a statement so that the rationale is captured.
6. Piggyback off one another's statements – encourage them to use the unfolding material as a set of prompts – tapping new thoughts and considerations. This is often worth doing towards the end of the generation stage when contributions are

drying up. Try asking "what might be some of the possible alternatives for achieving X" or "what other consequences might occur", etc.

7. Explain the role of the facilitator(s) – noting that the facilitator is not there to provide substance but rather work to cluster the material to help them make sense of it. If there are two facilitators (one capturing the material into *Decision Explorer* and the other moving the material around and encouraging contributions) then explain this process and purpose.

8. Issue pens, and ovals – it is important to provide all participants with the same pens; partly to make sure that the nibs are large enough to ensure that the writing can be read by all, and partly to provide some anonymity. Most people can't recognize one another's handwriting but if someone is working with a distinctive pen then this will highlight ownership.

9. Ask participants, once they have written down a few statements on to the ovals, to put them on the wall. This way other participants can piggyback off the contributions.

Running an OMT Workshop

When running the session be prepared for the first few moments to be a little 'quiet' as participants begin to think about what is important, and write down their contributions. There is often a slight hesitation to be the first to put up a contribution but once the group gets started then there is often a rush of contributions being placed on the wall. This initial generation stage may last for up to 30 min but typically the group starts to slow down before that. A good way of prompting for more material is to ask participants to review the material already posted and consider possible consequences, explanations and constraints. This not only increases the breadth of material but also increases the chance that participants read the contributions of others.

During this period of generation try to cluster the material into groups of similar material e.g. a cluster on staff, competition, funding, etc. Don't get too concerned about getting ovals into the 'right' cluster – the group can review and confirm (or change) the clusters and it is important that they feel they are able to do this. The objective here is to help the group manage the extensiveness of the material and thus reduce the cognitive load. The more the material is broken down into clear clusters the more they feel they can contribute. One tip to identifying clusters is to try moving contributions around to see where they fit. Also be prepared to change clusters if new material emerges suggesting different groupings. Where clusters become very large (30+ statements) see if you can break them down into sub-clusters. Encourage the participants to put their ovals into the clusters – it makes your job easier and gets them further involved in the emerging picture. Remember that these clusters will get modified as they become causal clusters rather than topic clusters (see the analysis section above).

Once the group has exhausted all the contributions they can make – at least initially – try to position the ovals so that in each cluster the most hierarchically super-ordinate is at the top and those that are more detailed are at the bottom. A tea or coffee break is a good time to do this.

The next stage moves away from apparent brainstorming to the structuring process and it is here that the most value emerges. With the group's help begin to confirm that the statements in the cluster belong there by reviewing the material in each cluster. The next stage which further helps sharpen the meaning of the clusters is to begin to start linking the ovals – building up the chains of argument. At this point further material will be generated as participants, when explaining how one oval links to another, provide detailed explanation. This in turn prompts another participant to realise that their perception is quite different – they saw a completely different chain of argument. When different arguments are identified it is important to avoid arguing about which is correct and capture both views.

The linking process therefore helps move the group from what is essentially a divergent picture to one that is a shared picture of the situation which can reveal quite important insights. For example, the cluster might expose a totally different understanding of a term or process. When eliciting these additional views, it is important to get the participants to write up the new material on new ovals – partly as it reduces the load from the facilitator but more significantly because it ensures that the contributions are in their handwriting gaining further ownership. Additionally it is worth using this period of the workshop to convert any statements that are not currently action oriented into a more action oriented phraseology and elaborate any single or two worded statements. Figure 4.15 shows the process of working through the clusters and Fig. 4.16 shows a cluster of material.

One tip that facilitates the linking process is to number all of the ovals as the links are made. This allows links from an oval in one cluster to be easily linked to an oval in another cluster some distance away. Rather than drawing in a long link, a small arrow with the oval's number can be written onto the flip chart. This process helps the group begin to see how the initial topic clusters they have identified interrelate whilst keeping the picture relatively tidy and amenable to effective working. The numbering also helps let the group know how many contributions they have made and if entering the map into *Decision Explorer* facilitates that process too – particularly if it is being done during the OMT workshop (as the ovals move around and are therefore difficult to capture).

Don't worry if it takes quite a bit of time to review, extend and link the first cluster – the first few always take the longest. As the group becomes more familiar with the process, and more of the material is worked through, then the process becomes quicker. Encourage discussion and make sure that all participants are able to feel part of the process.

Finishing an OMT Workshop

Reaching agreements follows from the continued exploration of the material generated. Each of the clusters is continuously reviewed to confirm that the material is captured accurately and linked appropriately. Check whether anything is missing. During this stage (or earlier when working through the clusters) it is a good idea to identify the 'head' (top point) of each cluster and with the group determining whether it forms a good title for the cluster.

Fig. 4.15 Working through the clusters

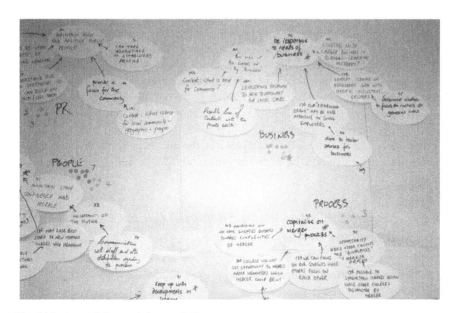

Fig. 4.16 A set of clusters being worked up

The forms of analysis discussed earlier (for using the software) are an appropriate way to begin identifying key issues and potent options. Although the analyses cannot be undertaken thoroughly it is possible to get the group to work together with the principles of analysis introduced to them by the facilitator. The process will usually seek to have the group (a) identify busy ovals (with lots of ins and outs), (b) look for options that hit many clusters (and the 'heads' of clusters), (c) gather together all of the heads of clusters and check them as a possible goal system (set of multiple criteria), and d) look for any feedback loops. Each of these provides a deeper understanding of the nature of the problem being addressed. In addition the analyses give some clues about where priority actions might lie. As with mapping in individual interviews using asterisks when using Decision Explorer, different colours can be used to distinguish statements that have different kinds of status.

Needless to say none of these analyses replaces the judgment of the group, but each does lead the group towards discussing possible agreements about a way forward to resolve the problem.

Concluding the workshop with some form of prioritisation of the options can be helpful. Within each of the clusters, identify those statements that potentially are options (or can be rewritten as options). Then provide each participant with a number of self-adhesive dots (see Fig. 4.16) and ask them to attach them to the options they think are the most important. If they believe that a particular option is very important then they can allocate more of the dots (resources) to this option. In addition, two colours can be used – one to determine short term and the other long term. This provides an indication of consensus and resource allocation by forcing a choice about what to focus on as solutions. Other criteria include having one colour of dot to indicate degree of leverage and another to show degree of practicality. Finally, when there are likely to be considerable disagreements it also can help to use one colour of dots as a veto. Although social pressures may reduce its effectiveness providing the opportunity to veto is an important aspect to procedural justice.

The conclusion of the workshop relies upon reaching reasonable consensus about priorities for action – full consensus is an ideal but is difficult to detect and usually impossible to attain.

Photographs of the final stages of the workshop provide un-manipulated 'minutes' for agreements and context.

For more details and case examples on the practice of Oval mapping see Ackermann and Eden (2001a, b) and Bryson et al. (2004a, b).

4.2.7   Working in a Facilitator Supported (Single User) Visual Interactive Model

4.2.7.1   Introduction to Facilitator Supported Modelling

The facilitator supported mode of working with *Decision Explorer* can run in four different ways. It can follow on from a series of interviews involving cognitive mapping (where the resultant maps have been entered into *Decision Explorer* and woven together as a group causal map using the analysis procedures mentioned above). It can also follow on from using the oval mapping technique (either during the same workshop or after and, potentially, with another group). A third possibility is where a model has been build from an analysis of documents (see Eden and Ackermann 2004a, b). Finally it can also be used as a starting point for the modelling exercise. This form, however, makes heavy demands on the facilitator to ensure that all the contributions are captured and linked appropriately. This is particularly the case at the start as contributions can be surfaced very quickly and discussion and debate generates considerable material.

Whereas the OMT or individual interviews act as powerful capturing and structuring opportunities, these facilitator driven workshops not only allow for development of the model in terms of content capture but also facilitate the development of common understandings and a shared language. As with OMT, participants are able to see their ideas within the context of those of others, thus extending an individual's understanding of different perspectives. In both cases having the material projected on to a public screen or wall helps separate the proponent from the contribution and thus helps the contribution to be judged on its merit. Capturing ideas into a publicly viewable map also allows participants to be able to move from a physiological 'knee-jerk' stance to one that is more thoughtful as participants do not have to immediately respond to the material. Thus the model becomes a 'negotiative' device allowing participants to listen to one another, to have time to mentally digest different views and therefore work more gently towards an agreement. Techniques of successful negotiation – both social and psychological – therefore play a prominent role in this form of SODA workshop.

4.2.7.2   Why Use the Software Supported Mode?

There are a number of reasons for choosing to use the single user mode of working. These include:

- The ability for participants to focus on the issue at hand rather than being distracted by ovals. When facilitated effectively it also reduces the risk of contributions being lost – the facilitator works to capture them rather than requiring participants to write them on ovals.
- Tighter adherence to the mapping guidelines – the facilitator is able to ensure compliance and take the cognitive load. In OMT mode, participants generate material that requires considerable tidying up to extract its full impact – this is particularly the case when entering links. Because of the ability to edit and re-edit on a continuous basis, flexibility in presentation is easy.
- Increased productivity through being able to exert greater concentration on the issue/situation. Being able to watch the map develop helps to avoid distractions such as trying to "get a word in edgeways", or to think through the implications of what is being said. It also helps to avoid the frustrations of long debates around a single non-contextualized point of view. Most participants at the end of a workshop report that although they feel exhausted they genuinely believe that they have made progress despite previous struggles (Eden and Galer 1990).

Fig. 4.17 A group focusing on the main screen working on a model produced from the morning's OMT session, which can be seen on the wall

• Like OMT it is relatively easy to set up and run. All that is required is a laptop computer, data projector with good resolution (preferably better than XGA), and a large screen (see Fig. 4.17). The better the resolution of the projector the more 'readable' are the statements – as well as allowing more to be brought on to the screen (this can be up to 50+ statements as the group slowly increases the material represented on a single view).

4.2.7.3   Running a Single User Workshop

As noted above, the set up demands for single user working are relatively straight forward.

In terms of layout of the workshop location, seating participants in a semi circle around a central screen/projected image is a good starting point as it enables all to easily read what is on the screen and see one another (keeping the social context). It is also important to have comfortable seats and appropriate refreshments (see Hickling 1990, for more details on good room design). Avoiding interruptions from the 'day to day' work can further help concentration and so running the session off site or in another office building may be considered. Getting the 'trivialities' of workshop design right will increase the probability of other, more important, activities working as planned.

When starting with a new map, it is worth being clear what the focal point of the intervention is and displaying it in the centre of the public screen. Where the model is already in existence, it is important firstly to review the existing material so that participants have an overview of what is in the model (see section 4.2.5.7 on producing an overview). The first part of an overview typically comprises a map of key/central issues and goals. This helps the group make sense of the complex material without feeling too overwhelmed. Having pre-worked up views that depict the material supporting each key issue (the equivalent of a 'hieset' – see section 4.2.5.6) also helps when working through the model's existing content. Finally having a set of text styles that not only comprise goals, key issues, and potent options but also a style that depicts agreed strategies (differentiated from key issues, but often the consequence of rewording key issues into strategy statements) and agreed actions (green for go) facilitates seamless working.

In both cases the participants will cycle between generation of new material, tentative agreements, digestion, and back to generation. Therefore designing the workshop to work on a cycle of around 20–30 min for each area of consideration (possibly clusters or hiesets) allows participants to explore, reflect, and move on with a sense of progression.

A few hints and tips for working in the software supported mode.

- Set up styles in advance (without borders – borders make it more difficult to see the box appearing around 'selected concepts') – use clear, easy to read fonts (Times Roman and Arial work best – try them out with the projector being used).
- Start with a few concepts on the screen (~15). This helps avoid participants being overwhelmed and not knowing where to start reading. Bring more material on as the group 'digests' the initial material. Try to avoid moving concepts around too frequently – whilst there is always the temptation to 'tidy' up the view, it can be distracting and frustrating to participants who have just worked out where statements are, to discover that they are no longer there!
- Turn off menus (where possible) as they can be very distracting! When first working with *Decision Explorer* having menus available is probably necessary. However, once more familiarity with 'hot-keys' has been gained, removing the menus provides: a) more screen room to view statements, and b) less distraction as the group doesn't usually need to see the menus.
- Work in 'fit to view' mode – as it will allow participants to see the whole of a map and it is possible to dynamically capture and review all of the material. When the statements become unreadable then it is likely to be an indication that a new view is needed.
- Capture as much of the dialogue as possible – as with doing interviews it is worth capturing the statements and then reviewing the links with the group.
- Review progress approximately every 20 min – this allows the group to go through a process of generation/creation/development/agreement and then digestion. It also helps the facilitator ensure that all the relevant material has

been captured along with any links to statements in the current view or to other parts of the model.

- Use views to 'drill down' and look at areas in more depth. As noted above, a view for each key issue can be helpful, as can views for loops.
- Analysis – should be used sparingly during the workshop. However, gaps such as coffee and lunch breaks can provide opportunities to see what emerges from the use of analysis tools.
- Have printed copies of 'starter' maps to hand so that you can easily refer to them – copies might also be useful for group members. Save regularly – it is software!

4.2.7.4 Summary

At the end of a workshop, it is helpful to reflect with the group on the progress to date and to clarify next steps. Building in sufficient time for the group to review agreements is important as it provides not only a sense of closure but also ensures that the messages taken back to others are consistent. Providing a set of print outs of all the material provides a very tangible deliverable – even if a more refined and 'tidied up' set is provided later.

For more information on the use of software supported workshops see Ackermann and Eden (1997)

4.2.8 Reflections on the Method

SODA therefore expects to provide the following benefits

- *Problem structuring* (through the capture and structuring process) and analysis of aggregated maps.
- Ability to help members of the group *change their minds* about the nature of the situation through seeing what others perceive and not having to respond immediately – time to think and act more cognitively than physiologically.
- The ability to *negotiate* a group view of the problem through appreciating the different perspectives, considering all options and their associated ramifications, and developing a sense of shared ownership and commitment.
- More *creativity* in option generation – through the ability to continue to build on one another's contributions rather than be reduced to just working with those that can be held on to mentally.
- *Real-time interaction* with the model. The ability to play with contributions, explore them, and dynamically amend and extend the model ensures greater understanding and ownership.
- *On-line minutes* and post workshop *review* – an organizational memory that can easily be referred to – particularly in the case of exploring why a particular option has been chosen (through looking at the consequences and explanations).
- Reduce the impact of dysfunctional *interpersonal dynamics*. By allowing all views to be heard, and appreciating the different rationales, etc.

- Gain enough commitment to *devote time and energy* to getting it right. The sense of being able to manage the complexity, and the feeling that progress is being made energizes the group to continue the work.

4.3 Developments in the Uses of SODA

The foundations of SODA lie in the use of cognitive mapping as an important early stage in capturing subjectivism. Section 4.2 explored the skills needed for creating cognitive maps. In this section we explore the development of SODA over the last 15 years. As we will see, most of these developments are related to using the principles of SODA within the context of a group setting only. This orientation has been driven significantly by seeking to meet the challenge of undertaking effective problem-solving directly with a group and within the context of achieving significant outcomes in half a day or less.

The structure of this last section starts with a focus on the more effective management of social processes and negotiation within organisations, within the context of higher group productivity with respect to problem-solving. This focus introduces the potential of SODA in the broader-based application of strategy making. In particular, we discuss two applications of a developed SODA methodology with respect to exploring future scenarios and stakeholder management. We also consider some of the ways in which SODA has been integrated with other operational research techniques, specifically system dynamics modelling. Finally we consider some of the ways in which SODA can be implemented in low risk problem-solving projects.

4.3.1 Managing Social Processes

4.3.1.1 Increasing Social and Psychological Negotiation

A significant foundation for the development of SODA was the view of organisations as negotiated enterprises where each participant in an organisation subjectively defines problems. That is to say, each member of a management team has a different perspective on any problem as a result of their particular role, experience, education, and setting within the organisation. Members of the team are conscious that they need to continue to coexist at the level of social relationships as well as with respect to solving problems together. We have called these two aspects negotiated social order and socially negotiated order (Eden and Ackermann 1998). Negotiated social order suggests that problem solving depends upon negotiating new social relationships in order for implementation to occur. Socially negotiated order implies that problem solving is a social process where solutions are the result of social negotiation.

However, alongside a recognition of the significance of social negotiation was also the recognition that problem solving is about members of the team changing their mind -- psychological negotiation. Thus, one emphasis in the development of SODA must always be on facilitating more effective social and psychological negotiation.

The construction of a causal map, as a model amenable to analysis, is an important part of negotiation. Negotiation depends upon people gradually shifting their positions and so the model, and the results of analysis, should be continuously in transition. For many, the use of SODA is focused upon the construction of static cognitive maps which are then merged into a static group map. The static nature of these maps, as models, is largely the result of the technology available for constructing maps – typically, a pencil and large piece of paper for constructing cognitive maps in an interview situation, the use of post-its or Ovals displayed on flipchart sheets on the wall for group work. In both of these cases it is possible to envisage changing both the wording of nodes and the placement of causal links. However, time pressures tend to discourage keeping the model in continuous transition, even though the productive outcomes of doing so usually make it worthwhile. In a group situation it is even more important to allow for changing wording to reflect increased ownership and changing causal links to reflect discussion and elaboration. Rewriting of a post-it or oval takes time which interrupts the flow of a meeting and so is not done often enough.

An additional, and important, aspect of good negotiation is the need to pay attention to anonymity when appropriate. The merging of maps into one group map retains some important aspects of anonymity, however, working with a group directly using post-it or ovals cannot ensure absolute anonymity. Nevertheless, anonymity plays an important role in successful negotiation.

4.3.1.2 Group Productivity Issues

Techniques such as SODA are of most use in the context of complex and messy problems. Dealing with these sorts of problems typically involves managers and experts who are short of time. Over the past 15 years the need to find ways of increasing the productivity of group problem-solving episodes has become increasingly important (Eden and Ackermann 2004). There have been two distinct approaches to addressing this problem: (a) working to a cycle of providing a deliverable – a 'take-away' approximately every hour, and (b) developing and using a computer based Group Decision Support System (GDSS) specifically designed to support SODA. The first of these approaches seeks to ensure that it is possible to design a problem-solving workshop that can be completed in one hour, where the deliverable at the end of the hour can inform the next stage of problem-solving. Each stage allows for a more thorough development. The second approach allows for parallel processing, computer supported analysis, and organisational memory in the form of a computer file.

4.3.1.3   Negotiation and Productivity: Using a Group Decision Support System (GDSS)

In the early 1990s the first version of a SODA based group decision support system was developed. Given the nature of technology at that time the system was based upon a hardwired network of laptop computers each running specially designed software. The laptop computers acted as consoles – one for each participant – and permitted direct communication with causal mapping software (*Decision Explorer*). The communication was controlled through the use of specially designed computer software that acted as a chauffeur. The chauffeur controlled the network and retained statistics about progress. In addition the chauffeur controlled electronic preferencing and rating, where participants were able to express their preferences with respect to options (the equivalent of using sticky dots in the low-tech version), and rate options with respect to, for example, the degree of leverage in relation to goals. The system was tested over a period of 5 years before being redeveloped at a professional level.

The group decision support system – called *Group Explorer* – permitted the achievement of a number of important objectives: (a) a causal map that could be in continuous transition where statements could be quickly and easily edited and causal links modified, (b) anonymity of contribution of statements or arrows, (c) the use of all the facilities available in *Decision Explorer*, particularly the use of styles to indicate different types of statement (goals, options, strategies, agreed actions, etc.). Significantly, the parallel processing possibilities increased the productivity of the group.

The system has now been used extensively with a wide range of different groups: top management teams in multinationals, small and medium-size enterprises, and public and not-for-profit organisations. Participants are consistently amazed at the progress that can be made in short periods of time using a combination of the SODA methodology alongside the group decision support system (see, for example, Andersen et al. 2010).

The use of a group decision support system replicates the use of oval mapping with a group without the requirement for initial one-to-one cognitive mapping interviews. Using SODA directly with the group is less expensive on participant and facilitator time, but does reduce the degree of richness that can be obtained through one-to-one interviews. It is also more demanding on the facilitator.

4.3.1.4   New and Better Researched Applications

Since the introduction of SODA as a soft-Operational Research methodology in the 1980s many of the principles have been extended and developed in other applications.

4.3.1.5 Strategy Making

The acronym, SODA, implies that the methodology is likely to be most applicable in exploring strategic options. Since strategic options are usually explored in relation to messy and complex problems, it is not surprising that situation exploration was likely to be relevant to strategy development. Indeed, many management teams who had been exposed to the use of SODA for exploring strategic problems wanted to continue using the techniques and processes as a part of strategic thinking and the development of strategy.

The structure of strategy (Eden and Ackermann 2001) – a network of goals, supported by a network of strategies, supported by a hierarchy of tangible actions – was similar to the hierarchy used in strategic problem-solving (see Fig. 4.9).

A significant area of concern in strategic planning had been the likelihood of a well-developed rationalistic strategic plan being ignored by those with power. The lack of ownership of a strategy by members of the top management team was a matter of great concern. The interactive way of working that is a strong feature of SODA was an attractive way of engaging a management team directly in the development of their own strategies.

Thus, during the mid to late 1990s the SODA method began to morph into a method for developing strategy. 1998 saw the publication of *Making Strategy: the Journey of Strategic Management* (Eden and Ackermann 1998) which discussed developments of SODA that addressed important concepts from strategic management. In particular, it became clear that the early stages of strategy making should include paying attention to the organisation's existing *emergent* strategy as well as to the development of any new strategic plans. The way in which members of the strategy making team defined important issues that needed to be addressed in order to create a successful strategic future was taken to be an indicator of emergent strategy. The issues and their relationships were easily depicted through a map. Exploring networks of issues was a straightforward development of the early stages of a SODA intervention.

Similarly, developments in addressing competitive advantage through the exploration of patterns of distinctive competences were articulated through the exploration and analysis of causal maps. The causal maps allowed for the identification of patterns of competences where it was the pattern that was distinctive (Bryson et al. 2007; Eden and Ackermann 2000, 2010b). The process was designed to pay particular attention to self-sustaining distinctiveness through the identification of feedback loops. In considering strategic management, the journey additionally encompassed consideration of the strategic management of stakeholders (Ackermann and Eden 2010). In particular the exploration of stakeholders involved participants surfacing various formal and informal relationships which once captured were amendable to analysis. Similarly the exploration of alternative futures – scenario building – became an exploration of the links between possible future events. The particular characteristics that followed from SODA as a methodology being adapted for the development of strategy was a focus upon the *systemicity* of issues, competences, goals, and stakeholders.

The notion of strategy making being a journey reflects the two significant concepts of negotiated social order and socially negotiated order that were central to SODA as a methodology. In other words, the process followed – the journey – is as important as the outcome. In addition, 'Journey' represented an important acronym to describe jointly understanding, reflecting upon, and negotiating strategy: JoURNeY. By expressing strategy development as a social process, the SODA methodology moved forward by paying respect to the importance of procedural justice (Kim and Mauborgne 1995) in encouraging consensus building and ownership.

The journey making process was further elaborated through the publication of *The Practice of Making Strategy* (Ackermann et al. 2005). Here was a focus on the incremental development of a strategy through a series of manageable tasks. The final outcome of the tasks was to be a "statement of strategic intent" for an organization, but each of the tasks led to a continuing refinement of the strategy. In this way the intention was to break up the process of strategy making into 'bite-size' chunks.

4.3.1.6   Informing Strategy Through the Development of Scenarios: One Specific Strategy Example

A key aspect of developing robust and practical strategies lies in understanding some of the significant changes that could happen to the environment during the period of time in which a strategy is being implemented. It is typical for us to think about the future as the trend development of the present. In other words, the future is projected from the present. Clearly a trend projected future is both possible and highly probable. However, such a future depends upon the structural characteristics of the past and present remaining in place. It is also possible the future may be determined by a number of critical events that break the trend. Of course, the critical event can arise when a trend variable reaches a critical point. For example, the demand in taking journeys by train may be forecast to continue growing but nevertheless reach a point of overcrowding where 'riots' are likely. The event of a 'riot' may lead to the destruction of train rolling stock, which may in turn lead to further overcrowding. Extensive overcrowding, and the disruption caused to passengers, may lead to government renationalising the railway network. A sequence of causally related events can gradually develop into a story about the future.

The process of envisaging possible alternative futures is encompassed within the well-established technique of scenario planning (van der Heijden 1996). However, most of the published techniques are resource intensive. Often it is simply impossible to devote high levels of resource to considering what are often seen as highly improbable scenarios, when set against simple trend forecasting. The use of causal mapping and the simple group process exemplified by SODA can provide a basis for undertaking some limited scenario development as a two hour workshop (see Eden and Ackermann 1998, Chapter C8 for an example).

In brief, the process involves group participants in suggesting possible future events that could have a serious impact on the success of any proposed strategy. Participants write out each event on a separate 'oval' as with oval mapping.

Only after participants have contributed all the events they can think of are the ovals linked together through causality. The causal map produced in this manner now encompasses a variety of future stories. Some of these stories cluster together as a relatively isolated scenario, others are highly interwoven. Some stories are triggered by, and totally dependent upon, a single starting event. Others encompass a portfolio of events. Thus, the peace scenario for Northern Ireland that is presented in *Making Strategy* (1998, p. 153) shows a series of linked stories all of which follow from the trigger event of an amnesty agreed for large numbers of paramilitary prisoners coupled with the government agreeing a ceasefire with republican paramilitaries. Three significant, but at the time surprising, event outcomes arise from these triggers: worsening industrial relations within the Northern Ireland prison service, a rising population of ordinary criminal (as opposed to political) prisoners, and prison staff fears of contamination from AIDS. The development of the stories depended upon linking together a set of suggested future events that had been treated as if they were independent during the first stage of the scenario development process.

In developing possible scenarios it is not necessary to make judgements about the probabilities of their occurrence. However, probabilistic forecasting could follow from the development of such maps through the use of Bayesian statistics and Monte Carlo simulation. However, the main purpose of developing scenarios is to explore the robustness of strategy with respect to unexpected futures. In doing so strategies can be refined and sensitivities developed. The process of exploring alternative futures means that managers are more likely to see futures unfolding earlier than would otherwise be the case, and this provides competitive advantage.

4.3.1.7 Multimethod Models: SD and Project Management

An essential aspect of SODA is that part which is about problem structuring. Delivering the structure of a problem through cognitive or causal mapping invites the identification of possible feedback loops. Earlier in this chapter we have discussed the potential for identifying false feedback loops, where the feedback depends upon a causal link which is incorrect. However, as we have also suggested, legitimate feedback suggests dynamic behaviour in the system. Feedback may suggest self-sustaining behaviour or controlling behaviour. If feedback is self-sustaining the behaviour may be vicious or virtuous. Alternatively, controlling feedback (a negative feedback loop) means that any shift in the state of a variable in the feedback loop results in the system returning to its original state.

The qualitative feedback structures that can be identified through the application of SODA will suggest obvious interventions that might reinforce a virtuous cycle, ensure that controlling feedback continues to work as long as it is desired, or look for ways of destroying a vicious cycle. However, as we mentioned earlier, it is sometimes appropriate to develop a simulation model of such dynamic behaviour to deepen understanding. Because the process of identifying feedback in the system is the process of identifying system dynamics, then system dynamics simulation methods are the appropriate way of exploring policy options through computer simulation.

The translation of cognitive maps, to causal maps, to influence diagrams, to the formal structure and system dynamics models and stocks, flows, and auxiliary variables requires considerable effort. Indeed the process of estimating the quantitative parameters of a system dynamics model is a skilled process. Nevertheless, it can be seen as a designed process (Howick et al. 2008) where each step introduces important analytical questions that will help resolve policy questions (see Eden et al. 2009).

4.3.1.8   Cognitive Change/Negotiation

Causal mapping has been consistently used to facilitate negotiation both within and across organisations. In recent years there have been careful studies of the implications for negotiation of understanding the processes by which participants contribute their views and causally link them together (Shaw 2003; Ackermann and Eden 2007). In the field of social psychology there have been a number of studies that suggest that participants in group decision making largely ignore the views of others unless those views match their own. Stasser and Titus (2003) provide a good summary of this stream of research. The use of causal mapping, and the process of mapping based upon the principles of SODA, appears to address some of the issues raised in this psychology based research.

In particular, the *gradual* shift in meaning of any statement on a causal map as causally related statements are added and as changes to the context and content occurs, enables cognitive change to occur. Rather than information being seen as isolated chunks, the mapping process facilitates a degree of equivocality that 'oils the wheels' of negotiation.

There appears to be considerable promise in the use of mapping as a way of facilitating negotiation in situations of overt conflict (Ackermann and Eden, 2010c).

4.3.1.9   Small Steps in Application: Low Risk Projects

One of the difficulties for potential users of methodologies such as SODA relates to the level of risk associated with trying to use a reasonably complex methodology with a real group for the first time. In the main part of this chapter (section 4.2.2.9) we have suggested a number of approaches to gaining experience in mapping. Undoubtedly, this must be a first step in developing the appropriate skills in the application of SODA. However, assuming a reasonable level of mapping skills, where formalities are adhered to, then the next step is to undertake some problem solving with a real group. Keeping risks down by advertising a reduced level of expectation of the group is an obvious first step (see also Eden and Ackermann 2004; Ackermann and Eden 2004).

Establishing frequent milestones, where each milestone produces a group deliverable, can be helpful. This means that the SODA episode can be designed in a manner that does not indicate premature closure as far as the group is concerned. An initial first milestone can be related to the surfacing of statements and agreeing their linkage. The first deliverable becomes the outcome of crude clustering and the identification of central nodes. The clusters provide for an overview of the problem, and the identification of central nodes provides an indication of where the 'nub of the issue' lies. The basis for establishing priorities will have been established. This milestone can be reached through the use of oval mapping or the use of *Decision Explorer* linked to a data projector. If this first milestone is reached in a satisfactory manner it is likely that the group would want to pursue matters further.

Earlier in this chapter we discussed the process of mapping the contents of a document. In particular, we discussed this activity in the context of learning how to do mapping. However, exploring the published goals system of an organisation by reverse engineering it into a causal map can often be extremely revealing and helpful. Goals statements often do not present the ways in which one goal supports another and in turn is supported by others. Thus, readers get no sense of the means/end structure and so see each goal as relatively independent and do not appreciate its overall purpose. Reverse engineering a goals statement into a map typically identifies strange means/end links and isolated statements. This process can work as the basis of the guiding group discussion about the redevelopment of the more carefully worded goals system. It is relatively low risk because it can be exploratory rather than being set up as an attack on the current goals statement.

References

Ackermann, F. 1996. Participants Perceptions on the Role of Facilitators using Group Decision Support Systems. *Group Decision and Negotiation*, 5: 93–112.

Ackermann, F. and Eden, C. 1994. Issues in Computer and Non-Computer Supported GDSSs. *International Journal of Decision Support Systems*, 12: 381–390.

Ackermann, F. and Eden, C. 1997. Contrasting GDSSs and GSSs in the Context of Strategic Change: Implications for Facilitation. *Journal of Decision Systems*, 6: 221–250.

Ackermann, F. and Eden, C. 2001a. Contrasting Single User and Networked Group Decision Support Systems for Strategy Making. *Group Decision and Negotiation*, 10: 47–66.

Ackermann, F. and Eden, C. 2001b. SODA – Journey Making and Mapping in Practice. In Rosenhead, J. and Mingers, J. (Eds.), *Rational Analysis in a Problematic World Revisited*: 43–60. London: Wiley.

Ackermann, F. and Eden, C. 2004. Using Causal mapping: individual and group; traditional and new. In Pidd, M. (Eds.), *Systems Modelling: Theory and Practice*: 127–145. Chichester: Wiley.

Ackermann, F. and Eden, C. 2010a. Strategic Management of Stakeholders: theory and practice. *Long Range Planning*, forthcoming.

Ackermann, F. and Eden, C. 2010b. Negotiation in Strategy Making Teams: Group Support Systems and the Process of Cognitive Change. *Group Decision and Negotiation*, forthcoming.

Ackermann, F. and Eden, C. 2010c. The Role of Group Decision Support Systems: negotiating safe energy. In Kilgour, M. and Eden, C. (Eds.), *Handbook for Group Decision and Negotiation*: Dordrecht: Springer.

Ackermann, F., Eden, C., and Williams, T. 1997. Modeling for Litigation: Mixing Qualitative and Quantitative Approaches. *Interfaces*, 27: 48–65.

Ackermann, F., Eden, C., with Brown, I. 2005. *The Practice of Making Strategy: A Step by Step Guide*. London: Sage.

Ackoff, R. L. 1981. *Creating the Corporate Future*. New York: Wiley.

Andersen, D., Richardson, G. P., Ackermann, F., and Eden, C. Using the *Group Explorer* Group Support System to Add Value to Group Model Building. *System Dynamics Review*, Forthcoming.

Belton, V., Ackermann, F., and Shepherd, I. 1997. Integrated Support from Problem Structuring through to Alternative Evaluation Using COPE and V.I.S.A. *Journal of Multi-Criteria Decision Analysis*, 6: 115–130.

Bougon, M., Weick, K., and Binkhorst, D. 1977. Cognition in organizations: analysis of the Utrecht Jazz Orchestra. *Administrative Science Quarterly*, 22: 609–632.

Bryson, J. B., Ackermann, F., Eden, C., and Finn, C. 2004a. The Oval Mapping Process: Identifying Strategic Issues and Formulating Effective Strategies. In *Strategic Planning for Public and Non-Profit Organisations*: 355–376. San Francisco: Jossey Bass.

Bryson, J., Ackermann, F., Eden, C., and Finn, C. 2004b. *Visible Thinking: Unlocking Causal Mapping for Practical Business Results*. Chichester: Wiley.

Bryson, J. M., Ackermann, F., and Eden, C. 2007. Putting the Resource-Based View of Strategy and Distinctive Competencies To Work in Public Organizations. *Public Administration Review*, July.

Buzan, T. and Buzan, B. 1993. *The mind map book*. London: BBC Books.

Eden, C. 1987. Problem Solving or Problem Finishing? In Jackson, M. C. Keys P. (Eds.), *New Directions in Management Science*: 97–107. Hants: Gower.

Eden, C. 1988. Cognitive Mapping: a review. *European Journal of Operational Research*, 36: 1–13.

Eden, C. 1990. The Unfolding Nature of Group Decision Support. In Eden, C. and Radford, J. (Eds.), *Tackling Strategic Problems: the role of group decision support*: 48–52. London: Sage.

Eden, C. 2004. Analyzing Cognitive Maps to Help Structure Issues or Problems. *European Journal of Operational Research*, 159: 673–686.

Eden, C. and Ackermann, F. 1998. *Making Strategy: The Journey of Strategic Management*. London: Sage.

Eden, C. and Ackermann, F. 2000. Mapping distinctive competencies: a systemic approach. *Journal of the Operational Research Society*, 51: 12–20.

Eden, C. and Ackermann, F. 2001. A Mapping Framework for Strategy Making. In Huff, A. and Jenkins, M. (Eds.), *Mapping Strategy*: 173–195. London: Wiley.

Eden, C. and Ackermann, F. 2004a. Cognitive Mapping Expert Views for Policy Analysis in the Public Sector. *European Journal of Operational Research*, 152: 615–630.

Eden, C. and Ackermann, F. 2004b. Use of 'soft-OR' models by clients – what do they want from them? In Pidd, M. (Eds.), *Systems Modelling: Theory and Practice*: 146–163. Chichester: Wiley.

Eden, C. and Ackermann, F. 2007. The Resource Based View: theory and practice. *Presented to Academy of Management Conference Philadelphia*.

Eden, C. and Ackermann, F. 2010. Competences, Distinctive Competences, and Core Competences. In Sanchez, R. and Heene, A. (Eds.), *Contemporary Perspectives on Competence-Based Management, Advances in Applied Business Strategy*, Volume 12: Bingley: Emerald Group.

Eden, C. and Galer, G. 1990. A Client's perspective. *Long Range Planning*, 23: 42–43.

Eden, C., Jones, S., and Sims, D. 1979. *Thinking in Organisations*. London: Macmillan.

Eden, C., Jones, S., and Sims, D. 1983. *Messing about in problems; an informal structured approach to their identification and management,* Oxford: Pergamon.

Eden, C., Jones, S., and Sims, D. 1994. Misunderstandings: understanding problems and the problems of misunderstanding. In Armson, R. and Paton, R. (Eds.), *Organizations: cases, issues, concepts*: London: Paul Chapman Publishing.

Eden, C., Ackermann, F., Bryson, J., Richardson, G., Andersen, D., and Finn, C. 2009. Integrating Modes of Policy Analysis and Strategic Management Practice: Requisite Elements and Dilemmas. *Journal of the Operational Research Society*, 60: 2–13.

Friend, J. and Hickling, A. 1987. *Planning Under Pressure: The Strategic Choice Approach*. Oxford: Pergamon.

Harvey, J. 1988. The Abilene Paradox: the management of agreement. *Organizational Dynamics*, Summer: 17–34.

Hickling, A. 1990. 'Decision Spaces': A Scenario about Designing Appropriate Rooms for Group Decision Management. *Tackling Strategic Problems: the role of group decision support*, 169–177.

Hofstede, G. 1980. *Cultures Consequences*. London: Sage.

Howick, S., Eden, C., Ackermann, F., and Williams, T. 2008. Building Confidence in Models for Multiple Audiences: the Modelling Cascade. *European Journal of Operational Research*, 186: 1068–1083.

Huff A. (Editor) 1990. *Mapping Strategic Thought*. New York: Wiley.

Huff, A. and Jenkins, M. 2002. *Mapping Strategic Knowledge*. London: Sage.

Janis, I. L. 1972. *Victims of Group Think*. Boston: Houghton Mifflin.

Kelly, G. A. 1955. *The Psychology of Personal Constructs*. New York: Norton.

Kim, W. C. and Mauborgne, R. A. 1995. A Procedural Justice Model of Strategic Decision Making. *Organization Science*, 6: 44–61.

Langfield-Smith, K. and Wirth, A. 1992. Measuring Differences between Cognitive Maps. *Journal of the Operational Research Society*, 43: 1135–1150.

Laukannen, M. 1998. Conducting Causal Mapping Research: Opportunities and Challenges. In Eden, C. Spender J. C. (Eds.), *Managerial and Organizational Cognition*: London: Sage.

Lindblom, C. E. 1959. The Science of Muddling Through. *Public Administration Review*, 19: 79–88.

McFadzean, E. S. and Nelson, T. 1998. Facilitating Problem Solving Groups: A Conceptual Model. *Leadership and Organization Development Journal*, 19: 6–13.

Nutt, P. C. 2002. *Why Decisions Fail: Avoiding the Blunders and Traps that lead to debacles*. San Franscisco: Berrett-Koehler Publishers Inc.

Phillips, L. and Phillips, M. C. 1993. Facilitated Work Groups: Theory and Practice. *Journal of the Operational Research Society*, 44.

Pidd, M. 2003. *Tools for Thinking: Modelling in Management Science*. Chicester: Wiley.

Richardson, G. and Pugh, A. L. III 1981. *Introduction to System Dynamics Modeling*. Boston, MA: Productivity Press.

Rittel, H. W. J. and Webber, M. M. 1973. Dilemmas in a general theory of planning. *Policy Sciences*, 4: 155–169.

Shaw, D. 2003. Evaluating electronic workshops through analysing the 'brainstormed' ideas. *Journal of the Operational Research Society*, 54: 692–705.

Simon, H. A. 1976. From substantive to procedural rationality. In Latsis, S. J. (Eds.), *Method and Appraisal in Economics*: Cambridge: Cambridge University Press.

Stasser, G. and Titus, W. 2003. Hidden Profiles: A Brief History. *Psychological Inquiry*, 14: 304–313.

Thomas, W. I. and Thomas, D. S. 1928. *The Child in America: Behavior Problems and Programs*. New York: Knopf.

van der Heijden, K. 1996. *Scenarios: the art of strategic conversation*. Chichester: Wiley.

Weick, K. E. 1979. *The Social Psychology of Organizing*. Reading, MA: Addison-Wesley.

Note

Decision Explorer can be obtained from www.banxia.com. It runs in Windows. Group Explorer can be obtained from the authors at Strathclyde Business School, Glasgow, UK. It requires Windows Server and a local area network of laptop computers able to run Internet Explorer.

Chapter 5
Soft Systems Methodology[1]

Peter Checkland and John Poulter

Abstract Soft systems methodology (SSM) is an approach for tackling problematical, messy situations of all kinds. It is an action-oriented process of inquiry into problematic situations in which users learn their way from finding out about the situation, to taking action to improve it. The learning emerges via an organised process in which the situation is explored using a set of models of purposeful action (each built to encapsulate a single worldview) as intellectual devices, or tools, to inform and structure discussion about a situation and how it might be improved. This paper, written by the original developer Peter Checkland and practitioner John Poulter, gives a clear and concise account of the approach that covers SSM's specific techniques, the learning cycle process of the methodology and the craft skills which practitioners develop. This concise but theoretically robust account nevertheless includes the fundamental concepts, techniques, core tenets described through a wide range of settings.

5.1 Introduction

- We all live in the midst of a complex interacting flux of changing events and ideas which unrolls through time. We call it 'everyday life', both personal and professional. Within that flux we frequently see situations which cause us to think: 'Something needs to be done about this, it needs to be improved.' Think of these as 'problematical situations', avoiding the word 'problem' since this implies 'solution', which eliminates the problem for ever. Real life is more complex than that!

---

[1] This chapter uses edited excerpts and selected figures from Checkland, P. and Poulter, J. (2006) *Learning for Action: A Short Definitive Account of Soft Systems Methodology and its use for Practitioners*, copyright of John Wiley and Sons Limited. Reproduced with permission.

P. Checkland (✉)
Emeritus Professor of Systems, Lancaster University, University House
Bailrigg, Lancaster, LA1 4YW

J. Poulter
Independent Consultant

M. Reynolds and S. Holwell (eds.), *Systems Approaches to Managing Change: A Practical Guide*, DOI 10.1007/978-1-84882-809-4_5, © The Open University 2010.
Published in Association with Springer-Verlag London Limited

- Soft Systems Methodology (SSM) is an organized way of tackling perceived problematical (social) situations. It is action-oriented. It organizes thinking about such situations so that action to bring about improvement can be taken.
- The complexity of problematical situations in real life stems from the fact that not only are they never static, they also contain multiple interacting perceptions of 'reality'. This comes about because different people have different taken-as-given (and often unexamined) assumptions about the world. This causes them to see it in a particular way. One person's 'terrorism' is another's 'freedom fighting'; one person sees a prison in terms of punishment, another sees it as seeking rehabilitation. These people have different *worldviews*. Tackling problematical situations has to accept this, and has to pitch analysis at a level that allows worldviews to be surfaced and examined. For many people worldviews are relatively fixed; but they can change over time. Sometimes a dramatic event can change them very quickly.
- All problematical situations, as well as containing different worldviews, have a second important characteristic. They always contain people who are trying to act *purposefully*, with intention, not simply acting by instinct or randomly thrashing about – though there is always plenty of that too in human affairs.
- The previous two points – the existence of conflicting worldviews and the ubiquity of would-be purposeful action – lead the way to tackling problematical situations. They underpin the SSM approach, a process of inquiry which, through social learning, works its way to taking 'action to improve'. Its shape is as follows:

1. Find out about both the problematical situation and the characteristics of the intervention to improve it: the issues, the prevailing culture and the disposition of power within the overall situation (its politics). Ways of doing these things are provided.
2. From the finding out, decide upon some relevant purposeful activities, relevant that is to exploring the situation deeply, and remembering that the ultimate aim is to define and take 'action to improve'. Express these relevant purposeful activities as activity *models*, each made to encapsulate a declared worldview, the model being a cluster of linked activities which together make up a purposeful whole. (For example, one model could express in terms of activities the notion 'prison' as if it were only 'a punishment system', another could express it as 'a rehabilitation system'.) Such models never describe the real world, simply because they are based on one pure worldview. They are devices, or tools, to explore it in an organized way. Techniques for building and using such models have been developed.
3. Use the models as a source of questions to ask of the real-world situation. This provides a coherent structure to a discussion or debate about both the situation and how it might be changed, a discussion which will surface worldviews and generate ideas for change and improvement.
4. In the course of the discussion, continually bring together the results of the 'finding out' in (1) and the ideas for change in (3). The purpose now is to find changes which are both arguably *desirable* (given these models) but also culturally *feasible* for these people in this particular situation with its particular

history, culture and politics. This is a process of seeking accommodations between different worldviews. That is to say, it is a process of finding versions of the to-be-changed situation which different people with conflicting worldviews could nevertheless *live with*. (Don't expect the worldviews to go away, nor wish that they would. Clashing worldviews, always present in human affairs, stimulate energy and ideas for change.)

- The elements (1) to (4) above constitute a *learning cycle*. They have necessarily been described linearly here but in use there is much iteration within the cycle as learning occurs. It is never followed in the flat-footed way in which it has been laid out here for explanatory purposes. Also it is apparent that it is essentially a group process leading to *group learning*. It is best carried out by people in the problematical situation itself, not left to an outside 'expert', though knowledgeable people can facilitate the process.
- Taking action to improve a problematical situation will of course itself change that situation, so that the learning cycle could in principle begin again. In any case the changing flux of everyday life will itself bring new events and new ideas, so that no human situation could ever be rendered static. In this sense SSM's learning cycle can be seen as never-ending. It ultimately offers a way of continuously managing any ongoing human situation. It does this by helping understanding of complex situations, encouraging multiple perspectives to be taken into account, and bringing rigour to processes of analysis, debate and taking 'action to improve'.

The seven points made above are presented pictorially in Fig. 5.1.

5.1.1 What Can SSM Be Used for?

The application area for SSM is very broad. This is not due to megalomania on the authors' part. Rather it stems from the wide applicability of two key ideas behind SSM. One of these is to create a process of *learning your way* through problematical situations to 'action to improve' – a very general concept indeed. The other is the idea that you can make sure this learning is organized and structured by using, as a source of questions to ask in the real situation, models (systems models) of purposeful activity. This is because every real-world situation contains people trying to act purposely, intentionally. It is the sheer generality of purposeful action – the core of being human – that makes the area in which SSM can be used so huge.

Stories of SSM use come from all sizes of company from small firms to large corporations, from organizations in both private and public sectors including the National Health Service. SSM is much used in the world of information systems and information technology. This derives from the fact that for any purposeful activity model (Fig. 5.7 being a very simple example) you can ask of each activity: What information would support doing this activity? And what information would be

Fig. 5.1 SSM's cycle of learning for action

generated by doing it? Since information is what you get when you attribute meaning to data in a particular context, and meaning attribution depends upon worldview, SSM's strong emphasis on worldview explains its relevance to this field.

In summary, SSM can be used in any human situation which entails thinking about acting purposefully, and is especially useful in any situation in which it is helpful to lift the level of discussion from that of everyday opinions and dogma to that level at which you are asking: What taken-as-given worldview lies behind these assertions of opinion?

5.1.2   Is SSM Mature?

Obviously it is never possible to claim that the development of any approach to human inquiry is 'finished', though some features of any such process may become so taken-as-given as to appear permanent. For example, in the inquiry process of natural science, if you are testing a new drug you give some patients the drug while others receive a placebo. The difference between the group ingesting the drug and the so-called 'control' group taking the placebo tells you what effects the drug produces (given a statistically significant sample size). This pattern would seem to be a permanent feature of scientific experiment. In applied social science, where SSM sits, the situation is less definite. Nevertheless, after hundreds of studies the core processes of SSM do now appear to be well-established, though the application area continues to expand. In the early days each significant study was likely to cause some rethinking of the process itself; but such changes became increasingly rare over the 30-year development period. We now regard it as a mature process.

The most recent addition to the literature about its development describes the use of SSM both in relation to the perceived content of the situation in question – SSM (c) and in relation to the process of carrying out the inquiry itself – SSM (p). This is in a paper published in 2006.[2] But this is a case of the literature lagging behind practice, as these twin uses of SSM have been recognized and exploited by those developing the approach since the early 1980s.

So SSM is now considered mature enough to justify inclusion in this book.

5.1.3   How Was SSM Created?

The classic way of doing research comes from natural science: set up a hypothesis and then test it experimentally. It is not easy to transfer this model of research to the gloriously rich social and human arena, though strenuous efforts to do that

---

[2] Checkland P.B. and Winter M.C. 2006 'Process and content: two ways of using SSM', Journal of the Operational Research Society vol. 57 (12) pp. 1435–1441

have been made over many years. SSM was developed using an alternative model of research, one more suitable for 'social' research at the level of a situation, group or organization, namely 'action research'. In this kind of research you accept the great difficulty of scientific experimental work in human situations, since each human situation is not only unique, but changes through time and exhibits multiple conflicting worldviews. Hence the pattern for the action researcher is to enter a human situation, *take part* in its activity, and use that experience as the research object. In order to do that, to do more than simply return from the research with a one-off story to tell, it is necessary to declare in advance the intellectual framework you, the researcher, will use to try to make sense of the experience gained. Given such an explicit framework, you can then describe the research experience in the well-defined language of the framework. This makes it possible for anyone outside the work to 'recover' it, to see exactly what was done and how the conclusions were reached. This 'recoverability' requirement is obviously not as strong as the 'repeatability' criterion for scientific findings within natural science. But then human situations are very much more complex than the phenomena studied in physics and chemistry labs! It is the declared framework and recoverability criterion which clearly separate accounts of well-organized action research from novel writing – which, alas, too much published social research resembles.

In the action research which produced SSM the initial declared framework was the Systems Engineering approach developed by the Bell Telephone Company from their own case histories. Systems Engineering (SE) is a process of naming a 'system' (assumed to be some complex object which exists or could exist in the real world), defining its objectives, and then using an array of techniques developed in the 1950s and 1960s to 'engineer' the system to meet its objectives. This framework was rapidly found to be poverty-stricken when faced with the complexity of human situations. It was too thin, not rich enough to deal with fizzing social complexity.

The SE framework was modified (and enriched) in the light of and in direct response to real-life experiences. Eventually, we had in our hands an adequately rich framework, but it was far removed from the starting point in SE. It became known as Soft Systems Methodology. It then took some time for even its pioneers to realize just how radical the shift had been from SE to SSM. Having introduced the notion of 'worldview' – essential in dealing with human social complexity – we were thereafter thinking of systems models not as descriptions of something in the real world but simply as devices (based on worldview) to organize a debate about 'change to bring about improvement'. That was the key step in finding our way to SSM. This important shift in thinking is not abstruse, but it turns out to be very difficult for many people to grasp, simply because everyone is so used to the casual everyday-language use of the word 'system'. In ordinary talk we constantly refer to complex chunks of the everyday world as systems, even though they do not come close to meeting the requirements of that concept. We speak of 'the education system', 'health-care systems', 'the prison system ', etc. using the word 'system' simply to indicate a chunk of reality which seems to be very complex but is, in some vague sense,

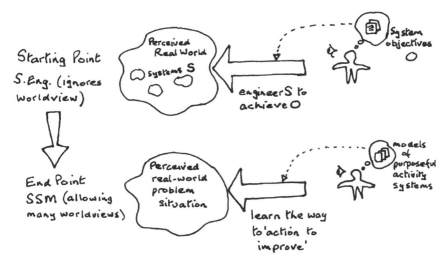

Fig. 5.2 The shift in thinking entailed in developing SSM

a whole, something which might be better 'engineered'. Figure 5.2 gives a visual indication of the shift in thinking as SE was transformed into SSM.

At the starting point (S.Eng.) in Fig. 5.2 (which ignores world views), 'systems' are names for things in the world which, given precise objectives, can be engineered to achieve them. At the end point (which accepts different world-views) 'systems' are devices used in a learning process to define desirable and feasible 'action to improve'.

Once the end point in Fig. 5.2 was reached, and the SSM framework had been established, it was further developed, modified and honed in a few hundred new experiences. Out of this came a model which captures all of these developmental experiences. The model, known as the LUMAS model is shown in Fig. 5.3. (It is in fact a generic model for making sense of any real-world application of any *methodology*, remembering that that word covers a set of principles which need to be embodied in an application tailored to meet the unique features of a particular situation.)

LUMAS stands for Learning for a User by a Methodology-informed Approach to a Situation. In order to 'read' this model, start from the user (U) in the centre. He or she, perceiving a problem situation (S) and appreciating the methodology (M), tailors the latter to the former to produce the specific approach (A) to be used in this situation (S). This not only produces an improved situation but also yields learning (L). This will change the user, who has gained this experience, and may also modify or enrich appreciation of the methodology. Every use of SSM can in principle be described in the language of this model. It is the gradually diminishing activity, over the years, of development occurring along the arrow which links L and M that makes it legitimate to describe SSM as mature.

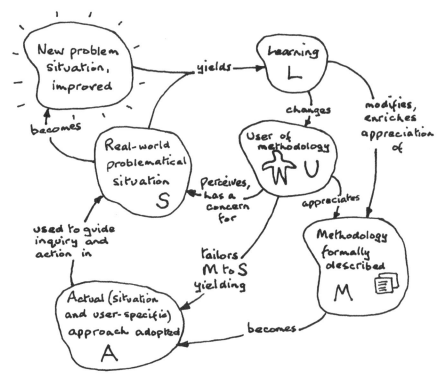

Fig. 5.3 The LUMAS model – learning for a user by a methodically-informed approach to a situation

5.1.4 How Does SSM Differ from Other Systems Approaches?

As described above, changes had to be made to Systems Engineering when it proved too blunt an instrument to deal with the complexity of human situations. Those changes explain SSM's difference from the other systems approaches developed in the 1950s and 1960s. SE is an archetypal example of what is now known as 'hard' systems thinking. Its belief is: the world contains interacting systems. They can be 'engineered' to achieve their objectives. This is the stance not only of SE; this thinking also underpins classic Operational Research, RAND Corporation 'systems analysis', the Viable System Model, early applications of System Dynamics and the original forms of computer systems analysis. None of these approaches pays attention to the existence of conflicting worldviews, something which characterizes all social interactions. In order to incorporate the concept of worldview into the approach being developed, it was necessary to abandon the idea that the world is a set of systems. In SSM the (social) world is taken to be very complex, problematical, mysterious, characterized by clashes of worldview. It is continually being

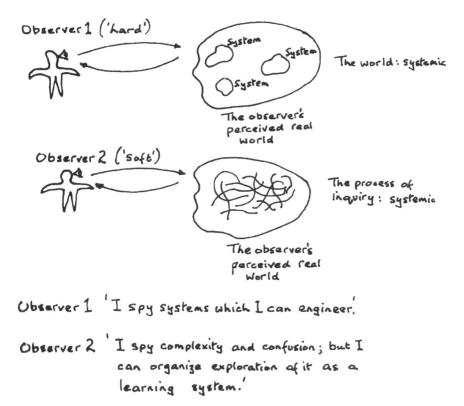

Fig. 5.4 The 'hard' and 'soft' systems stances

created and recreated by people thinking, talking and taking action. However, our coping with it, our process of inquiry into it, can itself be organized as a learning *system*. So the notion of systemicity ('systemness') appears in the process of inquiry into the world, rather than in the world itself. This shift created 'soft' as opposed to 'hard' systems thinking, the different stances adopted by the two being shown in Fig. 5.4, itself another version of Fig. 5.2.

This brings us to the end of a skeletal account of SSM as a whole. The next sections expand on this, describing the techniques used in the cyclic process in detail. Meanwhile it seems worthwhile to try to summarize the broad account of SSM in a couple of sentences.

> SSM is an action-oriented process of inquiry into problematical situations in the everyday world; users learn their way from finding out about the situation to defining/taking action to improve it. The learning emerges via an organized process in which the real situation is explored, using as intellectual devices - which serve to provide structure to discussion - models of purposeful activity built to encapsulate pure, stated worldviews.

5.2   SSM in Practice

The aim of the work which led to the development of Soft Systems Methodology
(Checkland 1981) was to find a better way of dealing with a kind of situation we
continually find ourselves facing in everyday life: a situation about which we
have the feeling that 'something needs to be done about this'. We shall call such
situations 'problematical', rather than describing them as 'problem situations',
since they may not present a well-defined 'problem' to be 'solved' out of existence – everyday life is more complex than that! A company might feel that it
needs to stimulate sales, perhaps by introducing a new product; or should they bid
for the equity of a smaller rival? A university may feel that its student intake is
too biased towards students from middle-class homes. What are the implications
of changing that? A government may struggle to define legislation which would
increase the feeling of security on the streets, given the threat of terrorism, without diminishing civil liberties. A local council may be receiving complaints that
the delivery of its services is not sufficiently 'citizen-friendly'. What should it
do? A head teacher may wonder how to decide whether to take on the responsibility for providing school meals (the school benefiting from any surplus generated)
or to leave that function to the local education authority. An individual may
develop a sense of unease about the future viability of the firm he or she works
for, and wonder whether to look for a job elsewhere. All these are 'problematical
situations'. They could be tackled in various ways: by appealing to previous
experience; intuitively; by randomly thrashing about (never a shortage of that in
human situations); by responding emotionally; or they could be addressed by
using SSM.

So what is it? It is an organized, flexible process for dealing with situations
which someone sees as problematical, situations which call for action to be taken
to improve them, to make them more acceptable, less full of tensions and unan-
swered questions. The 'process' referred to is an organized process of thinking your
way to taking sensible 'action to improve' the situation; and, finally, it is a process
based on a particular body of ideas, namely *systems* ideas.

That these ideas have proved themselves to be useful in dealing with the complexity of the social world is hardly surprising. Social situations are always complex
due to multiple interactions between different elements in a problematical situation
as a whole, and systems ideas are fundamentally concerned with the *interactions*
between parts of a whole. So it is systems ideas which help to structure the thinking.
(However, the way systems ideas are used within SSM is fundamentally different
from the way they inform the various earlier systems approaches developed in the
1950s and 1960s).

In order to ensure that the previous two paragraphs are clear, we need to unpack
them somewhat, and say a little more about the crucial elements within them. Four
elements in the paragraphs above will be expanded: 'everyday life and problematical situations'; 'tackling such situations'; a 'flexible process', and 'the use of systems ideas'.

5.2.1 *Everyday Life and Problematical Situations*

As members of the human tribe we experience everyday life as being quite exceptionally complex. We feel ourselves to be carried along on an on-rushing turbulent stream, a flux of happenings, ideas, emotions, actions, all mediated through the slippery agency of language, all continually changing. Our response to our immersion in this stream is not simply to experience it. Beyond that, we have an innate desire to try to see it, if we can, as *meaningful*. We *attribute* meaning to it – the ability to do this being one of the characteristics which marks us out as human. Part of this meaning attribution is to see chunks of the ongoing flux as 'situations'. Nothing is intrinsically 'a situation'; it is our perceptions which create them as such, and in doing that we know that they are not static; their boundaries and their content will change over time. Some of the situations we perceive, because they affect us in some way, cause us to feel a need to tackle them, to do something about them, to improve them.

5.2.2 *Tackling Problematical Situations*

As we tackle a situation we see as problematical, we are intervening in order to take action intended to bring about improvement. In order to do that sensibly we need to have a clear idea of what it is we are intervening in. This means having a clear view of the nature of the flux which constitutes everyday life. We have already described it as complex, changing, and having multiple strands: events, ideas, emotions, actions. To this we can add an answer to the question: What then happens when we intervene in a part of the flux seen as a problematical situation?

When we interact with real-world situations we *make judgements about them*: are they 'good' or 'bad', 'acceptable' or 'unacceptable', 'permanent' or 'transient'? Now, to make any judgement we have to appeal to some criteria or standards, these being the characteristics which define 'good' or 'bad' etc. for us. For example an 'eco-warrior' would judge any economic activity 'good' only if it met the environmentalists' criteria for 'good', namely 'environmentally friendly' and 'sustainable'. A 'capitalist' would see an economic activity as 'good' if it were 'profitable'. And where do such criteria come from? They will be formed partially by our genetic inheritance from our parents, the kind of person we are innately – and, most significantly, from our previous experience of the world. Over time these criteria and the interpretations they lead to will tend to firm up into a relatively stable outlook *through which* we then perceive the world. We develop 'worldviews', built-in tendencies to see the world in a particular way. It is different worldviews which make one person 'liberal', another 'reactionary'. Worldviews cause one observer's 'terrorism' to be another's 'freedom fighting'. Such world-views are relatively stable but can change over time. Thus a paranoid person whose worldview is 'this hostile world owes me a living' might become a more integrated member of society as a result of experiencing love and generosity.

This concept of worldview (the German *Weltanschauung* being the best technical word for it) is the most important concept in understanding the complexity of human situations, and indeed, the nature and form of SSM.

5.2.3   A Flexible Process

It is obvious from the argument so far that any approach able to deal with the changing complexity of real life will have to be flexible. It could never be reduced to a sequence of steps, which might be handed over to an intelligently programmed robot. It needs to be flexible enough to cope with the fact that every situation involving human beings is unique. The human world is one in which nothing ever happens twice, not in *exactly* the same way. This means that an approach to problematical human situations has to be a methodology rather than a method, or technique. A methodology, as the word indicates, is a logos of method; that is to say it is a set of ongoing principles which can be adapted for use in a way which suits the specific nature of each situation in which it is used. SSM provides a set of principles which can be both adopted and adapted for use in any real situation in which people are intent on taking action to improve it.

5.2.4   The Use of Systems Ideas

As stated above, systems ideas concern interaction between parts which make up a whole; also, the complexity of real situations is always to a large extent due to the many interactions between different elements in human situations. So it is not surprising that systems ideas have some relevance to dealing with real-world complexity (though they are only very rarely useful in *describing* that complexity).

The core systems idea or concept is that of an adaptive whole (a 'system') which can survive through time by adapting to changes in its environment. The concept is illustrated in Fig. 5.5. A system S receives shocks from its changing environment E. If it is to survive, it requires *communication processes* (to know what is going on) and *control processes* (possible adaptive responses to the shocks). Also, the system may contain sub-systems SS, or may itself be seen by a different observer as only a sub-system of some wider system. The idea of a *layered structure* is thus fundamental in systems thinking. Finally, what is said to be a system must have some properties as a single whole, so-called *emergent properties*.

(Thus the parts of a bicycle, when assembled correctly, and only then, produce a whole which has the emergent property of being a vehicle, the concept 'vehicle' being meaningful only in relation to the whole.) These four italicized phrases represent the core of systems thinking. So how can it be used here?

The relevance of this kind of thinking to SSM emerged when it was realised that every single real-world problematical situation, whether in a small firm making

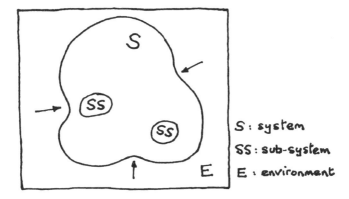

Fig. 5.5   The core systems concept: an adaptive whole

wheelbarrows, a multi-national oil company, or in the National Health Service (which employs more than a million people) has one characteristic in common. All such situations contain people trying to act *purposefully* not simply acting by instinct or splashing about at random. From this observation comes the key idea of *treating purposeful action as a system*. A way of representing purposeful action as a system, i.e. an adaptive whole (in line with Fig. 5.5) was invented. Figure 5.6 shows its general form.

A logically linked set of activities constitute a whole – its emergent property being its purposefulness. The activities concerned with achieving the purpose (the operations) are monitored against defined measures of performance so that adaptive control action (to make changes) can be taken if necessary.

Figure 5.7 shows a trivial example to illustrate the concept. With regard to Fig. 5.6, the 'measure of performance' might be the degree to which fence painting enhances the appearance of the property or, perhaps, 'good' or 'bad' might be defined according to whether or not the neighbours complain about it. This model, then is a 'purposeful activity model'.

The model in Fig. 5.7 is essentially within the worldview of whoever would do the fence painting. It is an instrumental model which spells out what is entailed in painting a garden fence. It could express the householder's worldview: 'I can do useful DIY jobs to improve my property.' However, if painting the fence were an issue in a real situation other worldviews would be relevant, even in an example as

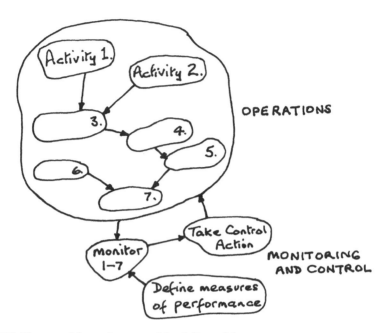

Fig. 5.6 The general form of a purposeful activity model

trivial as this – for example, in this case, those of the neighbours or the partner of
the fence-painter. In general there will always be a number of worldviews which
could be taken into account leading to a number of relevant models.

Suppose, for example, you were carrying out an SSM study of the future of the
Olympic Games. For anything as complex as this global phenomenon it is obvious
that it could be looked at from the perspective of worldviews attributed to the
International Olympic Committee, the host country, the host city, the athletes, the
athletes' coaches, the spectators, hot dog sellers, commercial sponsors, those responsible
for security, television companies, a terrorist group seeking publicity for their
cause, etc. This list could go on and on; there could never be a single model relevant
to all these different interests.

An important consequence flows from this: these purposeful activity models *can
never be descriptions* of (part of) the real world. Each of them expresses *one way
of looking at and thinking about* the real situation, and there will be multiple possibilities. So how can such models be made useful? The answer is to see them as
devices (intellectual devices) which are a source of *good questions to ask about the
real situation*, enabling it to be explored richly. For example, we could focus on the
differences between a model and the situation, and ask whether we would like

Fig. 5.7 A simple example of an activity model: a system to paint the garden fence by hand painting

activity in the situation to be more, or less, like that in the model. Such questioning organizes and structures a discussion/debate about the real-world situation, the purpose of that discussion being to surface different worldviews and to seek possible ways of changing the problematical situation for the better. This means finding an accommodation, that is to say a version of the situation which different people with different worldviews could nevertheless live with. Given the different worldviews which will always be present in any human situation, this means finding possible changes which meet two criteria simultaneously. They must be arguably *desirable*, given the outcomes of using the models to question the real situation, but must also be culturally *feasible* for these particular people in this particular situation with unique history and the unique narrative which its participants will have constructed over time in order to make sense of their experience. Figure 5.8 illustrates this.

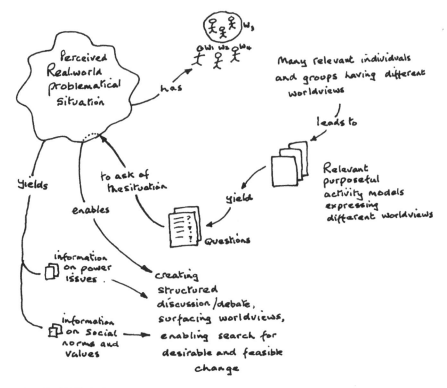

Fig. 5.8 SSM's basic process

In summary, then, we have:

- A problematical real-world situation seen as calling for action to improve it
- Models of purposeful activity *relevant* to this situation (not describing it)
- A process of using the models as devices to explore the situation
- A structured debate about desirable and feasible change

This gives the bare bones of the process of SSM, whose shape can now be described.

5.2.5   What Is the SSM Process?

The SSM process takes the form of a cycle. It is, properly used, a cycle of learning which goes from finding out about a problematical situation to defining/taking action to improve it. The learning which takes place is social learning of the group undertaking the study, though each individual's learning will be, to a greater or lesser extent, personal to them given their different experiences of the world, and hence the different worldviews which they will bring to the study. Taking action as a result of the study will of course change the starting situation into a new situation,

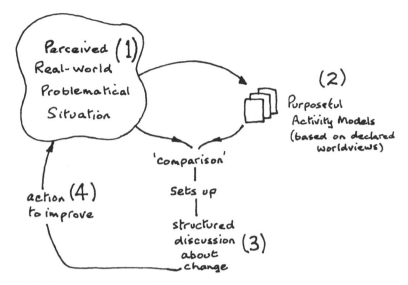

Fig. 5.9 The iconic representation of SSM's learning cycle

so that in principle the cycle could begin again (a relevant system then being 'a system to make these changes'). SSM is thus not only a methodology for a specially set-up study or project; it is, more generally, a way of managing any real-world purposeful activity in an ongoing sense.

The SSM cycle is shown in Fig. 5.9, which eventually emerged as its classic representation. It contains four different kinds of activity:

1. Finding out about the initial situation which is seen as problematical.
2. Making some purposeful activity models judged to be relevant to the situation; each model as an intellectual device, being built on the basis of a particular pure worldview.
3. Using the models to question the real situation. This brings structure to a discussion about the situation, the aim of the discussion being to find changes which are both arguably desirable and also culturally feasible in this particular situation.
4. Define/take the action to improve the situation. Since the learning cycle is in principle never-ending it is an arbitrary distinction as to whether the end of a study is taken to be defining the action or actually carrying it out.

Some studies will be ended after defining the action, some after implementing it.

This description of the cycle as activities (1) to (4) may give a false impression that we are describing a sequence of steps. Not so. Although virtually all investigations will be initiated by finding out about the problematical situation, once SSM is being used, activity will go on simultaneously in more than one of the 'steps'. For example, starting the organized discussion about the situation (3) will normally lead not only to further new finding out (1), perhaps focused on aspects previously ignored, but also to further new choices of 'relevant' systems to model. In real life,

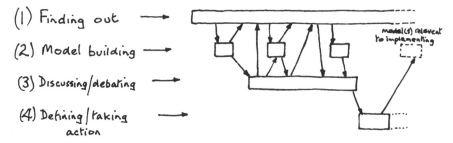

(1) Finding out ⟶

(2) Model building ⟶

(3) Discussing/debating ⟶

(4) Defining/taking ⟶
        action

Fig. 5.10 A typical pattern of activity during an SSM investigation

an investigation which sets out narrowly to improve, say, aspects of product distribution in a manufacturing company's distribution department, may well later sweep in issues concerning, perhaps, communications between production and marketing departments. Figure 5.10 illustrates a typical pattern of activity of the kind which emerges as an investigation digs deeper.

Figure 5.10 shows an on-going 'finding out' activity, three bursts of model building, discussion fed by both the models and the finding out, which itself leads to more finding out and more modelling. The final (fourth) burst of modelling shown here as an example follows from defining the 'action to improve' and would consist of purposeful activity models relevant to carrying out the action agreed.

Finally, in describing the SSM cycle, we could add (though this is really a point from the end of this chapter) that as users of SSM become more sophisticated they treat Fig. 5.9 not at all as a prescription to be followed, but as a model to make sense of their experience as they mentally negotiate their way through the problematical situation.

The previous sections have still focused on the basic question about SSM – what is it? Additionally, they have provided some context for its development, its application areas and the crucial difference from the systems approaches of the 1950s and 1960s. In the next sections the focus shifts more to 'how' rather than 'what': How exactly does the user move through the learning cycle of SSM, shown in Fig. 5.9, in order to define useful change? Which techniques for finding out, modelling and using models to question the real situation have shown themselves robust enough to survive in many different circumstances, so that they have become part of the classic approach?

The account here will follow the four basic activities of the broad-brush account (finding out, modelling, using the models to structure debate, and defining/taking action), with the usual reminder that activity in any project using SSM will reflect the kind of pattern shown in Fig. 5.10 rather than a stately linear progress.

5.2.6 The SSM Learning Cycle: Finding Out

Four ways of finding out about a problematical situation have survived many tests and become a normal part of using SSM. In the language of SSM they are known as 'making Rich Pictures' and carrying out three kinds of inquiry, known as 'Analyses One, Two and Three'. These focus, respectively, on the intervention itself, a social analysis (What kind of 'culture' is this?) and a political analysis (What is the disposition of power here?). They will be described in turn.

5.2.6.1 Making Rich Pictures

Entering a real situation in order first to understand it and then to begin to change it in the direction of 'improvement' calls for a particular frame of mind in the user of SSM. On the one hand the enquirer needs to be sponge-like, soaking up as much as possible of what the situation presents to someone who may be initially an outsider. On the other hand, although holding back from imposing a favoured pattern on the first impressions, the enquirer needs to have in mind a range of 'prompts' which will ensure that a wide range of aspects are looked at. Initially two dense and cogent questions were used as a prompt:

- What resources are deployed in what operational processes under what planning procedures within what structures, in what environments and wider systems, by whom?
- How is resource deployment monitored and controlled?

Certainly, if you can answer these questions you know quite a lot about the situation addressed. But these questions did not survive as a formal part of SSM. The problem with them is that when they were formulated, in the early days of SSM development, the thinking of the pioneers had not sufficiently divorced itself from thinking of the world as a set of systems.

The questions imply intervention in some real-world system – hence the references to 'wider systems' and to monitoring and control – rather than the intervention being addressed to *a situation*. The questions would no doubt have been changed eventually as the true nature of SSM was realized. However, what happened instead was that the questions were dropped because the phrase 'rich picture' quickly moved from being a metaphor to being a literal description of an account of the situation *as a picture*.

The rationale behind this was as follows. The complexity of human situations is always one of multiple interacting relationships. A picture is a good way to show relationships; in fact it is a much better medium for that purpose than linear prose. Hence as knowledge of a situation was assembled – by talking to people, by conducting more formal interviews, by attending meetings, by reading documents, etc. – it became normal to begin to draw simple pictures of the situation. These became richer as inquiry proceeded, and so such pictures are never finished in any ultimate sense. But they were found invaluable for expressing crucial relationships in the situation and, most importantly, for providing something which could be tabled as a basis for discussion. Users would say: 'This is how we are seeing your situation. Could we talk you through it so that you can comment on it and draw attention to anything you see as errors or omissions?'

In making a Rich Picture the aim is to capture, informally, the main entities, structures and viewpoints in the situation, the processes going on, the current recognized issues and any potential ones.

Here is a real-world problematical situation described in a paragraph of prose:

> The newly appointed headteacher of an 11s-to-18s school, which has overspent its budget in the last year or two, finds herself, in her first term, facing an issue concerning the provision of school meals. Currently these are provided by the county education authority through their catering services company, the contract being renewed annually. A member of that company who is leaving to set up her own catering company urges the headteacher to make a contract with her instead of the county, suggesting the school could save money on this. Some staff members agree with this, others want to stick with the status quo. Some parents, alerted by a national debate about school meals, want more nutritious meals as long as they don't cost more. Pupils say: 'We like burgers and chips.' The school governors are discussing this issue; the Chairman, himself MD of a catering company, is urging the headteacher to be entrepreneurial and to take on responsibility for the provision of school meals, believing this could be profitable for the school.

Figure 5.11 represents this situation in a Rich Picture. Our point is that this picture is a more useful piece of paper than the prose account. It could lead to better-than-usual level of discussion because not only can it be taken in as a whole but also it

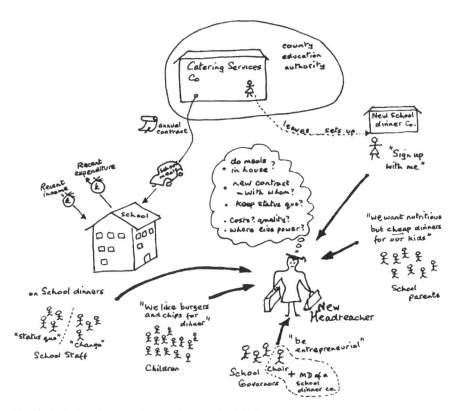

Fig. 5.11 A rich picture of the situation described in the text

displays the multiple *relationships* which the head teacher has to manage, not just immediately, but through time. That is the power of such pictures, though we have to remember that however rich they are they could be richer, and that such pictures record a snapshot of a situation which will itself not remain static for very long. Wise practitioners continually produce such pictures as an aid to thinking. They become a normal way of capturing impressions and insights.

5.2.6.2 Carrying Out Analysis One (The Intervention Itself)

Whenever SSM is used to try and improve a problematical situation three elements – the methodology, the use of the methodology by a practitioner and the situation – are brought together in a particular relationship, namely that shown in Fig. 5.12 The practitioner will adapt the principles and techniques of the methodology to organize the task of addressing and intervening in the situation, aiming at taking action to improve it. In developing SSM, this process was organized in a sequence of real situations, and it was quickly found useful to think about Fig. 5.12, in a particular way. Three key roles were always present:

1. There was some person (or group of persons) who had *caused the intervention to happen*, someone without whom, there would not be an investigation at all – this was the role 'client'.
2. There was some person (or group of persons) who were *conducting the investigation* – this was the role 'practitioner'.
3. Most importantly, whoever was in the practitioner role could choose, and list, a number of people who could be regarded as being *concerned about or affected by the situation and the outcome* of the effort to improve it – this was the role 'owner of the issue(s) addressed'.

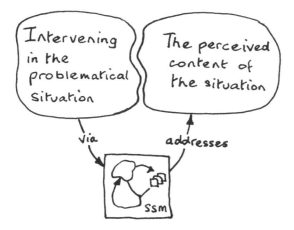

Fig. 5.12 The three elements in any SSM investigation

It is important to see why these are named as 'roles' rather than particular people. It is because one person (or group) might be in more than one role. For example, if the head teacher in the Rich Picture (Fig. 5.11) were to herself carry out an SSM-based study of her complex situation, she would not only be both 'client' and 'practitioner', she would also be one of the people in the list of 'issue owners' who care about the outcome. Sometimes a manager who causes an intervention to take place delegates detailed involvement in it to others, and so is only in the role 'client'. In this case the person(s) in the 'practitioner' role needs to take steps to ensure that the 'client' is kept informed about the course of the intervention so that the outcome when it emerges does not come as a big surprise. In every case the 'practitioner' needs to make sure that the resources available to carry out the investigation are in line with its ambition. Don't undertake a study of 'the future of the A-level examination in British education' if you have only got one man and a boy to work on it between now and next Thursday.

SSM's 'Analysis One', then, consists of thinking about the situation displayed in Fig. 5.12 in the way shown in Fig. 5.13, asking: Who are in the roles 'client' and 'practitioner'? and Who could usefully be included in the list of 'issue owner'?

Much learning came out of the simple thinking which led to this 'Analysis One'. For example, it was always useful to think about the client's aspirations for the intervention.

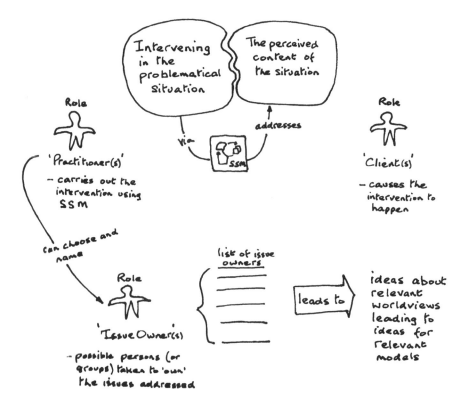

Fig. 5.13 SSM's Analysis One

They should always be taken seriously but should not be the sole focus of the work done. Thus, the person(s) in the 'client' role should be in the list of possible 'issue owners' but should very definitely not be the only one in the list. In this connection it was interesting to hear a senior manager from the RAND Corporation declare, some years ago, 'The RAND analyst places his or her expertise at the disposal of a real-world decision-taker who has to be a legitimate holder of power.' In the language of Fig. 5.13 this was to declare that for RAND the client *is* the issue owner, full stop. This cuts off all the richness which comes from the practitioner compiling a list of persons or groups *who could be taken to be* issue owners; for it is that list which introduces multiple worldviews. They in turn open up the chance of a richness of learning at a deep level for all involved in the intervention, leading, perhaps, to major change. The RAND manager's statement would define the practitioner as only a servant to the legitimately powerful. In the situation shown in Fig. 5.12, for example, 'issue owners' might include: the head teacher; the school governors, staff and pupils; parents; the county education authority and their catering services company; other catering companies, etc. The many worldviews from such a list give a chance that the richness of the inquiry can cope with the complexity of the real situation. They suggest ideas for 'relevant' activity models – ones likely to be insightful.

Some final learning, which is important in understanding SSM as a whole, comes from the fact that the person(s) in the 'practitioner' role can include *themselves* in the list of possible 'issue owners'. Normally SSM is thought of as a means of addressing the problematical content of the situation, which will include would-be purposeful action by people in the situation. It *is* that, of course. However, the practitioner(s) is about to carry out another purposeful activity, that of *doing the study*, which is a task always associated with the practitioner role. Carrying out the investigation can be thought about, and planned, using models relevant to doing this. Thus SSM can be applied both to grappling with the content of the situation and to deciding how to carry it out. These two kinds of use of the methodology are known as 'SSM (c)' and 'SSM (p)' – c for content, p for process. Use of SSM (p) often leads to the first models made in the course of an intervention being models related to doing the study. Figure 5.14 illustrates these two ways of using SSM.

5.2.6.3   Carrying Out Analysis Two (Social)

It might seem obvious that if you are going to intervene in, and change, a human situation, you ought to have a clear idea about what it is you are intervening in. You should have some sense of what you take 'social reality' to be. However, this is not too obvious! The Management Science field, for example, tries to get by through concentrating almost entirely on the *logic* of situations, even though the motivators of much human action lie outside logic, in cultural norms or emotions. So, if we are to be effective in social situations, we have to take 'culture' seriously and decide what we mean by it. This is especially important for SSM as an action-oriented approach.

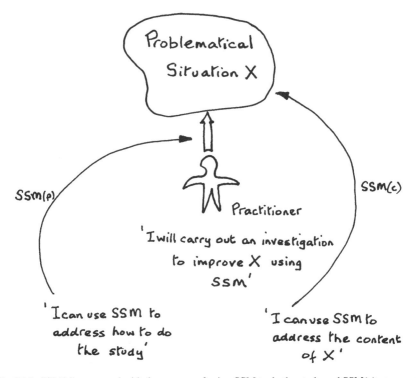

Fig. 5.14 SSM(p) concerned with the process of using SSM to do the study and SSM(c) concerned with the problematical content

If we are to learn our way to practical action which will improve a situation under investigation, then the changes involved in 'improvement' have to be not only arguably desirable but also *culturally feasible*. They need to be possible for these particular people, with their particular history and their particular ways of looking at the world. We have to understand the local 'culture', at a level beyond that of individual worldviews.

This might be straightforward if there were an agreed definition of exactly what we mean by 'culture'. However, there is no agreed definition, though the concept is much discussed by anthropologists, sociologists and people writing in the management literature. By the 1950s, a survey (by Kluckhohn and Kroeber) found 300 different definitions, and no agreement has been reached since then! In spite of that, everyone has a general, diffuse sense of what the word means. If you say "This is a 'can-do' culture", or "This is a 'buttoned-up culture'", or assert that 'The Civil Service is a punishment-avoiding, rather than a reward-seeking culture' then it will be accepted that you have said something meaningful. To anyone familiar with the society in question, those statements will have conveyed some sense of the 'feel', or 'flavour', of the situation: its social texture. In order to pin down such feelings more firmly, in a way which makes practical sense, SSM makes use of a particular model. This is a model which does not claim the status of rounded theory, but it has

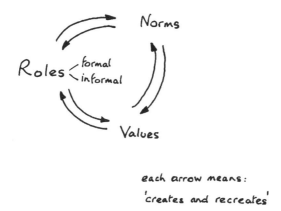

each arrow means:
'creates and recreates'

Fig. 5.15 SSM's model for getting a sense of the social texture of a human situation

proved itself useful in situations from small firms dominated by individuals to large corporations which develop and (partially) impose their own norms.

The model is at the same time simple (you can keep it in your head) but also subtle. It consists of only three elements – roles, norms, values – but the subtlety comes from the fact that none of these elements is static. Each, over time, continually helps to create and modify the other two elements, as shown in Fig. 5.15.

Together the three elements help to create the social texture of a human situation, something which will both endure *and* change over time. Consider the three elements in turn.

Roles are social positions which mark differences between members of a group or organization. They may be formally recognized, as when a large organization has, say, a chief executive, directors, department heads, section heads and members of sections. But in any local culture informal roles also develop. Individuals may develop a reputation as 'a boat-rocker', or 'a licensed jester' – someone who can get away with saying things others would suppress. The informal roles which are recognized in a given culture tell you a lot about it.

Norms are the expected behaviours associated with, and helping to define, a role. Suppose you told a friend you were going to meet 'the vice-chancellor of a UK university' next day. If you returned from the meeting and said that the VC sat picking her teeth, with her feet on the table, and was very foul-mouthed, your friend would be flabbergasted. Such behaviour is way outside the expected behaviour of someone in the role of VC in British society.

Values are the standards – the criteria – by which behaviour-in-role gets judged. In all human groups there is always plenty of gossip related to this. People love to discuss behaviour in role and reach judgements which praise or disparage: 'He's a very efficient town clerk who services committees well'; 'She's an ineffective vice-chancellor who won't take decisions.'

It is obvious from these definitions that the three elements – roles, norms, values – are closely related to each other, dynamically, and that they change over time as the world moves on. Anyone who has ever been promoted within an organization will know that occupying the new role changes them, as they adopt a new perspective appropriate to the role. Equally, how they enact the new role will have its effect, in future, on the local norm – the behaviour which people expect from whoever fills that role. The elements also change over time at a macro level. For example, when the authors were growing up in British society the worst role for a young woman to find herself in was to be an unmarried mother. At that time, society judged harshly the behaviour which led to this. Not anymore; the social stigma attached to the role has disappeared in the UK over the last 50 years.

So how exactly is the model of linked roles, norms and values in Fig. 5.15 used in SSM? At the start of an intervention open a file marked 'Analysis Two'. Then, every time you interact with the situation – talking to people informally, reading a document, sitting in a meeting, conducting an interview, having a drink in the pub after work – ask yourself afterwards whether that taught you anything about the roles, norms and values which are taken seriously here and characterize this particular group. Record the finding in the 'Analysis Two' file. Carry on doing this throughout the engagement, and put a date on every entry so that later on you can recover the progress of your learning, and reflect upon it. Figure 5.16 summarizes Analysis Two.

5.2.6.4 Carrying Out Analysis Three (Political)

The experienced reader will have noticed that so far in this discussion of 'Finding Out' about a problematical situation we have made no mention of the *politics* of a situation, an aspect which is always powerful in deciding what does or does not get

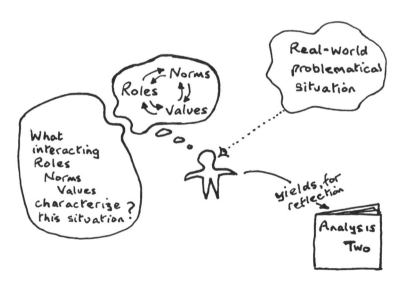

Fig. 5.16 SSM's Analysis Two

done. That is the focus of Analysis Three: to find out the disposition of power in a situation and the processes for containing it. That is always a powerful element in determining what is 'culturally feasible', politics being a part of culture not addressed directly in the examination of roles, norms and values of Analysis Two.

The 'political science' literature contains many models – usually fairly complex ones – which set out to express the nature of polities. The model used in SSM, in Analysis Three, does not come from that literature but from some basic ideas found in the work of the founding father of the field: Aristotle.

Aristotle argues that in any society (for him, the Greek city-state) in which human beings constantly interact, different interests will be being pursued. If the society as a whole is to remain coherent over time, not breaking up into destructive factions, then those differing interests will have to be accommodated; they will never go away. Accommodating different interests is the concern of politics; this entails creating a power-based structure within which potentially destructive power-play in pursuit of interests can nevertheless be contained. This is a general requirement in all human groups which endure, not only in societies as a whole. There will be an unavoidable political dimension in companies, in international sport, in health-care provision, in the local tennis club – in fact in any human affairs which involve deliberate action by people who can hold different worldviews and hence pursue different interests.

Analysis Three in SSM asks: How is power expressed in this situation? This is tackled through the metaphor of a 'commodity' which embodies power. What are the 'commodities' which signal that power is possessed in this situation? Then: What are the processes, by which these commodities are obtained, used, protected, defended, passed on, relinquished, etc.? Figure 5.17 summarizes Analysis Three. The commodities

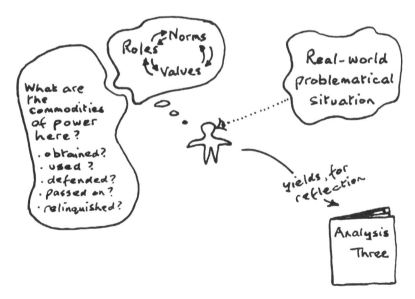

Fig. 5.17 SSM's Analysis Three

which indicate power in human groups are, of course, many and various. There is a link here to Analysis Two, since occupying a particular role embodies power: the chief constable has more power than a detective sergeant, by virtue of his role. Other common commodities of power include, for example: personal charisma; membership of various committees in organizations; having regular access to powerful role-holders; in knowledge-based settings, having intellectual authority and reputation; having authority to prepare the minutes of meetings – a chore, perhaps, but it gives you some power! Many commodities of power derive from information. Having access to important information, or being able to prevent others from having access to certain information, is a much-used commodity of power in most organizations.

A dramatic example of an unusual commodity of power in a specific SSM project was revealed when two managers in a consultancy company were being interviewed as a pair. They began to disagree with each other and, in a deliberate bit of power-play, one of them suddenly said: 'You say that, but you're NKT; I'm KT'. This local private language within this company referred to those partners who 'knew Tom' and those, more recent joiners, who 'never knew Tom', Tom being the charismatic founder of the company, now deceased. This taught those facilitating this use of SSM that there was an unstated but very real hierarchy here. The KTs, Tom's original disciples, were much more influential than the come-lately NKTs. This indicated that the only changes likely to be culturally feasible in this situation would be those supported by the KTs, whose power stemmed from their association with the charismatic Tom. This is an interesting example of a commodity of power which would gradually fade over time. And this itself reminds us that, as with Analysis Two, Analysis Three deals with elements which are continually being redefined as life moves on.

The way of doing this analysis echoes that of Analysis Two: open a file and record in it – with a date – any learning gained about power and the processes through which it is exercised. Do this, and reflect upon it, over the whole course of an investigation.

5.2.7   The SSM Learning Cycle: Making Purposeful Activity Models

As explained earlier, in order to ensure that learning can be captured, SSM users create an *organized* process of enquiry and learning. They do this by making models of purposeful activity and using them as a basis for asking questions of the real-world situation. This kind of model is used because every human situation reveals people trying to act purposefully. Since each model is built according to a declared single worldview (e.g. 'the Olympic Games from the perspective of the host city') such models could never be definitive descriptions of the real world. They model *one way* of looking at complex reality. They exist only as devices whose job is to make sure the learning process is not random, but organized, one which can be recovered and reflected on. This section describes how to make these devices.

The task is to construct a model of a purposeful 'activity system' viewed through the perspective of a pure, declared worldview, one which has been fingered as relevant to this investigation. In order to do that we need a statement describing the activity system to be modelled. Such descriptions are known in SSM as Root Definitions (RDs), the metaphor 'root' conveying that this is only one, core way of describing the system. A too-simple example would be: 'A system to paint the garden fence'. Here the worldview is unclear, and it is obvious that a richer description would lead to a richer outcome when the model is used as a source of questions to ask of the real situation. A number of ways of enriching an RD have shown themselves to be useful. For example, we could more richly express the RD above as: 'A householder-owned and staffed system to paint the garden fence, by hand-painting, in keeping with the overall decoration scheme of the property in order to enhance the appearance of the property'. This makes clear that the model takes a householder's worldview as given, and that that particular householder believes in DIY activity to improve it. In addition it not only describes *what* the system does (paint the fence); it also says *how* (by hand-painting) and *why* (to enhance the appearance of the property). (Also the worldview assumes a link between painting and improving appearance.) Clearly this would lead to a richer questioning of the real situation to which this purposeful activity was thought to be relevant as a device to structure the questioning.

The whole set of guidelines of this kind – there to help the modelling process – will now be described. They are set out in Fig. 5.18; the five numbered elements in the figure will be described in turn.

1. The PQR formula: The formula followed in enriching the fence-painting RD above is always helpful, and can apply to every RD ever written. It is known in SSM as 'the PQR formula': do P, by Q, in order to help achieve R, where PQR answer the questions: What? How? and Why? PQR provides a useful shape for any and every RD. Remember, though, in using PQR, that if the formula is complete, with all three elements defined, then the transforming process is captured in Q, the declared 'how'. In the simple example above the Q is 'hand-painting' (not simply 'painting'). Also, though it is not an issue in this example, the model builder has to be able to defend Q as a plausible 'how' for the 'what' defined by P. If you were to write 'define health-care needs' as P and then define Q *only* as 'by asking patients for their views' this would not be easily defensible.

2. The Root Definition: The PQR formula allows you to write out the RD as a statement. This always describes the purposeful activity being modelled as a transformation process, one in which some entity (in the example an 'unpainted fence') is transformed into a different state (here, a 'painted fence'). Any purposeful activity you can think of can be expressed in this way, which is useful because it makes model building a straightforward process. For complex activities the entity being transformed will probably be best expressed in an abstract way, for example: 'the health-care needs of Coketown citizens' transformed into 'the health-care needs of Coketown citizens met'. But the idea of purposeful activity as a transformation always holds, whether the transformation is concrete or abstract. Putting together

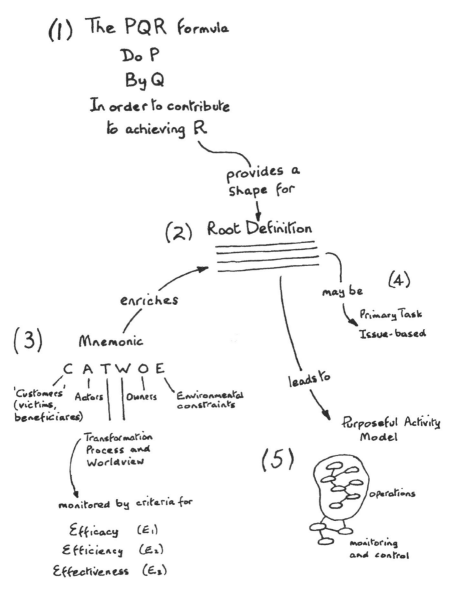

Fig. 5.18 Guidelines which help with building models of purposeful activity

the activities needed to describe the transforming process (i.e. 'building the model')
can begin when an RD is complete, but before moving on to this, elements 3 and 4
in Fig. 5.18 should be considered. They further enrich the modelling and improve
it as a source of questions to ask in the real situation.

3. CATWOE: When the idea of working with RDs as a source of models was being
   developed, a further enrichment of the thinking came from having, as a reference, a

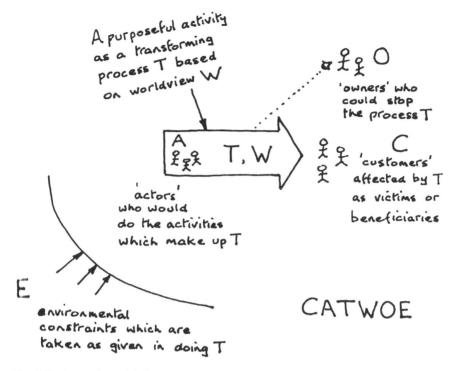

Fig. 5.19 A generic model of any purposeful activity, which yields the mnemonic CATWOE

completely general model of any purposeful activity. (This was a way of declaring exactly what we meant by 'purposeful activity'.) The general model is shown in Fig. 5.19. It contains elements which can usefully be thought about for any purposeful (transforming) activity.

The model provides the mnemonic CATWOE, defined as in Fig. 5.19. The concept here is that purposeful activity, defined by a transformation process and a worldview (a T and a W):

- Will require people (A) to do the activities which make up T
- Will affect people (C) outside itself who are its beneficiaries or victims (C for 'Customers')
- Will take as given various constraints from the environment outside itself (E) (such as a body of law, or a finite budget)
- Could be stopped or changed by some person or persons (O) who can be regarded as 'owning' it

Many people find it useful, when model building, to start the process by defining first T and W, then the other CATWOE elements. Experience suggests, though, that it is still useful to write out the RD as a statement which gives a holistic account of the concept being modelled.

Finally, within the guidelines which CATWOE provides, it is useful to think ahead to the model and ask yourself: What would be the measures of performance by which the operation of the notional system would be judged? Thinking out what those criteria would be really sharpens up the thinking about the purposeful activity being modelled. Three criteria are relevant in every case, and should always be named. We need:

- Criteria to tell whether the transformation T is working, in the sense of producing its intended outcome, i.e. criteria for *efficacy*
- Criteria to tell whether the transformation is being achieved with a minimum use of resources, i.e. criteria for *efficiency*; and
- Criteria to tell whether this transformation is helping achieve some higher-level or longer-term aim, i.e. criteria for *effectiveness*

In the case of the simple fence-painting system the criteria address, respectively, the questions: Does this count as 'a painted fence' (human judgement would decide)? Is the painting being done with minimum use of the resources of materials and time (these might be expressed as costs)? and Does the painted fence enhance the appearance of the property (again human judgement would decide)? These three criteria are always independent of each other. Thus, for example, the purposeful act of taking a drug to relieve your headache might be efficacious if the headache goes. But it could be inefficient if the drug cost too much or was very slow-acting. And it could also be ineffective, medically, if treating the symptom of the headache was unwise because the headache actually signalled a more serious complaint.

These 'three Es' will always be relevant in building any model, but in particular circumstances other criteria might also apply, such as *elegance* (Is this a beautiful transformation?) or *ethicality* (Is this a morally correct transformation?). The judgement is yours as to what criteria are needed.

4. Primary Task vs. Issue-based: The final consideration in Fig. 5.19 when formulating RDs prior to model building concerns RDs as a whole. Are they 'Primary Task' or 'Issue-based' definitions? This useful distinction (though it does not affect model building technique) arose through experience, like most developments in SSM. In the early days, when the legacy of Systems Engineering hung heavy over the new approach, the models built were always of purposeful activity of a kind that was present in the real world in the form of departments, divisions, sections, etc.; that is to say it was institutionalized. Thus, if working in a company with functional sections – production, marketing, research and development, etc. – we would in the early days of developing SSM make models only of a production system, a marketing system, an R&D system, etc. In these cases the boundary of the models we built would coincide with internal organizational boundaries. This is not 'wrong', but it puts limitations on the thinking of the team carrying out the investigation, which may go unnoticed. Every organization has to carry out many, many purposeful activities as it goes about its business. Only a few of these can be captured in the organization structure as departments, etc. These organizational boundaries are, in the last analysis, arbitrary, and could be changed.

Experience quickly showed that to stimulate the thinking of everyone involved in the investigation it was useful to make models of purposeful activity whose boundaries *cut across organizational boundaries*. These are 'Issue-based' models from 'Issue-based' RDs, models whose boundaries do not coincide with organizational boundaries. When such models are used to ask questions in the situation, interest and attention are always increased. This brings in broader considerations than is the case with a model which accepts organizational boundaries as a given. This is because the questions about what departments, sections, etc. should exist, and what their boundaries should be are always bound up in the power-play going on in organizations. That catches everyone's attention!

As a generalization we can suggest one choice of Issue-based RD which is always worth considering. In virtually all organized human groups there will always be contentious issues concerned with allocating resources. This is something which affects all members, leads to wide discussion, and is not usually assigned as an activity to a particular sub-group. An issue-based model based on transforming unallocated into allocated resources will be worth considering as a stimulant in most investigations. The general rule is: never work exclusively with either Primary Task (PT) or Issue-based (IB) RDs. Most investigations will best feature a mixture of both types.

5. Putting it all together – Conceptual Models: Earlier in this section, in point 2 above, model building was described as 'putting together the activities needed to describe the transforming process', in other words defining and linking the activities needed to achieve the transforming process. Given the guidelines provided by PQR, an RD, CATWOE, the 3Es and PT/IB, this task should not be a difficult one. The only skill called for is logical thinking. The most common error – even among logical thinkers – is to take your eye off the root definition and start modelling some real-world version of the purposeful activity being modelled. In work in a medium-sized manufacturing company, concerned with various issues regarding product distribution, it was easier for the SSM practitioners to build relevant models than it was for the distribution manager. He kept slipping into modelling the current ways of working in his department rather than the concepts in RDs. If you do this, of course, you find yourself not questioning current practice but comparing X with X – not very profitable!

People find their own way of making the selected relevant models, but a logical sequence to follow, or to refer to if in difficulty, is as follows:

1. Assemble the guidelines: PQR, CATWOE, the RD, etc.
2. Write down three groups of activities – those which concern the thing which gets transformed (the 'unpainted fence', or the 'health needs of the citizens of Coketown', in the examples above); those activities which *do* the transforming; and any activities concerned with dealing with the transformed entity (e.g. judging if it improves the appearance of the property, in the fence-painting example); this will give you a cluster of activities.
3. Connect the activities by arrows which indicate the dependency of one activity upon another; for example, you can't *use* a raw material to make something

before you've *obtained* it, so an arrow goes from an 'obtain' activity to the 'use' activity. In Fig. 5.7 activity 7 (paint the fence) depends upon both activities 4, 5 and 6, since you can't paint the fence until you've obtained both brush and paint and prepared the fence.

4. Add the three monitoring and control activities, which always have the structure shown in Figs. 5.6 and 5.7

Check the model against the guidelines. Ask yourself: Does every phrase in the RD lead to something in the model? And: Can every activity in the model be linked back to something in the RD or CATWOE, etc.? If the answer to both questions is 'Yes', then you have a defensible model. Note that the word used here is 'defensible' rather than 'correct'. This is because everyday words have different connotations for different people. Competent SSM practitioners working from the same RD might well produce somewhat different models; this is because they are interpreting the words in the RD, etc. somewhat differently. The important thing is that you can defend your model as representing what is in your RD, PQR, CATWOE, etc. Figure 5.20 summarizes the model building process.

Finally, on model building, there is one more guideline worth taking seriously. Aim to capture the activity in the operational part of the model in 'the magical number 7 ± 2' activities (but do break the 'rule' if necessary). This famous phrase comes from a celebrated paper in cognitive psychology. George Miller, based on laboratory work, suggests that the human brain may have the capacity to cope with around seven concepts simultaneously. Whether or not this is true it is certainly the case that a set of 7 ± 2 activities can be thought about holistically. If the number seems low, this is not a problem. Any activity in a model can itself, at a more detailed level, become the source of an RD and a model. Thus, in Fig. 5.7, activity 6 (obtain paint) could itself be expanded into a model which set out the connected, more-detailed activities which together combine to constitute 'obtain paint' – activities concerned with checking out suppliers, their prices, selecting one, etc. If this model were built, its activities would be numbered 6.1, 6.2, 6.3, etc. since they all derive from activity 6 in the parent model. In this way coherence is maintained no matter how many levels it may be necessary to go to in a particular investigation. In the authors' experience of more than a 100 studies it has never been necessary to expand beyond two levels below that of the parent model, and even then expanding only a few activities at the lower levels.

The first model presented here, to illustrate the idea of purposeful activity models, was that in Fig. 5.7. This was presented without a Root Definition, but now that this has been defined (above) we can present part of the model in a more developed form. This is done in Fig. 5.21 which makes one particular change. It would have been possible to include in the 'operations' part of the model an activity such as 'ascertain the judgement about the enhanced appearance of the property'. Another way of bringing in the R of PQR (the higher-level, or longer-term aim of the transforming process, judged by the criteria for effectiveness) is shown in Fig. 5.21. The monitoring and control activity has been split into two, with the monitoring for effectiveness having the added activity: 'Appreciate householder's aspirations for the fence painting.' This leaves open who would make the judgement about the hoped-for enhancement of the

1. Assemble guidelines : TandW
                           PQR ; PT/$_{1B}$
                           CATWOE , $E_1 E_2 E_3$

2. Starting from T and W name the purposeful action as a transformation:

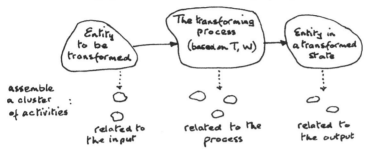

assemble a cluster of activities :   related to   related to the   related to
                                       the input   process   the output

3. Structure the activities according to dependency of one on another

aim for 7±2

4. Add the monitoring and control activities

5. Check the mutual dependency of guidelines and model

Fig. 5.20 A logical process for building SSM's activity models

appearance of the property – the householder? his or her partner? the neighbours? a prospective purchaser? This is probably, in this instance, the most elegant way of bringing all the elements in the guidelines into the model.

5.2.8   The SSM Learning Cycle: Using Models to Structure Discussion About the Situation and Its Improvement

When we enter a problematical situation and start drawing rich pictures and carrying out preliminary versions of Analyses One, Two and Three, we begin to build up what can become a rich appreciation of the situation. This appreciation – helped

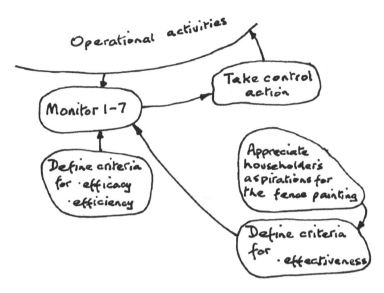

Fig. 5.21 A variant of part of the model in Fig. 5.7

especially by the list of possible 'issue owners' from Analysis One – enables us to begin to name some models which might be helpful in deepening our understanding of the situation and beginning to learn our way to taking 'action to improve'. Having built a hopefully relevant model or two, we are then ready to begin the structured discussion about the situation, and how it could be changed, which will eventually lead to action being taken. The models are the devices which enable that discussion to be a structured rather than a random one.

In everyday situations, typical discussions among professionals are characterized by a remarkable lack of clarity. In a typical 'management' discussion in an organization, unless there is a chairperson of near-genius, different voices will be addressing different issues; different levels, from the short-term tactical to the long-term strategic, will be being addressed; different speakers will assume different timescales. The resulting confusion will then provide splendid cover for personal and private agendas to be advanced. Use of the models to help structure discussion enables us to do rather better than this.

Structure to the discussion is provided by using the models as a source of questions to ask about the situation. This phase of SSM has usually been referred to as a 'comparison' between situation and models, but this wording is truly dangerous if it is taken to imply that the discussion focuses on deficiencies in the situation when set against the 'perfect' models. *The models do not purport to be accounts of what we would wish the real world to be like.* They could not, since they are artificial devices based on a pure worldview, whereas human groups are always characterized by multiple conflicting worldviews (even within one individual!) which themselves change over time – sometimes slowly, sometimes remarkably quickly. (It is those conflicting worldviews which are the fundamental cause of the confusion in most 'management' discussion.)

No, the purposeful activity models simply enable our organized discussion to take place. From the model we can define a set of questions to ask. For example: 'Here is an activity in this model; does it exist in the real situation? Who does it? How? When? Who else could do it? How else could it be done?'... etc. Or: 'This activity in the model is dependent upon these other two activities; is it like this in the real situation?' There is no shortage of possible questions, and practitioners quickly develop the knack of passing in a light-footed way over many possibilities and resting on those questions which are likely to generate attention, excitement or emotion. The questions can be about activities or the dependence of one activity upon another or upon the measures of performance by which purposeful activity is judged.

A general finding is that groups find it very difficult to answer questions derived from the measures of performance in a model. 'What criteria would indicate the degree to which this activity (either individual, or the set of operational activities as a whole) is efficacious, efficient and effective?' This is usually a difficult question to answer in most real-world situations, due to their complexity, but it usefully draws attention to the need for organized processes of monitoring, something which is often given scant attention in organizations of all kinds. At a broader level, the fact that a given model is based upon a declared (pure) worldview will draw attention to other, usually implicit, worldviews which may underlie what is actually going on in the situation. This may serve to define other relevant models worth building and also helps to raise the level of discussion to that at which previously taken-as-given assumptions are now questioned. This will usually wake up anyone who is sleep-walking through the discussion, not least because differences of worldview always provoke *feelings*, not simply mental activity. (Also, incidentally, experience in developing SSM suggests that the stimulation of emotion is probably, for most people, a powerful trigger for significant learning to occur.)

In practice, several ways of conducting the questioning of the situation have emerged. An informal approach is to have a discussion about improving the situation in the presence of the models. If some relevant models are on flip charts on the wall, they can be referred to and brought into the discussion at appropriate moments. This has been found useful in situations in which detailed discussion of the SSM approach is inappropriate or is not feasible for cultural reasons. It was effective in a situation in a giant publishing/printing company which was characterized by an operation – publishing, printing and selling consumer magazines – which combined two very separate cultures who found it difficult to appreciate each other's worlds. The editor/publisher culture contained people very different from those in the printing culture, though they worked in the same company. Models which related to the whole operation of commissioning material, editing and assembling magazine issues, printing them and marketing them, proved useful here as a background, rather than as a source of specific detailed questioning. They were on flip charts on the wall, and could be referred to during discussion.

A more formal approach, probably the most commonly used, is to create a chart matrix as in Fig. 5.22. The model provides the left-hand column, consisting of activities and connections from the model, while the other axis contains questions to ask about those elements (which may vary depending on the investigation underway). The task is then to fill in the matrix by answering the questions.

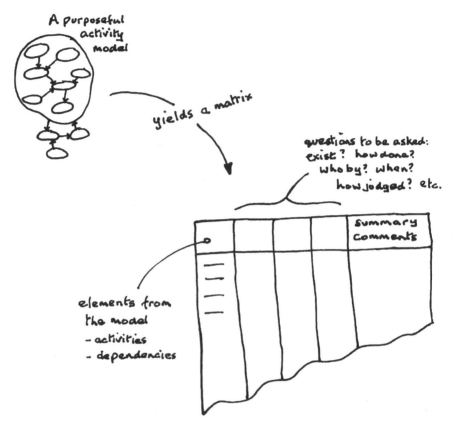

Fig. 5.22 A formal process for using models to question the real-world situation

An important warning here is that this process should not be allowed to become mechanical drudgery. This is where a light-footed approach is needed, glancing quickly at many activities and questions, making judgements, and avoiding getting bogged down. Experience quickly develops this craft skill. In fact, experience suggests that this business of seeking to avoid plodding through every cell in the matrix itself helps develop insights into 'the real issues in this situation' – though such judgements have to be tested.

A third way of using models to question reality is to use a model as a basis for writing an account of how some purposeful action would be done according to the model, and comparing this story, or scenario, with a real-world account of something similar happening in the real world. For example, work with SSM was carried out in a chemical company which treated every plant start-up as if it were the first they had ever carried out. It was very useful in that situation to make a basic generic model of 'a system to start up a new chemical plant' and then write a story from this pure (instrumental) model which could be compared with the real-world stories of previous plant start-ups, usually stories of delays and cock-ups.

The company was right in saying that every plant start-up revealed unique features. But this work also showed that it was useful to have a generic model to hand when planning for a new start-up. This model could then be enriched by new experiences, so that the chance of future surprises in plant start-up could be diminished.

Figure 5.23 summarizes different ways of using models in the context of SSM as a whole.

Whichever way the models are used to structure discussion, the aim is the same: to find a version of the real situation and ways to improve it which different people with different worldviews can nevertheless *live with*. Outside of the arbitrary exercise of power, this is the necessary condition which must be met in any human group if agreed 'action to improve' is to be defined.

5.2.9   *The SSM Learning Cycle: Defining 'Action to Improve'*

When describing the discussion/debate in SSM, much – perhaps most – of the secondary literature about the approach makes a remarkable and fundamental error. It assumes that the purpose of the discussion/debate is to find *consensus*. It is a 'remarkable' mistake in that anyone who had read the primary literature with care would not make it, and it is 'fundamental' because, in order to cope with the complexity of human affairs, SSM uses a much more subtle idea than 'consensus'. It works with the idea of finding an *accommodation* among a group of people with a common concern. This does not abandon the possibility of consensus; rather it subsumes it in the more general idea of accommodation. A true consensus is the rare, special case among groups of people, and usually occurs only with respect to issues which are trivial or not contentious; issues which people do not feel particularly strongly about. In the general case, however, because individuals enter the world with different genetic dispositions and then have different experiences in the world, there will always be differences of opinion resulting from different worldviews. So, if a group of people are to achieve agreed corporate action in response to a problematical situation, they will have to find an accommodation. That is to say they will have to find a version of the situation which they can all live with. These accommodations will of course involve either compromise or some yielding of position. A compromise may give no member of the group all they personally would look for in action to improve the situation. But finding an accommodation is usually a necessary condition for moving to deciding 'what we will now do' in the situation.

The idea of finding accommodations is probably most familiar to us in our personal lives. Any family, as long as it is not of the classic Victorian kind, run by a (male) tyrant who decides everything, will have to continually find versions of the family situation which the different members can accept and live with. This is a necessary characteristic if families are to stick together over a long period. But the idea is also relevant to our professional lives, and to public life. A dramatic illustration of the latter is provided by some British political history. In the UK in the

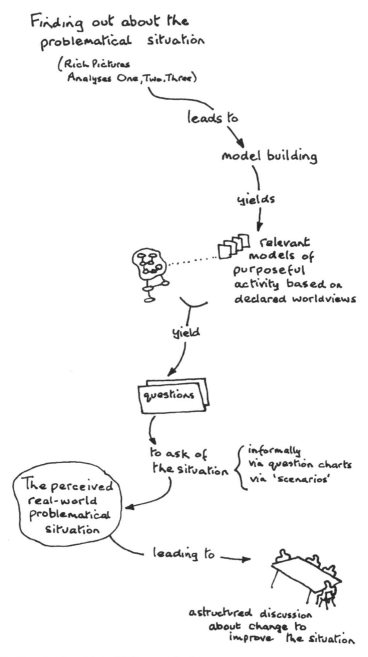

Fig. 5.23 The role of models in SSM summarized

1970s there were a number of major strikes in the coal industry, the disputes usually involving pay. One of those strikes lasted for a year. Now, the interesting thing about these disputes was that they were conducted within an accommodation between the two sides, the Coal Board and the National Union of Miners (NUM). Although the miners were on strike, members of the NUM nevertheless went down every mine in the country, every day, in order to keep the pumps running, since if you don't continuously pump water out of a coal mine you lose the mine. Although both sides regretted, but were prepared to have the dispute, there was an accommodation between them at a higher level: neither was prepared to live with the idea of the conflict destroying the whole industry. (It took political action to do that some years later!)

This view taken within SSM – that consensus is rare in human affairs, due to clashing worldviews – is not to be regretted. Clashing worldviews, always present, are a source of strong feelings, energy, motivation and creativity. If you find that the models you've built are not leading to *energetic* discussion, abandon them and formulate some more radical Root Definitions.

As discussion based on using models to question the problematical situation proceeds, worldviews will be surfaced, entrenched positions may shift, and possible accommodations may emerge. Any such accommodation will entail making changes to the situation, if it is to become less problematical, and discussion can begin to focus on finding some changes which are both arguably desirable and culturally feasible. In practical terms it is a good idea not to try and discuss the abstract idea 'accommodation' directly. It is best approached obliquely through considering what changes might be made in the situation and what consequences would follow. The relations between accommodations, consensus and changes is summarized in Fig. 5.24, and the practical way forward in seeking accommodation is by exploring possible changes and noting reactions to them.

In doing this it is best to think richly about change in human situations, separating the concept into three parts for analytical purposes, even though any significant change in real situations will usually entail all three elements. These are: making changes to *structures*; changing *processes* or procedures; and changing *attitudes*.

Obviously the easiest element to change is structure, which can often be done by decree through the exercise of legitimate power. Researchers have noted, for example, that large organizations tend to reorganize themselves structurally about every 18 months to 2 years. In the UK, governments have imposed structural change upon the National Health Service more than 20 times since it was established in 1948. That is the easy part, for governments. But of course new structures usually require both new processes and new attitudes on the part of those carrying out the processes or being affected by them. Organizations (and governments) find it much harder to think out the necessary new processes; and no one can be sure, in a unique social situation, about what to do to change attitudes in a particular direction. (In our current culture, obsessed with economics, the usual mechanism for trying to change attitudes is to provide material incentives, but this reflects acceptance of a bleak model of human beings as creatures responding only to sticks and carrots. Human beings are more complex than that.)

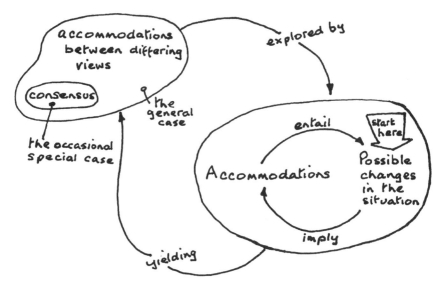

Fig. 5.24 Seeking accommodations or (rarely) consensus by exploring implications of possible changes

Figure 5.25 illustrates the stance on 'change' taken within SSM. It represents a reminder of things to think about when considering changes which are both desirable and feasible. It is self-explanatory, but two points are worth making. There is a question concerning the 'enabling action' which may be necessary if a potential change is to be accepted. This recognizes the social *context* in which any change will sit. Because of this context, introducing the change may require other action, enabling action, which is not directly part of the change itself. For example, when working within the UK National Health Service for the first time, in the early 1970s, the authors quickly found that in an acute hospital no proposed change would get accepted unless it had the support of senior hospital consultants. Shifts in the disposition of power have now modified that, but at that time in the history of the NHS, enabling action to secure the support of senior doctors was essential if any change of any kind was to occur in a hospital! The second point concerns trying to define the criteria by which a change can be judged as 'completed' and 'successful/unsuccessful'. This point has already been made above in connection with asking about 'monitor-and-control' activities in a real situation: well worth doing, but don't expect people in the situation to have any ready answers.

As we come to the end of this section's exposition of a 'fleshed-out' account of SSM, the discussion has become less detailed, in the sense that there are more detailed guidelines for finding out about a real-world situation, and building models used to question it, than there are for taking action to improve the situation. This is inevitable, and is due simply to the fact that no human situation is ever exactly the same as any other. Once we start exploring the real complexity of a human situation, not simply its logic, then formulae, algorithms and ready-made solutions are not available.

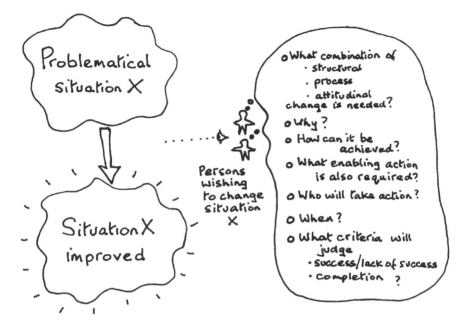

Fig. 5.25 SSM's stance on introducing change in human situations

Even guidelines become fewer. That being so, it seems helpful to give here, a real example of these ideas about change in action.

In the work mentioned earlier in the publishing-printing industry, the company carried out both of these major activities in selling a large range of consumer magazines. Publishing and printing were organizationally separate, and were in the hands of two very different cultures: on the one hand 'media-folk', on the other 'technologists'. There were many issues in the company concerning investment, pricing, and the placing and scheduling of work. For example, the printers thought of themselves as 'jobbing printers', making no distinction between printing one of the company's titles or that of a competitor. Publishers had ill-defined freedom to print within the company or externally. There were many rows about 'where to print', for example. This was an occasion in which the least-formal way of using models to question the situation was used: discussion in the presence of the models, which were on flip charts on the walls. In the discussion stimulated by the models the end point finally reached, subsequently approved by the board, was that there should be structural change. A new unit within the company was set up. This unit was centrally placed, and was staffed (part-time – it was not permanently in session) by people from both publishing and printing. This structural change was just about culturally feasible (where a fully integrated magazine-producing operation was out of the question) and the processes within the new unit were defined. As far as changes of attitude were concerned, the chief executive, who understood the difficulties of forcing change of that kind, wrote in the in-house company 'newspaper':

'Primarily the new unit is concerned with trying to develop a more effective relationship between our publishers and printers.' He was hoping that each of the two cultures would, through working together on some issues, begin to see the world through the eyes of the other.

5.2.10   The Whole SSM Learning Cycle Revisited: Seven Principles, Five Actions

We can now summarize the whole learning cycle of the SSM approach. In a concise account of SSM, which is as spare as we can make it, seven principles lead to five actions. These are based only on findings which, through many experiences over a long period, always turned out to be helpful. They are the end product of the several hundred cycles through the LUMAS model (Fig. 5.3).

The seven principles which underlie SSM are set out first.

1. The idea 'real-world problem' is subsumed in the broader concept of 'real-world *problematical situation*'; that is to say, a real situation which someone thinks needs attention and action.
2. All thinking and talking about problematical situations will be conditioned by the *worldviews* (*Weltanschauungen*) of the people doing the thinking and talking. These worldviews are the internalized taken-as-given assumptions which cause us to see and interpret the world in a particular way (one observer's 'terrorism' being another's 'freedom fighting').
3. Every real-world problematical situation will contain people trying to act *purposefully*, with intent. This means that *models of purposeful activity*, in the form of systems models built to express a particular worldview, can be used as *devices* to explore the qualities and characteristics of any problematical human situation.
4. *Discussion and debate* about such a situation can be *structured* by using the models in (3) as a source of questions to ask about the situation.
5. Acting to improve a real-world situation entails finding, in the course of the discussion/debate in (4), *accommodations* among different world-views. An accommodation entails finding a version of the situation addressed which different people, with different worldviews, can nevertheless live with.
6. The *inquiry* created by principles (1)–(5) is in principle a *never-ending process of learning*. It is never-ending since taking action to improve the situation will change its characteristics. It becomes a new (less problematical) situation, and the process in (3), (4) and (5) could begin again. Learning is never finished!
7. Explicit organization of the process which embodies principles (1)–(6) enables and embodies *conscious critical reflection* about both the situation itself and also about the thinking about it. This reflection which leads to learning, can (and should) take place prior to, during and after intervening in the situation in order to improve it. The process thus itself virtually ensures *reflective practice* by those who make use of it. Once the practitioner has internalized the SSM process,

so that he or she no longer has to stop and ask questions about it ('Remind me again what did PQR stand for?') then reflective practice becomes built-in too. The SSM user becomes a reflective practitioner.

These seven principles clearly underlie the four actions which define the classic shape of SSM in Fig. 5.9: finding out about a problematical situation; making models relevant to exploring it, based on different worldviews; questioning the situation using the models, in order to find desirable and feasible change; and defining/taking action to change the situation for the better. The seventh principle itself defines a fifth action which ensures cycling round the primary four, namely critical reflection on the whole process. This fifth action is at a different level from the other four. It is *about* the other four, i.e. at a meta-level. It is the activity which ensures that the lessons learned are captured, in the way that the LUMAS model of Fig. 5.3 indicates. Figure 5.26 expresses these five activities at their two levels.

Finally, in completing this more detailed account of SSM, it is worth re-emphasizing some of its core ideas. It does not seek 'solutions' which 'solve' real-world problems. Those ideas are a mirage when faced with real-life complexity, with its multiple perceptions and agendas. Instead SSM focuses on the process of engaging

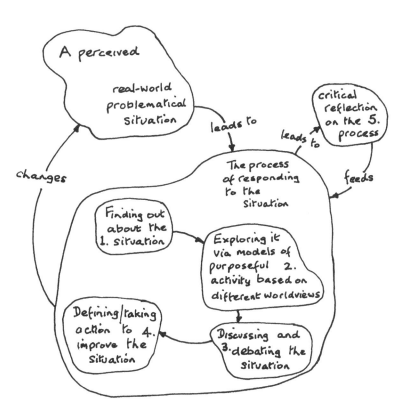

Fig. 5.26 The five activities which flow from SSM's seven principles

with that complexity. It offers an organized process of thinking which enables a group of people to learn their way to taking 'action to improve'; and it does that by means of a well-defined, explicit process which makes it possible to recover the course of the thinking which leads to action. This makes sure that every use of the approach produces learning which will accumulate over time, leaving the user better equipped to cope with future complexities.

5.3 Reflection

In this short finale we reflect on some aspects of Soft Systems Methodology practice. First we look at the issue of practice skills. Then we suggest some features of the appropriate mindset when approaching SSM. Finally, we provide a diagram summarizing SSM as a whole, Fig. 5.29.

5.3.1 Craft Skills in SSM Use

It is not easy to talk or write clearly and explicitly about craft skills, for the phrase conveys the idea of something which cannot be pinned down explicitly, something rather mysterious which cannot be completely analysed. Craft skills can be acquired through experience, but cannot entirely be taught, not in the way that 'How to solve simultaneous equations' or 'How to set up a website' can. The response to this in everyday life is the idea of 'apprenticeship'. The would-be young potter works alongside the skilled potter and eventually may be able to produce high-quality pots, having absorbed much from his or her mentor in terms of both explicit and tacit (unexpressed) knowledge. Now, we are not claiming that apprenticeship is necessary to become a competent SSM practitioner. There are many examples of people who have made excellent use of SSM based on written accounts of it. But we use this example to illustrate the fact that the process of using a methodology is much richer than the biff-bang application of a technique. What we *are* claiming is that with experience the user of SSM will both find a way of using the methodology that they are personally comfortable with (which fits with their cast of mind) *and* improve their use of SSM as experience accumulates.

Meanwhile we can offer some advice from experience which may help with the process of internalizing SSM, so that attention can be directed wholly to the situation addressed, rather than addressed to the methodology. Progress in that is signalled by no longer having to ask such questions as: Remind me again, what was the difference between Primary-task and Issue-based Root Definitions? Get over that hurdle and you can really begin to use the methodology effectively. In fact worrying about the methodology or its tools can hinder the learning process. The best advice about SSM is: dive in, tackle real situations and learn about SSM along the way.

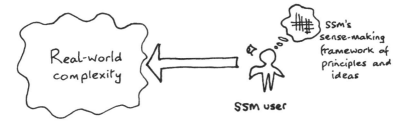

Fig. 5.27 SSM's basic stance – using a particular set of principles and ideas to make sense of real-world complexity

The craft skills in SSM use are thinking skills, rather than physical skills, and so can be thought about while sitting at a desk, going for a walk or lying in the bath. Here, from experience are some remarks about the practitioner state of mind which will make it easier to develop SSM's craft skills.

1. Always remain conscious of the fact that the process in which the user of SSM is engaged is one of addressing a complex human situation, mentally, by the conscious organized use of particular ideas and principles in order to achieve sense-making, as shown in Fig. 5.27.

This implies what is probably the key step in really understanding SSM and its use: grasping that the user in Fig. 5.27 is *consciously thinking about his or her own thinking*. This 'meta-level' thinking is not all that common. Some extremely intelligent people go through life in the stance shown as (a) in Fig. 5.28, never thinking about themselves as thinkers.

They perceive complexity in the world outside themselves and, *at the same mental level as that perception*, think 'I could do this, that, or the other…'

The experienced SSM user is in the stance shown as (b) in Fig. 5.28. This lifts the thinking to a level above that of simply perceiving the complexity. It lifts it to a meta-level, and makes the user able to inspect their own thinking and then think about it. It is this shift from stance (a) to stance (b) which increases the richness of thinking and enables insights to emerge and formula-driven thinking to be avoided. It is the (a) to (b) shift which turns a practitioner into a reflective practitioner and define SSM as an articulation of reflective practice.

2. Banish all thought of finding a permanent 'solution' or the optimum way of doing something in any human situation. No such situation is ever *exactly* like another; nothing ever happens twice in human situations, not in exactly the same way, and no such situation is ever static. (If 'a problem' can be stated *as if* human situations were unchanging, then you are dealing not with the unique [human] features of a situation but only with the logic of a situation – which may well apply to a general class of problem. For example if 'the problem' is 'where to site the new warehouse, given the shape of our market', then the depot-location

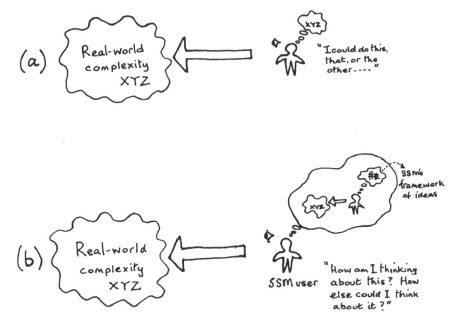

Fig. 5.28 SSM, as reflective practice, entails consciously thinking about your own thinking, i.e. moving to stance (b)

algorithm from 1960s Management Science may help. But do remember that the actual location of the new warehouse may be decided on the basis of human judgements which are far from rational.)

3. Try not to *impose* a structure on the situation. Rather, let it 'speak to you' as you tease out the strands of thinking within it. The attitude to adopt is that implied by the Scottish phrase 'I hear you'. This means withholding judgement, neither approving nor disapproving of what you find but allowing the situation to reveal its patterns. And know that this pattern can (probably will) change within the course of an investigation. So, be positive in forming judgements about the situation but tentative about hanging on to those judgements. Also, revisit your thinking continually to see how both the situation and your thinking about it is changing.

4. Remember that no methodology can do your thinking for you, and lead inevitably to a unique and successful outcome. What it can do is structure your thinking, or that of a team carrying out an investigation, so that you and/or the team's capabilities are used to the full. Also, in the team case, it will *enable* a group of people to become a real team much more easily than would be the case if no declared methodological principles were being followed. In virtually all case studies undertaken by the authors, SSM acted in this way, providing shared concepts and a shared language which helped team coherence. In one example, a team of civil servants and outside consultants carried out an SSM-based study of the personal taxation arrangements in the UK. An SSM (p) model of 'a system to do the study' was built at the start, based on the study's terms of reference,

which were treated as a Root Definition. It was used continually as a sense-making device as the study unfolded (rather than as a plan), and ensured that there were no communication issues in the disparate but united team.

5. When facilitating an investigation being carried out by people in the situation, always keep in mind that your aim is to *give away* the approach being used to the people in the situation itself. Don't hang on to ownership. In the rethinking of the role of Shell's manufacturing function, an investigation was truly carried out, with facilitating help, by the participants in the workshops, not only by the facilitators. In the rethink of an Information and Library Services Department the three members of the department who were seconded to carry out the study part-time wished to give the internal presentation on the finished work without help from the facilitators. This was an important signal that the higher-level aim of the study (to increase the department's 'problem solving skills') was being achieved.

6. Be ready to be surprised by the turns which the investigations take. As world views are surfaced and questioned there is no knowing which way the work will go, or what the final outcome will be. In some work with a publishing and printing corporation the outcome of structural change was in no way envisaged at the start of the work. Outcomes derive from no formula, they arise from the idiosyncrasies of the situations addressed. They derive in part from the always-present tension between the glorious mix of altruistic behaviour directed to group aims and the selfish pursuit of personal agendas which is never absent from human affairs.

7. Be aware that the action emerging as desirable and feasible from an investigation will frequently not be implementable by those undertaking the study, who may not have the necessary power. Because of this the investigators need continually to be making judgements about possible outcomes and asking themselves who would be in a position to cause or authorize action to be taken. Then make sure that those people are as closely involved as possible in the course of the investigation. It may not be possible to draw them into participation (they may well be senior people with wide agendas and full diaries); but as a minimum make sure that the outcome of an investigation does not come as a big surprise, out of a clear sky. Take whatever enabling action is necessary to avoid that.

8. Don't let the work done as part of an investigation ever feel like 'work', grinding along under grey skies. If it does feel like a grind, rather than an intellectual adventure, then stir things up. Try some outrageous Root Definitions, redefine CATWOE elements, think of new possible (if improbable) 'issue owners' in Analysis One. Do whatever you have to do to recapture zest. SSM should never feel like a grim or plodding experience; it should always be fun, serious fun, and a rewarding experience.

5.3.2 Approaching SSM: The Mindset

It is not very usual in Western thought to devote much attention to thinking about thinking. In most subject areas the focus is always on the substantive content, while 'how to think about this' is neglected. It is assumed that serious attention to the subject matter will somehow also inculcate 'how to think about it' by some kind of osmosis. However, the output generated by SSM's 30-year programme of action research in problematical real-life situations was precisely *an explicit way of thinking about*, and hence a process for dealing with, the kind of complexity found in human affairs. (The unusual nature of this outcome is probably what can make it difficult for some people to understand it.) The nature of SSM as a methodology implies a particular view of social reality but also implies that a would-be user should approach it in a particular frame of mind, which is summarized here in seven pieces of advice.

- *Reflect* on the fact that most discussion in human situations is of poor quality. Different topics interact, participants speak at different levels (from tactical to strategic) and bring different judgements to bear, based on different (unacknowledged) worldviews.
- *Know* that SSM can make such discussion much more coherent, and will deepen the level of thinking due to its surfacing of worldviews, since these govern how issues are both perceived and judged.
- *Accept* that no methodology can on its own lead to some first-rate outcome, but know also that even rough-and-ready use of SSM will improve the quality of the thinking of the participants and increase the quality of the discussion which they generate.
- *Know* that methodology should be treated for what it is, a set of principles which need to be tailored to a method for *this* situation with these participants, with their history, now. And remain oriented to the problem situation, not to the methodology, using SSM for making sense of real-life complexity.
- *Know* that the best way to learn about SSM is to use it, however crudely you do this at first.
- *Know*, when having a go at using it, that its principles are very resilient, capable of standing up to a good deal of rough use. (Models which might not get high marks in a university exam can, in real life, be helpful!)
- *Know* that the understanding of a situation gained through use of SSM is not gained for its own sake, but to become a spring for action. This is an action-oriented approach.

Given the frame of mind outlined above, any problematical situation in human affairs may be tackled with some confidence.

The outcome of any use of SSM will depend upon a number of factors whose effects cannot easily be disentangled. These include: the characteristics and abilities of the people carrying out the investigation; the characteristics of the situation as perceived by those who care about it; and the methodology itself. To this we can add that the very best uses of the approach seem to exhibit a certain style. At the end of the 1990 book describing twelve uses of mature SSM (Peter Checkland and Jim Scholes, *SSM in Action* [John Wiley and Sons, Ltd]), this was stated in the following terms:

> The very best uses of SSM seem always to exhibit a certain dash, a light-footedness, a deft charm. In this sense the role of the approach is akin to that of the cavalry in nineteenth century war: it can add a certain tone to what might otherwise be a vulgar brawl (p. 302).

A Basic outline of Soft Systems Methodology

o Think : 'problem situation'
     not 'problem'

o Find out about it :
     Rich Pictures
     Analysis One (the intervention)
          Two (social)
          Three (political)

o Think of some 'relevant systems'
  of purposeful activity ; name
  the worldviews they encapsulate

Activities
constituting
a purposeful
whole

take
control
action

monitor

define
measures
of performance

o Build the models of these notional
  systems (as on the left)
          · Root Definitions (PT/18)
          . PQR
          . CATWOE
          · 3Es   efficacy
                   efficiency
                   effectiveness

structured
debate about
change

o Use the models to question the
  perceived real-world situation,
     structuring a debate about
          change

action to
improve

accommodations
enabling change
to occur

o Seek accommodations which
  meet criteria: systemically desirable
  (based on these models) and culturally
  feasible (for these people in their
  situation). An accommodation is
  a version of the situation which
  different people (different worldviews)
  can nevertheless live with.

Fig. 5.29 A basic outline of soft systems methodology

To this we can add that the confidence which comes from SSM once it is internalised can help you, in the midst of the turmoil of everyday life, to demonstrate one highly desirable and productive end: grace under pressure.

Figure 5.29 is a one-page aide-memoire of the key elements in SSM's learning cycle, and their relationships within the whole. Good luck with it!

References

Checkland, P. (1981), *Systems Thinking, Systems Practice,* Chichester, UK: Wiley.

Checkland, P., Poulter, J. (2006), *Learning for Action: A Short Definitive Account of Soft Systems Methodology, and Its Use Practitioners, Teachers and Students,* Chichester, UK: Wiley.

Checkland, P., Scholes, J. (1990), *Soft Systems Methodology in Action,* Chichester, UK: Wiley.

Chapter 6
Critical Systems Heuristics[1]

Werner Ulrich and Martin Reynolds

Abstract Critical systems heuristics (CSH) is a framework for reflective professional practice organised around the central tool of boundary critique. This paper, written jointly by the original developer, Werner Ulrich, and Martin Reynolds, an experienced practitioner of CSH, offers a systematic introduction to the idea and use of boundary critique. Its core concepts are explained in detail and their use is illustrated by means of two case studies from the domain of environmental planning and management. A particular focus is on working constructively with tensions between opposing perspectives as they arise in many situations of professional intervention. These include tensions such as 'situation' versus 'system', 'is' versus 'ought' judgements, concerns of 'those involved' versus 'those affected but not involved', stakeholders' 'stakes' versus 'stakeholding issues', and others. Accordingly, boundary critique is presented as a participatory process of unfolding and questioning boundary judgements rather than as an expert-driven process of boundary setting. The paper concludes with a discussion of some essential skills and considerations regarding the practice of boundary critique.

6.1 What Is CSH?

A systems approach begins when first you see the world through the eyes of another.

(C.W. Churchman 1968, p. 231)

We do not need the systems concept at all if we are not interested in handling systems boundaries critically.

(W. Ulrich 1996, p. 17)

Critical systems heuristics (CSH) as developed by one of the authors (Ulrich 1983) is a philosophical framework to support reflective practice. In its most simple

---

[1] Parts of the account of the NRUA-Botswana study in Section 6.2 of the present paper are reproduced from an earlier publication by one of the authors (Reynolds 2007); we are grateful to the publishers of Edge Press, Point Reyes, CA, for granting us permission to reproduce this material.

W. Ulrich (✉) and M. Reynolds
The Open University, Walton Hall, Milton Keynes MK7 6AA.
e-mail: wulrich@gmx.ch and m.d.reynolds@open.ac.uk

M. Reynolds and S. Holwell (eds.), *Systems Approaches to Managing Change: A Practical Guide*, DOI 10.1007/978-1-84882-809-4_6, © The Open University 2010.
Published in Association with Springer-Verlag London Limited

formulation, CSH uses a set of 12 questions to make explicit the everyday judgements on which we rely (consciously or not) to understand situations and to design systems for improving them. Table 6.1 describes the 12 questions.

The precise nature and use of these so-called *boundary questions* will be explained later. For now we can briefly summarise three basic reasons for raising them and hence, three reasons for using CSH.

Table 6.1 The boundary categories and questions of CSH (Adapted from Ulrich 1996, p. 44)

Sources of influence	Boundary judgements informing a system of interest (S)			
	Social roles (Stakeholders)	*Specific concerns (Stakes)*	*Key problems (Stakeholding issues)*	
Sources of motivation	1. *Beneficiary* Who ought to be/ is the intended beneficiary of the system (S)?	2. *Purpose* What ought to be/is the purpose of S?	3. *Measure of improvement* What ought to be/is S's measure of success	**The involved**
Sources of control	4. *Decision maker* Who ought to be/is in control of the conditions of success of S?	5. *Resources* What conditions of success ought to be/are under the control of S?	6. *Decision environment* What conditions of success ought to be/are outside the control of the decision maker?	
Sources of knowledge	7. *Expert* Who ought to be/is providing relevant knowledge and skills for S?	8. *Expertise* What ought to be/are relevant new knowledge and skills for S?	9. *Guarantor* What ought to be/are regarded as assurances of successful implementation?	
Sources of legitimacy	10. *Witness* Who ought to be/ is representing the interests of those negatively affected by but not involved with S?	11. *Emancipation* What ought to be/are the opportunities for the interests of those negatively affected to have expression and freedom from the worldview of S?	12. *Worldview* What space ought to be/ is available for reconciling differing worldviews regarding S among those involved and affected?	**The affected**

1. Making sense of situations: understanding assumptions and appreciating the bigger picture

The boundary questions try to make sense of a situation by making explicit the *boundaries* that circumscribe our understanding. Such boundaries inform all our thinking about situations and systems; they constitute what in CSH we call our 'reference systems' (a concept to be introduced a little later). Broadly speaking, the boundary questions may be understood to cultivate a more holistic awareness of situations with regard to these wide-ranging issues:

– *Values and motivations* built into our views of situations and efforts to 'improve' them
– *Power structures* influencing what is considered a 'problem' and what may be done about it
– *The knowledge basis* defining what counts as relevant 'information', including experience and skills; and
– *The moral basis* on which we expect 'third parties' (i.e., stakeholders not involved yet in some way concerned) to bear with the consequences of what we do, or fail to do, about the situation in question

In CSH, these four dimensions of problems or problem situations are called *sources of motivation, control, knowledge, and legitimacy*, respectively (see column 'sources of influence' in Table 6.1). In sum, the 12 questions prompt an understanding of the 'bigger picture'.

2. Unfolding multiple perspectives: promoting mutual understanding

The boundary questions (hereafter referred to as CSHq1–12) reveal *contrasting* judgements as to what aspects of a situation ought to be/are part of the picture we make ourselves of it and what other aspects ought to be/are left out. CSH calls these judgements *boundary judgements*. They offer a way to examine how we frame situations. When people talk about situations, it often happens that their views differ simply because they frame the situations differently; more often than not, people are unaware of this source of misunderstanding and conflict, and even if they are vaguely aware of it they do not know how to examine its influence systematically. Thus seen, CSH offers a tool for understanding the *multiple perspectives* people bring into situations. By examining the different underlying boundary judgements, we can better understand people's differences and handle them more constructively.

As Table 6.1 suggests, we can identify and examine boundary judgements by asking different kinds of questions. First, for each boundary category there are two modes of question, a normative, ideal mode (i.e., what 'ought' to be…) contrasting with a descriptive, more realistic mode (what 'is' …). Second, judgements can be contrasted among the four stakeholder groups associated with the four sources of influence. So the set of judgements relating to intended beneficiaries (CSHq1–3) can be compared with those relating to decision makers (CSHq4–6), or experts (CSHq7–9), and/or witnesses (CSHq10–12). Third, at a more generalised level of analysis, judgements can be contrasted between those stakeholders 'involved' in the system design (CSHq1–9) and those 'affected' by its consequences but not involved (CSHq10–12). Fourth and last, moving onto an even further generalised level, we can review an entire set of boundary judgements (CSHq1–12) associated with any one reference system in the light of another set of boundary judgements belonging to a different reference system. It is at this last level of contrast that we can best begin to appreciate the phenomenon of people talking at cross purposes or talking past each other. Put quite simply, such arguments occur because people are using different reference systems. CSH helps to reveal such practice.

3. Promoting reflective practice: analysing situations – and changing them

The boundary questions support first of all an *analytical focus* on understanding situations, by revealing to ourselves and to others the boundary judgements at work and allowing everyone to understand their implications. Such understanding then also enables a *practical focus* on ways to improve a situation, by engaging with people having different perspectives. The aim in both cases is to enable *reflective practice*, in a way that reaches beyond the usual, mainly psychological-introspective understanding of the concept (see Ulrich 2000; 2008). Beyond supporting us (say, as professionals or managers involved in an intervention) in disclosing and reviewing our boundary judgements, CSH also supports uninvolved people in uncovering undisclosed boundary judgements imposed on them by not so reflective professional or managerial practice. The boundary questions can thus also be used with an *emancipatory focus* – allowing people to make their own authentic boundary judgements.

Before examining how CSH can be used in pursuing these three endeavours, it may be helpful to situate CSH in the two main traditions of thought on which it draws. The first is the tradition of *systems thinking* of which the work of C. West Churchman (1968; 1971; 1979) is representative. The widely cited remark of Churchman opening this chapter invites the question of the lens through which one might see the world differently. In CSH such a lens is referred to as a *reference system* – a conceptual device circumscribed by the 12 boundary categories which in turn are defined in Table 6.1 by the boundary questions for which they stand. While Churchman preferred to envisage systems as real-world entities, he nevertheless provided the initial foundation categories adapted later for delineating a CSH reference system. He first identified nine 'necessary conditions' (approximately aligned with CSHq1–9) for conceiving of anything as a system in his book *The Design of Inquiring Systems* (Churchman 1971, p. 43), and later extended these to 12 'planning categories' in a book entitled *The Systems Approach and Its Enemies* (Churchman 1979, p. 79f.). The three additional conditions are 'systems philosophers', 'enemies of the systems approach', and 'significance'; Churchman understands them to raise issues related to the significance of a systems perspective as distinguished from the partial (because non-holist) perspectives of the 'enemies' (i.e., politics, morality, religion, and aesthetics; cf. Churchman 1979, p. 80 and p. 156). In strict CSH terms, they are critical 'ideas' for meta-level reflection about the meaning of a systems approach rather than 'categories' for mapping any specific system (which is why CSHq10–12 are defined differently, as categories that are indeed constitutive of systems).

Despite this difference of understanding, Churchman's theme of the 'enemies' pointed the way to CSH's notion of boundary critique, in an effort to give a precise methodological meaning to his credo 'know (and love) thy enemy'. It also engendered an important heuristic device of CSH, the idea of maintaining tensions between contrasting perspectives for critical purposes; "we have to maintain the contradiction or else we allow ourselves to be overwhelmed by the consistent" (Churchman 1968, p. 229; Ulrich 1983, p. 275; Reynolds 2004, p. 542).

The second main tradition picked up in CSH is the tradition of *practical philosophy*. This comprises two largely independent strands of philosophical thought. On the one hand, there is the tradition of American *philosophical pragmatism* as rooted in the works of Charles Peirce (1878), William James (1907) and John Dewey (1925). On the other hand there is the European tradition of *critical social theory* as found particularly in the works of Jurgen Habermas (e.g. 1972 and 1984/87). Both strands of practical philosophy are to an important degree rooted in Immanuel Kant's (1787) *critical philosophy*, from which CSH derives many of its central concepts (see Ulrich 1983, Chapters 3–5). The 'American' pragmatic perspective of CSH means that it is oriented towards practical rather than theoretical ends; accordingly, CSH employs an *action-theoretical* framework, that is, it looks at situations from the point of view of an agent rather than an observer. Its 'European' critical perspective means that CSH considers values – and value conflicts – as integral part of all claims to rational practice; it relies on a *discourse-theoretical* (or 'discursive') framework to assist users in dealing openly and critically with the value implications of boundary judgements. All these influences have been detailed elsewhere (see Ulrich 1983; 1987; 1988a; 2001; 2003; 2004; 2006). Ulrich is now developing the two pillars of pragmatism and critique into an integrated framework of *critical pragmatism*, as a basis for a future 'philosophy for professionals' (see 2006; 2007a, b).

The peculiar combination of these very rich traditions has enabled CSH to significantly influence a strand of systems thinking and practice known as *critical systems thinking*. The point of departure for a critical systems approach as we understand it lies in the simple notion that all approaches, methodologies, methods, whether described as systems or something else, are partial, in the dual sense of (i) representing only a section rather than the whole of the total universe of possibly relevant considerations, and (ii) serving some parties better than others (Ulrich 2002, p. 41; 2005, p. 2). No specific proposal, no decision, no action, no system can get a total grip on the situation and get it right for everyone (Reynolds 2008a). The implication is that using a 'systems approach' requires us (i) to consider systematically what our systems maps or designs may leave out and (ii) to always examine them from multiple perspectives.

CSH is a critical systems approach developed to embrace this dual sense of partiality head-on. Let us see, then, how it attempts to provide this reflective lens.

6.2 Applying CSH

6.2.1 *Two Studies in Applying CSH*

CSH can support professional interventions in two general ways: it can help us to *evaluate* an intervention, or it can *inform* the methodologies used for intervention. The two interventions we describe are similar in that they both deal with complex situations of natural resources planning and management; they differ, however, in that they employ CSH for these two alternative purposes. The first project, an evaluation study of NRUA ('Natural Resource-Use Appraisal'), was part of a wider study by Reynolds (1998) exploring participatory planning for rural development in Botswana. The NRUA study examined how CSH could help evaluate existing practices in natural resource-use management with a particular view to poverty alleviation. The second project, ECOSENSUS – an acronym for 'Electronic/ Ecological Collaborative Sensemaking Support System' – involved both authors and explored how a number of computer-assisted tools, among them CSH, could support participatory environmental decision making by geographically distributed stakeholder groups in remote rural areas of Guyana (Berardi et al. 2006; Reynolds et al. 2007). Before discussing the use of CSH in these two projects, a brief general description of their context and of the reasons for employing CSH may be useful.

6.2.1.1 NRUA-Botswana

Botswana is about the size of France or Kenya, despite supporting a relatively small population of less than two million people. It is classified as being semi-arid with most of the surface area being a harsh environment of land covered by the Kalahari sands, making it difficult to practice commercially sustainable agriculture. Natural resource use involving agriculture (livestock and arable) and wildlife utilisation is constrained further by a shortage of surface water, along with low and variable patterns of rainfall. The country's relative political stability in a volatile region is underpinned by the wealth generated by the *non-renewable* natural resource sector – particularly diamonds. However, over two thirds of the population live in rural areas and are variously engaged with livelihood activities based on *renewable* natural resource use.

Since the early 1990s considerable attention has been given to promoting participatory planning in less-developed countries as a means of alleviating poverty in the rural areas and protecting the natural environment. During the 1990s the national government in Botswana, in partnership with a number of donor agencies, was actively piloting participatory forms of rural appraisal, as an alternative to conventional large-scale survey techniques and scientific monitoring procedures. The idea was to rely less on scientific techniques such as large-scale surveys and monitoring, and more on the knowledge and concerns of local people. The most popular approach amongst development practitioners at the time was Participatory Rural

Appraisal (PRA), an approach known mainly through the work of Robert Chambers (1994a, b; 1997). PRA can be described as a set of participatory methods and techniques, from visualization and interview techniques to group-dynamic methods, used to elicit and structure the knowledge and concerns of stakeholders.

Referring to the two kinds of applications mentioned at the outset, CSH could basically support PRA interventions in two ways:

1. We might want to use CSH *within* the framework of PRA, as yet another method for eliciting and structuring responses. Such a use might not do full justice to the larger philosophical framework and spirit of CSH; but it might still complement PRA's basket of methods in some essential ways, by adding the missing dimension of critically-discursive tools (i.e., tools to support processes of critical reflection and discourse on the value implications of alternative proposals) and indirectly also by drawing the attention of facilitators and users of PRA to this dimension. CSH would thus *inform* the use of PRA in a way that might make a real difference.

2. We might want to use CSH *in addition* to approaches like PRA, as a wider philosophical and methodological framework for analyzing the process and outcome of PRA interventions. This use is independent of the previous one – it makes sense regardless of whether CSH was used in the analyzed interventions themselves. CSH would thus serve to *evaluate* the use of PRA and similar participatory approaches in specific interventions, with a view to assessing their outcomes as well as modifying participatory planning in general.

The use of CSH in the NRUA study reported here was of the second kind; the aim was not to modify PRA but rather, to evaluate its use and outcome in three participatory planning projects of that time in Botswana. CSH served as the principal framework for all three evaluations.

The reasons for applying CSH as a framework for evaluating participatory planning in Botswana were:

- CSH should help reveal the limitations of the NRUA project projects with regard to its claim of being inclusive and holistic;
- CSH should prompt a critical awareness among those involved in participatory development projects such as NRUA as to what interests were given prominence and which others were marginalised; and
- CSH should suggest ways in which 'participatory' planning might be improved to incorporate more responsible professional intervention.

6.2.1.2   ECOSENSUS-Guyana

The Makushi tribal region situated in the Rupununi River catchment area in Guyana is the size of south east England and contains one of the highest diversities of animal and plant species in the world. The region is under intense pressure by government as well as international corporations to expand the exploitation of its natural resources, including timber, gold, and commercially viable fish species.

The indigenous Makushi Amerindians in Guyana are personally affected by many of the land-use projects in Guyana's North Rupununi District without being directly involved.

ECOSENSUS was conceived as a preliminary study to explore the potential of providing better support to such communities than is possible with conventional project-orientated management and its predominant reliance on scientific and technological expertise. For example, conventional GIS (geographic information system) applications as well as other e-science tools have largely focused on scientific and technological issues, whereas wider socio-economic issues that arise with land-use and development planning have traditionally been beyond the reach of such tools. Along with participants drawn from the community of Makushi Amerindians and the two authors, the study involved a small number of environmental scientists and software experts from Europe and Guyana.

The reasons for applying CSH in ECOCENSUS were:

- CSH should offer an opportunity for revealing and promoting wider stakeholder interests in the preservation and development of the Rupununi wetlands;
- CSH should serve as a meaningful tool for communicating about the use and preservation of natural resources; and
- CSH should enable more sustainable planning and sustainable development of the wetlands.

6.2.2   Using CSH as an Intervention Tool: Some Basic Concepts

The descriptions above give the broad contexts in which CSH was applied, along with the reasons why in each case CSH was considered relevant. But what methodological conjectures make us believe that CSH is an intervention tool that supports such demanding aims? Before examining the two studies in detail, it is necessary to first clarify some basic concepts associated with the use of CSH.

We have already hinted at the basic aims that we associate with CSH (see What is CSH?). With its conceptual framework of boundary categories and questions (as shown in Table 6.1 above) and a number of supporting concepts and guidelines, CSH offers a systematic structure for making sense of situations, unfolding multiple perspectives, and promoting reflective practice. Methodologically speaking, CSH uses the boundary questions to uncover the *reference systems* that inform our views of both problem situations and options for improving them. In the form of explicit reference systems, CSH provides a means of well-structured 'conversation' between *systems and situations*. In the language of CSH, the aim and nature of that conversation consists in *systematic boundary critique*. The relationship of 'systems' and 'situations' and the concept of 'reference systems' will be introduced first; 'boundary critique' will then be explained in the subsequent main section 6.2.3 titled *A core concept of CSH: systematic boundary critique*.

6.2.2.1   Systems Versus Situations

Among contemporary systems practitioners – particularly in the two traditions of soft and critical systems thinking – it is widely acknowledged that 'systems' are essentially *conceptual* constructs rather than real-world entities. Systems concepts and other constructs help us describe and understand the complex realities of real-world situations, including natural, technical, social, psychological or any other aspects that might potentially or actually be relevant at any one time.

Acknowledging the *fundamental divide between systems and reality* is basic to contemporary systems practice. Particularly SSM (soft systems methodology; Checkland 1981) and CSH understand systems as conceptual tools for learning *about* reality, rather than as being part *of* reality itself. However, CSH handles the distinction a bit differently from SSM. While in soft systems thinking, practitioners are supposed to reflect on their systems conceptions, and feasible interventions to be based on them, by 'comparing' them with the real-world situation perceived to be problematic, CSH interrogates the notion of a 'perceived situation' itself. CSH makes problematic 'the situation perceived to be problematic', so as to help practitioners see through their underpinning assumptions. In doing so, CSH handles the distinction of 'system' and 'situation' not so much as an absolute opposition between an epistemological construct and an ontological reality but rather as a *continuum* between two poles of contrasting proximity to reality; one pole being closer to the 'real' than the other but both belonging to an epistemological domain of talking about a reality that we cannot grasp in any direct and strictly objective way. The reason is, whenever we talk of 'situations' and 'systems' we are always already abstracting from the infinitely rich 'real world' and using judgement to *select* some aspects we assume to be particularly relevant. That is, both poles are always involved, although to a different extent – with varying degrees of proximity and selectivity – and in different ways – with a descriptive versus prescriptive intent. CSH uses three interrelated terms to refer to varying degrees of proximity to reality:

1. *Maps:* These commonly (but not necessarily always) assume quite close proximity to reality. Typical examples can be found in everyday life (e.g. road maps), in regional and environmental planning (e.g. zone maps), and in the natural sciences (e.g. in biology, maps of cellular organisation or the double-helix of DNA). A good map tries to approximate some section of reality as much as is feasible *and* required by the map's purpose; but it should not have us take the map for the reality itself. A good map will therefore make explicit its underlying assumptions (e.g. in a geographical map, its coordinates, scale, and symbols). Maps should serve as signposts to reality but should never be taken for that reality itself.
2. *Designs:* These are less proximate to reality than are maps; they serve as signposts pointing to how the real world *might* be or *'ought'* to be, which includes everything from detail improvements in existing maps to radically new and encompassing visions for the future (also called 'ideal maps' in CSH). A good design tries to give us critical distance to reality, as a basis for developing alternative futures. Designs embody an implicit critique of the present, for we cannot understand what constitutes an improvement over the present without seeing its shortcomings.

3. *Models:* These are heuristic devices for engaging with reality in terms of mapping or design. 'Model' is a generic term that emphasises the abstraction from reality involved rather than the specific purpose for which the abstraction is made. 'Model' is the least specific term of the three. Among the heuristic devices to which it refers, we might also count the methods we use to construct maps and designs. CSH would then itself be a model.

To avoid a blurring of terms, CSH refers to the notions we make ourselves of a relevant context of intervention as 'maps' or 'designs' and of CSH itself as a *framework* for reflective practice or a *methodology* of critical systems thinking.

The important point in conceiving of professional intervention in terms of mapping and design is this. However close to reality our maps and designs may be or claim to be, we must never, as Alfred Korzybski (1933, p. 750) once famously said, confuse the 'map' with the 'territory'. Now this applies also to our perception of the territory, which is itself a kind of map! Accordingly, CSH assumes that "all our knowledge is in terms of maps" (Ulrich 1983, p. 185). Counter to what is often assumed, we can then not simply align 'situations' with the 'territory' and 'systems' with the 'maps' or 'designs' we make of it. Whatever we can think and say about a situation, it already contains some mapping and/or design elements. 'Situations' and 'systems' stand for different degrees of abstraction and conceptualisation rather than for a strict opposition of the 'territory' (an ontological concept) and 'maps' or designs (an epistemological concept). We might say we speak of 'situations' when we mean a low-level conceptualisation – a notion of the real world that remains close to ordinary perception – whereas when we speak of 'systems', we mean a higher-level conceptualisation in which we make conscious and careful use of the systems concept along with other abstractions.

We should, then, not expect that we can ever validate or test systems maps and designs by comparing them with 'the situation', as if the latter provided an independent touchstone. Rather, from a critical point of view, our notion of the situation is itself a map and thus is likely to be conditioned by the same sort of selectivity that informs the map or design in question. We can, however, use differences between maps (or between designs) to drive our thinking about the underlying judgements that lead to these different models.

Ultimately, what matters is not the terms we use but the way we use them. For example, terms such as hydraulic systems, legal systems, ecosystems, inventory systems, financial systems etc. are often used as descriptors ('maps') of the real world, and there is no reason why we should ignore such common use of language or deviate from it. Likewise, systems for traffic control, for timetabling, for mitigating climate change, for poverty alleviation, for bringing up children etc. are often expressed as planning devices ('designs'). And of course, all such systems might also be regarded as 'models'. For the sake of simplicity, we may even continue to refer to the 'territory' as the 'situation' or 'context', as it is common practice in the systems literature, at least so long as we mean to refer to its basically ill-defined and ill-structured nature which still awaits careful definition – the 'mess', using Ackoff's (1981) well-known term. But as soon as we begin to define and structure the situation in some way, for example as a *problem* situation, or as a certain context *that matters*, or as *relevant* territory, then systems conceptions of some kind are already at play. In CSH terms these are called *reference systems*.

6.2.2.2 Reference Systems

To say that all our knowledge is in terms of maps is equivalent to saying that it is selective with regard to the aspects of the (undefined) territory or (defined) situation that it considers. Consequently, the crucial methodological issue for CSH is that in everything that we can think and say about the 'situation' at issue or a 'system' of concern, *selectivity* is at work. Reflective practice requires that we make ourselves and everyone concerned aware of this selectivity; for once our systems maps and designs become a basis for action, selectivity turns into *partiality* – it means that some parties will be better served than others, and still others may merely have to bear disadvantages.

The point is not that we ought to avoid selectivity – we can't. The point is, rather, that we should handle the selectivity of our maps and designs carefully, lest we deceive ourselves and others about their meaning and validity. Identifying and analysing our reference systems systematically is a methodologically rigorous way of putting into practice Churchman's observation cited at the outset: "A systems approach begins when first you see the world through the eyes of another."

By analogy, a *critical* systems approach begins when we first appreciate the ways our systems maps or designs depend on the reference systems we assume, whether consciously so or not. This does justice to the insight that the real world as such (the territory) is beyond what any conceivable method of inquiry can reveal to us in a secure and definitive way. Any conception we may have of it remains for ever open to doubt, contestation, and redefinition. There is an element of freedom involved: nobody can claim to advance the single right and objective map! This element of freedom does not imply, however, that all reasonable discussion about different maps and designs must stop here. The contrary is true: we may and should indeed argue and discourse about different maps and designs, to make sure we understand why and how exactly they differ – the different lenses they use to grasp the territory, as it were – and what implications these differences may have for all the parties concerned. The only 'stop signal' is one that prohibits indifference and intolerance in the way we handle our boundary judgements; for once we have understood the role of the reference systems they constitute, we can never again reasonably claim to own a monopoly for the single right view of the situation or the way to improve it – a common shortcoming even in professional practice.

In a sense, then, we can agree with Slavoj Žižek (1989, p. 21), who in his psychoanalytical work observes that 'the Real' is an extra-discursive realm, a realm apart from any of the constructs of 'realities' that we can talk about and which at bottom are inevitably ideological ('ideological' in the widest sense of the word: we make up 'reality' through our own ideas, depending on our interests and needs).

"Ideology is not simply a 'false consciousness', an illusory representation of reality, it is rather this reality itself which is already to be conceived as 'ideological'." Simply put, what is real we cannot talk about except through some lens, and the lens is at bottom ideological.

Žižek's observation is another way to remind us that in all our efforts to grasp situations, we map reality through some lens, the origin and exact nature of which lies in an extra-discursive realm. What is new in CSH is that it offers us a way of drawing the lens at least partly into the discursive realm. Through the analysis of underpinning reference systems, we acquire a shared language or literacy by means of which we can identify and unfold the normative implications of the lens systematically. In the language of CSH, we can thus understand partiality in terms of underlying selectivity. Although we may not ultimately fully understand the psychological and ideological forces behind that selectivity, we can and should nevertheless undertake a systematic effort to make ourselves and all those concerned aware of the partiality that it implies in a specific situation. Furthermore, although we cannot claim to talk about reality as such, it makes nevertheless sense – and is indispensable from a critical point of view – to talk about the different lenses people use, namely, in the form of (conscious or unconscious) reference systems. After all, what other means do we have, if not reflection and discourse, to improve mutual understanding about our differences?

How, then, does CSH operationalise this notion of a reference system? A basic definition is this: *a reference system is 'the context that matters when it comes to assessing the merits and defects of a proposition'* (Ulrich 2000, p. 251). 'Context' here means quite generally all those aspects of a situation that influence our appreciation of it, before and beyond any particular conceptualisation or modelling effort; whereas by 'reference system' we mean an explicit conceptualisation of 'a context that matters' as circumscribed by the four sources of influence (Table 6.1).

A specific reference system can thus also be described as *the set of answers that we give to the 12 boundary questions* and by which we determine the basic sources of selectivity at work in our systems' maps and designs – the sources of motivation, of control, of knowledge and of legitimacy informing our views. Note, however, that the purpose of the boundary questions is a purely critical one: the aim is boundary surfacing and review (i.e., making us aware of and reflect on boundary assumptions) rather than boundary setting (i.e., doing away with boundary questions by fixing the answers) – a frequent misunderstanding of CSH that we need to avoid. The point is not that we should claim we have the answers but rather, that we should uncover the inevitable selectivity of all our claims.

The idea that reference systems, as operationalised in CSH, inform all our maps of situations or designs for changing them, can shed some new light on the tension of 'system' and 'situation' about which we have been talking. Figures 6.1 and 6.2 illustrate the different light CSH sheds on the issue of handling the map-territory distinction, as compared to conventional systems thinking.

In the terms of Fig. 6.2, where might we locate problem situations and reference systems in the two case studies? In the NRUA-Botswana study, the problem

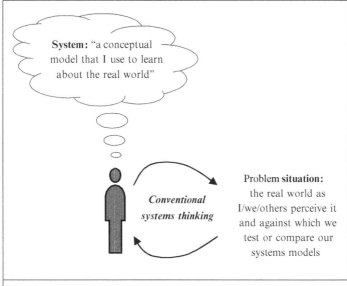

Fig. 6.1 System and situation in 'conventional' systems thinking

situation can be described in terms of the role of participatory planning in rural development. The central issue was, how did participatory planning in Botswana change the ways in which issues of value, power, expertise and moral engagement were handled; did it actually create opportunities to improve the reference systems at work? The focus was on evaluating existing systems of participatory planning.

In the ECOSENSUS-Guyana study, the problem situation might be described in more challenging terms which include the possibility of impoverished marginalised groups to have a greater 'say' (or meaningful involvement) in the mapping, design, and modelling of their livelihood strategies. The central issue was, how might stakeholders in a situation of marginalisation better engage with issues of value, power, expertise and moral dilemmas as they arise with their use of natural resources in fragile ecosystems? The focus was on learning to question the reference systems at work and to make transparent and constructive use of them in communicating with other stakeholders.

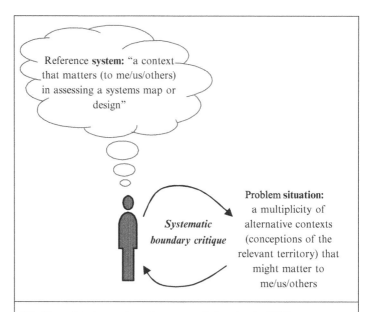

Reference **system:** "a context that matters (to me/us/others) in assessing a systems map or design"

Systematic boundary critique

Problem situation: a multiplicity of alternative contexts (conceptions of the relevant territory) that might matter to me/us/others

Working with the tension of system and situation in CSH:
Situations as well as systems maps or designs are understood as expressions of an underlying reference system, by which people frame situations differently and selectively. Systematic analysis and discussion requires boundary critique, an effort to unfold the built-in selectivity of people's grasp of situations, so as to appreciate the resulting partiality of systems maps or designs and to improve mutual understanding of differences and options for cooperative action.

Fig. 6.2 System and situation in 'critical' systems thinking

6.2.3   A Core Concept of CSH: Systematic Boundary Critique

Boundary critique is defined in CSH as a systematic – reflective and discursive – effort of handling boundary judgements critically, whereby 'critically' means both 'self-critically' questioning one's *own* claims and 'thinking for oneself' before adopting the claims of *others*. Boundary critique involves first of all a *process of unfolding*, that is, making ourselves and others aware of the boundary judgments assumed with respect to the 12 kinds of boundary judgements listed in Table 6.1. The concept of unfolding is adopted from the writings of Churchman (esp. 1979; cf. Ulrich 1988b, and Reynolds 1998). But Churchman used it in a somewhat different sense. In Churchman's systems thinking, 'unfolding' was essentially a metaphor for the holistic orientation of what he called more accurately the *sweep-in* process; the aim was to include in our systems notions ever more aspects of the real world so as to achieve a 'whole systems' view of a problem situation. In CSH, by contrast, the process of unfolding is a specific tool for uncovering the inevitable *selectivity* of all our systems maps and designs; that is, it serves a critical purpose against all holistic pretensions (cf. Ulrich 2004, p. 1127f). Behind this distinction are two different strategies for dealing with the unavoidable tension between systems and situations: overcoming or minimizing selectivity in Churchman's systems thinking, embracing selectivity openly and critically in CSH.

In addition to the process of unfolding, systematic boundary critique involves a second effort, the systematic *questioning* of boundary judgements with respect to their adequacy in terms of relevance, justification, and ethical defendability. Whereas the aim of 'unfolding' consists in uncovering the selectivity of the reference systems at work in our claims, the aim of 'questioning' consists in exploring and, if necessary, challenging their resulting partiality. To this end, boundary questioning requires that we thoroughly analyse actual and possible consequences and ask what they may mean for all the parties concerned; and furthermore, that we examine what options may be available that might provide a better basis for mutual understanding and cooperative action towards 'improving' the situation. Note that once again, in pursuing this quest for value clarification, the strategy of CSH is different from that of Churchman's systems approach: while Churchman sought the source of rationality for our claims in systems thinking itself, CSH seeks it in legitimate processes of discourse and decision-making *informed* by critical systems thinking (for a full discussion of CSH's underlying concept of a merely 'critical solution' of the problem of boundary judgements, see Ulrich 1983, entire Chapter 5). The step from holistic to critical systems thinking implies that "systems practice should not misunderstand itself as a guarantor of socially rational decision making; it cannot, and need not, 'monologically' justify the social acceptability of its designs." (Ulrich 1988a, p. 158)

6.2.3.1 Unfolding Boundary Judgements

We have understood that the process of unfolding aims to uncover the *selectivity* of the reference systems at work in our systems maps and designs or in any other propositions we make or face in a professional intervention, for example, problem definitions, criteria for improvement, proposals for action, evaluations of success, etc. For the sake of both simplicity and accuracy, CSH refers to all these propositions as *'claims'*, for they all imply a claim to the validity and relevance of what is proposed. We constantly need to judge the validity and relevance of claims; but we can reasonably do this only to the extent we are aware of the selectivity built into them in the form of boundary judgements. Only then can we fully understand the *partiality* that such selectivity implies in a specific context of application (the intervention context), in the form of consequences with which the different parties concerned may have to live with.

How, then, can we learn to unfold selectivity? The basic idea should be clear by now: we can do this by examining the ways in which specific claims are conditioned by boundary judgements. For example, the claim that participatory planning in NRUA-Botswana is 'good' might be revised when examining the various boundary judgements associated with the claim in a particular context. Similarly, in ECOSENSUS-Guyana, a claim that environmental planners work on behalf of marginalised communities may be quite a partial view when examined in the context of other reference systems.

To help us identify and unfold boundary judgements *systematically*, CSH proposes the 12 boundary questions listed in Table 6.1. They are methodologically grounded in a reconstruction of Kantian *a priori* science, which represents the epistemological basis of Kant's critical philosophy (see Ulrich 1983, Chapters 3–5); but this philosophical justification need not concern us here, as it is quite sufficient for convincing ourselves of their critical relevance that we start applying them to situations of professional or everyday decision-making and thus experience that they do indeed make a difference to our accustomed ways of thinking and arguing about problem situations and solution proposals. You will soon discover that thinking in terms of boundary questions allows you to come up with new and relevant conjectures and questions. At the very latest when others first ask you how it is you come up with such questions, you know you are on your way to becoming a practitioner of boundary critique!

In what order should one try to answer the boundary questions? Basically, due to the interdependence of the boundary categories, we may begin the process of unfolding with any one of the boundary categories that we find particularly relevant or easy to specify, and can then follow the line of thought that develops. However, beginners find it often useful to follow a *standard sequence*. We have found it useful (both in our teaching and professional practice of boundary critique) to follow the sequence suggested in Fig. 6.3, beginning with the interests of intended or actual beneficiaries (the sources of motivation, that is) and then thinking through the sources of control, knowledge, and legitimacy in this order, each time beginning with the concerns of the relevant stakeholders. Box 6.1 takes you through a corresponding short narrative of unfolding CSH questions.

The sequence works both with the 'is' and the 'ought' boundary questions. Experience suggests it is easier for many people to begin reflecting and communicating about their 'ought' answers, that is, their hopes and visions for the kind of change to be brought about in a situation, rather than analysing 'is' boundary judgements at the outset. This holds true especially in group settings; people who do not know one another well can 'warm up' and develop a sense of mutual trust and cooperation as they reveal to each other their visions for improvement, while at the same time familiarizing themselves with the spirit of boundary critique. Furthermore, this way of proceeding has the advantage that when it comes to the 'is' questions, the normative basis from which 'is' answers are to be assessed has already been clarified, so that an illusion of objectivity is avoided from the start.

Let us briefly highlight the material issues at which the 12 boundary questions aim. As you may recall, they are grouped into four basic sets of boundary issues or *sources of selectivity* that inform any reference system:

Sources of influence	Social roles (Stakeholders)	Specific concerns (Stakes)	Key problems (Stakeholding issues)

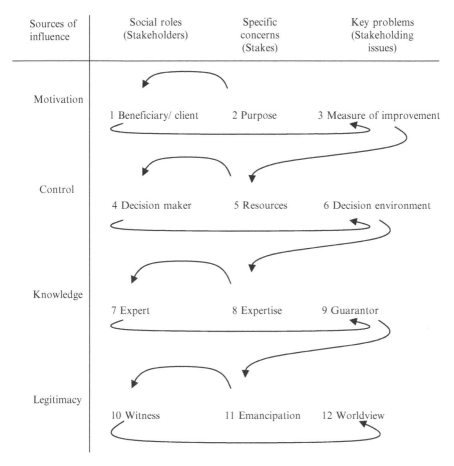

Motivation

1 Beneficiary/ client   2 Purpose   3 Measure of improvement

Control

4 Decision maker   5 Resources   6 Decision environment

Knowledge

7 Expert   8 Expertise   9 Guarantor

Legitimacy

10 Witness   11 Emancipation   12 Worldview

Fig. 6.3 Standard sequence for unfolding the boundary questions of CSH (Adapted from Reynolds 2007, p. 106)

1. Sources of *motivation* – where a sense of purposefulness and principle value comes from
2. Sources of *control* – where the necessary resources and power are located
3. Sources of *knowledge* – where sufficient expertise and experience is assumed to be available
4. Sources of *legitimacy* – where social and legal approval is assumed to reside

Identifying these four sources of selectivity is essential for gaining a sense of orientation: *"What is the intervention all about?"* It is equally essential for assessing and qualifying the claims that we or others associate with the intervention: *"What exactly does the intervention claim to achieve and what are its built-in limitations, that is, the assumptions and conditions on which its 'success' depends?"*

It is always recommended to consider all four sources of selectivity, for *together* they constitute the reference system assumed. They embody the four basic and unavoidable kinds of boundary issues that we need to understand if we wish to grasp an intervention's built-in selectivity.

Each of the four boundary issues is then further structured into three boundary categories, the first standing for a social group or *role* (stakeholder), the second for a *role-specific concern* (what's at stake), and the third for a *key problem* in reconciling clashes between such concerns (a stakeholding issue). (The term 'role' is to remind us that any one person or group of people may in a specific intervention hold several roles, that is, role-specific concerns.) These 12 kinds of boundary judgements, or the boundary categories to which they refer, signal what we must be looking for in order to make a system meaningful and to validate or challenge the claims we associate with it. Taken together, they define the selectivity of the reference system at work.

Box 6.1 An unfolding narrative of CSH

Notes:

(a) The example is for the purpose of 'ideal mapping', as explained in sections 6.2.4.1 (on 'Ideal Mapping') and 6.2.5.1 (on 'Developing CSH Literacy').
(b) The numbers in brackets refer to CSH categories 1–12.

Any human reference system might start with questions regarding some notion of 'purpose' in order to provide some initial sense of orientation. This then prompts the question regarding 'whose purpose?' An underpinning purpose reflects embedded values associated with some person or persons (even if that someone is representing the intrinsic value of non-human nature). Identifying first the *ideal* purpose (2) of the reference system in the 'ought' mode therefore suggests who the *intended* beneficiaries should be (1). This in turn suggests what might be appropriate measures of success in securing some improvement (3). In other words, how might the underpinning values be given formal expression (quantifiably or qualitatively) – through evaluation – to gauge improvement? Such questions make transparent the *value basis* of the ideal system.

Unfolding questions of motivation leads to questions regarding the necessary resources or components needed for success (5). Financial capital and other forms of tangible assets like natural, physical, and human capital might be complemented with less tangible factors such as social capital (access to networks of influence); but who is in control of such resources and might thus best be placed to provide them (4)? This in turn prompts questions as to what should be left *outside* the control of such decision makers in order to ensure some level of accountability. What *relevant* factors having an important potential impact on the system ought to lie outside the system, lest all the parties concerned depend entirely on those in control? In other words, what

(continued)

Box 6.1 (continued)

should be part of the system's decision environment (6) in order to keep it in check and accountable? What should be relevant but not component? So for example, if a system initiated with good intention becomes malignant, corrupt or disabling because of changing circumstances, are there factors in the environment that might ensure that the system deemed appropriate for one context and time is prevented from continuing indefinitely? Such questions help to make transparent the *power-basis* of the system.

One such set of factors requiring independence from the decision maker is 'knowledge' or expertise. That is, in an ideal setting human 'capital' (embodying expertise) ought not to be under the sole control of the decision maker but should have some independence. So what are the necessary types and levels of competent knowledge and experiential know-how (8) to ensure that the reference system actually has practical applicability and works towards its ideal purpose? Who ought to provide such expertise (7)? How might such expert support prove to be an effective guarantor; a provider of some assurance of success (9)? This invites the need to look out for false guarantors – that is, sources of deception. False guarantors are manifest by, for example, having expertise being incomplete and/or incompetent in terms of a specialised field, or more generally through assuming a dogmatic authority and complacency (e.g. a technocratic viewpoint) that does not allow for inevitable uncertainties (unforeseen events and unexpected consequences) and/or for the validity of other viewpoints and perspectives. Such questions help to make transparent the *knowledge-basis* of the system.

Finally, given the inevitable bias regarding values (motivation), power (control) and even knowledge (expertise) associated with any reference system, what is the legitimacy of such a system within wider spheres of human interests? In other words, if the reference system is looked at from a different, opposing viewpoint, in what ways might the activities be considered as coercive or malignant rather than emancipatory or benign (11)? Who (or what – for example non-human nature) hold such concerns, that is, who are the 'victims' of the system – and, importantly, what type of representation ought to be made on their behalf? That is, who may regard themselves capable of making representations on the victims' behalf and on what basis would they make this claim (10)? Finally, how might the underlying worldview associated with the reference system be reconciled with opposing worldviews (12)? Where might representation of opposing views be expressed, and what action ought to happen as a result? Such questions help to make transparent the reference system's *basis of legitimacy*, with special regard for the underpinning worldviews and moral assumptions, in dealing with the concerns of third parties and with long-term social and ecological implications.

The narrative in Box 6.1 illustrates a gradually unfolding shift in emphasis and concern from core constituents of a system of interest to features of its environment. In this way an unfolding (or peeling back, as it were) of successive sources of influence enables us to step out of the immediate point of reference in order to see 'the bigger picture' – a first step in reflective practice.

With Churchman, CSH operationalises this quest for the bigger picture as a dialogue (or in CSH terms, a reflective and discursive effort) among increasingly wider conceptualisations of the system of concern, as embodied in the three perspectives of *goal planning, objective-planning*, and *ideal planning* (see Churchman 1979, p. 82f; Ulrich 1983, p. 263 and 1988b, pp. 425–427). However, in line with its different understanding of the process of unfolding, the focus in CSH shifts from Churchman's quest for holistic thinking – for expanding system boundaries ever more – to the critical purpose of uncovering the unavoidable selectivity of our claims, whatever the underlying boundary judgements may be. This new focus on boundary critique rather than boundary expansion developed from the author's experience as a policy analyst:

> My personal conclusion is that dealing rationally with the problem of boundary judgements depends not so much on a never-ending sweep-in process – a heroic enterprise – but on a conscious and critical employment of boundary judgements. *Not what our boundary judgements are but how we treat them will determine the quality of our systems thinking in the first place.* For example, do we as policy analysts hide disputable boundary judgements ... behind a façade of expertise or do we really seek to make them transparent to everybody concerned? Any other conclusion would imply that the best systems thinker is the one who deals with the biggest problems. I think, rather, that the best systems thinker is the one who deals most consciously and overtly with the way in which s/he bounds the problem. (Ulrich 1988b, p. 420, slightly edited)

That is, unfolding in CSH is about value clarification rather than a hopeless (because never-ending) quest for comprehensiveness. The search for a whole-systems view of problems, while all right as an ideal, does not free us from the need to reflect on the selectivity of whatever standpoint we assume for grasping and assessing a situation as comprehensively as possible. But we cannot properly appreciate our standpoint without first gaining some critical distance – which is what the process of unfolding selectivity is all about.

6.2.3.2   Questioning Boundary Judgements

In CSH the process of questioning boundary judgements is crucial, and it is to this second level of boundary critique that we can now turn. Boundary questioning consists in analysing, evaluating and challenging the rightness of boundary assumptions; in one word: in testing rather than settling them, which would mean to fix them and thereby to turn them into 'givens' or even to withdraw them from any further critical discussion. Obviously, boundary questioning presupposes some previous awareness and unfolding of boundary judgements; which is to say, the distinction between boundary unfolding and questioning is an analytic one rather than a practical one.

In practice, unfolding and questioning boundaries inform and support one another in a closely interrelated way.

The basic idea is this. When it comes to boundary judgements, no one can claim to have the single right answers; therein consists the basic problem raised by the unavoidability of boundary judgements. The only practical approach is to examine the different selectivity of *alternative* proposals, as a basis for well-informed and transparent processes of opinion forming and decision making within democratically legitimate institutional settings. This is why CSH gives priority to *boundary questioning* (also referred to as 'boundary testing' in some sources) rather than to an illusory attempt to overcome selectivity through some kind of 'whole-systems' perspective.

Once we have found tentative responses to the 'is' and 'ought' boundary questions through the process of unfolding, the next task consists in questioning their validity. How can we be confident that the boundary judgements in question are right? What alternatives might be found more adequate? How would we want to defend them if challenged to do so? This sort of questions requires us to identify the exact nature and scope of the claims to which the boundary judgements give rise – for example, what is claimed to be achieved and who is supposed to benefit, and how can this choice be justified rationally? – and to submit these claims to the critique of the different parties concerned. Ultimately, since there are no objectively right or wrong answers to such questions, only legitimate processes of decision-making informed by such critique can achieve this. Not unlike a good map, a good process of decision-making should make transparent the boundary judgements on which the claims to be decided upon rely, and should also shed light on how different these claims may look in the light of alternative boundary judgements. In short, when we subject a claim to 'boundary questioning', we examine its consequences in the light of alternative sets of boundary judgements (those it assumes as well as options).

To be sure, clarifying consequences may require careful inquiry, at times with professional support. However, this is not to reserve boundary questioning to a setting in which professional expertise is available. We are dealing with an in-principle requirement rather than an absolute necessity. Where consequences are reasonably clear, say in everyday situations in which those involved oversee the implications of their propositions, it may be perfectly feasible to question boundary assumptions on the basis of knowledge available to everyone. For example, knowing something about the possible climate effects of fuel consumption may be sufficient to change our views about what 'improvement' means in the design of traffic policies, so we will revise our measure of improvement (CSHq3). Revision of boundary assumptions takes place quite naturally in everyday life as soon as our attention is drawn to previously neglected circumstances that in some way matter to us. We practice boundary critique every day without being aware of it! The difference is only that we do not practice it consciously and systematically. Once we become aware of the basic idea, we will be able to question boundary judgements so much more effectively, both in individual reflection and in dialogue with others:

1. *Boundary reflection:* Do my/our/their current 'is' boundary judgements agree with my/our/their 'ought' boundary judgements? That is, is there a discrepancy between what I/we have identified as my/our/their actual boundary judgements on the one hand and what we would consider adequate, if not ideal, boundary judgements on the other hand? If so, should I/we revise my/our boundary assumptions?

2. *Boundary discourse:* Do my/our boundary judgements conflict with yours? If so, may this help us understand why we disagree about what is the problem or what to do about it? Can we revise our boundary judgements so that we then agree about the issues, although perhaps still not about solutions? (cf. Ulrich 2000, p. 255)

The first mode of boundary questioning aims at handling boundary judgements *self-critically*, the second at using them *dialogically* so as to improve mutual understanding and, where necessary, to challenge those who may not handle their boundary judgements so self-critically. (It should again be clear that these two modes of boundary questioning are closely interrelated and support each other, and that a similar distinction applies to the boundary unfolding that is presupposed in boundary questioning.) Figures 6.4 and 6.5 illustrate the two modes of boundary questioning.

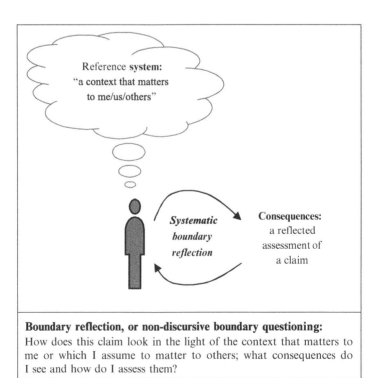

Fig. 6.4 Boundary reflection: first of two complementary forms of boundary questioning.

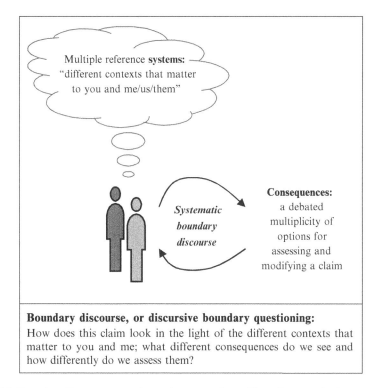

Fig. 6.5 Boundary discourse: second complementary form of boundary questioning

Through both boundary reflection and boundary discourse, we can make ourselves and everyone else concerned aware of the ways in which all proposals and claims are conditioned by boundary judgements, and can on this basis begin to be more open to alternative proposals and appreciate the reasoning behind them. Once it becomes apparent that there are options for the boundary assumptions in question, it is no longer necessary and meaningful for anyone to claim objectivity for their specific reference systems; we can gain a new level of mutual understanding and tolerance in dealing with the often conflictual nature of interventions. Through boundary *reflection*, we can achieve a new quality of professional self-reflection; through boundary *discourse*, a new quality of communication in and about professional interventions.

The two case studies, to which we now turn, exemplify both modes of boundary critique, the quest for professional self-reflection as well as for improved communication. They also address both levels of boundary critique, unfolding and questioning. Combining the two distinctions, the NRUA-Botswana study exemplifies mainly a reflective mode of boundary unfolding, whereas the ECOSENSUS-Guyana study exemplifies more a discursive mode of boundary questioning.

6.2.4   Boundary Critique Applied to NRUA-Botswana

The Botswana study (for a full account, see Reynolds 1998) aimed to evaluate three projects that were all concerned with participatory planning in rural development:

– Participatory Rural Appraisal (PRA) Pilot Project
– Natural Resource Management Project (NRMP)
– Botswana Range Inventory and Monitoring Project (BRIMP)

Each project was considered as an effort to design a system of interest that could meaningfully be examined in the terms of boundary critique, by identifying and unfolding its major sources of influence:

– Motivation: the prime stated objectives were centred on promoting participatory planning
– Control: along with government, donor agencies provided significant resources (finance, infrastructure etc).
– Knowledge: significant expertise came from non-governmental sources (such as NGOs, private consultants and parastatal organisations)
– Legitimacy: the prime stated objectives were more aligned with social and environmental improvement rather than conventional drivers of economic improvement

The basis for evaluating the projects was to be furnished by field research; its results were then to be assessed against the researcher's own ideal reference system. Accordingly, the evaluation started with an effort by the author (*qua* evaluator) to map out both an 'ideal map' and an 'actual map' of the situation he encountered in Botswana. Not unlike the way Ulrich had used these two kinds of maps in the two case studies that are included in *Critical Heuristics* (1983, Chapters 8 and 9), the ideal (or normative) map was to clarify the evaluator's 'ought' reference system whereas the actual (or descriptive) map was to identify major boundary judgements built into the current situation. Our account therefore starts with ideal mapping.

6.2.4.1   Ideal Mapping (Identifying the 'Ought')

As a first step, the evaluator reflected on his personal reference system for evaluating natural resource-use appraisal (NRUA) and participatory planning for rural development in Botswana. Wherein consisted his preconception (or perhaps bias) as to what such planning was all about? How *should* he understand the relevant context, and thus the reference system of his evaluative endeavour? Based mainly on preparatory background reading, as well as some previous personal familiarity with the situation in Botswana, he tentatively defined his reference system as follows: '*a system to enhance natural resource-use appraisal (NRUA) through participatory planning for assisting rural poverty alleviation and protection of the natural environment in Botswana*'.

Next, a reflective exercise of ideal mapping was to clarify the normative orientation to be associated with this reference system for the purpose of the evaluation. Obviously, this normative orientation might later change, but an evaluation has to start with *some* normative assumptions and these should be clear from the start.

Table 6.2 illustrates the result of this ideal mapping exercise, constructed by means of the 12 boundary categories of CSH; the categories were unfolded following the sequence recommended in Fig. 6.2.

In an ideal world of purposeful human activity, the roles of beneficiary, decision maker, expert and witness are closely interrelated and ultimately converge (Ulrich 1996, p. 40f). For natural resource-use appraisal, a system of self-organisation and appraisal involving conscientious natural resource users (sharing communal land) might be considered as such an ideal situation. The point is not that we should assume we live in an ideal world; the point is that ideal mapping provides us with critical distance to what is real. With this aim in mind, the ideal map summarised in Table 6.2 provided a helpful point of reference for subsequently constructing and questioning descriptive maps (or 'actual maps', in the terms of CSH) of each of the three projects.

6.2.4.2   Descriptive Mapping (The 'Is' Analyses)

The descriptive mapping in the NRUA study occurred in two stages: firstly, it was to identify the relevant stakeholder groups for each project; and secondly, it was to specify the role-concerns of all identified stakeholders and surface key problems in reconciling these concerns.

Stage 1: Identifying Stakeholder Groups

It was found that in all three projects, the social roles of beneficiary, decision maker, expert and witness were largely played out by four main kinds of institutional agents. These were, respectively, government departments, donor agencies, consultants, and non-government organisations (see Table 6.3). Whilst impoverished natural resource users would clearly represent the *ultimate intended* (or 'ideal') beneficiaries (see Table 6.2), for the purpose of identifying *actual* stakeholders associated with each project there was a need to address and interview the *immediate* beneficiaries of NRUA – the various government departments who would claim to be working on behalf of the rural poor. During the later evaluation, the author kept in check and made transparent in fieldwork notes the assumptions (a) that government authorities would indeed ensure appropriate representation of such stakeholders and (b), to the extent they would fail to do so, that NGOs would provide such representation.

The primary roles and role-related concerns assigned to the four major institutional agents are not to be understood as being mutually exclusive. While there was considerable overlap among the stakeholders' concerns, it was useful to have this first mapping of stakeholders as a basis for starting a more detailed evaluation of NRUA associated with each project.

Table 6.2 Ideal map of participatory natural resource-use appraisal in Botswana

Sources of influence	Social roles (*Stakeholders*)	Role-specific concerns (*Stakes*)	Key problems (*Stakeholding issues*)
Motivation	*Beneficiary* Rural poor, future generations and non-human nature	*Purpose* To improve natural resource use planning in addressing needs of the vulnerable	*Measure of improvement* Indices of (i) Rural poverty alleviation (ii) Enhanced condition of natural resources
Control	*Decision-maker* Communal resource users	*Resources* Necessary components to enable NRUA, including: (i) Project/ finance/human (ii) Social networks	*Decision environment* (i) Interest groups affected by NRUA (ii) Expertise not be-holden to decision maker
Expertise	*Expert* Communal resource users informed by natural and social scientists and other sources of relevant knowledge and experience	*Expertise* Technical/experiential/ social knowledge and skills, including (i) Rural peoples' knowledge and experience (ii) Interdisciplinary and intersectoral facilitation skills (iii) Social and environ-mental responsibility	*Guarantor* Competent professional and non-professional knowledge, avoiding: (i) 'Scientism' (sole reliance on objective and statistical 'fact') (ii) 'Managerialism' (sole reliance on facilitating communication) (iii) 'Populism' (allowing loudest collective voice as sole guarantor)
Legitimation	*Witness* Collective citizenry representing interests of all (including private sector) affected by NRUA, both local and global, and present and future generations	*Emancipation* NRUA open to challenge from those adversely affected, including interests of private land owners and diamond industry competing for access to communal resources	*Worldview* Manage conflicts of interest between: (i) National economic growth, privatization and fencing policies (ii) Vulnerable rural livelihoods and nature

Stage 2: Eliciting Concerns and Key Problems in Each System of Interest

The crux of the study then consisted in identifying precise stakeholder representatives from each of the four institutional agents for each of the three projects, and eliciting from these representatives information on the concerns and key problems they associated with participatory NRUA practice, and perhaps also with participatory

Table 6.3   Actual stakeholder map of natural resource-use appraisal in Botswana in the 1990s

Major stakeholders (primary roles of the institutional agents identified)	Major stakeholder roles (primary concerns of the institutional agents identified)
Government departments	Beneficiary: getting chances to participate in improved NRUA practice for better delivery on, and design of, government policy, on behalf of rural constituency
Donor agency	Decision maker: providing resources efficiently for effective NRUA practice
Consultancy (academic or private business)	Expert (professional): ensuring impartial production of knowledge for sustainable and ethical natural resource use
Non-government organisations (NGOs)	Witness: representing interests of impoverished natural resource users, future generations, and non-human nature

planning in Botswana in general. The fieldwork of gathering this information occupied the most time in the study and correspondingly generated the most data. There is no need (nor space) here to go through the descriptive maps assembled for each of the three projects. Neither is there space for detailing the process of critiquing each descriptive map against the corresponding/respective ideal map of NRUA. More important is that readers get a feel for the outputs of this systematic boundary critique.

6.2.4.3   Critique: 'Ought' and 'Is'

Boxes 6.2–6.4 provide brief summaries of the final critique resulting for each project which was presented in more detailed form to the project personnel. Each Box summarises some descriptive mapping and specific critique of 'role', 'role-specific concern' and 'key problems' associated with each source of influence.

It may appear that the critiques presented for each project are very negative. The summaries provided here do not give justice to the creative aspects of each project which were also detailed in the reports to project personnel. Nevertheless a central task of CSH is to nurture an attitude of creative disruption. From a critical systems perspective critique does not equate to being negative, but rather should provide a platform for *improving* understanding and practice associated with a situation of interest or a context that matters.

6.2.4.4   Extra-discursive and Discursive Evaluation

The NRUA-Botswana study represents an example of systematic boundary critique adopting a largely extra-discursive, 'expert-driven' use of CSH categories. In other words, the use of CSH categories was reserved for the author's own purposes. For example, interview schedules were designed around CSH questions; not organised in terms of systematically going through each CSH question but rather customised according to

Box 6.2 Participatory Rural Appraisal (PRA) Pilot Project

Motivation *critique*	Local government *extension officers* were immediate beneficiaries rewarded with facilitation skills to enable greater involvement of local people in extension work. But to what extent might *alleviating perceived rural social inertia* lead to poverty alleviation? The key measure of success for the project was centred on *high levels of participation* and generation of *self-help projects*. Perhaps instead, rural poor might benefit from better access to and control over resources rather than being subject to further consolidation of government extension practices.
Control *critique*	Under trajectory of (i) increased privatisation and fencing of communal land resulting in further alienation of natural resource, and (ii) reduced government assistance for local development projects, rural poor livelihoods are increasingly dependent on contracts with landowners and donor support for collective projects. Is there a risk that rural people's knowledge loses its independence in becoming increasingly subject to government extension practice which itself is circumscribed by government central policy?
Expertise *critique*	To what extent might participation levels amongst rural poor in PRA exercises provide a guarantee for poverty alleviation? Might this guarantor attribute distract from large body of empirical data and experience suggesting significant correlation between rural poverty and land fencing policy since the mid-1970s?
Legitimacy *critique*	Dominant underpinning belief that benevolent government (through tradition of generous handouts and transfer of technology projects) has been responsible for generating rural social inertia, hence the need for government to step back and allow 'development from within'. Danger of further marginalising rural poor through not appreciating perceived root cause relating to control and access to land.

(i) the perceived stakeholder role (beneficiary, decision maker etc.), (ii) the particular project being focused upon (often, interviewees would have a stake in several projects at the same time), and (iii) information arising from prior interviews with other stakeholders and/or relevant grey literature. During the course of this study three separate

Box 6.3 Natural Resource Management Project (NRMP)

Motivation *critique*	Key beneficiaries of NRMP appear to be management staff of community based natural resource management (CBNRM) projects responsible for eliciting support/ resources from different line Ministries (e.g. Wildlife and Tourism, Agriculture, Water Affairs, Local Government). But to what extent might improved *multisectoral planning* address rural poverty and communal land degradation? Key measure of success is the number of CBNRM projects, primarily as indices of improved intersectoral collaboration. But do CBNRM projects (i) use or simply bypass line ministries? (ii) elicit collaboration with government or dependency on donors? and (iii) serve the *very* poor?
Control *critique*	Have CBNRM projects become new currency for rural development? Whilst CBNRM might appear to be better grounded in local needs, are there greater levels of accountability in use of financial resources as compared with government extension programmes? Does short term funding support from donor agencies allow government to divert resource support away from local rural development?
Expertise *critique*	CBNRM management requires multidisciplinary expertise and skills in facilitation. But to what extent are participatory techniques involving rural participants a useful trigger for intersectoral collaboration and communication between traditional sector and disciplinary based experts? Rural people's knowledge may be regarded as a useful check on professional judgements but how far is it appreciated as a potential driver for rural development initiatives?
Legitimacy *critique*	Dominant underpinning belief that appropriate expertise ought to drive rural development rather than traditional dependence on civil service sector-based bureaucratic functions that inevitably create the closed 'silo' mentality. Possible conflict with local understandings of the need for greater autonomy and control over development amongst rural participants in conjunction *with* locally-elected government officials rather than donor-promoted project managers.

Box 6.4 Botswana Range Inventory and Monitoring Project (BRIMP)

Motivation *critique*	Immediate beneficiaries are *policy advisors* wishing to *instil longer-term coordinated planning* to address problems of previous piecemeal development in rural sector. BRIMP is housed in the Ministry of Agriculture, dominated by free market neo-liberal economic development planning and policies associated with fencing communal rangeland. So how likely is it that such coordinated planning might benefit rural poor? Do economic measures of success associated with gross national (agricultural) product equate with rural poverty alleviation and enhanced condition of natural environment?
Control *critique*	Commoditised resources provide the most appropriate means for economic planning. Thus fencing of communal land, privatising water supply, project-oriented development, and having rural participants on-tap for consultations during monitoring and evaluation efforts, might be considered as important measures of control; consolidating existing relations of economic power rather than empowering the rural communities (?). Are there risks of further disenfranchising rural communities through consolidating private ownership of land?
Expertise *critique*	Central guarantee for ensuring properly co-ordinated efforts is through purposive *monitoring and evaluation* using econometric indices based on criteria of efficiency and effectiveness in terms of generating economic wealth from natural resources. Participatory techniques using rural people's knowledge are regarded as a means of (in PRA terms) 'ground-truthing' or checking information arising from more technically oriented surveillance systems like remote sensing.
Legitimacy *critique*	Dominant belief that free-market determinism using econometric devices applied to natural resource-use provide most effective means for reducing poverty and protecting the natural environment. Needs reconciling with the Botswana tradition in communal rangeland management, and primacy of democratic debate as a means of determining policy.

learning journals were kept – one for each of the NRUA projects being evaluated. The material in each of the three journals provided an essential resource for writing up an 'is' analysis (descriptive map) of each project. The ensuing critique was generated largely from individual reflection on the data gathered and experiences gained.

But the real value of boundary critique lies in its dialogical use to test other stakeholders' reference systems. Despite the methodological conception of the evaluation study itself as an extra-discursive intervention, in the sense that CSH was employed in a monological (problem-structuring and practice-reflecting) way, that is, as a tool of post-hoc boundary reflection, an important dialogical component came into play though the process of sharing the findings with the project personnel. This was done, firstly, through formal interviewing; secondly, through informal engagement amongst stakeholders involved with actual PRA activities; and thirdly, through the interim reporting stage where feedback from stakeholders was sought.

How did CSH inform the interviews with 78 stakeholders associated with the three projects? Each interview began with questions relating to what the stakeholders considered to be their main role, their main concerns and key problems in fulfilling their role. Wider questions were then asked about relationships with other stakeholders and *their* perceived roles, concerns and key problems. These responses were mapped in the form of initial ideal ('ought') and actual ('is') maps, which then provided further prompts in developing the conversation throught further interviews. Conflicts coming to the fore among respondents belonging to same stakeholder group were recorded and used for further enquiry and/or included in interim reports. Some of the interviewees were further interviewed less formally during subsequent fieldwork.

In recording all these conversations, it proved useful to continually update the respondents' ideal and actual maps. The mapping of stakeholder views was found to be a continually evolving exercise during conversations and accompanying reading of informal grey literature made available through the conversations. At the same time, critiques were emerging which equally needed continual recording. Again, this was essentially a subjective exercise on the part of the evaluator, although other ways of handling the critical process are of course conceivable, for example, making it a central concern of some (moderated) groups of stakeholders. In any case, it was important to keep a record of the developing critique as a basis for reporting back.

Reporting back on a CSH-based evaluation clearly involves transparency. As well as revealing contrasting values, power-relations, expert-biases, and questions regarding the wider legitimacy of NRUA practice, the evaluation also invoked the transparency of the evaluator regarding the reference system that informed the evaluation. Skills in translating findings and impressions into a mutually appreciated vocabulary and narrative were equally required, remembering that stakeholders are not conversant with CSH terminology. A key to successful evaluation lies in eliciting critical appreciation and further engagement among stakeholders. All stakeholders were invited to comment on the interim reports either orally or in writing, which generated considerable feedback. Finally, a specially convened seminar at the University of Botswana provided further opportunity for dialogue among more than 50 participants from all three projects.

Each report began with an explicit statement of (i) what the author's perception was on the main issues of the evaluation, including underlying values and purposes of the project, issues of power and decision making, relevant knowledge, and moral underpinnings; and (ii) the author's own role and purpose with respect to the evaluation exercise. Respondents should be made aware that scientific data and statistics, while useful to support the output of a CSH evaluation, provided only one element in the overall evaluation; its core was a qualitative exercise primarily aimed towards collaborative improvement of, and developing responsibility over, the situation.

6.2.5   Boundary Critique Applied to ECOSENSUS-Guyana[2]

In the ECOSENSUS study, the discursive mode of boundary critique moved into the centre. Whereas in Botswana CSH served as a framework for evaluating the use of participatory planning, in Guyana it was to serve as a framework for engaging underprivileged stakeholders along with researchers and planners in participatory processes of decision making, by giving them a new language for articulating their concerns. To put it differently: whereas the Botswana study used boundary critique directly to formulate reference systems for evaluative research, ECOSENSUS wanted to make a start towards generating *CSH literacy* among stakeholders. It should be said though that this was not the main aim of the project; it primarily was a pilot study for developing and testing new software tools to support participatory planning and management of natural resource use among geographically distributed stakeholders and professionals. The connection between the two aims was the idea that the software tools might incorporate concepts of boundary discourse, so as to encourage and facilitate a critical handling of stakeholding issues.

The stakeholders involved included Makushi Amerindians and their NGO representatives in the Rupununi wetlands; planners and other experts in the field of environmental management and computational software development; University of Guyana postgraduate students, and project funders.

Given that the project was conceived as an exploratory pilot study, its financial and time frame were rather limited and its level of ambition was accordingly modest. Within this frame, ECOSENSUS had two specific objectives:

1. To help develop open-source software tools that should enable marginalised communities to engage with partners and experts elsewhere in shared, Internet supported processes of decision making about environmental issues
2. To develop open content learning units able to support the use of the software tools developed in the project, thereby also promoting collaborative skills in managing natural resource dilemmas.

With a view to the first objective, the technical basis was provided by *uDig*, an open-source graphic surface for geographical information systems (GIS) – from where comes the name 'uDig' (= user-friendly Desktop/Internet GIS, see http://udig.refractions.net/). A second technical basis consisted in *Compendium*, an open-source software for *dialogue mapping* developed at the Open University on the basis of Kunz and Rittel's (1970) concept of issue-based information systems (IBIS), (see Conklin 2005 and http://projects.kmi.open.ac.uk/compendium/). ECOSENSUS should achieve an integration of Compendium with uDig, so as to facilitate their simultaneous use. At the same time, the project should explore possibilities to extend Compendium with mapping tools developed on the basis of CSH, so as to help users unfold the vital stakeholding issues involved in the aim of supporting marginalised

---

[2] We are indebted to colleagues working with us on the ECOSENSUS project for some of the ideas expressed in this chapter. ECOSENSUS was supported by the United Kingdom's Economic and Social Research Council (ESRC), Project Reference Number RES-149-25-1017.

communities. Finally, the project should pilot-test whether such software applications would indeed enable the stakeholders to adopt a wider problem perspective and unfold it in a well-structured, graphically supported, manner.

With a view to the second objective, the project began developing and testing a pilot online course with participants from Guyana, as an opportunity for them to develop some initial practice in using the software tools as well as in boundary discourse. The course was provisionally entitled *Team Building for Sustainable Natural Resource Management*. The participants included NGO representatives of the Amerindian community and students at the University of Guyana, two staff members from the University of Guyana acted as tutors. The authors were part of a wider course development team with colleagues from the Open University, the University of London and the University of Guyana.

The project thus comprised a number of interrelated endeavours which, though often running concurrently and being very iterative, may nevertheless be laid out in rough chronological order:

1. Initial team building and familiarisation with existing software tools (uDig, Compendium, video conferencing software) and systems ideas (CSH) among distributed team members
2. Technical integration of uDig with Compendium and testing with the team
3. Development of CSH templates for Compendium
4. Empirical testing of CSH templates in Guyana
5. Development and testing of open content learning material for team building

For the present purpose we need not concern ourselves with the technical side of the project (which progressed satisfactorily) but can focus on endeavours 3 and 4. We can also briefly explore the intent and challenges behind using CSH as an input to building open educational resources (OERs) for the wider purpose of team building (endeavour 5).

6.2.5.1   Developing CSH Literacy

Since in Guyana CSH was to serve mainly as a discursive framework for mediating conversation, language issues became central. While in Botswana the evaluator was reasonably familiar with the language of CSH, in ECOSENSUS the intended users were new to boundary critique. It was necessary to 'translate' CSH in two respects – firstly, into short expressions that could easily be captured in the graphic surface of uDig and Compendium, and secondly, into terms accessible to a marginalised non-European community accustomed more to verbal and visual communication than to written literacy. Other studies have equally reported on the importance of adapting the tools of boundary critique to specific users groups; compare, for example, Carr and Oreszczyn (2003) and Achterkamp and Vos (2007).

In promoting CSH literacy among specific users, an immediate question arises: Why might they wish to engage in boundary conversation? We found it useful to 'pick up' our intended users by responding to specific motives they might have for engaging in boundary reflection and discourse. We thus developed *four basic templates for boundary critique*, each relating to a particular motive or purpose (see Box 6.5).

Box 6.5 Templates for four basic applications of boundary critique (Adapted from Ulrich 2005, p. 12)

Template (a):	*Ideal Mapping*
Purpose:	'Vision building'
Guiding question:	'What's our vision?'
	(or: Where do we want to go from here?)
Template (b):	*Evaluation*
Purpose:	'Value clarification'
Guiding question:	'Where are we standing?'
	(or: How satisfied are we with the state of affairs?)
Template (c):	*Reframing*
Purpose:	'Boundary revision'
Guiding question:	'What's the relevant context?'
	(or: How else can we frame the picture?)
Template (d):	*Challenge*
Purpose:	'Emancipation'
Guiding question:	'Don't you claim too much?'
	(or: How can we rationally claim this is right?)

Once stakeholders can see a purpose behind the use of a particular language tool, the motivation to engage increases. Moreover, the templates offer some direction for training and practice, in that they stand for increasingly demanding uses of boundary critique. They thus also represent levels of increasing competence in boundary reflection and discourse. The first two templates (a) and (b) represent an elementary use of boundary questions – in the 'ought' mode for (a) and in both the 'ought' and 'is' modes for (b) – which we have found easiest to learn for most users of CSH. The third template – (c) reframing – additionally involves a critique of 'ought' and 'is', with the aim of providing an alternative reference system (i.e. another set of answers to the boundary questions). Template (d), finally, represents a more advanced, argumentative use of boundary critique, where any one of the responses to a question might be countered by, say:

- A suggestion: e.g. "I see young people as beneficiaries but I don't see them included at present"
- A doubt: e.g. "I wonder about the assumed assurances of success, what if you ignore…?"
- A contradiction: e.g. "if this is the client, we will not accomplish the right thing, because…" or finally
- A simple what-if inquiry: e.g. "what if we would redefine expertise as…?"

So much for the basic issue of providing impetus for boundary reflection and discourse. The next issue was testing how the intended users understood the boundary questions. In a field test with participants in Guyana, we first found considerable variability in their understanding of the questions. But when we subsequently applied the questions more specifically to one of the four purposes (a)–(d) mentioned above, rather than simply testing CSH's language without a clear end in mind, there was more appreciation and comprehension. Box 6.6 illustrates some responses of 18

Box 6.6 Getting familiar with CSH questions

(Selected responses from 18 participants of the ECOSENSUS-Guyana study to boundary questions relating to land-use planning for the North Rupununi wetlands)

Responses to questions about motivation (CSHq1–3)

"There shouldn't be one client in all of this. There should be a sort of a continuum where 'clients' are of different [and] varying levels of importance, and the dependency on the Rupununi should be the tool that identifies these levels. For example, a villager in the Rupununi seeking economic gain, so that he can send his children to school, should be able to use the [natural] resources in the area to do this."

"The researchers ought to be the client because they are the ones who provide information [for] the both local communities and the world – the purpose is for people to have knowledge of the project, their objective and purpose."

"National institutions in terms of meeting their CBD [community based development] [with] objectives having more information for decision-making – information is power"

"It should serve everyone's interest, even though this project involves few groups of people, e.g. the communities, field staff, [and] scientists but in the long term the purpose is for everyone. So it should serve everyone's purpose."

Responses to questions about control (CSHq4–6)

"The decision makers now are project managers, and to some extent field researchers. For example, with the water chemistry kit being broken, the data on water quality is not being collected."

"Project coordinators, researchers the people living in the communities must work to make decisions."

"The immediate clients working with the wetlands project [ought to be decision makers]"

"The North Rupununi District Development Board ought to be the decision maker."

(continued)

Box 6.6 (continued)

Responses to questions about expertise (CSHq7–9)

"Those who ought to be considered [as] professional [are] communities of
the north Rupununi [and] field researchers."
"Expertise of research, planning, consulting"
"Everyone's expertise [should] be consulted because everyone's knowledge [should
be] considered. The project would [then] have a better impact to everyone and
this would be a better understanding among different groups of people."
"[The actual source of expertise comes from] Conservation International,
Guyana Foundation."

Responses to questions about legitimacy (CSHq10–12)

"One of the things that is affecting how stakeholders [feel] is that they buy into
what the project is about but their vision may be different from the people that
conceptualised it."
"Having everyone involve to understand [how] to manage what is there for
everyone's benefit."
"The worldview that is determining is … land as sustainable wetlands area."
"Sustainable development is possible."
"Viewing the scientific knowledge is important. Use of scientific data is the
professional thing to [do] in decision making."

---

respondents who were asked to try and use the questions as a help to voice their concerns about current land-use development plans for the North Rupununi wetlands.

Not all 18 respondents were equally articulate. English was a second language
for most and cultural differences made some questions more challenging than others
to them. The questions on legitimacy for example recorded a relatively low
response – a difficulty to be expected as questions of legitimacy are not easily
raised in the Amerindian culture (legitimacy resides with the authority of the village
elders). Despite such obstacles, there was evidence among the responses that with
appropriate facilitation, meaningful stakeholder dialogue might develop.

Turning now to the four purposes (a)–(d) mentioned above, it proved easiest to
achieve a basic degree of CSH literacy in having the Amerindian participants talk
about their visions for the future of the Rupununi wetland ('ideal mapping' as an
entry-level use of boundary discourse, as suggested in Box 6.6 above).

But how should we structure templates for ideal mapping and the other purposes
specifically for stakeholders accustomed to oral and visual rather than written communication? Clearly, the templates needed to use terms that would help the
Amerindian participants relate the boundary questions directly to their experience;
as well as provide a basis for visualising the sequence of unfolding suggested earlier (Fig. 6.3) within the Compendium software. As a basis for formulating such
templates we used the kind of decision (or deliberation) trees reproduced in
Table 6.4 (the example shows a tree for an ideal-mapping template).

Table 6.4 Specification of CSH questions for an ideal-mapping template ("What's our vision?")

Boundary issues	Root issues	Main questions	Specified prompts
Sources of motivation	What are the motivating factors?	Whom do we want to serve?	Primary clients? Secondary clients? Whom can't we realistically serve although ideally we would?
		What do we want to achieve?	Primary aims? Secondary aims? Unrealistic aims?
		What should be our measure of improvement?	Quantitative measure(s) of improvement? Qualitative aspects of improvement?
Sources of control	Who's in control?	Whom do we want to decide?	Those able to stop us Those able to change or redefine our measures of improvement Those already in control of resources
		What resources do we aim to have available?	Financial Material Political/social Other
		What conditions of success should rightly be controlled by third parties?	Public sector authorities Private sector organisations Individual stakeholders not involved Nature/chance
Sources of knowledge	What information and skills are relevant?	Whom do we want to contribute their experience and expertise?	Indispensable experts Desirable experts Impossible experts Undesirable experts
		What information and skills do we want them to contribute?	Ordinary experience Professional know-how Professional skills Other
		Where should we look for some guarantee of success?	True guarantors False guarantors Doubtful/potential guarantors
Sources of legitimacy	What stakeholders should be considered?	Whom do we want to voice the concerns of those not involved?	Those affected but not involved Those concerned but not directly affected Those normally without voice (future generations, non-human nature etc.)
		What do we want to do to emancipate stakeholders from our premises and promises?	In terms of rights In terms of compensation Other
		What worldview do we want to rely on/privilege?	Privileged view Clashing views

The template-trees were then translated into the Compendium dialogue mapping software. Answers, questions or conjectures arising in a conversation can be noted directly in the software.

6.2.5.2 Team Building for and by Using Boundary Critique

In addition to software support, appropriate facilitation and team-building efforts were explored so as to help the participants in familiarizing themselves with the spirit of boundary critique. Some local meetings were held in different locations in Guyana, offering a facilitated opportunity to practice the software tools and simultaneously to express feedback on the draft templates. Later, the focus shifted to the development of an open educational resource. A pilot course on *Team Working for Natural Resource Management* should offer the participants both an introduction to natural resource management issues and another opportunity to practice the new software tools.

The course development relied on a conceptual framework drawing on two traditions: systems thinking informed by CSH, and participatory action research (PAR, cf. Fals-Borda 1996) partly informed by critical pedagogy (Freire 1970). CSH appeared relevant to address both the earlier-discussed duality between systems and situations as well as the PAR dimension of the project, as it has explicitly addressed such contexts (see Ulrich 1996); PAR appeared relevant to encourage active participation of the Guyana stakeholders.

We mapped these two dimensions of systems thinking and participation onto a standard project management and learning cycle involving the four basic activities of *observing, evaluating, planning* and *acting*. This yielded the framework shown in Fig. 6.4.

The framework understands systems thinking and participation as involving *two basic tensions* that need to be dealt with in most professional interventions (see Reynolds 2008b for a similar framework application to project management in international development programmes). The first, horizontal dimension represents the *tension of 'system' versus 'situation'* (cf. Figures 6.1 and 6.2). The second, vertical dimension represents the *clash of multiple perspectives* that tends to make it difficult in practice to achieve mutual understanding among stakeholders, regarding both their different views and concerns ('stakes') and alternative ways to develop these into joint action for improvement ('stakeholding development').

The two dimensions may be combined with our earlier distinction of non-discursive versus discursive boundary questioning (cf. Figs. 6.4 and 6.5). *Boundary reflection* may then be said to focus attention on the reference systems that inform our understanding of situations, for example, when it comes to evaluating the real-world consequences of action ('system' versus 'situation'); whereas *boundary discourse* would focus more on the conflicts arising between stakeholders due to different reference systems informing their view of the situation and of options for improving it, and on the consequent need for acquiring some mutual understanding. Taken together, these two basic tensions thus also capture the familiar and rarely avoidable tension between *individual* appreciation of situations and the need for *cooperative* action. Even though we rarely achieve shared understanding in the sense of consensus, we have to achieve some kind of shared practice, through decision making based at least on mutual (though not shared) understanding – which is what we expect boundary discourse to facilitate.

We used this framework to inform the development of on-line course material structured around three main topics: (i) learning to identify stakes and stakeholders; (ii) unfolding stakeholding issues; and (iii) developing an individual project dealing with a problem situation in Guyana. All three parts should provide practice in boundary reflection and discourse, partly supported by the software tools. The project ended before the course had been completed, but some of the material is now available as an open educational resource (OER). ECOSENSUS became one of the first content providers of the Open University's OER initiative called OpenLearn (www.open.ac.uk/openlearn); see the site's experimental 'LabSpace' section.

The hope is for some of the ECOSENSUS ideas to be taken up by users in the growing open-access community and to be adapted for users in different contexts. Some of the course material has already been taken up in a subsequent development of OERs for the North Rupununi Adaptive Management Plan (NRAMP), again using the LabSpace facility of OpenLearn.

6.2.5.3 Final Reflection

Looking back on the 18-month ECOSENSUS-Guyana study, what have we learned about the use of CSH? It was clear from the outset that the project was to explore new territory rather than implementing anything definitive; our hope was to learn about the limitations in transposing our tools into a totally different cultural context. We certainly did!

Here is a brief summary of the limitations we learned about, structured around the four basic CSH sources of influence (which may inform limitations no less than success in achieving improvement):

1. *Motivation*: There was a certain technocratic bias built into the project to fulfill predetermined objectives around the development of electronic tools (Compendium and uDig) for our sponsor, rather than first exploring the needs of the intended users.
2. *Control*: There were limitations on time, staffing and other resources (particularly local facilitation and Internet access for our Amerindian colleagues) that had been underestimated in the project design and turned out to impede the 'distributed' stakeholder dialogue we aimed to support.
3. *Knowledge*: There was little experience and expertise with the use of software tools such as uDig and Compendium to support dialogue on issues of natural resource management among marginalised stakeholders. For example, it proved to be difficult to record the content of such conversations in a (partly graphic) form and language that would be easily accessible for all participants despite differing technical equipment, skills, and cultural backgrounds.
4. *Legitimacy*: Raising questions of legitimacy proved difficult for some of the participants, but also for the authors as there were limited opportunities to gauge

effects of the project on third parties, including likely 'victims' such as conventional environmental planners.

Despite such limitations, we found that the use of CSH did make a difference in the way software tools and other planning tools were used in this project. It made sure that in the course of the project, the original focus on technical issues gradually shifted to substantive issues of the stakeholder discourse to be facilitated. In particular, it created space for such crucial issues to be deliberated upon as, for example, what views and concerns were to inform the maps of the Rupununi land-use situation drawn by means of these tools, rather than allowing them (as is more usual) to remain hidden away or being treated as mere inconveniences.

On the other hand, we do not feel we managed to mobilize as much involvement on the part of the Amerindian participants as we might have hoped. This may be due in part to the cultural differences we have mentioned, along with the dominance of software-related technical and conceptual concerns and the limited reach of a short-term project such as ECOSENSUS. Even so we believe that ECOSENSUS demonstrated the feasibility of supporting project management by e-social science tools such as those we explored. Just as important, it demonstrated a simultaneous need for basing professional intervention and project management on enlarged frameworks such as the one envisaged in Fig. 6.6. ECOSENSUS certainly made us aware of how

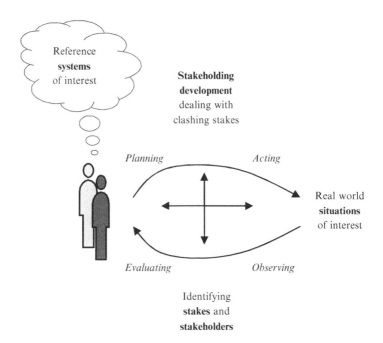

Fig. 6.6 ECOSENSUS Framework (Adapted from Reynolds 2008b, p. 779). "Reframing expert support for development management", *Journal of International Development*, Pergamon, with permission from Elsevier

long a way current managerial and e-science approaches still have to go so as to really create spaces for an open and reflective handling of crucial stakeholding issues.

In this early phase of their development it is probably inevitable that the tools themselves, rather than the processes they ought to facilitate, are in the centre. As long as this is so, boundary critique is better thought of as a personal stance and competence that is acquired primarily through personal study and practice along with dialogue with others, rather than through intermediate software applications. The third and final section of this introduction to CSH discusses some of the personal skills in question.

6.3   Developing CSH Skills and Significance

6.3.1   Boundary Critique and Personal Competence

Understanding methodological ideas is not enough, we must also develop some personal competencies and attitudes in applying them. As we have thus far focused on introducing some core concepts of CSH and reviewing two case studies in their light, let us now consider some of the skills and virtues involved in practicing boundary critique.

The basic theme of this concluding section is that boundary reflection and discourse have a lot to do with who we are and how we work as professionals, that is, with our sense of professional identity and competence. Readers may find it meaningful to reflect on the degree to which they are already on their way to acquiring such competence, or what they can do to become competent practitioners of boundary critique.

6.3.2   Recognising Boundary Judgements – and Keeping Them Fluid

Learning to practice boundary critique begins with understanding the role boundary judgements play, that is, with reading some of the sources on CSH. In addition, it helps to listen attentively to how people talk and argue in everyday conversations, on the bus, at work or in TV discussions; try to *hear* the boundary judgements they make without apparently being aware of them, and discover how they consequently misunderstand one another and talk at cross-purposes.

Once you have understood the importance of boundary judgements as a factor that conditions all our thinking, a *critical* impetus comes into play: you will then no longer want them to operate unrecognised in your thinking. You will prefer to control *them*, rather than allowing them to control you. Likewise, in discussions with others, you will probably no longer want their boundary judgements to go unrecognised or be imposed on you and others as 'given'. Rather than seeing them withdrawn from any critical consideration, you will want them to be transparent and open to revision. *To understand the role of boundary judgements means to keep them under review and fluid rather than allowing them to become 'hard' and taken for granted.* In this respect, we may indeed take the talk of a shift from 'hard' to critical systems thinking quite literally!

But what is it that contributes towards rendering boundary judgements visible and fluid? All the skills that we are going to discuss are contributing to this aim, but perhaps the two most basic ones are what CSH calls 'systematic iteration' and 'systemic triangulation'.

6.3.2.1   Systematic Iteration of Boundary Judgements

Our reference systems change over time, as do the situations to which we apply them. Some of our boundary judgements may be put into question by the way a situation of concern evolves, others by new knowledge we acquire or in discussion with others, or we gain new experience through other situations in which we are professionally or privately involved, and so on.

An important point in this natural evolution of our thinking is this: all our boundary judgements are interdependent. We cannot simply adapt a boundary judgement (say, as to who should belong to the beneficiaries) to some new piece of information and for the rest continue with our previous understanding of the situation, without revising the other boundary judgements that constitute our reference system (e.g. our measure of improvement might need to be adapted, and consequently the resources needed, the decision maker controlling them, the kind of expertise called for, and so on). *Whenever we change any one boundary judgement, all the others may be in need of change, too.*

Consequently, the process of unfolding and questioning boundary judgements is not a simple matter of observing a standard sequence of boundary questions such as Table 6.1 and Fig. 6.3 may be understood to suggest it in two slightly different versions. Rather, boundary critique becomes a cycle of multiple revisions which may take us through *several* and *changing* sequences of boundary reflection. This is what we mean by describing boundary critique as an *iterative process*.

In the NRUA-Botswana study, the process of evaluating each of the three projects was essentially iterative in that new insights about any one of the three projects prompted the evaluator to revise his reference system for each of the other two projects, too. In the ECOSENSUS-Guyana study, it was the gradual progress of mutual understanding and better communication, along with equally growing awareness of obstacles and difficulties, which provided a main driver for revising the authors' reference systems.

There are three important aspects to this basic skill of iterating boundary judgements:

– Since new insights into the limitations or arbitrariness of our reference system may at all times prompt us to revise our boundary judgements, we need not worry so much about 'getting them right' from the outset. What matters more is that we start developing a sense of the *different* kinds of reference system that might guide us, before we invest too much time and effort for inquiry and reflection about any particular boundary judgement.

– Since the answers we give to the 12 boundary questions are interdependent, it does not really matter where we start. Rather than following some predefined order mechanically, we can start with any boundary question that we find particularly interesting or relevant, or easy to answer, or helpful to stimulate discussion, and so on. The ensuing boundary reflection or dialogue can then follow where the process takes it, as the interdependence of the boundary judgements will quite naturally lead us to previously unconsidered boundary issues and make sure that we clarify our reference system in terms of all 12 boundary issues.

– Similarly, since boundary revision is an iterative process, when the need for revising our reference system arises we may start with any of the boundary judgements concerned. We will then usually see some of our other previous boundary judgements in a new light, or new boundary issues emerge. So we can move to those other boundary issues and examine how our reference system is changing. Likewise, moving back and forth between 'ought' and 'is' answers may drive the process of revision, as may any other kind of input that can help us better understand the conditioned nature of our boundary judgements.

This is not to say that it is not a good idea for beginners to start with a standard sequence such as the one suggested in Fig. 6.3. However, you need not be its slave. Use it as long as it proves helpful; drop it when it becomes a constraint. As we grow more accustomed to thinking in terms of boundary critique, we can free ourselves from following a fixed order and allow more naturally flowing reflection and discussion.

6.3.2.2 Systemic Triangulation

The boundary judgements that we continually make (whether consciously or otherwise) are influenced by two other sets of judgements that are continually at play. Firstly there are judgements on what we take to constitute reality, for example, based on what we observe or expect to happen in consequence of our actions. We call such observations and anticipations *judgements of 'fact'*. In NRUA-Botswana, they involved, for example, the monitoring of land use through extensive surveys and geographic information systems (GIS). Likewise, for ECOSENSUS-Guyana, the importance of uDiG as a device for accessing and making immediate judgements on the ecological well-being of local ecosystems, was integral to the study.

Secondly, and just as importantly, there are more intuitive judgements on what we take to constitute improvement, that is, what we individually and collectively ascribe to the real world in terms of measures of worth. We call such assessments *judgements of 'value'.* In both NRUA-Botswana and ECOSENSUS-Guyana there was to be expected considerable variability in value judgements regarding, for instance, the worth of some notion of pristine nature as compared with the worth of, say, a natural 'resource' such as timber or other forms of land use for human development.

We have thus three sets of judgements that condition the ways we conceive of situations and systems: factual judgements, value judgements, and boundary judgements. Judgements of fact and judgements of value are often said to be interdependent, but it usually remains unclear what exactly that means and how it is to be explained. CSH gives us a precise explanation: 'facts' and 'values' depend on one another as both are conditioned by the same boundary judgements. For example, when we expand our boundary judgements regarding what belongs to the relevant situation (say, when we recognise a previously ignored condition of success), previously ignored facts may become relevant; but in the light of new facts, our value judgements may suddenly look different and need revision. Similarly, when our value judgements change, we will need to revise our boundary judgements accordingly, and in consequence new or different facts become relevant.

CSH refers to this triadic interplay of reference system, relevant facts and values as an *eternal triangle* that we need to think through, and to its methodological employment for critical purposes as *systemic triangulation* (Ulrich 2000, p. 251f; 2003, p. 334; and 2005, p. 6). The term 'triangulation' originally refers to the need for using at least three triangulation points for surveying land; in the empirical social sciences it has come to mean the use of different data bases (gained preferably by different research approaches) to describe and analyse social issues. 'Systemic' triangulation goes beyond this concept by combining different data bases (judgements of fact) with different reference systems (boundary judgements) and value sets (judgements of value) to gain a deeper understanding of the selectivity of claims.

Systemic triangulation can also be understood as an extended form of systematic iteration of boundary judgements. Whereas in the basic form the iteration takes place among changing boundary judgements, in the extended form it takes place among boundary judgements, factual judgements and value judgements.

Stepping back from one's reference system in order to appreciate other perspectives is perhaps the most challenging attribute of a systems practitioner. This is what systemic triangulation is all about. It is a core skill we need to develop in order to become competent in boundary critique. The eternal triangle suggests a way to do this: we can make it a habit to consider each corner of the triangle in the light of the other two, by asking questions such as these: "What new facts become relevant if we expand the boundaries of the reference system or modify our value judgements? How do our valuations look if we consider new facts that refer to a modified reference system? In what way may our reference system fail to do justice to the perspective of different stakeholder groups? Any claim that does not reflect on the underpinning 'triangle' of boundary judgements, judgements of facts and value judgements, risks claiming too much, by not disclosing its built-in selectivity." (Ulrich 2002, p. 42; similarly 2003, p. 334, and 2005, p. 6).

Systemic triangulation is indeed highly relevant from a critical point of view. It serves several critical ends:

- It helps us in becoming *aware* of, and thinking through, the selectivity of our claims – a basis for cultivating reflective practice.
- It allows us to *explain* to others our bias – how our views and claims are conditioned by our assumptions. We can thus qualify our proposals carefully, so that they gain in credibility.
- It allows us to *see through* the selectivity of the claims of *others* and thus to be better prepared to assess their merits and limitations properly.
- It improves *communication*, for it enables us to better understand our differences with others. When we find it impossible to reach through rational discussion some shared views and proposals, this is not necessarily so because some of the parties do not want to listen to us or have bad intentions but more often, because the parties are arguing from a basis of diverging boundary judgements and thus cannot reasonably expect to arrive at identical judgements of fact and value. And finally, as a result of all the above implications
- It is apt to promote among all the parties involved a sense of modesty and mutual *tolerance* that may facilitate productive cooperation; for once we have understood the principle of systemic triangulation, we cannot help but realise that nobody has a monopoly for getting their facts and values right, and that accordingly it is of little help simply to accuse those who disagree with us to have got their facts and values wrong!

6.3.3 Towards a New Ethos of Professional Responsibility

The five critical elements mentioned above amount to a *new ethos of responsibility* for systems practice, and for professional practice in general. It says that the rationality of professional claims and arguments is to be measured not by the impossible avoidance of justification deficits but by the degree to which we deal with such deficits in a transparent, self-critical, and self-limiting way (Ulrich 1993, p. 587). It is a stance that takes the 'enemies of the systems approach' no less seriously than the different reference systems of those involved in an intervention (cf. Reynolds 2004, p. 550f). Let us conclude with three pertinent reflections.

6.3.3.1 "Context Matters": Working with the Tension of System and Situation

The phrase 'context matters' provides perhaps the simplest and most generic description of what it means to develop competence in boundary critique. First, it prompts the question: What is the relevant context? or simply: *Which context matters?* Second, it prompts the question: What makes this context matter more than other conceivable ones? or simply: *Why does it matter?* The first question raises issues of meaning and relevance; it invites us to reflect on our understanding of 'the problem' (the 'situation') and ways to improve it. The second question raises issues of validity and rationality; it urges us to reflect on the validity claims involved in our 'systems' maps and designs and to examine the arguments that support or challenge them.

As evidenced in the two case studies, getting to grips with real-world situations of intervention does not usually allow us to stay within the pristine conceptual world of our systems methodologies. Rather, it compels us to face the basic tension between 'system' and 'situation', by continuously questioning our systems maps and designs as to how selective they are in capturing the situation, and our notion of the situation as to what options there are for our underlying reference system. By consciously working with the tension of 'system' and 'situation', either can play a critical role for the other; together, they can help us develop and maintain some healthy self-critical distance to our own professional assumptions, findings, and conclusions.

Boundary critique, then, is not just a process of delimiting and arguing our *systems* conceptions. It should equally inform our notion of the relevant problem *situation* – of the 'context that matters'. Our systems maps and designs can hardly be better than the notion of the context that informs them! But whereas in the case of our systems maps and designs, boundary critique will usually require a systematic and explicit effort of boundary unfolding and questioning, in the case of our notion of the context it will often tend to be more intuitive and implicit. We all bring into professional interventions a background of personal experiences and skills that shape our views of the context, and it will hardly ever be possible that we render all those background assumptions fully explicit. What matters more is that we develop a sense of openness and flexibility with respect to the differing contexts that matter to different people, and are prepared to revise our initial notion of the relevant context.

Regarding this important aspect of personal competence, our experience is that boundary critique works best as a reflective framework that most of the time operates in the *background* – a set of concepts and questions we need not talk about all the time but should simply allow to inform our critical thinking. In our communication with others, we can probably best convey the spirit of boundary critique by the example we give in handling our boundary judgements carefully and limiting our claims accordingly, whereas constant talk about boundary judgements may only cause others to switch off. Even in individual reflection, once we have understood the role of boundary assumptions it is hardly possible to 'forget' their importance.

Thus seen, boundary critique ultimately becomes a Socratic professional stance rather than an explicit technique. It encourages a *new methodological modesty* that expresses itself in the way we qualify our claims and deal with those of others. Such a stance will also make a difference in the way we meet people concerned about a situation who have no special expertise and skills: we will understand *and let them feel* that we are prepared to meet them on an equal footing. Rather than putting them in a situation of incompetence, as professional practice often does, we will treat them as competent partners in exploring the context that matters (Ulrich 2000). When it comes to the contextual assumptions informing our views, ordinary citizens have no disadvantage as compared to the experts.

6.3.3.2   "Deep Complementarism": The Significance of Using CSH in Support of Other Methodologies and Methods

The new ethos of responsibility that we associate with boundary critique has also consequences for our cooperation with other professionals. It should inspire in us a *new openness regarding the methodologies others use*. Whatever our own preferred methodology may be in a certain situation, it cannot supersede a careful handling of the eternal triangle that is at work in all our professional findings and conclusions. In this respect, we all meet as equals, regardless of the methodologies we master. Consequently, we may develop and practice skills of boundary critique in conjunction with any kind of methodology, whether it is a 'hard', 'soft' or 'critical' systems methodology or any other kind of approach.

Developing competence in boundary critique thus goes hand in hand with a methodological stance of 'deep' methodological complementarism (Ulrich 2003, p. 337f): while the *problem situations* we face as professionals change and may require different methodologies, the *argumentation tasks* we face remain basically the same. Whatever professional tools we use, in the end we need to convince the parties concerned that we have got our 'facts', 'values' and 'boundary judgements' right, that is, conducive to improvement *in the eyes of the parties concerned*. Professionals cannot delegate this act of approval to themselves; no methodology, no method, no kind of expertise can justify it. All that professional competence can contribute is to lay open to those concerned the assumptions on which it relies, the consequences they may have, and the options available for alternative proposals. Since unfolding and questioning such selectivity is the core business of boundary critique, must we not conclude that all sound professional practice requires *some* skills of boundary critique, whether in explicit CSH terms or not?

CSH accordingly proposes that boundary critique should become part of the critically reflective skills of every professional and should also be considered a core competence of group leaders and facilitators. Particularly in interventions in which disagreements about essential questions arise, appropriate space for boundary reflection and discourse should be set up, both among those involved in the intervention on the one hand and among those involved and other parties concerned but not involved on the other hand.

Consequently, CSH aims not to replace but to *complement* the use of other methodologies, with a view to supporting reflective practice. We consider it one of the strengths of CSH that it is thoroughly grounded philosophically and methodologically yet does not constrain the user's flexibility with respect to the specific approaches and tools that one may prefer and master. It thus enlarges rather than replaces the specific professional skills of its users, and thereby also can provide a common language for reflective practice across different professions and methodologies.

6.3.3.3 "Seeing the World Through the Eyes of Others": Systems Thinking as Constructive Critique

Revisiting the two quotations introducing this chapter, we may finally ask: What insight and value is there in CSH that contributes to the aspiration of *'seeing the world through the eyes of another'*? And moreover: What insight and value does it contribute to the need for being *constructively critical* of the worlds we see 'through the eyes others', as well as of our own worlds?

Answering these two questions is the topic of the entire chapter. But perhaps we can summarise the particular competence and ethos boundary critique is meant to convey to the reader a bit differently. It starts by recognising that boundary judgements are not an invention of CSH but are operational out there in the messy world of professional practice, waiting to be unfolded and questioned! You may choose to ignore them, but does that make you a better researcher and professional? Remember the mountain climber who was asked why he had climbed a mountain; his answer was, 'because it exists'. Similarly, the fact that boundary judgements exist and underpin all our claims should be sufficient impetus to explore them. That they exist may be bad news at first, for they may put into question many of our cherished ideas about competent research and practice; but if we handle them carefully, they may also offer opportunities for gaining a deeper understanding of what it means to be a good professional.

As you, the reader, learn to practice boundary critique and grow more familiar with it, you will gradually discover its power to stimulate your thinking in new, constructively critical ways. You will discover that it helps you in better appreciating what others say and why it differs from your views, but also why people so often talk past one another and are intolerant. Likewise, you will discover that the cogency and credibility of your own proposals and arguments increase to the same degree to which boundary critique makes you appreciate their conditioned nature and limit them accordingly.

What is at stake is the quality of our professional thinking and communication with others. If that is reason enough for you to read more about boundary critique, you may want to start with a more comprehensive and detailed discussion of the quest for competence in systems research and practice than is possible here (Ulrich 2001). Some down-to-earth guidelines for getting started with boundary critique are equally available elsewhere (Ulrich 2000). But ultimately, as with all skills, the only way to learn boundary critique is by trying, and by experiencing the difference it makes in practice, for yourself. *"Dare to articulate your own boundary judgements and to question those of others!"* must be the beginner's motto.

Boundary critique (dare we say?) is never a bad idea. It reminds us that a well-understood systems approach begins and ends with the questions we ask, not with the answers we give.

References

Achterkamp, M.C., & Vos, J.F J. (2007). Critically identifying stakeholders: evaluating boundary critique as a vehicle for stakeholder identification. *Systems Research and Behavioral Science 24*(1), 3–14.

Ackoff, R.L. (1981). *Creating the Corporate Future: Plan or Be Planned For.* New York: Wiley.

Berardi, A., Bernard, C., Buckingham-Shum, S., Ganapathy, S., Mistry, J., Reynolds, M., Ulrich, W. (2006). The ECOSENSUS project: co-evolving tools, practices and open content for participatory natural resource management. *2nd International Conference on e-Social Science,* 28–30 June, Manchester, UK. Presentation and full paper available in the website of the *National Centre for e-Social Science (NCeSS)* of the Economic & Social Research Council (ESRC), http://www.ncess.ac.uk/research/sgp/ecocensus. Also available in the Open University's Open Research Online site, http://oro.open.ac.uk/2692/.

Carr, S. & Oreszczyn, S. (2003). Critical systems heuristics: a tool for the inclusion of ethics and values in complex policy decisions. In *Ethics as a Dimension of Agrifood Policy, Proceedings of the Fourth Congress of the European Society for Agricultural and Food Ethics, Toulouse, France, 20–22 March 2003.* Paper available in the website of the *European Society for Agricultural and Food Ethics (EurSafe),* http://technology.open.ac.uk/cts/EURSAFE4-CSH-paper.pdf.

Chambers, R. (1994a). The origin and practice of participatory rural appraisal. *World Development, 22*(7), 953–969.

Chambers, R. (1994b). Participatory rural appraisal: challenges, potentials and paradigm. *World Development 22*(10), 1437–1454.

Chambers, R. (1997). *Whose Reality Counts? Putting the Last First.* London: Intermediate Technology Publications.

Checkland, P.B. (1981). *Systems Thinking, Systems Practice.* Chichester, UK, Wiley.

Churchman, C.W. (1968). *The Systems Approach.* New York: Delta/Dell Publishing.

Churchman, C.W. (1971). *The Design of Inquiring Systems: Basic Concepts of Systems and Organizations.* New York: Basic Books.

Churchman, C.W. (1979). *The Systems Approach and its Enemies.* New York: Basic Books.

Conklin, J. (2005). *Dialogue Mapping.* Chichester, UK: Wiley.

Dewey, J. (1925). The development of American pragmatism. *Studies in the History of Ideas 2*(Supplement), 353–377.

Fals-Borda, O. (1996). Power/knowledge and emancipation. *Systems Practice 9*(2), 177–181.

Freire, P. (1970). *Pedagogy of the Oppressed.* New York and London: Continuum.

Habermas, J. (1972). *Knowledge and Human Interests.* London: Heinemann.

Habermas, J. (1984/87). *The Theory of Communicative Action.* 2 Volumes, Cambridge, UK: Polity Press.

James, W. (1907). *Pragmatism: A New Name for Some Old Ways of Thinking.* New York: Longman.

Kant, I. (1787). *Critique of Pure Reason* (2nd ed). Transl. by N.K. Smith, New York: St. Martin's Press, 1965 (orig. Macmillan, New York, 1929).

Korzybski, A. (1933). A Non-Aristotelian System and its necessity for rigour in mathematics and physics. In A. Korzybski, *Science and Sanity: An Introduction to Non-Aristotelian Systems and General Semantics,* Lakeville, CT: International Non-Aristotelian Library, pp. 747–761.

Peirce, C.S (1878). How to make our ideas clear. *Popular Science Monthly 12*(January), 386–302.

Reynolds, M. (1998). 'Unfolding' natural resource-use information systems: fieldwork in Botswana. *Systemic Practice and Action Research 11*(2), 127–152.

Reynolds, M. (2004). Churchman and Maturana: enriching the notion of self-organisation for social design. *Systemic Practice and Action Research 17*(6), 539–556.

Reynolds, M. (2007). Evaluation based on critical systems heuristics. In B. Williams and I. Imam (eds.), *Systems Concepts in Evaluation: An Expert Anthology,* Point Reyes, CA: Edge Press, pp. 101–122.

Reynolds, M. (2008a). Getting a grip: a critical systems framework for corporate responsibility. *Systems Research and Behavioral Science 25*(3), 383–395.

Reynolds, M. (2008b). Reframing expert support for development management. *Journal of International Development 20*(6), 768–782.

Reynolds, M., Berardi, A., Bernard, C., Bachler, M., Buckingham-Shum, S., Mistry, J., Ulrich, W. (2007). ECOSENSUS: developing collaborative learning systems for stakeholding development in environmental planning. *Curriculum, Teaching & Student Support Conference,* The Open University, Milton Keynes, 1–2 May 2007. Paper available in the Open University's Open Research Online site, http://oro.open.ac.uk/8580/. Also available through the site of the Knowledge Media Institute, http://oro.open.ac.uk/view/faculty_dept/kmi.html.

Ulrich, W. (1983). *Critical Heuristics of Social Planning: A New Approach to Practical Philosophy.* Bern, Switzerland, and Stuttgart, Germany: Haupt. Paperback reprint version, Chichester, UK: Wiley, 1994 (same pagination).

Ulrich, W. (1987). Critical heuristics of social systems design. *European Journal of Operational Research 31*(3), 276–283.

Ulrich, W. (1988a). Systems thinking, systems practice, and practical philosophy: a programme of research. *Systems Practice 1*(2), 137–163.

Ulrich, W. (1988b). Churchman's 'process of unfolding' – its significance for policy analysis and evaluation. *Systems Practice 1*(4), 415–428.

Ulrich, W. (1993). Some difficulties of ecological thinking, considered from a critical systems perspective: a plea for critical holism. *Systems Practice 6*(6), 583–611.

Ulrich, W. (1996). *A Primer to Critical Systems Heuristics for Action Researchers.* Hull, UK: University of Hull, Centre for Systems Studies.

Ulrich, W. (2000). Reflective practice in the civil society: the contribution of critically systemic thinking. *Reflective Practice 1*(2), 247–268.

Ulrich, W. (2001). The quest for competence in systemic research and practice. *Systems Research and Behavioral Science 18*(1), 3–28.

Ulrich, W. (2002). Boundary critique. In H.G. Daellenbach and R.L. Flood (eds.), *The Informed Student Guide to Management Science,* London: Thomson Learning, pp. 41–42.

Ulrich, W. (2003). Beyond methodology choice: critical systems thinking as critically systemic discourse. *Journal of the Operational Research Society 54*(4), 325–342.

Ulrich, W. (2004). C. West Churchman, 1913-2004 (obituary). *Journal of the Operational Research Society, 55*(11), 1123–1129.

Ulrich, W. (2005). A brief introduction to critical systems heuristics (CSH). Paper available in the Open University's *ECOSENSUS project web site,* http://projects.kmi.open.ac.uk/ecosensus/about/csh.html, or in the CSH section of *Werner Ulrich's Home Page,* http://wulrich.com/csh.html.

Ulrich, W. (2006). Critical pragmatism: a new approach to professional and business ethics. In L. Zsolnai (ed.), *Interdisciplinary Yearbook of Business Ethics, Vol. 1,* Oxford, UK, and Bern, Switzerland: Peter Lang, pp. 53–85.

Ulrich, W. (2007a). Philosophy for professionals: towards critical pragmatism. *Journal of the Operational Research Society, 58*(8), 1109–1113.

Ulrich, W. (2007b). The greening of pragmatism (three reflections on the past, present, and future of critical pragmatism). *Ulrich's Bimonthly,* March–April, May–June, and September–October 2007, http://wulrich.com/bimonthly_march2007.html.

Ulrich, W. (2008). The mainstream concept of reflective practice and its blind spot. *Ulrich's Bimonthly,* March–April 2008, http://wulrich.com/bimonthly_march2008.html.

Žižek, S. (1989). *The Sublime Object of Ideology.* London: Verso.

Chapter 7
Epilogue: Systems Approaches and Systems Practice

Martin Reynolds and Sue Holwell

Abstract Each of the five systems approaches discussed in this volume: system dynamics (SD), the viable systems model (VSM), strategic options development and analysis (SODA), soft systems methodology (SSM) and critical systems heuristics (CSH) has a pedigree. Not in the sense of the sometimes absurd spectacle of animals paraded at dog shows. Rather, their pedigree derives from their systems foundations, their capacity to evolve and their flexibility in use. None of the five approaches has developed out of use in restricted and controlled contexts of *either* low *or* high levels of complicatedness. Neither has any one of them evolved as a consequence of being applied only to situations with *either* presumed stakeholder agreement on purpose, *or* courteous disagreement amongst stakeholders, *or* stakeholder coercion. The compilation is not a celebration of abstract 'methodologies', but of theoretically robust approaches that have a genuine pedigree in practice.

7.1 Reflections

The compilation of the five systems approaches discussed in this volume – system dynamics (SD), the viable systems model (VSM), strategic options development and analysis (SODA), soft systems methodology (SSM) and critical systems heuristics (CSH) – is not a celebration of abstract 'methodologies', but of theoretically robust approaches that have a genuine pedigree in practice. Their pedigree derives from their systems foundations; their capacity to evolve and their flexibility through a variety in contexts of use. There are three levels of rich practice enabling these five systems approaches to retain flexibility and continual development: firstly, the interaction amongst those sharing an enthusiasm for one particular approach; secondly, the interaction between practitioners from different communities of systems approaches; and thirdly the rich interaction between Systems and other communities

M. Reynolds (✉) and S. Holwell
The Open University, Walton Hall, Milton Keynes MK7 6AA

M. Reynolds and S. Holwell (eds.), *Systems Approaches to Managing Change: A Practical Guide*, DOI 10.1007/978-1-84882-809-4_7, © The Open University 2010.
Published in Association with Springer-Verlag London Limited

of practice associated with different professions. All five approaches deal with interrelationships, multiple perspectives and boundary judgements, but always with regard to the context of use – 'the way of the world'.

7.1.1 Taking Stock

This is a useful point at which to consolidate some of the core commonalities shared by the five approaches described in the preceding chapters. Firstly, and most importantly, they all are ways of dealing with complex situations and issues. Secondly, they are all rooted in the fundamental systems concepts of *emergence* (the property of a 'whole' that arises from the interaction of the parts and is more than the 'sum of the parts'); *hierarchy* (layers and/or levels); *communication* (the exchange of data, information, resources within the boundary as well as the development of mutual understandings and the power that genuine listening can offer); and finally *control* (the corrective actions necessary for long term survival). In Checkland's basic system metaphor, "of an adaptive whole, surviving over time in a changing environment," these fundamental notions are essential (Checkland 1981).

An essential corollary of the 'system' metaphor is that of inter-relationships, multiple perspectives and boundary judgements – the three generalized purposeful orientations behind any systems approach. Again, it is evident that all five approaches take connections and relationships seriously, although their focus of attention may be on different forms or kinds of connection and relationship. The drawing of a boundary, a demarcation between what is included and what is excluded is explicit and unavoidable in all systems practice; although the degree of attention given to this varies between the five approaches. This crucial point in any systems work – making the judgement about boundary – is discussed more fully shortly. Clearly, the fundamental systems concepts and the three 'purposeful orientations' are manifest in each of the approaches but in different ways and with different emphases.

Moreover, each of the approaches included here is the result of the cumulative experience of a community of practitioners that comprises people from many different professional backgrounds: some of whom, but not all, call themselves 'systems practitioners'. The practitioners who have contributed to this development work in many different fields and domains. The experienced complexity of the real situations through which the approaches have developed derives from there being both interrelatedness and interdependencies to deal with, and with there being many views on what 'improvement' could/should look like. Not surprisingly, through practice some now have recognizable variant forms; and in some instances, such as VSM and SD, there are distinct 'schools of approach'. For this book, practice has been given precedence although we acknowledge that some readers might have preferred a much closer adherence to theoretical definitions in some instances. We also acknowledge that all perspectives on use of all approaches have not been included. But our focus on practice, drawing on the reflections and experience of long-standing practitioners, provides a unique strength of perspective and portrayal of each approach.

7.1.2 Flexibility and Ongoing Development

The accounts of the approaches here, in general, bear little resemblance to the first expositions of the approach (see for example, the SSM account by Checkland in this volume and compare that to the first SSM paper published in 1972). As mentioned in the Introduction, similar evolutionary modifications are applicable to all five approaches. The ongoing development of each approach is a function of the variety in contexts of use. A contemporary list of application areas where SD is used – from modeling defence systems to use for fostering group dynamics – illustrates David Lane's point that System Dynamics is an approach that provides space for different contexts of use (Lane 2000). Whilst VSM is primarily used for organisational management, Patrick Hoverstadt in chapter 3 makes an important wider distinction: "I've talked about VSM in terms of an organisational model to look at "human activity" and the emphasis has been on formalised systems that the casual observer would recognise as entities in the real world – companies, hospitals, charities that sort of thing. But of course, VSM isn't just a model of organisations it's a model of *organisation* and as such is useful in other domains."

Both SODA with cognitive mapping, and SSM belong to a group of approaches that are frequently regarded as problem structuring methods (Rosenhead and Mingers 2001). They each have a rich historic tradition of being helpful in structuring problems in different domains (as against the more rigid exercise of solving problems, which tends to be more domain specific). In common with SD, SSM also emerged from another discipline – that of Systems Engineering. Peter Checkland found, when he and his colleagues tried to apply Systems Engineering to 'messy management' problems, that it failed. First, the learning from experiences that gave rise to SSM can be encapsulated in the key ideas of treating purposeful activity as a systems concept, and acknowledging that any purposeful activity is only meaningful when a worldview is declared. In other words, purposeful activity only makes sense when the view that frames the 'purpose' for the activity is understood and made explicit. Second, the models used in SSM were of concepts relevant to thinking about the problematic situation, and explicitly were not models of anything in the situation to be engineered. This 'shift of systemicity' from the world to thinking about the world, for Checkland differentiates 'hard systems approaches' from soft systems approaches. The third key thought that separated Systems Engineering from SSM was the realization that the 'intervention process' was organized as a learning system, a means of learning the way to what would count as an 'improvement'.

Finally, CSH shares some of its ancestry with SSM. It emerged directly from the ethical systems tradition and the works of C. West Churchman. Churchman himself began professional work as a systems engineer but was increasingly involved with applying systems ideas to wider ethical issues, ending his career with a professorship in peace and conflict studies at the University of Berkley, California. Werner Ulrich's work in developing CSH as a means of supporting reflective practice in all professional domains including social planning and environmental design was firmly rooted in this tradition.

7.1.3   Characteristics: Shared and Distinct

Moving beyond the common systems origins, the five approaches also share other characteristics, particularly at the more abstract level. All five assume that complex situations and messes cannot be resolved or improved without engaging in a process that is cyclic and iterative; recognizing that changes in perspective and level (in the hierarchy sense) reveal new insights that require revisiting earlier findings. This point is explicitly made, for example by Morecroft and Checkland, but is equally the case for all five.

The contributing authors are very clear that real improvements can only come when the richest understanding of the situation as a whole is achieved; that treating a situation such as the Somalia pirate 'problem' simply as a problem of bad people being pirates will only result in the on-going need for more fire-fighting at best, but will not improve the situation overall. This is reflected in the precise use of the language of 'situation' and not 'problem'; of 'improvement' and not 'resolution' or 'fix'. Simon Caulkin's comment in *The Observer* newspaper on the banking sector early in 2009 laments the prevailing fashion that in both its view and language is diametrically opposed to the approaches examined in this Reader:

> Ever in thrall to economics, today's management has faithfully reflected this.... Managers have grown – and been taught – to eschew messy reality in favour of managing by computer model and target.... Indeed, increasingly they don't know how to manage forward from reality rather than backward from the numbers. Thus the besetting sin of mistaking the map for the territory, the scorecard for the game, the representation for reality. Seize the chance to make banking dull again. (Simon Caulkin, management editor The Observer, Sunday 19 April, 2009)

The use of models and diagrams is integral to all five approaches. Crucially, all five regard the models as being 'conceptual constructs' and not representations of (or part of) reality in the way that in the UK we expect an ordnance survey map to be. All five approaches regard the use of models and diagrams as a means to facilitate *learning,* and not as ends in themselves.

However, even a cursory reading will reveal that at the more detailed level there are very distinct differences between the approaches. Clearly the content and appearance of the models and diagrams is very different: the straight lines and boxes in VSM, contrast with the curves of a cognitive map, and the 'clouds' in an SSM activity model. And while all of the models make clear the connections between the various elements, the nature of the connections varies considerably from variety equations in VSM, from influence of one variable on another in SD, and contingency in SSM. The entities being modeled are also quite different, for example, entities in SD, processes in VSM, issues and options in SODA, activities in SSM, and sources of influence in CSH.

The book chapters are descriptions or accounts of the different approaches, but they are no more than that and their use in practice is never as clean and tidy as a concise description might suggest.

The success of any systems approach discussed in these pages is ultimately dependent on the user of the approach in some context or setting. An approach of itself cannot guarantee, or even determine success. So whilst we may discuss different approaches in their abstract sense, any claims towards their value in improving or making change in a situation are dependent on several things: the context of use; the practitioner's purpose, skill and insights, and the level and quality of participation of those engaged in the problem situation itself. Indeed as Checkland describes see section 5.1.3 and Fig. 5.3 in the LUMAS diagram (Learner, User of methodology, Methodology, Actual approach adopted, real-world problem Situation) there is an ongoing definition and re-definition between the ideas, the situation and the practitioner for every approach in the hands of a skilled (or just knowledgeable) practitioner. Indeed this aspect, which one might term improvisation, is true of any approach to dealing with human situations. Donald Schön writes explicitly about the role of improvisation in professional practice:

> … Schön, who stresses reflection in the midst of action … frequently used jazz as an image of reflection-in-action: the process of improvisation in the moment based on a response to the situation (what other musicians are playing, the audience's response etc), to the established rhythm and melody of the piece, and also on one's own abilities and enthusiasms. (Ramage and Shipp 2009, p. 292)

The notion of improvisation is helpful in grasping some of the nuances of a good systems approach. But how might we understand this process more in order to help nurture and ensure future flexibility and development in systems approaches and still retain theoretical rigour? Two ideas in the wider systems tradition may help us. First, there is the widespread understanding of the tension between *practice and theory* expressed by practitioners like Donald Schön and others more specifically concerned with systems modeling (Pidd 2004). Second, there is the notion of *entrapment* in our ways of thinking and practice that is of interest to many systems practitioners including the authors in this compilation. We can briefly examine both.

7.2 Practice and the Skilled Practitioner

The notion of 'practice', and therefore 'practitioner' is somewhat slippery. Schön's writings on reflective practice may already be familiar. Writing on the 'crises-of-confidence' professionals were experiencing in the 1980s Schön argues that the process of 'reflection-in-action' by professionals is underpinned by four constants that only change relatively slowly. They are "the reliably solid references from which, in reflection-in-action, he [the professional] can allow his theories and frames to come apart" (Schön 1984, p. 270).

These constants are the:

1. Language, media and repertoires used to describe 'reality' and to conduct 'experiments'
2. Appreciative settings brought to the problem setting, to the evaluation of inquiry and to reflective conversation
3. Overarching theories by which sense is made of the phenomena
4. Role frames within which tasks are set and through which institutional settings are bound

A satisfactory account of the phenomena in the practice situation is not achieved until it is framed in terms of the overarching theory, and a cumulative repertoire of exemplars, facts and descriptions can be built against the institutional settings (Schön 1984, pp. 273-274).

A skilled practitioner is one who continually keeps alive the tension between practice and theory. This ongoing tension can be understood on different levels. At an individual level, our personal reflection-in-action continues all the time both consciously and sub-consciously. Past practices and experiences inform the way we think about things and the way that we think obviously influences practice. Beyond the individual level – what might be called 'practitioner community' levels – the dynamics of theory and practice become more intricate and three different levels are helpful. Our colleague, Karen Shipp, designed the three influence diagrams below to help illustrate these three levels of rich dialogue enabling systems approaches to retain flexibility and continual development.

7.2.1   Level 1 Interaction Within a Particular Methodology's Practitioner Community

Figure 7.1 illustrates the dynamics of interaction amongst a practitioner community such as, for example, VSM practitioners or SODA practitioners. The practitioners share an underlying methodology associated with the approach.

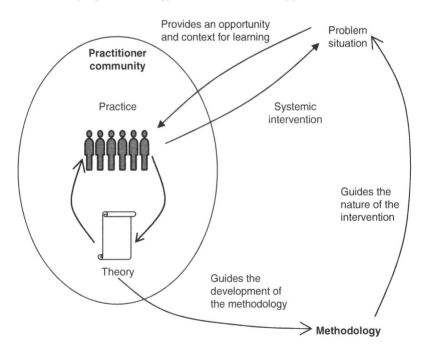

Fig. 7.1 Influence diagram illustrating the interplay between problem-situation, methodology and practitioner-community in the development of a methodology over time associated with a particular (systems) approach to intervention

This diagram shows the traditional cycle of learning from the interaction of theory and practice within the practitioner community associated with a particular methodology. When a practitioner makes an intervention in a problem situation, the methodology guides the nature of the intervention, and the situation provides the opportunity and context for the practitioner to learn from the experience. This learning influences the development of theory within the community, which in turn influences the development of the methodology itself.

7.2.2   *Level 2 Interaction Within the Wider Systems Community*

The next diagram is up a level from Fig. 7. 1 and illustrates two of the mechanisms by which methodologies develop as a result of learning transfer between *different* practitioner communities; say between SD practitioners, SSM practitioners and SODA practitioners.

Figure 7.2 shows three practitioner communities (PC1, PC2, PC3) for methodologies 1, 2, and 3. The overlapping circles of the practitioner communities

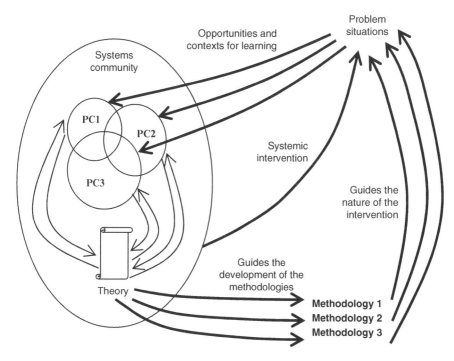

Fig. 7.2 Influence diagram illustrating two mechanisms by which methodologies develop as a result of learning transfer between different practitioner communities belonging to a shared family of approaches (e.g., systems approaches)

illustrate that individuals can, and do, belong to more than one practitioner community, perhaps practicing more than one approach. This co-membership is one mechanism by which different methodologies can, and do influence the development of others, in the interplay of practice and theory within the practitioner community.

The interaction between theory and practice is shown here between each practitioner community and an *external* body of theory, acknowledging that published theory is often read widely amongst a broad systems community (as well as in more specialist community publications). This illustrates a second mechanism by which the development of a methodology is likely to be influenced by *other* methodologies.

7.2.3   Level 3 Interaction Between Systems and Other Communities of Practice

Finally, there is an even wider influence on systems approaches. This involves the influence of practicing professionals and non-professional groupings – teachers, health workers, managers, planners, evaluators, public and private sector administrators, etc. that may or may not have any formalized 'methodological' traditions. Whether they have recognized formal methodologies or not, such groups and individuals have considerable influence on the way in which practitioner communities develop their skills (Fig. 7.3).

Fig 7.3 shows two routes by which a systems methodology can evolve as a result of influences from outside the systems community. When the practitioner community connected with a particular methodology is engaged in the continual cycle of learning from the interplay of theory and practice, the thinking and experiences of members cannot help but be drawn into this learning cycle. In particular, other ways of thinking and seeing – whether drawn in from conversation, everyday media or deeper reading – will influence the development of theory; while the close engagement with participants of all kinds – from their different professions, roles and fields of endeavor – when working in the field, will broaden and perhaps challenge the repertoire of practice that the practitioner has to draw on. The message to be taken for practitioners from the account of the five approaches given here is to avoid seeking some methodological purism in testing out any one systems approach, but rather to explore its validity and adaptation in conjunction with other approaches familiar to the user.

A particular feature of the five systems approaches discussed in these pages are the sought-after working relationships and dialogues with such communities and individuals. Such interactions enhance not only the practice but also serve to strengthen the theoretical underpinning associated with each methodology. They also serve to protect against the risk of becoming trapped in 'group-think' that can be a feature of long-standing communities.

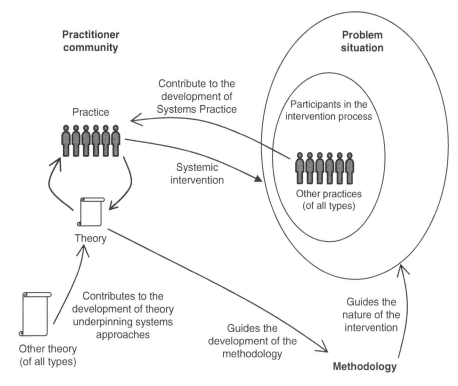

Fig. 7.3 Influence diagram illustrating how other types of professional practice and other fields of academic theory can contribute to the development of a methodology associated with a systems approach

7.2.4 Recognising the Possibility of Entrapment

A particularly helpful way of envisioning traps is through the practice of boundary critique (Ulrich 2000) described more fully in the CSH chapter. Making judgements is always central to practice. This is especially so for systems practice where the explicit drawing of boundaries is an integral part of the practice. But it is also important because practice of the systems approaches in this compilation involves understanding that the 'world' is not a given; it is not a once-and-for-all, unambiguous object. Systems approaches here recognise that there are unlikely to be single, and universally accepted solutions to the issues that engage people's attention.

Figure 7.4 illustrates not only the necessity for making judgements, of at least three different kinds, but reminds us that each kind of judgement affects other judgements in a never-ending cycle.

Similar ideas have been expressed in somewhat 'classical' prose by Geoffery Vickers (1987). In his description of an appreciative system: "… [It] seems to me to

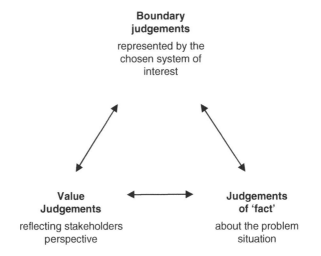

Fig. 7.4 Dynamics of systems thinking (Adapted from Ulrich 2000; Reynolds 2008a)

carry with those linked connotations of *interest, discrimination* and *valuation* which we bring to the exercise of judgement and which tacitly determine *what* we shall notice [judgements of fact], *how* we shall discriminate situations from the general confusion of ongoing events [boundary judgements] and how we shall *regard* them [value judgements]" (Vickers 1987, pp. 98–99; My italics). There is a resonance also with the 'triadicity' (between fact, value, and boundary judgements) in Charles Peirce's nineteenth century semiotics and theory of representation (objects being represented, those who make representation, and actual representations (Peirce 1878) and Habermas' three worlds (*the* natural world, *our* social world, and *my* internal world (Habermas 1984). There is also resonance with Peter Checkland's LUMAS model (Learning for a User by a Methodology-informed Approach to a problem Situation) distinguishing between 'methodology as words on paper' – *boundary judgements* –, the 'user of methodology' – *value judgements* – , and 'the situation addressed' – *judgements of 'fact'* (see section 5.1.3). Thus Vickers, Checkland and Ulrich in different ways highlight the need to continually question and review judgements, not least on systems boundaries during the course of any intervention.

Importantly, systems boundaries – that is, boundary judgements (whether in terms of models, methodologies, approaches, organisational practices etc.) – must never be allowed privilege to remain independent of changes in the context of use (judgements of 'fact') and the users themselves (value judgements).

Systems are of course abstractions – ways of framing – and the act of framing itself requires making judgements, especially boundary judgements. Different systems approaches can be considered as frameworks (Reynolds 2008a, b) in the sense that, as the name implies, *framework* has two interrelated parts; one, a cognitive or conceptual device – a *frame* of reference which, two, enables *work* through systems (plans, projects, programmes, etc.). Figure 7.5 is a development of Fig. 1.4 in the

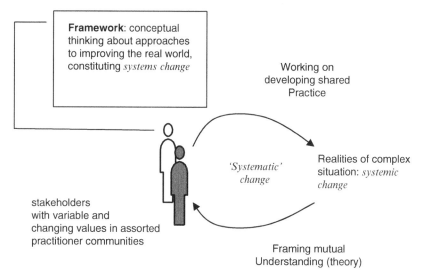

Fig. 7.5 Framing and systems change, systematic change and systemic change (Adapted from Reynolds 2008a)

introductory chapter to illustrate the dynamics of change in the development of systems approaches.

From Figs. 7.4 and 7.5, we are reminded that there is an imperative to continually ask questions of 'systems'; to appreciate them as *judgements* of fact rather than *matters* of fact. For example, when confronted with arguments of an iniquitous 'economic system' generating continual social and ecological impoverishment, or an 'education system' that systematically continues to marginalise particular sectors of our community, as systems practitioners we have an opportunity (some would say a responsibility) to create space for, and help support the framing of, better 'economic and education systems', rather than continuing as if they are given realities that we simply have to live with. The potential idea of 'systems' as conceptual tools of oppression rather than conceptual tools for liberation is captured in a familiar quote:

> To a man with a hammer, everything looks like a nail.

In the introductory chapter we talked of traps in conventional thinking, but are there also potential traps in our systems thinking? We previously identified two traps of conventional thinking – reductionism and dogmatism. We ought to acknowledge the second side of this coin now, and ask what it would mean to think of systems thinking as being subject to the risk of the two traps of holism and pluralism. How might these also become – in some situations or on some occasions – limitations rather than enhancements to our thinking? Could it be something akin to 'systems fixation' or even a 'fetishisation of systems'? There is always the potential of becoming too attached to our systems – whether these be conceptualized as rigidly bounded systems or indeed less overtly bounded systems approaches – they are only conceptualizations that help us on our way – they are not the (or even an) answer in themselves.

7.3   Context Always Matters

Let us finally return to the nature of the complex situations to which systems approaches generally make a claim towards improving. In the introduction we chose three stories prevalent in the UK during Easter 2009 to illustrate contrasting senses of complexity with which systems approaches might be of help: the remembrance of tragic events at Hillsborough in 1989, the continuing piracy off Somalia, and the discovery of relatively large numbers Orangutans – an endangered species – in Indonesia.

By way of review we will finish by re-visiting the media stories used in the Introduction to contextualize the relevance of these five approaches, but this time by reference to each story and the five approaches. This is intended to be illustrative only, and is not an exhaustive mapping of any one approach against a story.

System Dynamics, for example, might be used to examine the consequences of different configurations of the physical layout of a football stadium (the flow of patrons into and out of regions of the stadium under different conditions, in order to assess the risk of overcrowding, or speed of evacuation). It might be used to examine, say, the economic consequences of piracy in a particular geographically bounded region. Or it might be used to examine the dynamics of the interconnections between orangutang population size, the population of other predator or predated species, and human encroachment into the habitat. The VSM could be used to explore the organizational arrangements and governance for a football event from intelligence gathering to the operations necessary to accept tickets and seat patrons. VSM could provide insight to actual hierarchical relationships in the organisation of piracy. Or it might be used to model future design of species protection schemes. Cognitive mapping (from SODA) might be used with the police leaders who had been involved at Hillsborough to examine the thinking which lay behind some examples of faulty decision-making, perhaps for training purposes. This could be extended to reveal patterns of thinking prevalent in one stakeholder group (say football ground officials) to members of another stakeholder group (say victims' families) in order to facilitate understanding and thus a movement towards greater eventual peace of mind. SODA might be used to develop a strategy for protecting international waters from piracy, or the policing of illegal logging in Indonesia. SSM has already been used to think about Hillsborough (see Lea et. al. 1998). It could be used to think about improvements for the Somalia piracy using relevant models such as 'a system to improve living standards in Somalia', a 'system to reward pirates for safe escort of ships', a 'system to create new jobs'. Similarly, SSM models relevant to the protection of Orangutans could include – 'a system to provide ecotourist travels', or on a deeper learning level, a 'system to protect against the diminishment of biodiversity' or a 'system to promote a natural resource based economy in Indonesia and so on. Finally, the use of CSH could help in revealing the details and consequence of reference systems that perceive football supporters as 'hooligans'. CSH might be used as a discursive tool to enable meaningful conversation between those stakeholders involved with perpetuating sea piracy and those stakeholders affected by sea piracy. Similarly, CSH could be used to map out the different reference systems associated with the conservation of Indonesian forests, with a view to identifying contrasting stakeholders and collective stakeholdings around sources of motivation and values, control and the leverage of power, knowledge and 'expertise'; as well as sources of legitimacy in appreciating the moral consequences of conservation and non-conservation.

This superficial sketch of the approaches against the media stories only serves to illustrate the applicability of all of them to situations of different kinds. It does not say anything about situation of type A is suitable for approach X, and that situation type B is not suitable for approach X. In the hands of a skilful practitioner each of these approaches will give useful insights to any situation.

In conclusion we provide space for two other voices. First, our colleague, Robin Asby, describes the relevance of systems approaches in today's world:

> Too often, today's problems are solved by utilizing easy and comfortable approaches to obtain simple solutions. In reality as many discover, simplicity and common sense approaches are far from effective in dealing with complex, dynamic and diverse problems. Despite the initial apparent ease and comfort that this brings, focus tends to be on the elements of the perceived problem, rather than the 'bigger picture'; and typically there is no consideration of interactions, nor questioning the belief that there is one best solution. As more and more program failures escalate there is a growing need to improve and create better results through systems thinking. Systems thinking is a discipline of seeing the "whole" through a critical lens, recognizing patterns and interrelationships, appreciating other perspectives, and learning how to structure more effective, efficient and creative systems. (Robin Asby, 2009, personal communication)

Second, the great systems thinker and practitioner, Mary Catherine Bateson, reminds us of the 'way of the world' to which systems approaches covered in this compilation continue to serve as a continually creative endeavour:

> It's confusing, but we have a right to be confused. Perhaps even a need. The trick is to enjoy it: to savor complexity and resist the easy answers; to let diversity flower into creativity. (M.C. Bateson 2004, "Afterword: To Wander and Wonder", p. 410)

References

Bateson, M.C. (2004). *Willing to Learn: Passages of Personal Discovery*. Hanover, NH: Steerforth Press.

Checkland, P. B. (1981). *Systems Thinking Systems Practice*. Chichester: John Wiley.

Habermas, J. (1984/87), *The Theory of Communicative Action*, 2 Volumes, Cambridge, UK: Polity Press.

Lane, D. (2000). Should System Dynamics be Described as a 'Hard' or 'Deterministic' Systems Approach? *Systems Research and Behavioural Science* 17(1): 3–22.

Lea, W., Uttley, P., and Vasconcelos, A. C. (1998) "Mistakes, misjudgements and mischances: Using SSM to understand the Hillsborough disaster" *International Journal of Information Management*, 18(5): 345–357.

Peirce, C.S. (1878), "How to make our ideas clear". *Popular Science Monthly*, 12 (January); 386–402

Pidd, M., Ed. (2004). *Systems Modelling: Theory and Practice*. Chicheter: Wiley.

Ramage, M. & Shipp, K. (2009) *Systems Thinkers*. London: Springer and The Open University Press.

Reynolds, M. (2008a). Getting a grip: a critical systems framework for corporate responsibility. *Systems Research and Behavioural Science* 25(3): 383–395.

Reynolds, M. (2008b). Reframing expert support for development management. *Journal of International Development* 20: 768–782.

Rosenhead, J. and J. Mingers, Eds. (2001). *Rational Analysis for Problematic World Revisited.* Chichester, John Wiley & Sons.

Schön, D. (1984). *The reflective practitioner: how professionals think in action.* Aldershot, UK: Ashgate.

Ulrich, W. (2000). Reflective Practice in the Civil Society: the contribution of critically systemic thinking. *Reflective Practice* 1(2): 247–268.

Vickers, G. (1987). Essays of Sir Geoffrey Vickers. *Policymaking, Communication and Social Learning*. G. B. Adams, J. Forester and B. L. Catron (Eds). New Brunswick, NJ: Transaction Books.

Index

Lightning Source UK Ltd.
Milton Keynes UK
UKOW06f0607100116

266052UK00001B/12/P

9 781848 828087